Appomattox

Appomattox

*Victory, Defeat, and Freedom
at the End of the Civil War*

ELIZABETH R. VARON

OXFORD
UNIVERSITY PRESS

OXFORD
UNIVERSITY PRESS

Oxford University Press is a department of the University of Oxford.
It furthers the University's objective of excellence in research,
scholarship, and education by publishing worldwide.

Oxford   New York

Auckland   Cape Town   Dar es Salaam   Hong Kong   Karachi
Kuala Lumpur   Madrid   Melbourne   Mexico City   Nairobi
New Delhi   Shanghai   Taipei   Toronto

With offices in

Argentina   Austria   Brazil   Chile   Czech Republic   France   Greece
Guatemala   Hungary   Italy   Japan   Poland   Portugal   Singapore
South Korea   Switzerland   Thailand   Turkey   Ukraine   Vietnam

Oxford is a registered trade mark of Oxford University Press
in the UK and certain other countries.

Published in the United States of America by
Oxford University Press
198 Madison Avenue, New York, NY 10016

Library of Congress Cataloging-in-Publication Data
Varon, Elizabeth R., 1963–
Appomattox: victory, defeat, and freedom at the end of the Civil War / Elizabeth R. Varon.
pages cm
Includes bibliographical references and index.
ISBN 978-0-19-975171-6 (hardback)
1. Appomattox Campaign, 1865.
2. United States—History—Civil War, 1861–1865—Peace.
3. Lee, Robert E. (Robert Edward), 1807–1870.
4. Grant, Ulysses S. (Ulysses Simpson), 1822–1885.
5. Reconstruction (U.S. history, 1865–1877) I. Title.
E477.67.V37   2013
973.7'38—dc23   2013019903

1 3 5 7 9 8 6 4 2

Printed in the United States of America
on acid-free paper

CONTENTS

Acknowledgments   vii

Prologue   1

PART ONE   BATTLEFRONT

1. No Escape   7
2. Councils of War   23
3. The Surrender Conference   48
4. The Armies   79

PART TWO   HOME FRONT

5. Tidings of Peace   115
6. Victory and Martyrdom   135
7. Defeat and Liberation   157

PART THREE   AFTERMATH

8. The Trials of Robert E. Lee   183
9. The Promise Betrayed   208
Epilogue: The Apple Tree   244

Abbreviations   259
Notes   261
Index   293

ACKNOWLEDGMENTS

This project has its origins in an invitation I received in 2009 to speak on the subject of Juneteenth at the Library Company of Philadelphia; in the course of researching "emancipation day" celebrations, I learned of the centrality of Lee's surrender in postwar discourse on black liberation, and I began to see Appomattox in a new light. Given my long-standing fascination with Grant and Lee, I was eager to connect my new knowledge to my old interests. I thank my friend Julie Campbell at Washington & Lee University for joining me on a memorable outing to Appomattox for some early field research and for encouraging me to write this book. I am grateful for the chance I had to workshop my preliminary findings at colloquia at Princeton University and Georgetown University. And I thank my research assistant at Temple University, Dr. Zachary Lechner.

A stroke of good fortune brought me home to Virginia in the fall of 2010 and kicked the project into high gear. I benefited immensely from the expertise and generosity of three historians in particular: Christopher Calkins at Sailor's Creek Battlefield Historical State Park; Patrick Schroeder at Appomattox Court House National Historical Park; and John Coski at the Museum of the Confederacy. I found countless treasures at the Library of Virginia, the Virginia Historical Society, and special collections at Washington & Lee University, and I thank the staffs of these splendid institutions for their assistance.

Most especially, I am grateful for the resources of the University of Virginia: the vast Civil War holdings at Alderman Library and Small Special Collections; the research support of the College of Arts and Sciences; the example set by my colleagues in the Corcoran Department of History; the energy of my research assistants Jon Grinspan and Eric Sargent; and the friendship and wisdom of Gary Gallagher, who was kind enough to read my manuscript and share his singular command of the Civil War era. I am also grateful to the History Departments at Chestnut Hill College and George Mason University, and to the Society of Civil War Historians, for providing forums in which I could test my conclusions.

Susan Ferber at Oxford University Press brought her editorial expertise and deep knowledge of the field of nineteenth-century U.S. history to bear on the manuscript, rendering it more cogent and readable; the anonymous readers she chose for the manuscript's final vetting made many excellent suggestions for revisions.

I thank my husband, Will Hitchcock, for his unflagging support and enthusiasm; for his many insights on the historical themes of victory, defeat, and liberation; and for his skillful tweaking of some key passages in this book. I have drawn energy, as ever, from my father's abiding faith in the future. His ability to radiate love is at once humbling and inspiring. My brother and fellow historian Jeremy knows this better than anyone and knows, too, how much I treasure our sixth-sense sibling bond.

Most of all, I am grateful to my children, Ben and Emma, for the light and laughter, the sweetness and solidarity, they bring to our every day. This book is for them.

E.R.V.
Charlottesville, Virginia

Appomattox

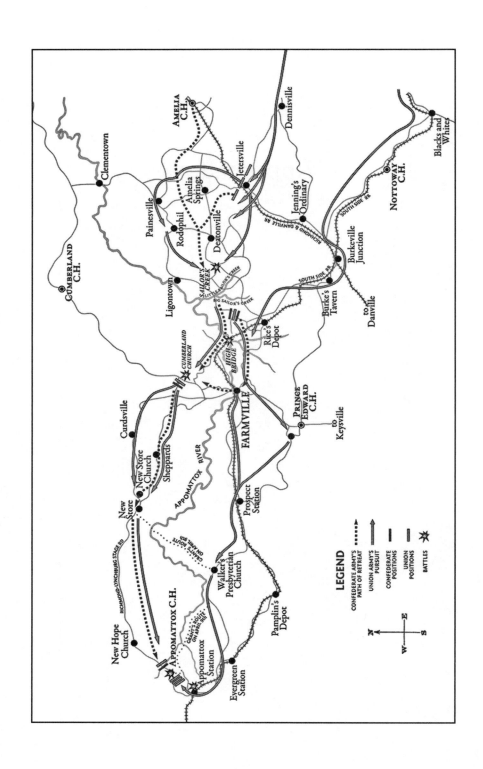

Prologue

On Palm Sunday, April 9, 1865, Ulysses S. Grant, general-in-chief of the Union army, met Robert E. Lee, his Confederate counterpart, in the modest parlor of Wilmer McLean, in the Southside Virginia village of Appomattox Court House. Lee was the very picture of dignity—wearing a solemn expression and fine dress uniform, he embodied the proud gentility of the South's planter elite. Grant, dressed casually in a mud-spattered uniform, embodied a dignity of an altogether different sort: that of the hardscrabble farmers and wage earners he had molded into a formidable fighting machine. After awkwardly exchanging some pleasantries about their service in the Mexican War, the two men agreed to the surrender terms that effectively ended the Civil War. In essence, Grant's terms set free the conquered soldiers of the Army of Northern Virginia, on the promise that they would never again take up arms against the United States. Grant's magnanimity in this hour, and Lee's stoic resignation in defeat, inaugurated a process of national healing that would not only restore the shattered Union but would also prepare the way for America's emergence as a world power.

This scene forms one of the most significant moments in the story Americans tell themselves about the meaning and legacy of the Civil War. Unfortunately, it is a myth. Grant and Lee *did* meet at Appomattox and sign the surrender terms in McLean's parlor. But the meaning of this event has never been fully understood. As Grant and Lee set their hands to the surrender terms, they positioned themselves at the center of a bitter and protracted contest over what exactly was decided that April day at Appomattox. The two men represented competing visions of the peace. For Grant, the Union victory was one of right over wrong. He believed that his magnanimity, no less than his victory, vindicated free society and the Union's way of war. Grant's eyes were on the future—a future in which Southerners, chastened and repentant, would join their Northern brethren in the march towards moral and material progress. Lee, by contrast, believed that the Union victory was one of might over right. In his view, Southerners had nothing to repent of and had survived the war with their honor and principles intact. He was intent on restoration—on turning the clock back, as much as possible, to the days when Virginia led the nation and before sectional extremism alienated the North from South.

Each man believed that he alone held the moral high ground. Each man hoped to win over the "reasonable" men among his former enemies. And each hoped, perhaps naively, that the other would be his first convert.

In peace as in war, the two men also represented different strategic styles. Lee's challenge once again was to make the best of a weak hand—and this he would do, in the surrender's aftermath, with characteristic creativity and audacity, understanding all along that his personal prestige was the greatest asset that the advocates of restoration possessed. Grant, by contrast, played the long game. A man whose generalship at times relied on power and persistence rather than on maneuver, Grant doggedly pressed the case that Appomattox signified a Union transformed—better than before and improving still.

These competing visions and strategies would exert a profound influence over postwar politics. White Union soldiers, Northern civilians in the Republican and War Democrat camps, and anti-Confederate Southerners rallied around the idea of the surrender as vindication. They saw the Union's mercy, exemplified by Lincoln and Grant, as a source of moral authority and as the best means to knit the country back together. Free blacks and former slaves, both soldiers and civilians, joined together with white abolitionists and with some radical Southern Unionists in staking out the argument, as a variation on the theme of vindication, that the war had struck a blow for human equality. The Union's magnanimity was, in their view, a means to secure the goals of black citizenship and of racial harmony. They too claimed Lincoln and Grant as the heroes who proved that victory favored the righteous.

But these victors' interpretations of Appomattox were fiercely contested from the start. Southerners who had supported the Confederacy, together with Northern antiwar ("Copperhead") Democrats who had deplored the Lincoln administration's policies, particularly emancipation, rallied around the theme of restoration. They believed that Grant's magnanimity was both a concession to the moral rectitude of the defeated Confederates and a promise that honorable men would not be treated dishonorably. Proponents of restoration saw Lee as their standard bearer and came to see Lincoln's successor, Andrew Johnson, as Lee's ally.

In the year after the war, Grant and Lee learned that the visions of the peace they had brought to the table at Appomattox were incompatible, and the two men grew further apart politically, as they and their countrymen and women grappled with the ambiguities, entailments, tensions, and possibilities in the surrender terms. This lesson of Appomattox runs counter to the myth that the surrender, as a moment of healing, transcended politics and frustrates our desire to believe that Grant and Lee embodied a special kind of patriotism untainted by ideology. But to understand the surrender's meaning for those who experienced it, we must see Grant and Lee and as their contemporaries did: as consummate leaders who had the power and responsibility to champion their respective causes in peace as they had in war. Americans looked to the rival generals, the two most prestigious men in the country, for guidance and inspiration as they sought to legitimate the cause for which each side had paid such a terrible price.

Confederates and Copperheads believed that Lee drew a line in the sand at Appomattox. White Southerners knew they must accept that the war was over and that secession and slavery were dead letters—but the North must ask nothing more of them. Northern Republicans and Southern Unionists, white and black, watched in disbelief and even horror as this narrow interpretation of what the Union had won and the Confederacy lost took root in the South, inspiring Southern resistance to Reconstruction and to Republican authority. In their eyes, Grant's victory at Appomattox had heralded a new era in American politics: no longer would the haughty Southern elite consider itself entitled to dominate the government; no longer would it feign superior gentility and virtue. Grant had spared the defeated Confederates their lives and had spared them punishment and humiliation—and for this white Southerners must show humility and gratitude. Although Lee technically observed the terms of his parole, he failed, most Northerners agreed, to show the required repentance; instead, he worked subtly to promote restoration as a political program. By the time of the surrender's first anniversary, Grant was deeply disappointed in Lee's refusal to give the victors their due. Confronted with white Southern intransigence, Grant came to see the necessity of black citizenship for the Union's full vindication.

The debates over the surrender were forged in battle, in the Union and Confederate armies' experience of Lee's desperate retreat. Aside from Grant and Lee, no Americans felt themselves closer to the truth than the small circle of men whom each commander counted as his military family: the field commanders and staff officers to whom Lee and Grant turned for counsel and entrusted the execution of their orders. And so this book begins with them, in the days before the surrender, with Lee's army intent on escape and Grant's on its annihilation. These men did not see the Appomattox campaign as the postscript to the great decisive battles of the war. They believed that the fate of the Union and of the Confederacy still hung in the balance in April 1865.

PART ONE

BATTLEFRONT

1

No Escape

"From present indications the retreat of the enemy is rapidly becoming a rout. We are shelling their trains and preparing to attack their infantry immediately." So Philip H. Sheridan wrote Grant on April 5, 1865, from Jetersville Depot, Virginia, three days after Lee's army had abandoned the trenches of the fallen cities of Richmond and Petersburg and begun its flight west. From the start, Grant's goal was not merely to pursue Lee's army but to intercept it: to cut Lee off and prevent him from veering South and joining the Confederate army of Joseph Johnston in North Carolina. Sheridan, commanding the Federal cavalry and Fifth Corps, led the way. Grant counted on him both to assess the deterioration of Lee's army and to take the tactical initiative, assuming command of infantry divisions as they joined him in the vanguard. This was a role that Sheridan relished.[1]

An ambitious Ohioan of Irish extraction, Sheridan had always dreamed of being a soldier; West Point had launched him on his way. In the war's last chapter, he was ablaze with confidence because he had fulfilled every assignment Grant had given him to the letter: Sheridan had reorganized the cavalry of the Army of the Potomac; bested the Confederate cavalry under his nemesis J. E. B. Stuart and left Stuart dead; foiled Jubal Early's plans to use the Shenandoah Valley as a base for offensive operations in the North; stripped the Valley, the "granary of the Confederacy," of valuable resources; and prompted the evacuation of Petersburg by routing Pickett's Confederates at Five Forks, on April 1, 1865. On the eve of the surrender, Sheridan, a major general at age 33, was not just Grant's right-hand man in Virginia but already a national hero. To the Northern public, the scrappy cavalryman—whose ferocity seemed all the more remarkable given his short-legged, five-foot-five frame—was their "Little Phil."[2]

Sheridan was determined to shape the course of the retreat by using his fast-moving cavalry to repeatedly strike Lee's columns, particularly his wagon trains. These aggressive tactics reflected Sheridan's restless, relentless nature; his utter fearlessness; and his deep distrust of and contempt for the enemy. That distrust and contempt was born of bitter experience: Sheridan's Valley campaigns had furnished him ample evidence of Southern ruthlessness in the form of murderous raids by guerrillas such as John Singleton Mosby, and evidence too of the stubborn defiance of Confederate civilians, and of the determined courage and yearning for freedom displayed by the countless slaves who flocked to his lines. Sheridan had come to see the entire Valley of Virginia as an "insurgent section" whose civilians no less than its soldiers had to be brought to heel. In the war's closing moments, Sheridan sought not only the final vindication of the "just cause of the Government" but personal vindication, too, against those in his own army who had doubted, back when J. E. B. Stuart seemed invincible, the efficacy of the Union cavalry.[3]

Sheridan's dispatches to Grant during Lee's retreat kept up a drumbeat: we must "exert ourselves," he urged, and move forward "with the utmost speed." If the Union army acted with urgency, Sheridan promised Grant on April 5, "I see no escape for Lee."[4]

Such appeals were based on Sheridan's awareness of Lee's tactical bind and of the desperate state of the rebel army. The last year of the war had been a prolonged nightmare for the Army of Northern Virginia. Under Grant's leadership, the Union had successfully prosecuted a "hard war" strategy, designed to deplete the resources and sap the morale of Southern soldiers and civilians alike, as well as to mobilize the Union's superior manpower. Since September of 1864, the Confederacy had experienced a crushing string of reverses: the surrender of Atlanta to Sherman's army; Lincoln's reelection; Sherman's march to the sea; Sheridan's Shenandoah campaign; the fall of Fort Fisher, the last viable supply line into the Confederacy; and the Union conquest, at the end of a grinding siege, of the Confederate capital of Richmond and of Petersburg, a vital rail junction and logistical lifeline. The government of President Jefferson Davis had evacuated the capital just in advance of the Union troops and fled to

Danville, Virginia, nearly 150 miles southwest of Richmond. On April 2, 1865, on the heels of Davis's flight, Lee withdrew some 60,000 troops from the trenches that ran from Richmond to Petersburg; the Federal army pursued Lee's retreating columns with a force of nearly 80,000.[5]

The main topographical features running west from the Richmond–Petersburg front were the Appomattox River and the South Side Railroad. As they left Petersburg, they veered away from each other, the river to the northwest and the railroad to the southwest, only to twist back and converge in the vicinity of Farmville. The river and railroad diverged again thereafter and nearly converged a second time near Appomattox Court House. Just beyond the end of the river, the railroad turned south at Lynchburg. As the retreat began, Lee's main columns moved parallel to the north bank of the Appomattox River; Grant and the Army of the James followed the tracks of the South Side Railroad; Sheridan's cavalry, along with infantry corps of the Army of the Potomac, took the straightest course due west, between Lee's line and Grant's. Success for Lee depended on his staying well ahead of the Federals, so that he could dip south at a point of his choosing; failing that, he would have to punch a hole in the Federal lines in order to effect his rendezvous with Johnston's army.[6]

Lee's opening gambit in the retreat failed. He intended for his columns to concentrate at Amelia Court House, where they would meet awaiting supply trains and pick up the tracks of the Richmond & Danville Railroad, which connected those two cities on a course running from the northeast to the southwest, across the Appomattox River and then the South Side Railroad en route to Danville. In short, the plan was for the army to head south from Amelia, along the railroad to Burkeville Junction, and then beyond the Virginia state line and on to North Carolina. But the provisions failed to materialize, and the Confederates wasted a day in fruitless foraging while awaiting General Richard Ewell's column from Richmond. Sheridan knew well that this was yet another severe setback for an army that was already physically and psychologically depleted by a year of trench warfare during Grant's prolonged siege of the Confederate capital; Lee's men had long been fighting the specter of hunger and malnutrition. He knew too, thanks to Union reconnaissance, that Lee had arranged for rations to be sent to Burkeville Junction, southwest of Amelia, so that the Confederate army could reprovision there and salvage Lee's original plan.

Brave Ulysses: Grant in 1864. (Library of Congress)

So the Federals concentrated at Jetersville Depot, a stop nearly halfway to Burkeville from Amelia, across Lee's projected line of march—and thus forced him to shift his course, first northward and then to the west, through Rice's Station toward Farmville, where rations would be waiting. Sheridan, it seemed, was anticipating Lee's every move.[7]

Lee's army endured a harrowing night march on April 5. Desertion had plagued the Army of Northern Virginia during the previous year, and by the early spring, it literally wore that army away, with thousands of Confederates drifting away from the retreat, driven by deprivation, despair, and thoughts of home. Meanwhile Grant, who had trailed 16 miles behind Sheridan's vanguard earlier that day but who had heeded Sheridan's summons that he race to the front, met with Sheridan at 10:00 p.m. at a makeshift headquarters "in a small log cabin in the middle of a tobacco patch." Grant poured over Sheridan's maps and heard his cavalry commander's plea: Grant should reject the proposal of Major General George G. Meade, head of the Army of the Potomac, who believed Lee had settled in around Amelia Court House and advocated attacking his right flank there. Sheridan was sure that Lee had tried to slip the Federal trap; Meade's advance on Amelia Court House would be useless. Sylvanus Cadwallader, a *New York Herald* correspondent attached to Grant's headquarters, witnessed this scene and commented that Sheridan was "enthusiastic, positive and not a little profane in expressing his opinions." Grant could not hide his "quiet enjoyment of Sheridan's impetuosity."[8]

Grant also had respect for Meade, with whom he had worked amicably in what could have been a fraught command arrangement. Upon his promotion to supreme commander of the Union forces, Grant had opted to travel with Meade's Army of the Potomac and to direct its operations in person. Despite the fact that this rendered the victor of Gettysburg a subordinate in his own army, Meade proved loyal to Grant and indispensable in executing Grant's strategic vision. Sheridan, by contrast, sparked Meade's notoriously volatile temper; Meade was visibly angered by Sheridan's rise as the "star among Grant's lieutenants in the East." Sheridan, in turn, was exasperated by Meade. Sapped by a respiratory illness since the fall of Petersburg, Meade seemed to Sheridan to have lost his fighting edge.[9]

Sheridan and Grant together met with Meade at midnight on April 5 and reminded him that the Federals' aim was not to follow Lee but rather to get in his front. Grant agreed with Sheridan that the Confederate retreat had become "a life and death struggle" for Lee to secure provisions for his army. Grant ordered Meade's infantry to advance on Amelia Court House and Sheridan's cavalry to head west; if Sheridan was correct—and Lee had resumed his westward march—the Union infantry could then veer to the left and fall in with Sheridan.[10]

The morning of April 6 vindicated Little Phil as the Federal infantry advance on Amelia confirmed that Lee's men, in a night march, had evacuated their former position. Sheridan's cavalry took up a hot pursuit, soon joined by Meade's hastily redeployed infantry. The Federals caught up with the Confederates in the muddy bottom lands of Big and Little Sailor's Creek, a tributary of the Appomattox swollen from recent heavy rains. The creek descended south from the river in a wishbone shape, with the handle of the wishbone opening into its two prongs: Little Sailor's Creek to the east and Big Sailor's Creek to the west. Lee, who rode with General Longstreet's First and Third Corps at the head of the Confederate line of march, made steady progress, moving without incident beyond the creek crossings toward Rice's Station—unaware, at first, of the descending chaos farther down the line, where the three interlocking Battles of Sailor's Creek were being joined under gray skies and spring showers.[11]

Union forces led by Sheridan's cavalry and the Army of the Potomac's Sixth Corps under Major General Horatio Wright and the Second Corps under Major General Andrew A. Humphreys converged on the Confederate forces of Lieutenant Generals Richard H. Anderson and Richard S. Ewell and Major General John B. Gordon. Anderson and Ewell, who held the second and third positions in Lee's marching order, had been harassed as they moved west by Sheridan's cavalry. In the afternoon of April 6, Anderson, after crossing Little Sailor's Creek, decided to stop and fight, drawing up a defensive line at Marshall's Cross Roads (also known as Harper's Farm) and bracing his men for the onslaught of Federal horsemen. The Union advance was initially driven back but soon broke the rebel line, with George Armstrong Custer leading the decisive charge. A brevet major general at the tender age of 25, Custer commanded the Third Division of Sheridan's cavalry and embodied the élan of the ideal cavalryman.

Bedecked in a custom-made uniform of gold-lace trimmed velvet, with a signature red necktie and wide brimmed hat, the golden-maned Custer cut a romantic figure—but it was his instinct for combat and his conspicuous bravery that endeared him to Sheridan and to his troops. Men were simply "ashamed to be cowardly" under such a leader as one of Custer's subordinates put it. On this day, the spoils of Custer's triumph included materiel of war Lee could ill afford to lose—about 800 horses and mules, 300 wagons, and 15 pieces of artillery. It also included bounty priceless in symbolic value: 31 banners of Confederate regiments.[12]

Ewell, for his part, after crossing Little Sailor's Creek a mile to the north of Marshall's Cross Roads, was chased down by the Federal infantry of Wright's Sixth Corps near Hillsman's Farm. Horatio Wright had taken command of the Sixth as part of Grant's shake-up of the senior command in Virginia; another West Pointer who ranked among Grant's favorite lieutenants, Wright had the good fortune to inherit a veteran corps that was already fabled for its aggressiveness, and he had fulfilled Grant's high expectations with a decisive attack on the Petersburg lines on April 2.[13]

In the late afternoon of April 6, Wright's army and Ewell's menaced each other from the heights on either side of the creek. Union artillery, only 800 yards from the Confederates' quickly improvised rail works, prepared the way for the infantry attack, which commenced at about 6:00 p.m. According to Brevet Brigadier General J. Warren Keifer, a careful chronicler of the battle, Union soldiers "descended into the valley" between the lines, moved steadily across the swampy creek bank "in the face of a destructive fire" from the enemy, "and, with shouldered guns and ammunition-boxes also, in most cases over the shoulder, waded through the flooded stream . . . without a halt or waver in the line." Once they made the crossing, the Federals reeled back in the face of a fierce volley from Ewell's entrenched line. Ewell's troops, flushed with their initial success, bounded over the rail works in pursuit of the fleeing Federals and drove the Union soldiers at bayonet point back over the creek. The Confederates' reckless countercharge, Keifer notes, made them vulnerable because they were in advance of their own defenses, and the Union seized the moment with a barrage of canister, announcing the start of a second Federal assault. Overwhelmed by a coordinated attack on both flanks and the center of their lines, the Confederates had no way to end this "bloody slaughter" but to surrender. In this segment of the battlefield, General Ewell himself was the prime quarry. He was swept up by the Federals— and soon his officers gave over their formal capitulation. Wright crowed in his report on the battle that the enemy had been "annihilated" by the "murderous" combination of Federal artillery, infantry, and cavalry fire- power. His Sixth Corps had "nobly sustained its well-earned reputation."[14]

As the diary entries of Colonel Elisha Hunt Rhodes of the 2nd Rhode Island infantry reveal, the junior officers of the Sixth Corps, too, knew well that they had just "won a victory that must help to bring the war to a close." But their joy at bagging Ewell and setting fire to captured Confed- erate wagons was tempered by their own losses—in the case of the 2nd Rhode Island, 44 killed and wounded. "So near the end and yet men must die," Rhodes lamented on April 7, in what would prove a fitting epitaph for the Appomattox campaign.[15]

More men were dying in the third of the battles, two miles to the north. Ewell had hoped to save the bulk of the Confederate wagon trains by directing them along the Jamestown Road to cross Sailor's Creek over the "double bridges" at the top of the wishbone. Gordon's Second Corps of the Army of Northern Virginia had followed that train— opening another breach in Lee's order of march. Union troops in Major General Andrew A. Humphrey's Second Corps kept Gordon in their sights. Humphreys, a West Point engineer who had formerly served as Meade's chief of staff, had assumed command of the Second Corps in the fall of 1864, replacing the wounded hero of Gettysburg, Winfield Scott Hancock. Humphreys was admired by his contemporaries for his intellectual precision, and this quality is displayed in his crisp dispatches to Meade's headquarters and in his detailed after-battle reports and postwar memoir. The Second Corps began its pursuit of Gordon on the morning of April 6 and kept up the chase all day, driving the enemy some 14 miles from Amelia Sulphur Springs to Sailor's Creek, "over every foot of which a running fight was kept up," Humphreys wrote. "The country was broken, and consisted of open fields alternating with forest with dense undergrowth, and swamps, over and through which lines of battle followed closely on the skirmish line with a rapidity and nearness of connection" that astonished him. The Confederates' desper- ation was evident, as their route of retreat was "literally lined with their tents, baggage, and cooking utensils," cast aside in the quest to stay a few steps ahead of their Union foes.[16]

The coup de grâce came just before dark. Capitalizing on the fact that the rebel wagon train had become mired in mud and backed up, the Union Second Corps assaulted Gordon's men, who had formed a battle line north and west of the congested double bridges. In the ensuing clash, the wagons themselves served as Confederate breastworks and abatis. As it had in the battles to the south, under Sheridan and Wright, the Union force again proved overpowering. The Confederates lost more than 200 wagons and 70 ambulances, as well as precious guns and ammunition. The human toll was no less staggering. While Gordon's command escaped, and the remnants of his Second Corps regrouped and moved west, thousands of less fortunate Confederates were captured by the Federals. By nightfall, the scope of the Union victory had become clear. The three Battles of Sailor's Creek had cost Lee nearly one-fifth of his remaining force. Confederate casualties numbered approximately 7,700 compared with 1,148 for the Union. Among the eight generals the Union captured was none other than Robert E. Lee's oldest son, George Washington Custis Lee.[17]

There were, on April 6, no intimations of mercy in the treatment accorded the Confederate captives. The day had witnessed, Sheridan insisted, "one of the severest conflicts of the war, for the enemy fought with desperation to escape capture, and we, bent on his destruction, were no less eager and determined." The rebel prisoners—one of the largest forces to surrender without terms in the entire war—were rounded up and sent to prison camps in the North. Lee, who rode east from Rice's Station only to witness his men fleeing the scene of battle, exclaimed, "My God! Has the army been dissolved?" Southerners mourning the demise of their cause would thereafter remember this day as "Black Thursday."[18]

Sheridan had been the mastermind of the battles, coordinating the infantry and cavalry assaults. His effort to take credit for the day incurred the wrath of Meade, who felt, with some justification, that Wright's infantry corps and Humphreys were given short shrift. No one could deny that Sheridan had performed brilliantly in deploying the cavalry as a strike force. As one Confederate artilleryman put it, Sheridan's horsemen called to mind the marauding Cossacks who had driven Napoleon from

Moscow: they would "make sudden swoops upon our wearied and half-starved lines," and then "sweep off in widening circles, only to return again when a favorable opportunity presented itself, and renew their harassing attacks." In keeping with the Union's hard-war strategy, these were tactics of intimidation, meant not only to deplete the rebels but also to unnerve them.[19]

Reporting to Grant that night that he had "routed [the enemy] handsomely," Sheridan delivered the lasting verdict on the day: "If the thing is pressed I think that Lee will surrender." Grant forwarded the message to Lincoln, who in a pithy response emblematic of his way with words and of the command harmony he shared with Grant and Sheridan, responded, laconically: "Let the thing be pressed."[20]

Sharing Sheridan's sense of urgency, Major General Edward O. C. Ord of the Army of the James had played a key role in the day's progress. Before sunrise on April 6, he had deployed a raiding party of two infantry

"Little Phil" Sheridan showed the reeling Confederates no intimation of mercy. (Library of Congress)

regiments and a cavalry detachment from his Army of the James north-west from Burkeville to destroy the South Side Railroad's High Bridge, one of the possible escape routes for the retreating Confederate columns. Ord, like Sheridan, was a West Pointer and part of Grant's inner circle. Although he could not boast Sheridan's record of victories, Ord had won Grant's trust with reliable service in the Army of the Tennessee—and like Sheridan, he came east at Grant's request. In January of 1865, Ord took command of the Army of the James. Although a temperamental and self-centered man, Ord was deeply loyal to Grant and preferable in Grant's eyes to his predecessor, the sour and unreliable Benjamin Butler.[21]

Ord's logistical target at this juncture, the High Bridge, was an elaborate structure—a 2,500-foot-long railroad bridge suspended 125 feet high on immense brick pillars, with a wagon bridge below it. The bridge carried the South Side Railroad across the Appomattox River to its north bank; the railroad then ran north of the river for a short stretch before crossing to the south bank again on bridges beyond Farmville. Eager to protect such a lifeline, Longstreet, who received intelligence of the Federal gambit, sought to counter it by sending the cavalry, under Major General Fitzhugh Lee (Lee's nephew) and including Major General Thomas L. Rosser (Custer's best friend at West Point), to the scene. In the ensuing clash on April 6, the Confederate cavalry surrounded the Union raiding party and not only preserved the bridge but also took roughly 780 Union men prisoner. This success promised initially to be a counterweight to the Sailor's Creek debacle. The Confederate army left the scene of those battles on the night of April 6 in two columns. One, consisting of Gordon's decimated command and Major General William Mahone's division of reinforcements, sought to use High Bridge to get north of the river; the other, led by Lee and Longstreet, proceeded south of the river to Farmville. By dividing the army this way, Lee hoped to avoid a scenario in which his forces were strung out—and vulnerable to Sheridan's swooping attacks—along a single route. Moreover, once Gordon and Mahone successfully crossed the High Bridge, the tables could be turned: Lee's men could destroy the structure to foil the trailing Federals.[22]

The first engagement at High Bridge proved to be a pyrrhic victory for the Confederates. As the main body of Ord's army moved north from Burkeville to pursue Longstreet toward Farmville, the Union Second

Corps under Humphreys moved out from Sailor's Creek in the early morning of April 7, and the Federals soon learned from local citizens that the main body of Confederate troops was headed to High Bridge. Humphreys was determined that his corps would again keep up a running fight with the Confederates. The Federals arrived at High Bridge at 7:00 a.m., not long after the last of Gordon's and Mahone's men had piled across it—and not long after Confederate engineers had set the spans to the torch. The Union infantry worked feverishly to extinguish the flames on the lower wagon bridge and to drive back the "considerable force of the enemy. . . . drawn up in a strong position on the heights of the opposite bank," as Humphreys noted. By 9:00 a.m., blue troops were making their way across the wagon bridge to continue their harassment of the Confederates.[23]

At that very hour, Longstreet's famished men were falling upon the rations issued them—their first in four and a half days—at Farmville on the south bank of the river. Soon they were ordered to move out, hungry still, as one of Sheridan's cavalry divisions and Ord's infantry swarmed in. Lee chose to direct his retreating columns back north across the Appomattox using the railroad and wagon bridges at Farmville and after burning those bridges, to use the river as a protective cordon as the Army of Northern Virginia moved toward Appomattox Station, where rations were sent from Lynchburg. In a rare lapse of judgment, Lee had rejected the advice of General Edward Porter Alexander, who had urged him to choose the more direct route, south of the river, to Appomattox Court House and then to the station. Unfortunately for Lee, Humphreys's Second Corps had successfully crossed the High Bridge, so he, too, was north of the river. He attacked Lee's flank at Cumberland Church, five miles away from the High Bridge crossing. In a fight that lasted from 1:00 p.m. until dark, Confederate forces under Mahone and Longstreet beat back a series of Federal attacks.[24]

This was another hollow victory. Meade and Grant recognized the need to reinforce Humphreys north of the river, and by day's end, help was on the way in the form of Wright's Sixth Corps, which improvised a foot bridge and commandeered a pontoon bridge to cross the Appomattox River at Farmville. The fighting on April 7 had not only foiled Lee's plan to use the river as a shield, but it also left the Federals massed in

Scene of another lost chance: the imposing High Bridge. (Library of Congress)

Farmville, with Sheridan already moving along the very route, south of the river, that Lee had rejected; Sheridan's intelligence reports confirmed his sense that "Lynchburg was undoubtedly [Lee's] objective point now." (Uniting with General Joseph Johnston's army in North Carolina remained Lee's ultimate objective.) Sheridan again was prescient and decisive: "Resolving to throw my cavalry again across his path, and hold him till the infantry could over take him, I directed everything on Appomattox depot," a rail stop on the South Side Railroad en route to Lynchburg, due west. Sheridan soon learned that his wily scouts, posing as Confederates and brandishing a purloined dispatch from Lee, had sent on seven boxcars of provisions for the Confederates from Lynchburg to the Appomattox depot. With advance notice of where the food stores were heading, Sheridan would have another chance to deprive Lee's men of sustenance.[25]

Grant arrived in Farmville on April 7 and set up headquarters at Randolph House. He still wore the same uniform—now spattered with mud—in which he had undertaken his night ride to Sheridan on April 5. He was soon joined in Farmville by Ord and by Ord's principal corps commander, Major General John Gibbon. Another career soldier who, like Sheridan, was independent and outspoken, Gibbon made his name as a brigade and division commander at the Second Battle of Bull Run, South Mountain, Antietam, Fredericksburg, Gettysburg, and the Virginia Overland campaign in the spring of 1864. Grant, historians agree, "ranked Gibbon as one of the finest commanders in the Army of the Potomac," and in January 1865, Gibbon was rewarded for his service with command of the newly created Twenty-fourth Corps of the Army of the James. Grant directed Ord and Gibbon to support Sheridan south of the river. Then he turned to them and said, "I have a great mind to summon Lee to surrender."[26]

As Gibbon recalls, Grant must have "had the matter already well prepared in his mind," for "very shortly" after this conversation, Grant penned a two sentence note to Lee:

April 7, 1865—5 p.m.

General R.E. LEE,
   Commanding C.S. Army:

GENERAL: The result of the last week must convince you of the hopelessness of further resistance on the part of the Army of Northern Virginia in this struggle. I feel that it is so, and regard it as my duty to shift from myself the responsibility of any further effusion of blood by asking of you the surrender of that portion of the C.S. army known as the Army of Northern Virginia.

Very respectfully, your obedient servant,
U. S. GRANT,
Lieutenant-General, Commanding Armies of the United States[27]

The delivery of this message was entrusted to Brigadier General Seth Williams, the inspector general on his headquarters staff. It was a savvy choice on Grant's part; Williams had served as adjutant for Lee at West Point. Williams was to make his way to Lee's lines via the Union's Second Army Corps headquarters.[28]

Grant's first note inaugurated a correspondence with Lee that ultimately comprised four exchanges of letters leading to the April 9 meeting at Appomattox. None of the letters was transparent in meaning. Rather they reflected complex military and political calculations, rooted not only in each man's assessment of the exigencies of the moment but also in his strategic vision, his deliberations with his key advisers, and his wartime experiences.

So what were Grant's calculations as he inscribed the April 7 note into his worn, yellowed dispatch book? His own accounts show that uppermost in his thoughts was the knowledge that Sheridan had a jump on Lee in the race to Appomattox Station. Shortly after he sent the note through the lines, Grant wrote orders for the following morning, specifying that Major General Charles Griffin's Fifth Army Corps would join Sheridan, Ord, and Gibbon in setting a trap for Lee. (A "proud, abrasive, and bellicose" former artillerist, Griffin was another veteran of the Overland campaign whom Grant had rewarded with a corps command, after Sheridan had relieved General Gouvernor K. Warren of command during the Battle of Five Forks, on April 1, 1865.) Meanwhile, Humphreys and Wright, with Grant and Meade in train, would track Lee north of the river and push him into the trap. Grant also had in mind a conversation he had the previous day with a captured Confederate officer. That officer revealed that Ewell and other Confederate prisoners believed the cause was lost and that any further bloodshed would be "very little better than murder." This evidence of disaffection within the Confederate high command confirmed Grant's sense, one shared by his inner circle of commanders, of the "hopelessness" of the Confederate cause.[29]

As he chose his words on April 7, Grant was not only sifting recent developments. At that moment, he felt the echoes of history. In his message to Lee, Grant invoked George Washington's correspondence with General Cornwallis at Yorktown in 1781. In his correspondence with Cornwallis, Washington had evinced his "ardent desire to spare the further effusion of blood." This phrasing was part of the American military lexicon, and it appeared in exchanges over the surrenders of Fort Sumter, Fort Pulaski, Vicksburg, and Atlanta, among other Civil War battle sites.[30]

Though formulaic, the "effusion" phrase had a special resonance for Grant. He had deeply personal reasons for wanting to shift to Lee the responsibility for further bloodshed. Lee's casualty rate, estimated from 18 percent to 20 percent, was much higher than Grant's (10.2 percent). But this fact was obscured by political rhetoric. During the Overland campaign the preceding spring and summer, as the Union army suffered horrific losses at the Wilderness, Spotsylvania Court House, Cold Harbor, and the Crater, the antiwar Copperhead press had fastened on Grant the epithet of "The Butcher." His tactics, they charged, had no purpose but to "gratify the ambition or malice of politicians and scoundrels." Grant had been stung by this criticism but not deterred. He knew the Union sacrifices served a higher purpose: to bring Lee to his knees. Vindication was close at hand. Whether Lee chose willfully to consign his army to certain destruction or he chose to surrender it, the mantle of "butcher" would necessarily fall, at last, from Grant's shoulders.[31]

2

Councils of War

Lee, at Blanton House in Cumberland County, received Grant's note at around 9:30 p.m. on April 7. The circumstances of its delivery were not auspicious; the bearer Seth Williams had run a gauntlet of diffident Confederate pickets, who opened fire on him and killed one of his orderlies. Longstreet, who was with Lee, recalls the scene: "I was sitting at his side when the note was delivered. He read it and handed it to me without referring to its contents. After reading it I gave it back, saying, 'Not yet.'" Lee instructed his aide-de-camp, Colonel Charles Marshall, to write out the following answer to Grant:

April 7, 1865

Lieut. Gen. U. S. GRANT,
    Commanding Armies of the United States:

GENERAL: I have received your note of this date. Though not entertaining the opinion you express of the hopelessness of further resistance on the part of the Army of Northern Virginia, I reciprocate your desire to avoid useless effusion of blood, and therefore, before considering your proposition, ask the terms you will offer on condition of its surrender.

R.E. LEE,
General[1]

Lee did not show the response to Longstreet, but Longstreet surmised, based on the orders Lee soon gave for another night march, that Lee had rejected Grant's overture. As Seth Williams rushed the response back to

Grant, the Confederate army moved out, toward the stage stop of New Store on the Richmond–Lynchburg Stage Road. That road would take Lee's troops to Appomattox and the South Side Railroad; if all went according to plan, the Southern army would reprovision at Appomattox Station; then make its way to Campbell Court House, 30 miles south of Lynchburg; and from there to Danville.[2]

Why did Lee and Longstreet decide to fight on? The two men shared a deep trust born of Longstreet's service as the "steadiest and most reliable officer in Lee's army." An imposing man of great mental and physical toughness, Longstreet had been a pillar of strength for Lee, particularly now, as Lee's strength was ebbing. Fifty-eight years of age in the spring of 1865, Lee was still described by contemporaries as a strikingly elegant and handsome man. But his command style—he shared the hardships of his soldiers on the march, rather than benefiting from superior food and accommodations; reconnoitered key enemy positions rather than relying on junior officers for such intelligence; and kept a small staff, which freed up men for fighting but burdened Lee with crushing administrative duties—had taken its toll. Lee had suffered two broken wrists, a heart attack, and chronic rheumatism over the course of the war and clearly could not take much more.[3]

Both men knew that the Confederate command structure had atrophied over the past week. Not only had Lee lost Ewell and seven other generals to capture at Sailor's Creek but he would soon also decide to relieve from their commands Anderson and Major Generals George E. Pickett and Bushrod Johnson for poor performance in the week's fighting. Lee's inner circle was reduced to his three stalwart Major Generals, Longstreet, Gordon, and Mahone; three artillery chiefs, Brigadier Generals William N. Pendleton, Edward Porter Alexander, and Armistead L. Long; his personal staff, led by Marshall, Colonel Charles S. Venable, and Colonel Walter H. Taylor; and his cavalry corps chief and nephew, Major General Fitzhugh Lee.

These men's unity of purpose had been somewhat frayed over the course of the retreat. Alexander, the most analytically astute of his lieutenants, was brooding over Lee's ill-fated decision to move the army north of the river; "no man who looked at our situation on a map," he averred, "could fail to see that Genl. Grant now had us completely in a trap." Moreover, in the hours before Grant's message arrived, Pendleton, claiming to represent a group of officers who had recently conferred and deemed the cause lost, met with Lee to raise the delicate subject of surrender. A classmate and close friend of Lee's from West Point, Pendleton was one of the war's "fighting parsons" (he was an Episcopal priest); his avowed purpose at that moment was to remove from Lee the stigma of broaching the subject of surrender himself.[4]

Lee would countenance no such martyrdom. He rejected the proposal, with the following rebuke to Pendleton: "General, we have yet too many bold men to think of laying down our arms. The enemy do not fight with spirit, while our boys still do." Here was Lee's famous faith in the ability of his "boys" to work miracles and his contempt for an enemy that had many times before—most notably at Antietam and Gettysburg—failed to pursue the Confederates with vigor and to finish them off. Lee trusted that there were enough "true men left," as the dogged Mahone put it, to revive the South's chances.[5]

Lee was not only acting on faith but also making political calculations. He continued, to Pendleton, "Besides, if I were to say a word to the Federal commander he would regard it as such a confession of weakness as to make it the condition of demanding unconditional surrender—a proposal to which I will never listen." His foe's reputation as "Unconditional Surrender" Grant was forged in the winter of 1862, when Grant captured Fort Donelson on the Cumberland River in Tennessee. He had rejected the Confederate commander's request for an "armistice . . . to settle terms of capitulation" with the terse, and soon famous, reply: "No terms except an unconditional and immediate surrender can be accepted." From that time on, Grant was the very picture, in Southern eyes, of mercilessness— an image enhanced by his relentless hammering of Lee's army in Virginia.[6]

Bristling at the thought of unconditional surrender, Lee at this key moment held out hopes for a negotiated peace: one in which the Confederacy, even if forced to capitulate, could still impose conditions on or extract concessions from the Yankees. Such hopes were rooted in Lee's understanding of Confederate war aims. Keenly aware, from the war's start, of the North's superiority in manpower and resources and of the fearful odds against his overwhelming the Federal army, Lee had long imagined that signal Confederate victories might bring the Northern people to their senses and cause them to repudiate the Lincoln administration and to concede Southern independence. This scenario for victory rested on the possibility that the Northern "Peace Democrats"—a faction that demanded the restoration of the Union "as it was" and promised to exact no punitive measures, perhaps not even emancipation itself, should the South come to the negotiating table—could be converted to an essentially pro-Southern position. The idea that decisive military triumphs could effect a revolution in Northern politics was behind Lee's two ill-fated invasions of the North in 1862 and 1863; nothing seemed better calculated to undermine the Republican regime than Southern victories on Northern soil. As Lee's aide-de-camp Charles Marshall put it, "The arguments for peace in the North would have been much more convincing if victory had placed Washington, Baltimore, or Philadelphia within our reach."[7]

Lee in 1864, when there was still hope for the Confederate cause. (Library of Congress)

The resounding reelection of Lincoln in the 1864 election—and the thorough discrediting of the Peace Democrats as treacherous Copperheads—dealt a blow to Southern hopes for a political revolution in the North. Those hopes received another blow at the Hampton Roads Peace Conference on February 3, 1865, where Lincoln brusquely disabused a delegation of Confederate commissioners of the idea that peace could come without reunion and emancipation. But these setbacks did not dispel the resilient Southern fantasy that men of good faith in the North might yet be persuaded to come to the negotiating table. What, exactly, might the South negotiate for? Jefferson Davis's vice president Alexander Stephens led a peace faction that sought a settlement recognizing the sovereignty of the individual Southern states; as the historian Steven E. Woodworth explains, such "an exceedingly ambiguous formula . . . could have embraced a restored Union, an independent Confederacy, or perhaps something in between." The last of Davis's five secretaries of war, John C. Breckinridge, nurtured his own conviction, in the war's final spring, that the cause was lost—the best course was to seek a favorable settlement before the army and government were snuffed out altogether. Even with Southern independence off the table, the Confederates could, he reasoned, still try to secure some concessions on the questions of the confiscation of Southern property, amnesty for leaders of the rebellion, and, perhaps, compensation for emancipated slaves. What Stephens and Breckinridge hoped for was a ceasefire, "expecting that once the guns stopped, the North would not have the will to start fighting again." An armistice could lead to an "honorable peace."[8]

Unfortunately for would-be negotiators, the man at the top, Jefferson Davis, insisted to the last that there could be no peace without Confederate independence. The lightning rod for all the political disaffection in the turbulent Confederate government, Davis had been seared by constant criticism from his Congress, Southern governors, and the press; that criticism exacerbated his tendency to be isolated, stubborn, and imperious. "As the war went on, Davis demonstrated more and more that he saw himself and the Confederacy as one and the same, inseparable," the historian William C. Davis has noted. The Confederate president summarily rejected any peace proposals that would concede independence, on the grounds that "he had no constitutional power to negotiate for his own suicide." Davis rejected the conditions for peace that Lincoln invoked at Hampton Roads—that Confederates accept emancipation and reunion—as "degrading" and "humiliating." He did not want Lincoln's pardon: "Amnesty," Davis fumed, "applies to criminals." Davis's defiant mentality was fueled, over the course of the conflict, by Lee's many odds-defying battlefield successes and by Davis's conviction that he best knew the mood of the public. This was the crippling irony at the heart of the Confederate debates over the prospect of peace: the moments when Confederate military victories gave the South the greatest potential bargaining power were the very moments when Davis and the Confederate public were surest of their ultimate victory and therefore most unwilling to negotiate.[9]

Lee seems to have tried to steer a course between the two alternatives of timely concession and inveterate defiance. His growing affinity for the rhetoric of an honorable peace and his determination to keep his options open are revealed by his reaction to a strange encounter, on February 25, 1865, between none other than Longstreet and Ord. The two opposing generals were old friends. When the Hampton Roads Conference failed, Longstreet and Ord met between the lines, and at Ord's urging agreed that they would propose a meeting of the senior officers of both armies to negotiate a settlement. Ord, a Maryland Democrat opposed to abolitionism, thought it best that the "slavery question" was "taken out of the hands of politicians"; Longstreet agreed that a "military convention" could best forge an honorable peace, in which, for example, Southerners might be remunerated for the loss of their slaves. Longstreet went so far as to pitch the idea of such a convention to Lee and Jefferson Davis. Lee, approving it, then wrote to Grant, on March 2, 1865, expressing his desire to "leave nothing untried which may put an end to the calamities of war." But the overture went nowhere, as Grant soon made it clear that political questions lay beyond his jurisdiction. He could only address subjects of "purely a military character." Ord and Longstreet took the fizzling of their scheme in stride and returned promptly to the business of fighting. Davis cynically held up the failure of the two February peace efforts as confirmation that the Lincoln administration simply would not negotiate in good faith and that the Confederacy must fight to the death.[10]

Lee, for his part, could accept neither the futility of negotiations nor the inevitability of defeat. Breckinridge, whose "settle before it is too late" position was informed by Lee's sobering reports on the depleted state of the Confederate army, tried in the war's final month to get Lee to recommend surrender. The secretary of war was sure Lee shared his conviction that the South would get more favorable terms if the government surrendered intact than it would if its leaders were hunted down in scattered outlaw bands. But Lee could not abandon the hope that his army might still win politically meaningful battlefield victories, ones that pulled the Confederacy back from the brink and gave it renewed leverage.[11] Even as late as April 7, 1865, in the wake of the Sailor's Creek debacle, Lee believed that something—the power to influence would-be negotiations and to shape public opinion itself— could still be gained by further resistance. The effusion of Confederate blood, as Lee implied in his message to Grant, and as Longstreet likewise suggested in his two-word rejoinder to Lee, was not yet "useless."

Even if political concessions regarding slavery and states' rights seemed only a remote possibility in April of 1865, national pride and personal pride were still very much at stake. Lee and Longstreet were keenly aware that other Confederates who had surrendered their commands, such as Brigadier General Simon Buckner of Fort Donelson, were held in low esteem by the Southern public.[12] And one can surmise, by the way Lee deprecated Grant's mere "opinion" that the Southern cause was hopeless, that Lee had no intention of letting Grant hand down a verdict on the state of the Southern army. Lee's April 7 message to Grant, in short, insisted on two things: Grant was wrong about the inevitability of Southern defeat and therefore right to open negotiations with Lee over the peace.

Seth Williams hastened the note to Grant, who received it at daybreak on April 8 and answered it that morning. To Lee's query about the nature of the terms proposed, Grant responded:

April 8, 1865

GENERAL R.E. LEE,
Commanding C.S. Army:

GENERAL: Your note of last evening, in reply to mine of same date, asking the condition on which I will accept surrender of the Army of Northern Virginia, is just received. In reply I would say that, peace being my great desire, there is but one condition I would insist upon, viz, that the men and officers surrendered shall be disqualified for taking up arms again against the Government of the United States until properly exchanged. I will meet you, or will designate officers to meet any officers you name for the same purpose, at any point agreeable to you, for the purpose of arranging definitely the terms upon which the surrender of the Army of Northern Virginia will be received.

Very respectfully, your obedient servant,
U. S. GRANT,
Commanding Armies of the United States[13]

In specifying these terms, Grant had both a precedent and a mandate in mind. The precedent, as the historian Joan Waugh has noted, was found in the terms Grant offered to Lieutenant General John C. Pemberton at Vicksburg, Mississippi, on July 4, 1863. There, nearly 30,000 Confederate survivors of Grant's prolonged siege were paroled: they were sent back to their lines on the promise, sworn to on each man's signed "parole," that they would not take up arms against the Union again until exchanged. Under the elaborate prison cartel system the two sides had established, a paroled prisoner of war either went to one of his own side's parole camps to be exchanged or went home, where he could, if he desired to get back into the fray, await word of and then report for an impending exchange. That system had broken down in the fall of 1863, in part because of the Confederates' breach of faith: they refused to treat African American soldiers, enlisted in the wake of Lincoln's Emancipation Proclamation, as paroled prisoners of war and instead enslaved or executed them. When the exchange system was suspended, prisoner of war camps filled up. Under mounting public pressure, the practice of exchanges was resumed in January of 1865.[14]

Grant had been quite forthright in the rationale for his Vicksburg terms. His leniency toward the prostrate Confederates would "make them less dangerous foes during the continuance of hostilities, and better citizens after the war was over." He hoped the parolees would melt into the countryside and into civilian life rather than report for exchange. The same logic—with an emphasis on the eventuality of peace—was at work in Grant's April 8 offer to Lee. Grant knew well that if Lee accepted his terms, the Army of Northern Virginia would never be "exchanged." Lee's paroled soldiers would be, instead, in perpetual limbo: prisoners of war whom the victorious Union had granted a conditional freedom from captivity. Grant trusted that these soldiers, even more than his Vicksburg parolees, would welcome the chance to go home and lay down their arms forever.[15]

Grant's mandate in April of 1865 was, paradoxically, to offer liberal terms of unconditional surrender to Lee's army. Lincoln had laid out the groundwork for this policy painstakingly and at great political risk. Through his bitter battle for reelection, in the face of Democratic charges that he was needlessly prolonging the war, Lincoln remained firm that the U.S. government alone would set the conditions for peace—and that those conditions were the reestablishment of national authority through-out all the states and the abandonment of slavery.

This stance accorded well with Grant's view of the North's evolving war aims. Grant's political affinities with Lincoln were deeply rooted but their political convergence was a long time in the making. Like Lincoln, Grant had favored the Whig Party before the war and had admired the "great compromiser" Henry Clay. Although Grant had distinguished himself as a junior officer in the Mexican War, he shared the Whig Party's view, one represented by Lincoln in Congress, that the war had been at its root an unjust Southern bid for more slave territory. Like Lincoln, Grant had a strong visceral dislike of slavery but also deep distrust of those radical ab-olitionists who called for immediate emancipation; like Lincoln, Grant had married into an elite Southern slaveholding family. But while Lincoln had been instrumental in the mid-1850s in defining the new Republican Party's doctrine of the nonextension (rather than the abolition) of slavery, Grant, on the political sidelines, had cast his ballot in 1856 for the Demo-crat James Buchanan, seeing in him, wishfully, a moderate alternative to the sectional extremes of abolitionism and secession. When Lincoln emerged as the Republican Party's standard bearer in 1860, Grant leaned toward the Democrat Stephen Douglas, fearful that Lincoln's election would push the South over the edge.[16]

The rush to secession in the wake of Lincoln's victory, and Lincoln's stern resistance to secession, sparked Grant's gradual conversion to the Republican

Party. Grant agreed wholeheartedly with Lincoln that the framers had designed a perpetual Union and that secession was unconstitutional and anarchical; Grant felt too that the secessionists were bullies and hypocrites, who claimed to defend state sovereignty but then herded the Southern states into the Confederacy using tactics of intimidation. These were Grant's political views. But what was his political role once the war started? Grant believed strongly both in the subordination of military to civil rule and in the close connection between politics and military success. He deviated from both the senior West Pointers, like Henry Halleck, who were committed to conventional warfare and disdained politics and from "political generals" drawn from the civilian ranks, such as Benjamin Butler, who lobbied openly to shape the Lincoln administration's political objectives. Grant instead pledged himself "to support the political goals of the administration as they were presented to him," as historian Thomas J. Goss has explained, and he "was willing to use unconventional tactics to achieve the desired end." By the summer of 1862, confronted by civilian resistance and guerrilla depredations in Union-occupied Tennessee, Grant had accepted the idea that the war was a contest between two societies, not just two armies. He embraced hard-war measures, most notably emancipation, as a military necessity. In 1864, Grant openly rejected the Democrats' peace platform as an attempted "counter revolution," and he strongly endorsed Lincoln's reelection. Moreover, Grant became a vocal supporter of the most important corollary to emancipation: the enlistment of black troops in the Union army.[17]

Like Lincoln, Grant understood the Civil War to be exceptional. While the Revolution, War of 1812, and Mexican War had been brought to a close by peace treaties, the United States could not negotiate such a treaty with the Confederacy, as that would implicitly recognize its sovereignty as a separate nation and thus confer legitimacy on disunion itself. "The American Civil War could not end with a negotiated peace," explains the historian James McPherson, "because the issues over which it was fought— Union versus Disunion, Freedom versus Slavery—proved to be non-negotiable." If the South embraced reunion and black freedom, the Union could act with leniency; indeed, Lincoln's December 1863 Proclamation of Amnesty and Reconstruction had offered to pardon Confederates who took an oath of allegiance to the United States and swore to abide by emancipation. But the rebels would not dictate the terms of peace to the Union.[18]

After Lincoln's electoral triumph, this policy was reiterated in his February 3, 1865, meeting with Confederate peace commissioners at Hampton Roads. On March 28, Lincoln clarified his position again, in a meeting on the *River Queen* with Grant, General Sherman, and Admiral David D. Porter. From that point on, there could be no mistaking Grant's brief. He was to secure the capitulation of Lee's army and then offer terms in the liberal spirit Lincoln intended. Those terms were to encompass the surrender of a hostile army and not seek to resolve the political questions of the defeated Confederates' civil rights (such as their enfranchisement and the restoration of their property) and criminal liabilities or of their pardon and amnesty; those questions would be taken up by the civil authorities, within the framework Lincoln had constructed. Hence, Grant's offer to Lee, on April 8, of surrender by parole. Like the Vicksburg terms, these were military in character and therefore well within Grant's warrant from Lincoln.[19]

As Grant's second message found Lee, on the afternoon of April 8, the first of the final two battles of the campaign was being joined. There was relatively little fighting that day until shortly after 4:00 p.m., at which point the lead elements of Sheridan's cavalry, under Brevet Major General Wesley Merritt and Custer, began attacking Confederate positions at the railroad depot of Appomattox Station, which lay roughly three miles to the southwest of the village of Appomattox Court House (also known as Clover Hill). At first they encountered only a small cavalry contingent, detailed to protect the trains loaded with Confederate provisions. Custer's brigade succeeded in driving the Confederates back, only to run headlong into the withering fire of General R. L. Walker's reserve Confederate artillery train—some 100 pieces of artillery arranged in a semicircle in a dense forest of scrub oak and blackjack pine, about a half-mile from the station. The Confederates had the high ground and over the course of several hours beat back the Union cavalry. But Custer rallied his men for one final concerted attack, and by 8:00 p.m. the Federals had won the day: the Union had seized the Confederate supply trains at Appomattox Station; captured numerous artillery pieces; and driven Lee's advance guard back toward the village of Appomattox Court House, north of the station. Merritt felt that it was "impossible to overestimate the value of this day's work." Not only had the cavalry again taken food from the mouths of Lee's men, but they had also seized the high ground west of Appomattox Court House and blocked the Richmond–Lynchburg Stage Road—the vital artery along which Lee's army had lumbered from New Store toward Campbell Court House. Lee would not be able to steal another night march on Grant. The Confederates, strung out for 10 miles along the stage road, now confronted a Federal force positioned squarely across their line of march.[20]

In order that the Confederates "might have no rest," Sheridan directed his men to "continue the skirmishing throughout the night." He would hold the line and wait for reinforcements. "The necessity of getting Ord's column up was so obvious now," Sheridan wrote, "that staff-officer after staff-officer was sent to him and to General Grant requesting that the

Custer: symbol of the Northern cavalry's élan. (Library of Congress)

infantry be pushed on, for if it could get to the front, all knew that the rebellion would be ended on the morrow." In Sheridan's view, Lee would
not surrender "until compelled to do so," as he put it in a dispatch that
evening to Grant; what the Union needed to deliver now was not a symbolic show of force but a final knockout blow. Sheridan and his division
commanders did not sleep a wink, as they were buzzing "at the prospect
that our weary work was about to end so happily." The contrast between
their condition and that of their foes could not have been starker. As Merritt put it, with a poetic touch, the night of April 8 fell "darkly and terribly
on the Army of Northern Virginia."[21]

That army had spent the day pushing on to Appomattox from New
Store. Saturday the 8th was the "first quiet day of the march," Longstreet's
artillery chief Edward Porter Alexander recalled, but the reason for "this
fatal quiet," he noted somberly, was that Union cavalry, rather than attacking the Confederate flanks, was "hurrying along" to "head us off." It was
not just the soundscape but the landscape that struck Confederates as
eerie and redolent of defeat. Mahone found Appomattox to be the "most
god forsaken neighborhood one can conceive." His headquarters for the
evening were "in a miserable long [log] hut occupied by a family of
deformed people—that made me shiver to behold, and whose deformity
and condition forcibly suggested we were near the end."[22]

Sometime around sunset, Grant's second message was delivered to
Lee. Lee rejected the suggestion of his staff officer Charles Venable that he
simply disregard it. Instead Lee wrote out this reply:

April 8, 1865

Lieutenant-General GRANT,
   Commanding Armies of the United States:

GENERAL: I received at a late hour your note of to-day. In mine
of yesterday I did not intend to propose the surrender of the Army
of Northern Virginia, but to ask the terms of your proposition. To
be frank, I do not think the emergency has arisen to call for the
surrender of this army; but as the restoration of peace should be
the sole object of all, I desired to know whether your proposals
would lead to that end. I cannot, therefore, meet you with a view

to surrender the Army of Northern Virginia; but as far as your
proposal may affect the C.S. forces under my command, and tend
to the restoration of peace, I should be pleased to meet you at 10
a.m. to-morrow, on the old stage road to Richmond, between the
picket-lines of the two armies.

> Very respectfully, your obedient servant,
> R.E. LEE,
> *General*[23]

While Grant had a precedent and mandate for offering terms of surrender to his foe, Lee had at this stage in their correspondence no clear
precedent or a mandate for accepting such terms. Richmond was in Federal hands and Jefferson Davis, who had taken flight from the capital, was
in Danville, able to keep up only sporadic communications with Lee.
Davis had issued a proclamation to his countrymen on April 4 vowing to
maintain the fight for Confederate independence, and his hope was that
Lee would reach Danville and protect this new seat of government. Lacking a clear channel of communication with his own government, Lee was
forced to improvise.[24]

In using the word "restoration" twice, in his second note to Grant, Lee
began to elaborate his vision of an honorable peace. Restoration was of
course the favorite theme of the Peace Democrats, who sought to return
the Union to the "way it was"; theirs was a platform of sectional equilibrium, of proslavery consensus, and of Democratic supremacy. But Lee's
understanding of restoration was distinct, rooted in his family culture and
in that of his native Virginia. Like many other Virginians of his generation
and elite bloodline, Lee was steeped in nostalgia for the days of the early
Republic, when the other states "almost took it for granted that Virginia
would be their leader" and when Virginians felt a proprietary pride in the
Union. Hailing from a Federalist/Whig family, Lee had been a reluctant
secessionist in 1861; he disparaged the extremism of Northern abolitionists and Deep South "fire-eaters" alike and came to accept Virginia's secession only when it was a fait accompli. Over the course of the secession
crisis, Lee had shown little enthusiasm for the extreme version promulgated by the "fire-eaters" of the states' rights doctrine—one that held the
Union to be a revocable treaty between sovereign states and secession to

be a constitutional remedy for breach of contract—and little enthusiasm for their militant demands, such as reopening the slave trade, or their litany of grievances. When Lee finally embraced secession, he did so in the name of state allegiance and self-defense—an awareness that long, long before there was a Union, there was Virginia, a veritable country of its own, with a claim on her citizens that stretched back to the seventeenth century. If Virginia lost its primacy in the Union, the Union was no longer sound. If their ancient mother called them back, men like Lee reasoned, they must heed the call.[25]

The war had quickly radicalized Lee, rendering him an ardent Southern nationalist and indeed the preeminent symbol of Southern nationalism. In the war's closing moments, Lee's political heritage—a strain of Unionism in which Virginians were at the center of the national experiment—represented an ideological fallback position for him. An honorable peace, for Lee, would be marked by moderation and restraint. It would restore to the Union the legitimacy and equilibrium and to the South the "prosperity & influence" he associated with the halcyon days of an imagined past, before the nation had drifted away from the principles of the Virginia founders and before the slavery controversy had attenuated the affective bonds between North and South. From April 1865 on, "restoration" would be Lee's political keyword.[26]

On April 8, he looked to Grant for signals that such an honorable peace was possible. Again Lee refused to concede that the Army of Northern Virginia was spent; if Grant could confirm that restoration was his "sole object," Lee would consider, for the greater good, and in his capacity as commander-in-chief of all Confederate forces, the "terms" of Grant's "proposition." Lee was, in effect, angling for an armistice as the prelude to possible negotiations.[27]

This remained a last resort. Knowing full well his army had one final chance to forestall surrender, Lee in the late evening of April 8, from his headquarters north of Appomattox Court House, called a council of war, to which he summoned Longstreet, Gordon, and Fitz Lee. Gordon, a charismatic Georgian, was not a professional soldier by training but had consistently exceeded expectations and had proven to be one of Lee's most capable commanders in the last harrowing year of the war. Fitz Lee was, like his uncle Robert, a consummate career soldier. A prodigy of sorts, he had risen to the rank of Major General at the age of 27. These men met, Gordon recalls, "in the woods at [Lee's] headquarters and by a low-burning bivouac-fire. There was no tent there, no chairs, and no camp-stools. On blankets spread upon the ground or on saddles at the roots of the trees, we sat around the great commander." The men felt "unutterable anguish" as they looked into Lee's "clouded" face. Lee shared with them his exchange of letters with Grant and reviewed their predicament. Together they decided that Fitz Lee and Gordon, with Longstreet in support, would try to break a hole in the Federal line at sunrise. If it was only the Union cavalry obstructing the way, the men wishfully stipulated, Lee and Gordon were to clear the foe from their path and open an escape route to Campbell Court House. But if there were Federal infantry massed in force, they were to notify Lee, "in order that a flag of truce should be sent," Fitz recalled, "to accede to the only alternative left us."[28]

While Lee's message was conveyed to the Union lines, Grant settled into the headquarters he shared with Meade and their respective staffs—a country homestead called Clifton House, on Humphrey's line of march. Grant was in the throes of a throbbing migraine, which he treated by soaking his feet in hot water and by applying mustard plasters to his wrists and neck, "hoping to be cured by morning." There was a piano in the home, and, as Meade's aide-de-camp Theodore Lyman noted, "It is a singular sign of forebearance that [Grant] allowed the staff officers to go on for a long time pounding the piano and singing choruses, without objecting." At around midnight, Lee's response arrived. Grant listened through the haze of pain to his chief of staff, Brigadier General John A. Rawlins, read it aloud. Rawlins was Grant's self-appointed guardian angel, who took it upon himself to shield the sometimes intemperate general-in-chief from alcohol and to protect his public image. According to *New York Herald* correspondent Sylvanus Cadwallader, who covered developments at Grant's headquarters, once Rawlins had finished reading Lee's letter, a spirited discussion ensued. Lee's "cool, disingenuous" tone threw Rawlins into "unusually bad temper." Lee "wants to entrap us into making a treaty of peace—something beyond and above the surrender of his army," Rawlins charged; his message was "cunningly worded" to "gain time, and better terms." Grant should not meet Lee under such an insulting premise.[29]

It was obvious to Grant, too, that Lee's phrasing in the second message announced "a different purpose from that of surrendering his army." Lee's rhetoric of restoration held no charm for Grant. Indeed, Grant, in expressing his support for Lincoln in the 1864 election, had publicly and explicitly rejected the equation of peace with restoration. He associated such language with the defeatism of the Peace Democrats and with the specter of the "restoration [to the South] of slaves already freed." Grant would be party to no rolling back of the transformations—the consolidation of Republican power, repudiation of the doctrine of secession, emancipation of the slaves, and enlistment of black troops—that the war had wrought.[30]

Although Grant was confident that once they met, Lee would agree to capitulate on Grant's term, at this moment, he yielded to Rawlins—and moved to reestablish control over the tenor of the correspondence. On the morning of April 9, Grant sent Lee this answer:

April 9, 1865

General R.E. LEE,
   Commanding C.S. Army:

GENERAL: Your note of yesterday is received. As I have no authority to treat on the subject of peace the meeting proposed for 10 a.m. to-day could lead to no good. I will state, however, general, that I am equally anxious for peace with yourself, and the whole North entertain the same feeling. The terms upon which peace can be had are well understood. By the South laying down their arms they will hasten that most desirable event, save thousands of human lives, and hundreds of millions of property not yet destroyed. Sincerely hoping that all our difficulties may be settled without the loss of another life, I subscribe myself,

Very respectfully, your obedient servant,
U. S. GRANT,
Lieutenant-General, U.S. Army[31]

Grant's message served to reassure Lee that the Northern public would greet his paroling of Lee's surrendered army with approbation and to remind him that Lincoln had already set the broader conditions of the peace. Grant also, with his reference to what the war had cost and might still cost the South, signaled that his merciful offer to Lee was not a repudiation of the hard-war strategy but rather an extension of it. Mercy would come only when Lee at last conceded that his cause had been rendered hopeless. After Grant sent this message through the lines, he then telegraphed Secretary of War Edwin M. Stanton, updating him on the correspondence and reassuring him that there "has been no relaxation in the pursuit during its pendency."[32]

The pursuit was coming to its dramatic close. Beginning at 2:00 a.m. on April 9, Gordon's infantry corps formed a line of battle along the western rim of the village, straddling the stage road. The battle line ran on the diagonal from the northwest to the southeast, with Fitz Lee's cavalry anchoring the right, northernmost flank, and Brigadier General Clement Evans's brigade, in Gordon's corps, anchoring the southernmost, left flank. Fitz Lee and Gordon had a hot argument about whether the cavalry or infantry should lead the Confederate attack, which was resolved when one of Gordon's division commanders, Major General Bryan Grimes, volunteered to take the lead. At daybreak, the Confederates began skirmishing with the Union cavalry, which was positioned astride the stage road to the west of the Confederate battle line. The Confederate advance unfolded from approximately 7:00 to 9:00 a.m., with Gordon's infantry lines swinging "out from Appomattox Court House like a door hinged to the southern edge of the village" in order to clear the stage road area of four Union regiments under Colonel Charles H. Smith—as the historian Noah Andre Trudeau has described the scene.[33]

While the cavalry fight was getting under way, Ord and Gibbon, whose forced march of nearly 20 hours straight had covered some 30 miles on April 8, arrived at Sheridan's headquarters, near Appomattox Station. They decided that Gibbon's Army of the James Twenty-fourth Corps (which recently absorbed two infantry brigades of the U.S. Colored Troops, from the Twenty-fifth Corps), followed by Griffin's Fifth Corps of the Army of the Potomac, would push forward at once to reinforce the cavalry.[34]

The infantry, marching at the double-quick, arrived at the front at approximately 9:30 a.m. While Ord felt they intervened "barely in time" to save the flustered cavalry, Sheridan felt that his plan had worked like clockwork—on his orders, the cavalry fell back purposefully, gradually, "to give time for the infantry to form its lines and march to the attack." The Federals, in other words, baited the Confederates with a seeming retreat and then sprang the trap: as the Confederates advanced into the breach, they "could see Ord's men emerging from the woods" to the south and pushing up toward the stage road. Gibbon directed Brigadier General Robert S. Foster's First Division of the Army of the James to form across the road and Brevet Major General John W. Turner's division to move forward on Foster's right. "These maneuvers were rapidly performed," wrote Gibbon, "and as soon as our infantry opened fire the enemy fell back."[35]

At long last the Union had forced the Confederates to confront the futility of continued resistance: "The hopelessness of a further attack being plain," Sheridan observed, "the gray lines instinctively halted" and retreated toward Appomattox Court House. The Confederates were encircled: Gibbon's and Griffin's infantry divisions controlled the stage road area and thus blocked the route leading southwest, while Sheridan's cavalry, positioned on Gibbon's left and Griffin's right, cut off any possible escape routes to the northwest or the southeast. Some three miles to the northeast, Humphreys' and Wright's infantry Corps were pressing Longstreet's men at New Hope Church, preventing Lee from using them to reinforce Gordon. Moreover, the Union now occupied the high ground, in the form of the hills ringing the village, while much of the Confederate infantry had fallen back into the "basin"-like low ground of the Appomattox River valley on the village's northeastern rim.[36]

Lee, who initially followed the morning's developments while positioned on a ridge roughly two miles beyond the village, knew by 8:00 a.m. that his army's attempted break out was failing. Even before the fight was truly under way, he had received a discouraging assessment from Gordon, who confessed that his corps had fought to a "frazzle" and could not succeed without reinforcement from Longstreet. Lee knew well, too, that Federal infantry had already reached Appomattox Station and were bound for the front. Steeling himself for what must necessarily come next, Lee held a series of conversations with his inner circle. Consulting first with Alexander, Lee asked: "The enemy seems to be across our road in force this morning. What have we got to do?" Alexander offered up his artillery, which had not yet been pressed into service that morning, but Lee responded that he simply could not concentrate from his scattered commands a sufficient force "to accomplish any valuable results."[37]

Alexander then decided to speak his mind freely. Rather than surrender, he argued, the Confederates should "take to the woods." If they scattered "like rabbits and partridges," the Union could not efficiently hunt them down. Such a strategy would buy valuable time—time in which individual Southern state governments could perhaps negotiate favorable terms of peace. "Grant is called 'Unconditional Surrender Grant,'" Alexander noted with dismay. "The men who have fought under you so long have the right to ask you to spare us the mortification of your asking Grant for terms and being told 'Unconditional surrender.'" Alexander implored Lee: "Save us from that!" The Confederates, he insisted, needed "*terms* to prevent vindictive trials and punishments."[38]

Lee, taking a tack both pragmatic and humane, gently persuaded Alexander that no good could come from dispersing the army. The Southern soldiers "were already demoralized by four years of war, and would supply their wants by violence and plunder," Lee noted, and the Union would inevitably adopt harsh countermeasures to roust the Confederates out. "A state of society would result, throughout the South, from which it would require years to recover." Besides, Lee added, "I am too old to go bushwhacking." Most important, Lee tried to comfort Alexander by assuring him that Grant intended to offer "honorable and liberal terms, simply requiring us not to take up arms again until exchanged." Alexander was duly reassured. He abandoned his plans to "take to the bushes on the first sign of a flag of truce." He would "stay and see it out."[39]

Lee himself took little comfort from the prospect of Grant's liberality. Struggling over what to do, Lee consulted Longstreet and then Mahone. According to Longstreet, Lee's "brave bearing failed to conceal his profound depression." Both men agreed the cause was lost. Mahone was particularly blunt. If Grant offered to pardon the Southern soldiers, they must accept such terms of surrender as honorable ones, he told Lee. In Mahone's view, "It would be criminal—murder to sacrifice another life in

Edward Porter Alexander, one of Lee's close confidantes in the final days.
(Museum of the Confederacy, Richmond, Virginia)

the hopeless cause." When Lee handed him the text of Grant's demands
for surrender, Mahone concluded that it was not yet clear, from what
Grant had written, "whether we were to [be] paroled to go [to] our
homes or to prison." There was only one way to find out: Lee must meet
with Grant.[40]

At 8:30 a.m. on April 9, Lee and a small entourage, under a makeshift flag
of truce, rode out north along the Richmond–Lynchburg Stage Road,
through his own rear guard toward Humphrey's lines, to keep the 10:00 a.m.
appointment he had proposed to Grant the previous evening. A Federal
courier, Lieutenant Colonel Charles A. Whittier of Humphrey's staff,
soon met Lee on the way with the letter Grant had written that morning,
declining any meeting to "treat on the subject of peace." Lee had his aide-
de-camp, Charles Marshall, prepare the following response:

April 9, 1865

Lieut. Gen. U.S. GRANT,
  Commanding U.S. Armies:

GENERAL: I received your note of this morning on the picket-
line, whither I had come to meet you and ascertain definitely
what terms were embraced in your proposal of yesterday with reference to the surrender of this army. I now request an interview in
accordance with the offer contained in your letter of yesterday for
that purpose.

Very respectfully, your obedient servant,
R.E. LEE
General[41]

This message, and a second one requesting a "suspension of hostilities
pending the adjustment of the terms of surrender," soon reached Meade—
who was sick and convalescing in an ambulance—but not Grant. After
sending his own note to Lee that morning, Grant had undertaken a circuitous
22-mile journey to Sheridan's lines, and the general-in-chief "consequently
could not be communicated with immediately." The fact that Grant was in
transit and out of touch consigned Lee to an awkward purgatory. Had Grant
broken off their correspondence and withdrawn his earlier offer of surrender
by parole? At Meade's urging, Lee sent an additional request for an interview
to Grant through Sheridan's lines; while the earlier request had proposed that
the two generals meet between the picket lines, on neutral ground, in this
letter Lee offered to meet wherever Grant chose. Lee then returned to his own
lines and informed Gordon that he should raise flags of truce on his front.
Meade and Sheridan, for their part, were in limbo too. "As they had heard
nothing of all this until the fighting had got to be severe and all going against
Lee, both of these commanders hesitated very considerably about suspend-
ing hostilities at all," Grant explained. "They were afraid it was not in good
faith, and we had the Army of Northern Virginia where it could not escape
except by some deception." The two commanders grudgingly consented to a
ceasefire of two hours, during which time Grant was to be tracked down.[42]
   Starting at about 10:00 a.m. on April 9, as Gordon's men began to withdraw from the front through Appomattox Court House, flags of truce

started to appear along the Union and Confederate lines. Their appearance came as a surprise, even to brigade and division commanders who had led troops in the morning's battle. For example, Brigadier General Joshua L. Chamberlain—the hero of Little Round Top at Gettysburg, who headed General Joseph J. Bartlett's First Brigade—was overwhelmed when he heard the bearer of a flag of truce declare that General Lee was to meet with General Grant over the proposed surrender: "What a word is this! So long so dearly fought for, so feverishly dreamed, but ever snatched away, held hidden and aloof; now smiting the senses with a dizzy flash! 'Surrender'? We had no rumor of this from the messages that had been passing between Grant and Lee, these two days, behind us." Chamberlain gathered himself, sent the message ahead to Griffin, and was left amazed at the "boding change."[43]

The flags could not diffuse the atmosphere of mistrust that hung over the scene. An incident involving Custer and Longstreet is a case in point. Longstreet sent Major Robert Sims of his staff to inform Gordon of the ceasefire, and Gordon then dispatched Sims to take the news to Sheridan's lines, under a makeshift flag of truce, a towel wrapped around a stick. There Sims encountered Custer, who told Sims, "We are behind your army now and it is at our mercy." Custer insisted on riding back to Confederate lines, brandishing a handkerchief wrapped around his sword, as his own flag of truce, to confront Longstreet with this same message. In Longstreet's account, Custer, with his "flaxen locks flowing over his shoulders," brusquely declared, "'In the name of General Sheridan I demand the unconditional surrender of this army.'" This was not uncharacteristic behavior from Custer, who had a history of nervy behavior and who, in order to dispel rumors that he was a Copperhead Democrat, had declared in 1864 that he opposed any peace settlement with the Confederates "except that which is offered at the point of the bayonet." Longstreet reminded Custer that Lee was in command of the army and that he was at that very moment on his way to Grant to negotiate a surrender. Yet Custer would not relent. Longstreet's aide, Major Thomas J. Goree, reveals what happened next: "Finally Genl. Longstreet seemed to lose his patience, and in substance told Genl. Custer that he could not and would not surrender the army, that he (Longstreet) was not half whipped yet, and if he (Custer) was not satisfied to await the result of the conference between Genl.

Lee and Genl. Grant, he could return to his command, and commence hostilities again as soon as he pleased, and he would see that he met with a warm reception." Custer stood down, knowing full well he would soon have the satisfaction of seeing Longstreet yield.[44]

Sheridan, for his part, exchanged tense words with Gordon after General Martin Gary's cavalry brigade fired on the Union general's entourage as he tried to ride, under flag of truce, through Gordon's lines to Appomattox Court House. Sheridan dispatched a messenger to the offending commander, the truculent Martin Gary, informing him of the ceasefire. Gary promptly declared the Federal envoy a prisoner and sent Sheridan the arch message, "I do not care for white flags: South Carolinians never surrender." Sheridan gave Merritt orders to attack Gary's position and finish him off. Then Little Phil lit into Gordon. When Gordon requested a suspension of hostilities, "pending the negotiations which [Lee] is having with General Grant," Sheridan replied indignantly that he thought it "singular that while such discussions are going on, General Lee should have continued his march and attempted to break through my lines this morning." If Lee did not accept the terms Grant offered, Sheridan warned, "We will renew hostilities." Sheridan's exchange thus had the same purpose as Grant's with Lee: to make his foe concede that surrender, and not a negotiated peace, was the only option left to the Confederacy. Gordon, who found Sheridan to be abrasive and lacking in "delicacy and consideration," nonetheless understood that the Federal commander had all the cards. "General Lee's army is exhausted," Gordon told Sheridan. "There is no doubt of his surrender to General Grant."[45]

About a half hour after this initial exchange, at approximately 11:00, in the midst of the ceasefire, Sheridan and Gordon reconvened in the village on the steps of the courthouse. They were joined by a handful of other Union officers, including Ord, Gibbon, and Merritt, and a group of their Confederate counterparts, including Longstreet, Major General Henry Heth, and Major General Cadmus M. Wilcox. As Gibbon explained, "The village was between the two picket lines and for the first time in four years prominent officers on both sides who had not met, except in battle, during that time, mingled together." Despite the fact that Union Brevet Major General Romeyn B. Ayres of Griffin's corps tried to encourage conviviality by passing a whisky flask around, a "first class article," by his lights, the mood was wary. "All wore an air of anxiety," Gibbon remembers, and "no one felt like talking much." They all knew that the prevailing quiet might yet be the prelude to the "reopening of the storm."[46]

Lee, for his part, sought a few moments of respite behind the lines. Along the stage road, north of the river, the Confederate commander rested under the shade of an apple tree as he awaited Grant's final reply. Earlier that morning, when he first received word that Gordon's effort to break the Federal line was in vain, Lee had confessed to Venable that he would rather "die a thousand deaths" than go see Grant. But in the ensuing hours, Grant's logic had proven as inescapable as his army. Lee realized, at last, that he could not spend a thousand lives, in vain, to spare his soul the agony of this reckoning.[47]

|| 3 ||

The Surrender Conference

Lee's retreat across central Virginia had been a drama of maneuver and counter-maneuver; so too had his correspondence with Grant. Their April 9 surrender conference and brief meeting on horseback the following day would be no different. The surrender was not just an ending but a beginning, an inherently political moment that set the terms of an unfolding debate about the meaning and implications of the war. Lee and Grant knew this. That is why each man moved, Lee more decisively at first, to stake out a position. Lee sought to turn military defeat into moral victory. In his view, the war—which was brought on by extremism and devolved, on the Union side, into a brutal contest of numbers—had cost America dearly. The peace was an opportunity for the country to obliterate the war's "grievous effects" and regain what it had lost: to restore the civic virtue Lee associated with the founders and the promising days of the early Republic, before the Union's fall from grace. Lee, at Appomattox, staked the claim that his army and not Grant's embodied such virtue, that something of the underdog courage and steadfastness of the Revolutionary generation survived among the Confederates, intact and purified. For Lee, the surrender was a negotiation in which he secured honorable terms for his blameless men, and the peace was contingent on the North's good behavior.[1]

Grant's position was diametrically opposed to Lee's. In his view, the Federal army's triumph flowed from the superior virtue of its cause. He believed that in the hands of the incomparable Lincoln and of his officers and troops, the Union war had been noble and ennobling. The Union's victory was proof of both the resilience and the adaptability of republican institutions. It meant that the Confederates must "yield principles that they had deemed dearer than life"; Grant knew this would not be easy, and so his magnanimous terms were designed to encourage Southern submission. The surrender was in no sense a negotiation. Grant could be merciful precisely because he had rendered Lee utterly powerless and his cause hopeless.[2]

At Appomattox, the stalwarts in each man's inner circle fell in line behind his particular interpretation of the surrender and took up a new task: that of inscribing the truth, as they saw it, into the public consciousness and the historical record. These men, knowing full well that they were eyewitnesses to monumental events, read meaning and purpose into every detail of the surrender conference, and their accounts reveal that the seeds of continuing strife were sown at the very moment of Union victory and Confederate defeat.

Lee's note requesting an interview with Grant finally caught up with the Union commander-in-chief shortly before noon on April 9, nearly two full hours after Lee had written it. Grant was still eight miles east or so from Appomattox Court House. He had been tracked down, with considerable effort, by Lieutenant Charles E. Pease of Meade's staff. "When the officer reached me I was still suffering with the sick headache," Grant would later recall, in one of his memoir's most enduring lines, "but the instant I saw the contents of the note I was cured."[3]

Grant turned off the road onto a grassy bank, where he consulted with his staff officers. Rawlins read the contents of Lee's note aloud. Remembering Rawlins's skeptical reaction to Lee's April 8 note, Grant asked him, wryly, "How will that do Rawlins?" Rawlins replied, "I think *that* will do."

Grant then directed his military secretary Ely S. Parker to write out his reply to Lee:

April 9, 1865

General R. E. LEE,
   Commanding C.S. Army:

Your note of this date is but this moment (11:50 a.m.) received. In consequence of my having passed from the Richmond and Lynchburg road to the Farmville and Lynchburg road I am at this writing about four miles west of Walker's Church, and will push forward to the front for the purpose of meeting you. Notice sent to me on this road where you wish the interview to take place will meet me.

Very respectfully, your obedient servant,

U. S. GRANT

Lieutenant-General[4]

Grant summoned his aide-de-camp Brevet Brigadier General Orville E. Babcock, who, like Rawlins, was a key figure in his personal staff of twelve officers—the hardworking and devoted aides-de camp, secretaries, adjutants, and inspectors general who served as the mobile administration of the U.S. army. These men were at Grant's side constantly during the grinding Overland campaign and the siege of Petersburg and Richmond, and they had unmatched access to him. At the Federal army's headquarters at City Point on the James River, and then again on the road to Appomattox, they often shared Grant's dinner table; fireside conversation; anxious sessions waiting for intelligence reports and word from the front; and consultations about tactics, strategy, and politics. Babcock, a West Point engineer from Vermont, would serve after the war as Grant's personal secretary. On this day, Grant instructed Babcock to convey his note to General Lee through Sheridan's headquarters near the battle lines. Babcock's detailed account, endorsed by Grant himself, captures the scene. When Babcock reached Sheridan's temporary headquarters near Appomattox Court House, he found the general "pacing backward and forward" in exasperation. "Genl. Sheridan said at once in emphatic language that he believed the truce was a game" and that Lee was still "playing to get time to escape." Babcock told Sheridan that he had in his possession Grant's most recent note to Lee, confirming that they were to meet, and verbal authorization to find a place for such a meeting. "Genl. Sheridan seemed disappointed," and said, "'Damn them, I wish they had held out one hour longer and I would have whipped the Hell out of them.'" But since he finally had unimpeachable proof of Lee's intentions to surrender, Sheridan relented. He assigned a member of his staff, Colonel J. W. Forsyth, to accompany Babcock on the mission to find Lee.[5]

Babcock and Forsyth, at around 1:00 p.m., found Lee sitting by the apple tree where he had stopped to rest; over the years wagon traffic along

the road "had cut away the dirt from the roots of the tree on one side, form-
ing a convenient bench for a seat." Lee was "surrounded by a number of his
Officers." Babcock handed Lee Grant's note and then, at Lee's suggestion,
wrote instructions to Meade to extend the ceasefire beyond 2:00 p.m.,
so that a renewal of hostilities would not disrupt the peace efforts of the
two commanders-in-chief. While Forsyth rode off with this message,
Babcock headed toward Appomattox Court House with Lee and with
Lee's aide-de-camp, Charles Marshall (and two orderlies).[6]

Grant, meanwhile, when he finally arrived at the front, met up with
Sheridan and Ord on the Richmond–Lynchburg Stage Road, the rutted,
grassy cart-path at the center of the village of Appomattox Court House.
The village was modest, consisting of merely a few dozen structures, most
prominent among them the courthouse and a tavern. According to Frederick Newhall, a Sheridan staff officer, Grant and Sheridan had the following understated exchange: "How are you, Sheridan?" "First rate,
thank you; how are you?" came the reply. "Is General Lee up there?"
Grant asked, referring to the designated meeting place. "Yes," said Sheridan. "Well then," Grant concluded, "we'll go up." Newhall found the two
men's economy of expression and emotional self-control characteristically
American and wholly admirable.[7]

Lee's mood as he set out for the meeting is captured by Longstreet.
While waiting under the apple tree for Grant's response, Lee had confided
to Longstreet that he feared his earlier rebuff to Grant might "cause him to
demand harsh terms." Lee knew that there was ample precedent in the
history of warfare for granting amnesty to the subjects of a defeated
state—for treaties that wiped the slate clean. But Lee knew too that civil
wars and insurrections, such as the English Civil War and guerrilla insur-
gencies against Napoleon, had ended with the execution of defeated
rebels. Lincoln's 1863 Amnesty Proclamation had seemed to preclude a
harsh regime of reprisals, but his administration's suspension of habeas
corpus and use of military commissions to prosecute those charged with
violation of the laws of war signaled his willingness to mete out stern punishments. Would Lee be tried for treason, and punished as a criminal?
Even Longstreet's reassurances as to Grant's character, based on their
friendship in their West Point days, could not dispel Lee's fear that Grant
aimed to humiliate him. Longstreet knew how to release Lee from the grip

of such fear. He suggested to his chief that if Grant's terms were harsh, Lee "should break off the interview and tell General Grant to do his worst." "The thought of another round seemed to brace him," Longstreet thought, for the grim business that lay ahead.[8]

Why did Lee choose Marshall as his escort to the meeting with Grant? A Baltimore-based lawyer before the war, Marshall, like Lee, had a distinguished Virginia lineage, being the great-nephew of the renowned Supreme Court Chief Justice John Marshall. During the war, Marshall secured a place in Lee's inner circle by judiciously managing the General's "enormous flow of correspondence." As the historian Gary W. Gallagher notes, "Marshall was so close to his commander for so long and so intimately involved in writing official reports that he better than almost anyone else could speak authoritatively about Lee's opinions, decisions, and reactions to events." Marshall was therefore the perfect witness to the surrender. Lee knew he would be able to count on his help in recording the event, contextualizing it, and assigning it meaning. Lee asked a second figure in his inner circle to accompany him to the meeting with Grant, Colonel Walter H. Taylor, who served as Lee's chief of staff. The scion of a well-to-do Norfolk family, Taylor was the youngest member of Lee's staff but the most skilled bureaucrat. He regarded his chieftain much like a devoted son would his father. Taylor was driven by the desire to please the "queer old genius," as he called Lee—and often was exasperated by Lee's temper (Lee loathed paperwork) and by his stinginess with praise. Taylor begged off the chance to ride with Lee and Marshall to the McLean house; he simply could not bear the thought of seeing Lee humiliated. Taylor would later regard this decision as indefensible, and it would haunt him.[9]

Taylor was not the only one of Lee's intimates who could not bear the thought of surrender. Just as flags of truce were going up along the lines, "once he was certain that his troopers were no longer needed," Fitzhugh Lee put into motion a plan he had aired at the Confederate council of war the previous evening. "If a surrender was compelled," Fitzhugh Lee was to "try and Extricate the cavalry." As it turned out, one of his three cavalry corps—the one under the command of Robert E. Lee's middle son William Henry Fitzhugh ("Rooney")—was hopelessly trapped by Ord's infantry on the morning of April 9. But the other two divisions, under Colonel Thomas T. Munford and Major General Thomas L. Rosser, on the outer flank of the Union infantry, seized the opportunity to slip the Federal trap and head to Lynchburg. Fitzhugh Lee's break out was inspired by his "fond, though forlorn *hope*, that future operations were still in store for the cavalry."[10]

And so it was Marshall at Lee's side—not Longstreet or Gordon, who kept the remnants of Confederate infantry in check during the tense cease-fire, nor his young protégé Taylor, who was unnerved by the prospect of surrender, nor Lee's nephew, who had taken flight. Marshall rode on ahead of Lee and Babcock to secure a site for the surrender. He found one at the residence of Wilmer McLean, a man with an exceedingly unlikely story. "McLean used to live on the first battle field of Manassas, at a house about a mile from Manassas Junction," Marshall learned. "He didn't like the war, and having seen the first battle of Manassas, he thought he would get away where there wouldn't be any more fighting, so he moved to Appomattox Court House." McLean's home was a three-level, symmetrical brick house in the Greek-revival style, with a short staircase leading up to a wooden porch that ran along the front of the house (with benches on either side) and was adorned by six columns. The front door, atop the external stair-case in the center of the porch, opened into an entrance hall that ran along the length of the house from front to back, in a popular Southern design meant to maximize airflow. At 3,300 square feet, it was the finest house in the town, three times the size of an average home. The property had an external kitchen, smokehouse, storehouse, and slave quarters. McLean had made a tidy sum during the war as a speculator in the sugar market and as a profiteer. His assets amounted to about $40,000—in soon-to-be worthless Confederate money.[11]

After making arrangements with McLean, Marshall and his orderly then doubled back and retrieved Lee and Babcock to escort them to McLean's home. They entered McLean's parlor, which was 17 by 19 feet, to the left of the central hallway. The room contained a turtle-top marble table positioned near the window that fronted the house; a couch along the interior wall to the right of the door; an oval, wood spool-leg table near the center of the room; and several chairs (in some accounts and depictions, there was a third free-standing table in the rear of the room; in others, a nearly ceiling-high secretary desk in the back corner). The long exterior wall of the room, running along the side of the house,

The McLean House, site of the surrender conference. (Library of Congress)

featured a fireplace, painted black, with white vases on both ends of the mantelpiece. According to Marshall, he, Lee, and Babcock passed the awkward minutes in which they awaited Grant's arrival by talking with each other in "an affable way." Babcock peered periodically out the front window for signs of Grant. After about a half an hour's wait, Grant arrived, at approximately 1:30, accompanied by Ord, Sheridan, Rawlins, and other members of his personal staff, including Assistant Adjutant General Colonel Theodore S. Bowers, military secretaries Captain Ely S. Parker and Lieutenant Colonel Adam Badeau, and aide-de-camp Lieutenant Colonel Horace Porter. Marshall and Lee were standing as Grant and his entourage entered the room.[12]

Grant was keenly aware of the poor figure he cut: "I had an old suit on, without my sword, and without any distinguishing mark of rank except the shoulder-straps of a lieutenant general on a woolen blouse. I was splashed with mud in my long ride." He worried that Lee might feel it was a "studied discourtesy" to appear this way, but Grant, who was away from his base of supplies, had had no opportunity to change into a dress uniform. Grant found Lee "in a fine, new, splendid uniform" and bearing a handsome ceremonial sword, a gift to Lee from an anonymous Marylander. The two commanders exchanged some pleasantries about the weather, their service in the Mexican War, and some mutual friends. Grant was surprised that Lee, who had outranked him during the Mexican War, claimed to remember Grant from those faraway days. He introduced several of the officers to Lee. "After being presented," Sheridan remembers, "Ord and I, and nearly all of General Grant's staff, withdrew to await the agreement as to terms." Some of these men milled about in the entrance hall while others joined their fellow staff officers on the piazza of the McLean parlor, where they nervously awaited word of the final terms. Conspicuously absent was Meade, who was too far away from Appomattox Court House to attend.[13]

A few Union officers—most likely Babcock, Bowers, and Ely S. Parker—stayed in the parlor for the entire duration of the meeting. Bowers, a Pennsylvanian who worked as a newspaper editor before the war, had risen up the ranks from clerk at Grant's headquarters to aide-de-camp to assistant adjutant general (i.e., senior administrative officer). By far the most remarkable individual on Grant's staff—and perhaps the most indispensable—was Parker. A Seneca Indian from upstate New York, Parker was a man of great eminence among his people: the last grand sachem of the Iroquois League of the Five Nations. Schooled as a boy by Baptist missionaries, Parker made it his life's work both to preserve and defend Iroquois culture and to represent the capacity of Native Americans to excel in the modern world. As a young man, he studied civil engineering and embarked on a successful career in that field. In 1857, he worked on the construction of a customs house and marine hospital in Galena, Illinois—the hometown, at the time, of none other than U. S. Grant, who had retired from military life and was working at his father's store. Parker and Grant became friends. When the war broke out, Parker hastened to seek a military commission, only to be turned away because he was Native American. His persistence and undeniable competence eventually landed him a commission as an army engineer, with the rank of captain and assistant adjutant general. He fulfilled that role expertly in the Tennessee theater in 1863 and 1864; in August of 1864, Grant appointed him as one of his military secretaries. Many of Grant's orders and reports in the last year of the war are in Parker's immaculate handwriting and bear his signature.[14]

By all accounts, it was Lee who turned the meeting away from social conventions and to the matter at hand. He said to Grant: "General, I have

Ely S. Parker (seated, facing left), flanked by John A. Rawlins and others of Grant's staff. (Library of Congress)

come to meet you in accordance with my letter to you this morning, to treat about the surrender of my army, and I think the best way would be for you to put your terms in writing." Grant verbally rehearsed what he had promised in their correspondence—that both enlisted men and officers would be paroled—and Lee, listening attentively, verbally assented. Grant called to Parker for his manifold order-book, a writing tablet twice the size of a business letter sheet that contains a stencil that imprints copies of whatever is inscribed in it. Parker prepared the book for three copies. Grant sat at the oval table, and in pencil, began to write the terms:

Appomattox Court House, Va., April 9, 1865

General R. E. LEE,
    Commanding C.S. Army

GENERAL: In accordance with the substance of my letter to you of the 8th instant, I propose to receive the surrender of the Army of Northern Virginia on the following terms, to wit: Rolls of all the officers and men to be made in duplicate—one copy to be given to an officer designated by me, the other to be retained by such officer or officers as you may designate; the officers to give their individual paroles not to take up arms against the Government of the United States until properly exchanged, and each company or regimental commander sign a like parole for the men of their commands. The arms, artillery, and public property to be parked and stacked, and turned over to the officers appointed by me to receive them. This will not embrace the side-arms of the officers, nor their private horses or baggage. This done, each officer and man will be allowed to return to their homes, not to be disturbed by United States authority so long as they observe their paroles and the laws in force where they may reside.

Very respectfully,
U. S. GRANT,
Lieutenant-General.[15]

After Grant finished writing, he looked over the draft with Parker, striking out a few extraneous words. Meanwhile, Babcock invited back into the room Ord, Sheridan, and other key officers. According to Newhall of Sheridan's staff, who waited with the lesser officers on the piazza, Babcock was downright jaunty: "He came out smiling, whirled his hat round his head once," and then beckoned Grant's inner circle into the parlor. The men who rejoined the scene included not only Sheridan, Ord, Rawlins, Porter, and Badeau, but also Abraham Lincoln's eldest son, Robert Todd Lincoln, a junior staff officer to Grant; Brigadier General Michael Ryan Morgan, commissary chief; Grant's inspector general, Major General Seth Williams; Brigadier General John G. Barnard, chief engineer; aide-de-camp Lieutenant Colonel Frederick T. Dent; Quartermaster General Rufus Ingalls; Brevet Brigadier General George H. Sharpe, head of the Bureau of Military Information (army intelligence); and *New York Herald* correspondent Sylvanus Cadwallader, Grant's favorite member of the press corps. Newhall, peering in from the outside, observed that they "walked on the floor silently, as people do who have a first peep at a baby." According to Porter, "We walked in softly, and ranged ourselves quietly about the sides of the room, very much as people enter a sick-chamber when they expect to find the patient dangerously ill."[16]

While much has been made of the contrasting physical appearance of Grant and Lee at their meeting, the appearance of these Union officers on the scene is just as revealing. They symbolized the might of the Federal army: its administrative and logistical prowess, command harmony, and its phalanxes of troops. They symbolized too the stark emotional realities at work: while Lee was eager to shield his inner circle from the mortifying experience of surrender, Grant was eager to include his men in this moment of triumph. More important still, the presence of these men represented the victor's power to shape public opinion of the surrender. Grant would have many sympathetic witnesses to attest to what had transpired at the McLean house.

Surrounded by his devoted compatriots, Grant took the manifold book to Lee, who rose from his seat to take the book and read the terms over. Grant said to Lee that he "hoped and believed this would be the close of the war." Lee remarked that Grant's stipulation that Confederate officers could keep their side-arms and horses and baggage would have a "very happy effect" on the Southern army. Lee then pointed out to Grant, the latter recalls, that "their army was organized a little differently from the army of the United States (still maintaining by implication that we were two countries)" insofar as Confederate cavalrymen and artillerists owned their own horses. Could they retain this private property, Lee asked? Grant at first reiterated the written terms he had just prepared, in which only officers would retain their mounts. But Grant then reconsidered the matter, musing that as most of the Confederates were small farmers, "it was doubtful whether they would be able to put in a crop . . . without the aid of the horses they were then riding." Grant told Lee that by special order he would instruct the officers who processed the paroles to let every Confederate who owned a horse or mule to take the animal home. Lee expressed his satisfaction with this.[17]

Grant instructed Bowers to copy the terms in ink in the manifold book. Although he was the senior and Parker the junior adjutant, Bowers was so nervous he could not write—so the task was turned over to Parker, who had the best handwriting of anyone on the staff. Parker carefully transcribed the terms for the official record. One copy would be sent to

Washington, D.C., one to the telegrapher, and the third was handed by
Grant to Lee. Lee instructed Marshall to draft his formal reply. It read:

> Headquarters Army of Northern Virginia
> April 9, 1865
>
> GENERAL:—I have received your letter of this date containing
> the terms of the surrender of the Army of Northern Virginia as
> proposed by you. As they are substantially the same as those
> expressed in your letter of the 8th instant, they are accepted. I will
> proceed to designate the proper officers to carry the stipulations
> into effect.
>
> Very respectfully, your obedient servant,
> R. E. LEE,
> *General*[18]

While Parker copied the terms, Grant, at Lee's request, consulted with
Sheridan and Morgan about procuring rations for Lee's starving troops;
they agreed that 25,000 Union rations would be directed from Sheridan's
commissary to Lee's. At around 3:00 p.m., Grant signed the ink copy of
his terms and Lee signed his acceptance letter, with no hint whatsoever
of "theatrical display," Marshall has noted, in the exchange. The two men
shook hands, and Lee and Marshall departed and returned to the Confederate lines. In Sheridan's words, Lee "mounted his chunky gray horse,
and lifting his hat as he passed out of the yard, rode off toward his army,
his arrival there being announced to us by cheering, which, as it pro-
gressed, varying in loudness, told he was riding through the bivouac of
the Army of Northern Virginia." After attending to some last details of
the surrender, Grant left the McLean house at approximately 4:15 p.m.
When news of the surrender reached the Union lines, the jubilant soldiers commenced firing a salute of 100 guns in honor of their victory.
But Grant "sent word . . . to have it stopped." "The Confederates were
now our prisoners," he explained, and there was no need to "exult over
their downfall."[19]

As his postwar memoirs reveal, Grant's own sense of exultation was tempered on April 9 by the solemnity and tense ambiguity of his meeting with

Lee. The Union commander had been "quite jubilant" when he received Lee's letter, conceding the need to capitulate, that morning. But the surrender conference itself left Grant strangely "sad and depressed." Although the Confederate cause was, in his view, among the "worst for which a people ever fought," there was no denying that Lee's men had fought "valiantly" and suffered much. As the two men conferred in the McLean parlor, Grant had struggled to read Lee. Lee's "impassable face" entirely concealed his emotions from Grant, who could not tell whether Lee "felt inwardly glad that the end had finally come." Lee's bearing did rehabilitate him somewhat in Grant's eyes. While Grant felt that Lee did "not appear well in the correspondence" they had exchanged over the previous two days—Lee's playing for time and advantage struck Grant as irresponsible—during their face-to-face meeting Lee appeared "concerned alone for the welfare of his

Union artist Alfred Waud's rendering of Lee's solemn ride away from the McLean House. (Library of Congress)

army and his State." Grant was painfully aware of the fact that over the course of the war, many Northerners, in the Union army, the government, and the press, had attributed to the formidable Lee "almost superhuman abilities." Grant knew all along that the rebel chief "was mortal," and the surrender vindicated that knowledge. Perhaps the surrender conference carried with it, too, intimations of Grant's own mortality: Grant's war and his victory were already, in this moment, passing into history.[20]

In another sense, however, Grant's victory was unambiguous, and his exultation unbounded. Grant understood the surrender to symbolize the defeat of not only Lee and of the Confederate army—for whom he could muster a soldier's empathy—but the defeat also of an altogether unsympathetic foe: the Copperheads on the Northern home front who had worked cynically to undermine the war effort. Grant felt undisguised contempt for such "stay-at-home traitors" and regarded them as nothing less than "an auxiliary to the Confederate army." Their presence had been a kind of handicap for the Northern army. Lee and the coercive Confederate regime could and did sternly command the loyalty of the South's pool of able-bodied white men; "the whole South was a military camp," as Grant saw it. The Union war effort by contrast had unfolded on two fronts: against the rebels in the field and the treacherous croakers at home. Grant had been keenly aware all along of his army's power and responsibility to win victories that would bolster the confidence of the Northern people in the "ultimate success of the cause." He and Lincoln had sustained each other's confidence: "There was never a day when the President did not think that, in some way or other, a cause so just as ours would come out triumphant," Grant reflected.[21]

In Grant's eyes, the Union's triumph vindicated the principle of "rule by the majority"; the founders' belief in a perpetual Union; and the capacity of citizen-soldiers, representing democracy, to outfight the conscripts and dupes of an autocratic society. The downfall of the Confederacy unburdened the South and the nation of slavery, "an institution abhorrent to all civilized people not brought up under it." Now the way was open for the Union's ethos of moral and material progress—and the mass of white Southerners could be disenthralled from their subservience to a slaveholding class whose alleged "patent of nobility" the Northern army had, at bayonet point, revoked.[22]

As for his surrender terms, Grant felt their meaning to be unmistakable and their logic unimpeachable. "There is nothing clearer in my mind than that the terms of the paroles given by officers and soldiers who were arrayed against the authority of the General Government of the United States prior to their surrender exempts them from trial or punishment for acts of legal warfare so long as they observe the conditions of their paroles," Grant wrote in the spring of 1866. He later elaborated: "I never claimed that the parole gave these prisoners any political rights whatever. I thought that that was a matter entirely with Congress, over which I had no control; that, simply, as general-in-chief commanding the army, I had a right to stipulate the surrender on terms which protected their lives." The terms rested on military calculations. Grant felt certain, on April 9, 1865, that should Lee surrender, "all the rebel armies would surrender, and that we would thus avoid bushwhacking and a continuation of the war," and he felt certain that Lee would not surrender if he "supposed that after the surrender he was going to be tried for treason and hanged." It made eminent sense, thought Grant, to spare the lives of a "few leaders" as a means of getting all of Lee's men and their arms "under control, bound by their oaths to obey the law."[23]

Grant was secure in the knowledge that the terms "met with the hearty approval of the President." He did not believe himself to be encroaching on the realm of politics; instead, he saw the Appomattox settlement as an extension of Lincoln's policy for amnesty and reconstruction, the premise of which was that once Southerners had seen—and admitted—the error of their ways, they could return to the national fold. Grant hoped that his lenient surrender terms, in keeping with Lincoln's political calculations and with his noble spirit, would hasten the conversion of the defeated Confederates to a creed of democratic self-government and freedom. On April 9, 1865, Grant seized the moral high ground. He made no concessions to the Confederates or the Copperheads in his magnanimous terms; his was the generosity of a conqueror whose victory was total.[24]

For the Union officers who witnessed the surrender conference, Grant himself embodied their just cause. They "felt the overpowering influence of the scene," as George Sharpe put it; they knew they were "witnessing the proceedings between two chief actors in one of the most remarkable transactions of the nineteenth century." The comportment of Grant filled these Union men with pride. They delighted in the details of his rough-and-ready image—Grant had seen fit to meet Lee in his "soldier's blouse," with his boots "nearly covered with mud," coat button "gone astray," thread gloves "soiled"—and his "cigar in his mouth during the whole time of the surrender." "The 'Old Man' paid but little attention to dress," General Morgan observed, but "on that day the appearance of our general whom we loved was good enough for me." These men believed that Grant had been the underdog in the fight against the fabled Lee. Lee's elite lineage, his long-standing reputation as a sterling soldier, his successes against a series of overmatched Union generals in the eastern theater, and his God-like status in the eyes of the Southern people—all these advantages had been neutralized by the brilliance and courage of humble, unpretentious U. S. Grant. Grant's magnanimous terms were the "legitimate outgrowth of Grant's judgment and feeling," as Adam Badeau of Grant's staff put it, and "the consequence of all that had gone before." Grant had so thoroughly defeated his nemesis that there was no need, at this moment of Lee's downfall, to exact further retributions or humiliation.[25]

As for their impressions of Lee, the Union witnesses ascribe to the rebel general profound sadness and abject powerlessness. In their view, the meeting was in no sense a negotiation, because Grant had all the cards. Take, for example, the account of Badeau, penned a few weeks after the surrender. Badeau had been Grant's military secretary since March of 1864 and had spent many a late night over the course of the war's final year writing out Grant's letters and keeping the general, who was a night owl, company. On April 9, Lee struck Badeau as a man whose spirit, as well as his misguided cause, had been utterly crushed. "He seemed depressed, and talked but little. Grant was perfect in his demeanor, because completely simple and natural. Lee made no demands whatever, [and] accepted whatever Grant suggested." Grant was "so touched" by Lee's "complete acquiescence," Badeau asserts, that Grant allowed officers to retain their side-arms and personal property. Morgan's account strikes a similar note. According to the Union commissary chief, when Grant asked Lee, "How many men have you?" during their discussion about providing rations for the Confederates, Lee answered despondently, evidently unsure how many Southern troops were left in the ranks: "We have nothing but what we have on our backs, our books are all lost, our companies are

mostly commanded by non-commissioned officers. We have nothing."
Out of generosity, to alleviate so pathetic a plight, Morgan and Grant
offered 25,000 rations to the prostrate rebel army.[26]

On the subject of whether cordiality was possible under such circumstances, the Union officers who were present at the conference disagree.
Babcock, Porter, Morgan, and Cadwallader suggest that Lee was visibly
relieved at Grant's terms and able to muster some social graces when
introduced to the Union officers in the room. Lee was "depressed in spirit,
but agreeable and pleasant in conversation," according to Babcock; the
Confederate general talked amiably with old army acquaintances such
as Seth Williams and Morgan. Sharpe and Badeau, by contrast, insist
that Lee "coldly rebuffed" the Federal officers' attempts to "revive old
memories." Lee's pride—all he had left now—verged, thought Sharpe, on
"haughtiness." The efforts of Grant and his men to "take away the great
awkwardness of the scene" were in vain.[27]

One introduction, more than any other, broke Lee's reserve: his introduction to Ely Parker. As Porter remembers it:

> Parker being a full-blooded Indian, when Lee saw his swarthy fea-
> tures he looked at him with evident surprise, and his eyes rested
> on him for several seconds. What was passing in his mind no one
> knew, but the natural surmise was that he at first mistook Parker
> for a negro, and was struck with astonishment to find that the
> commander of the Union armies had one of that race on his per-
> sonal staff.

Parker, in his telling of the scene, strikes an altogether different note:
"After Lee had stared at me for a moment . . . he extended his hand and
said, 'I am glad to see one real American here.' I shook his hand and said,
'We are all Americans.'" According to Parker, Lee's back was to everyone
else but Marshall at this moment—so none of the Union witnesses could
corroborate Parker's version of the story.[28]

We can never know for certain what transpired; it may be that both
stories are true and that Lee, after initially betraying his shock at Parker's
presence, gathered himself and made a redeeming gesture. We can specu-
late, however, about why each man, Porter and Parker, was so invested in

his own version of the encounter. In Porter's eyes, perhaps, Lee in this moment revealed something of what Sharpe observed: the condescension and conservatism of Southern society. In letting his disgust flash across his face, Lee demonstrated that his society was mired in the moral low ground. For Parker, the rebel general's gracious gesture of respect toward him may have dramatized how those who are defeated could nonetheless maintain their dignity and a measure of their moral integrity— as a spokesmen for the defeated Iroquois, Parker was, perhaps, especially attuned to Lee's plight. But Parker's account of his exchange with Lee also serves, paradoxically, to locate Parker fully with the victors' circle. In his response to Lee ("We are all Americans"), Parker was, in his own way, acting magnanimously to a defeated foe.

According to Union observers, Lee tried manfully to hide his emotions as he exited the McLean house but could not do so. "General Lee came out looking very red in the face," thought General George A. Forsyth, one of the officers who milled about outside while the meeting transpired. As he pulled on his gloves, Lee visibly smote his left palm with his right fist, in the frustrated spirit of what might have been. He looked toward the rebel lines and gave a "choked sigh." It was truly over now.[29]

Grant's circle of commanders believed that the Appomattox campaign ended the Civil War. At the time of Lee's surrender, Johnston's Army of Tennessee remained in the field, in North Carolina—but with the redoubtable Sherman bearing down on him, the Union men reckoned, the Confederate general would soon be forced to capitulate, as Lee had. Davis and his government were in flight but could not long elude the grasp of the Federals; the same was true of the remaining Confederate forces, scattered in Alabama, Mississippi, and the Trans-Mississippi theater.

As important as the victory itself, Grant's men insisted, was *how* it had been won. In the reports they submitted on the campaign and in their farewell orders to their troops, the Union generals who had effected Lee's surrender emphasized the privations, hardships, and severe loss of life the Federal army had suffered; the "gallant" heroics of the officer corps; and the unflagging "enthusiasm," "cheerfulness," and "noble spirits" of the rank and file. The cavalry commanders took special pride in the fact that their detachments of horsemen were "in most instances confronted by superior numbers" of enemy infantry and artillery, as Custer put it; as far as the cavalry's performance was concerned, Merritt averred, the Appomattox campaign had "scarcely a parallel in history." The message of these reports and orders was clear: the Union victory was hard earned and a testament to the courage and skill of the Federal army. And to its righteousness: "Your efficient services and gallant conduct in behalf of *human rights* and *human freedom*," General Keifer of the Sixth Army Corps proclaimed in his farewell order to his troops, "will not be overlooked by a grateful country."[30]

Grant recapitulated these themes in General Orders No. 108, his tribute to the Federal troops, issued on June 2, 1865, as they were being mustered out in the wake of the successive surrenders of the remaining Confederate forces. It began:

> Soldiers of the Armies of the United States! By your patriotic devotion to your country in the hour of danger and alarm—your magnificent fighting, bravery and endurance—you have maintained the supremacy of the Union and the Constitution, overthrown all armed opposition to the enforcement of the Law, and of the Proclamations forever Abolishing *Slavery*, the cause and pretext of the Rebellion, and opened the way to the Rightful Authorities to restore Order and inaugerate Peace on a permanent and enduring basis on every foot of American soil.
>
> Your Marches, Sieges, & Battles, in distance, duration, resolution and brilliancy of result, dim the luster of the world's past military achievements, and will be the Patriot's precedent in defense of Liberty and Right in all time to come.

Grant praised the Union soldiers for having "discharged the highest duty of American citizens" and having won the "highest honors a great and free nation can accord." He closed his address, "To achieve these glorious triumphs and secure to yourselves, your fellow-countrymen and posterity the blessings of free institutions, tens of thousands of your gallant comrades have fallen, and sealed the priceless legacy with their lives. The graves of these a grateful nation bedews with tears—honors their memories, and will ever cherish and support their stricken families."[31]

For Grant and his men, the Union's victory flowed from the superior valor of its troops and virtue of its cause: this was the self-evident truth of Appomattox. Such an understanding of the significance of the surrender was at odds with an interpretation that had already begun to take shape, on April 9, within Lee's inner circle. For Confederate perspectives on the surrender conference we must turn first to Marshall, because Lee—unlike Grant—never committed to paper a reminiscence of the scene, and no other Confederates had first-hand knowledge of what transpired within the McLean house. Not surprisingly, Marshall's account diverges sharply from those of Grant's cohort. In Marshall's telling, Lee was not depressed, powerless, and acquiescent, nor was he haughty and cold. Rather the surrender was a drama that illustrated the "great qualities" that "adorned Lee's character." The very fact that Lee chose to receive the terms in person was, for Marshall, richly symbolic. While Grant had offered in their correspondence to meet with designated Confederate officers rather than Lee himself, Lee had chosen the "path of duty" as if it had been the "Way of Triumph": by meeting in person with Grant, Lee implicitly insisted that his conduct and his cause were beyond reproach. Lee was unfailingly cordial to Grant and the Union troops, and that civility was returned by them, as a mark of their respect for so great an adversary. In Marshall's view, Lee was not a passive recipient of Grant's leniency but instead made a series of propositions, such as the suggestion that Confederates might retain their horses, to which Grant assented. Indeed, Grant agreed to distribute rations in part because Lee held "about a thousand or fifteen hundred" Yankee troops as prisoners, men who were suffering along with the starving Confederates.[32]

Marshall, like the Union witnesses, delighted in contrasting Lee's attire with Grant's. But for him, Grant suffered in the comparison. The Union general "looked as though he had had a pretty hard time," Marshall thought. When confronted with Lee's dazzling elegance—Lee had on the "handsomest uniform" Marshall had ever seen and carried a gleaming sword with an elegant gold and leather scabbard—Grant felt obliged to excuse himself and to explain that his own side-arms and dress uniform were still some ways off, with his wagon train. According to Marshall, Grant reckoned that "Lee would rather receive him as he was" than postpone the meeting. Lee had once chastised Grant for his informal attire eighteen years earlier, during the Mexican War; the Confederate defeat had not fully closed the gap in experience, authority, and social stature between the two men, and Lee still commanded Grant's deference. From April 9 on, in his speeches and articles and memoirs of the surrender conference, Marshall explicitly ascribed "kindness, and generosity, and magnanimity" to *both* Lee and Grant. Lee, who might have been justified in haughtiness, or coldness, had chosen the course of civility instead.[33]

Juxtaposing Marshall's reflections on the surrender conference with other Confederate sources on the Appomattox drama shows that Lee had much more on his mind, on April 9, than the imperatives of civility. Such sources reveal that Lee was preoccupied, as his army capitulated, with the condition of his own troops, with how he would justify the surrender to his contemporaries, and with the verdict of history. On the morning of April 9, Colonel Venable had asked Lee plaintively, "Oh, general, what will history say of the surrender of the army in the field?" Lee had responded: "I know they will say hard things of us; they will not understand how we are overwhelmed by numbers. But that is not the question, colonel; the question is, 'Is it right to surrender this army?' If it is right, then I will take all the responsibility!"[34]

In fact, for Lee the questions—"What will history say?" and "Was it right to surrender?"—were inextricably linked. In order to establish the rightness of the surrender, Lee would have to lead a new sort of campaign in the treacherous terrain of politics. Its strategic aims were to prove that the Army of Northern Virginia had, in the end, faced insurmountable odds, worse than the two-to-one odds Lee had faced over the course of the war, and also to demonstrate that Lee had secured for his men terms that were not just favorable but also honorable. Lee would depend on his lieutenants, as he had during the war, to take the tactical initiative. But in the battle for public opinion, their weapons were words and numbers.

The opening salvo of the campaign was Lee's Farewell Address to his troops. Marshall prepared a draft of it on the morning of April 10, in accordance with instructions Lee had given him the night before; Marshall then submitted the draft to Lee for his input and approval. The final version read:

HDQRS. ARMY OF NORTHERN VIRGINIA
April 10, 1865

GENERAL ORDERS,
No. 9

After four years of arduous service, marked by unsurpassed courage and fortitude, the Army of Northern Virginia has been compelled to yield to overwhelming numbers and resources. I need not tell the brave survivors of so many hard-fought battles, who have remained steadfast to the last, that I have consented to this result from no distrust of them. But feeling that valor and devotion could accomplish nothing that would compensate for the loss that must have attended the continuance of the contest, I determined to avoid the useless sacrifice of those whose past services have endeared them to their countrymen.

By the terms of the agreement, officers and men can return to their homes and remain until exchanged. You will take with you the satisfaction that proceeds from the consciousness of duty faithfully performed; and I earnestly pray that a merciful God will extend to you his blessing and protection.

With an increasing admiration of your constancy and devotion to your country, and a grateful remembrance of your kind and generous considerations for myself, I bid you an affectionate farewell.

R. E. Lee,
General[35]

The order was promptly copied for circulation among the corps commanders and staff of the army. Lee, as he rode among his troops, reprised its central theme: "the odds against us were too great." General Order No. 9 immediately took on an iconic status. On the face of it, the document was admirable for its brevity, simplicity, and transparency. It was altogether fitting that Lee should console his men by emphasizing their steadfast devotion to the cause and his own enduring gratitude to them. Lee's address had profound emotional resonance; to his starving and exhausted men, the Yankee army seemed endless and encompassing.[36]

Like the correspondence between Lee and Grant, and the surrender terms, Lee's Farewell Address had layers of meaning and deep, tangled roots. For white Southerners, the reference to "overwhelming numbers and resources" was a sort of code: in the context of proslavery ideology and of the Confederate creed, "numbers" conjured up a Northern army of mercenaries and hirelings, among them a vast cohort of recent immigrants, who had been seduced or coerced into service and had no real moral stake in the fight. "Resources" conjured up images of Northern factories and cities in which an exploited underclass churned out the materiel of war at the behest of rapacious capitalists and power-hungry politicians. Southern nationalists had seen the burgeoning wealth and population of the North as an indictment of Northern society: its social instability, ruthlessness, and obsession with the bottom line. The address's reference to the "unsurpassed courage and fortitude" of the Confederate troops was part and parcel of that same indictment of the North. Defenders of the "Southern way of life" had made a staple of the claim that Southern men—accustomed to mastery and the agrarian life—were made of sterner stuff than Northern "wage-slaves." Lee and Marshall, highly educated, sophisticated men, were well aware of this ideological freight. By implying that Union troops had not been the equals of Confederate ones in the essential attributes of manhood, the address made a political statement. The Union victory was one of might over right: the Northern war machine, not the skill and bravery of Grant and his men, had ground the South down. Only when the Confederacy had reached the point at which "valor and devotion could accomplish nothing" did Lee at last relent.[37]

Just how overwhelming had the Union force been? In the immediate aftermath of the surrender, Lee offered up a striking answer to that question: "The enemy were more than five times our numbers," he explained to Davis in an April 12 letter announcing the surrender. By his reckoning, the Confederates had fewer than 8,000 infantrymen and roughly 2,000 cavalrymen in fighting condition left on April 9. "If we could have forced our way one day longer it would have been at a great sacrifice of life, and at its end I did not see how a surrender could have been avoided." Such an assessment was based on estimates of how many Confederates had massed on Gordon's front in the final battle. Indeed Gordon, in his farewell address to his corps, anticipated Lee's General Order No. 9. "He gave the reasons for our surrender that our supplies had been exhausted and we had only seven thousand muskets & two thousand cavalry surrounded by an enemy sixty thousand strong," wrote a Confederate infantryman in his April 9 diary entry.[38]

Lee's other principal officers soon closed ranks around the idea that, in the end, they had faced odds of worse than five-to-one. They had begun the retreat with a force of merely 35,000 men, only to have it ground down by Grant's "countless hordes." Their "brave little army," as Pendleton put it, never lost its internal cohesion or its will to fight. It had simply been overpowered. Lee did what he could to insure that this interpretation would circulate through the Union as well as the Confederate ranks. On April 10, Meade visited Lee in the apple orchard, one of a string of such visits Lee would have to endure that day. Meade found Lee, he wrote his wife, Margaretta, on April 10, to be "old & feeble"; Lee "was very sick, and had not a mouthful to eat." But Lee had the presence of mind to press his case: he informed a surprised Meade that he had defended Richmond and Petersburg with only 35,000 men (Meade thought the number had been twice that). As to the endgame, "Lee's army was reduced to a force of less than 10,000 affective armed men," Meade explained to Margaretta. "We had at least 50,000 armed men, so that nothing but madness would have justified further resistance." Here, courtesy of Meade, were Lee's "overwhelming numbers."[39]

Even as the campaign to establish the odds unfolded, Lee moved on a second front, to cast the surrender terms in the best possible light. On the morning of April 10, Lee again met with Grant. The two men conversed on horseback. Grant brought along some of his principal officers, "all kept aloof in a sort of semi-circle" around their chieftain, "too far to hear the conversation," according to Badeau. This tableaux "was lighted up with the bright sunshine," Ely Parker would later recall; he could not "help but be struck by the beauty of the scene." Grant's agenda soon became clear. As the historian Gary W. Gallagher explains, Grant "asked Lee's help in securing the surrender of other Confederate military forces. Only President Davis could decide such questions, replied Lee, echoing Grant's comments on April 8 about the relative authority he and President Lincoln held." Lee had an agenda of his own. Hoping their paroles could confer on his men a measure of immunity from harassment or reprisals at the hands of the victorious Federals, he requested of Grant at this April 10 meeting that each individual Confederate be issued a printed certificate, signed by a Union officer, as proof that such a soldier came under the settlement of April 9.[40]

Gibbon, one of the three Union generals (along with Griffin and Merritt) to whom Grant had designated the task of finalizing the settlement, took the matter in hand. On April 10, his corps printing press, manned by a detail of printers he had rounded up, began churning out blank parole certificates. The presses were set up in the Clover Hill Tavern in the village, the temporary headquarters of George Sharpe, who was tasked with overseeing the distribution of the paroles. In most cases, Confederate officers rather than Union ones signed the parole passes—the most practical arrangement. By Grant's orders, Confederates with parole passes could pass through Union lines on their way home and ride for free on military railroads and government transports. The question of who exactly should be eligible for a parole was settled on April 10, when Grant's three designated officers met with their Confederate counterparts, Longstreet, Gordon, and Pendleton, to elaborate the details of the April 9 settlement. They were efficient and cordial; "I do not think that any six men could have had a more harmonious meeting," Gibbon would write to his mother the following day. At Gordon's urging, the six men decided on a "liberal" policy in keeping with Grant's liberal terms: the surrender of the Army of Northern Virginia was construed to include all Confederates forces operating on April 8 within a 20-mile radius of Appomattox.[41]

It is easy to see why Grant and Gibbon readily assented to Lee's request. A parole certificate vouchsafed that a soldier would "not be disturbed"—so long as he observed the "laws in force" where he resided. Union men put the emphasis on the second clause: the certificates would speed the Confederates' reintegration into civilian life and remind them of obligations attendant upon their status as prisoners.[42]

The Confederates emphasized the first clause: in their eyes, the paroles represented the promise that they would not be treated dishonorably. Edward Porter Alexander, for example, reckoned that the terms, in their simple brevity, "practically gave an amnesty to every surrendered soldier for all political offences." It was hard for him to imagine "that there would ever be any vindictive desire to hang or punish our prominent men for treason." Sharing this view of things, Fitz Lee, who with his cavalry had slipped away from the Federals on the morning of April 9, opted to turn back to Appomattox, to accept Grant's terms and be paroled. When he arrived at the village on April 11, Fitz Lee called on Gibbon at the McLean house; he had been a cadet under Gibbon at West Point. The wayward Confederate became his former commander's guest for the night. "Lying on the floor, [Fitz Lee] slept as soundly as a child, after, as he said, having had no sleep for a week," Gibbon would later recall. "He seemed to rejoice that the war was over."[43]

Just how a parole might confer practical advantages is illustrated by an incident involving one of Longstreet's brigadier generals, Henry A. Wise. A former governor of Virginia and leading secessionist, the flinty Wise was headed home to Norfolk from Appomattox when he had a telling encounter with a Yankee cavalryman. As that cavalryman tried to confiscate Wise's horse, Wise brandished his parole certificate, declaring that he had "Gen. Grant's safe-guard" and was "under its protection!" The Union man gave way. The notion that the parole certificates conferred protection on their bearers gained immediate currency among the Confederate troops. "It was very noticeable," observed Union Colonel A. B. Lawrence, quartermaster of the Twenty-fourth Corps, "how greedily the Confederates, rank and file especially, clutched at their 'protection papers' provided for them by the terms of the treaty." The parole slips "were eagerly sought for" as a shield against "punishment and vengeance."[44]

By April 15, roughly 28,000 Confederates had been paroled. Awkwardly for Lee and his lieutenants, this number far exceeded the figure

Protection papers: the Appomattox parole of Confederate surgeon Robert Poole Myers. (Museum of the Confederacy, Richmond, Virginia)

of 10,000 they offered as an estimate of Confederate strength. Had Lee's campaign to secure favorable terms undermined his campaign to prove that the Southern troops had faced insurmountable odds? The answer, he and his men insisted, was no. The discrepancy was "easily explainable." Most of the paroled men were "unarmed stragglers" and "extra-duty and detailed men" who "added nothing to the fighting capacity of the army." This was an ingenious argument, a final flourish to the Farewell Address: the men who reported for duty and took their place on the battle line on April 9 were not the main body of the army—they were its beating heart.[45]

It was not at all clear, in the raw, uncertain days after the surrender, if this argument would take. For one, it would be difficult to prove. Lee and his lieutenants did not know with certainty how many men had fought on Gordon's front; how many had straggled, clinging to the wagon trains that stretched to the rearguard; how many had deserted; how many were unarmed; how many were too hungry and foot-sore to fight. The final reports of Union and Confederate commanders had not yet been submitted and tabulated—and Lee had his headquarters papers, with official "records, returns, maps, plans etc.," destroyed during the retreat, right before the army reached Appomattox Court House, lest they fall into the hands of the Yankees.[46]

Then there was the problem of the holdouts. Lee's brave little army, it will be recalled, had splintered on the morning of April 9, as Fitz Lee's cavalry headed to the hills. While Fitz soon circled back to Appomattox, two of his division commanders, Thomas Rosser and Thomas T. Munford, fought on rather than turning back—they were determined to rally the rogue Confederates in Virginia who had not yet been paroled and then to report to General Johnston in North Carolina. Rosser and Munford considered themselves to be the beating heart of the Confederacy, and they rejected Lee's vision of an honorable peace. The Union's policy of conciliation, so Munford declared, was designed to lull the Confederates to sleep, so the Yankees could "rivet the chains they have been making such gigantic efforts to forge." True Southerners would not "kneel down" and "kiss the rod that smote them." Munford implored his fellow Virginians to "teach our children eternal hostility to our foes."[47]

Munford and Rosser were encouraged in their defiance by Jefferson Davis, who received unofficial reports of Lee's surrender on April 10 while in Danville. His fugitive government then made its way to North Carolina and set up a new provisional government seat in Greensboro. Despite the "chilly reception" from the inhabitants of that city, Davis maintained that "as long as the Confederacy had an organized army somewhere, the cause was not lost." Even after the rumors of Lee's surrender were confirmed, on April 12, Davis remained committed to "cobbling together scattered regular units . . . for a conventional defense," as the historian William B. Feis has explained; he hoped to link up Johnston's army with the Confederate forces in Alabama, Mississippi, and Louisiana.[48] This strategy of rallying the remnants cast a shadow of doubt over General Order No. 9 and its insistence that valor could no longer work miracles.

By far the most vexing problem, though, was this: the discrepancy between the number of "effective" troops and the number of parolees raised the specter of Confederate failure. Why, on April 9, had so many men languished or malingered behind the lines? How many of these were deserters—not simply tardy, but absent without leave? Why were so many men starving and unarmed? Why did Lee not have more "effectives" at his disposal?

Behind the scenes, Lee grappled with these questions. On April 10, he received Confederate visitors as well as Union ones in the apple orchard. While Lee was cordial, if guarded, in the presence of men like Meade, he was visibly agitated—by turns angry and sad—when surrounded only by his own men. According to Lieutenant Colonel William Blackford, one of his chief engineers, Lee was in "one of his savage moods" that day, pacing back and forth "like a caged lion." It was not just the humiliation of defeat that was unbearable, but the sense that somewhere along the line, the Confederate war effort had gone wrong. Right after Meade's visit to Lee, Mahone called on Lee to "bid him good bye." The Confederate warrior found that his beloved chief "was obviously full of grief," betrayed by his "watering eye." To Mahone, Lee revealed his doubts about the conduct of the Confederate war effort. "Genl Lee observed that he had advised the Confederate authorities at the start—that the contest on which we had entered could not be over estimated and our chance to win was to be found by throwing the whole military or fighting power of the Confederacy into the struggle." "While not saying so," Lee "manifestly thought [this] had not been done": the Confederacy had failed to mobilize the South's manpower and resources to the fullest.[49]

Ten days later, on April 20, Lee penned a letter to Jefferson Davis that plumbed the depths of his own disappointment and bitterness. He confided to the Confederate president that as the Army of Northern Virginia left the trenches of Richmond and Petersburg, it "began to disintegrate." The men had been "feeble" and demoralized in the last months of the war and lacked the "boldness and decision which formerly characterized them." Their want of confidence, Lee surmised, "was produced by the state of feeling in the country, and the communications received by the men from their homes": civilians on the home front, engulfed in misery and in the path of the Federal juggernaut, had beckoned the men to desert. Many of the stragglers who drifted back into the lines after the surrender conference "had left the ranks on the march." Invoking Grant's formula, Lee did as Grant had asked him to do on the morning of April 10. He rejected the option of guerrilla warfare and exerted his influence on behalf of peace. "To save useless effusion of blood," Lee wrote Davis, "I would recommend measures be taken for suspension of hostilities and the restoration of peace."[50]

In acknowledging the disintegration of his army, Lee was confessing, the historian Joseph T. Glatthaar has noted, that "Confederate defeat was no foregone conclusion." If that disintegration could have somehow been prevented, "the war might have turned out differently." Modern-day scholars, drawing on the parole lists and reams of official records and returns, have established that Lee began the retreat with 60,000 men (not 35,000) and ended it with 30,000 men within a four-mile radius of Appomattox. Grant had 60,000 men within a 10-mile radius. These statistics contradict Lee's claim of five-to-one odds; in the end, he faced two-to-one odds, the same he had faced all along. The statistics also encapsulate the story of his army's disintegration: over the course of the retreat, it had been cut in half, not only by battlefield debacles such as Sailor's Creek but also by mass desertion and starvation.[51]

The great irony of Lee's Farewell Address is that he knew, perhaps better than any other Civil War commander, that an army's strength was not measured in numbers. Rather its strength lay in its unity, confidence, aggressiveness, and élan. He knew that his army no longer possessed

enough of this sort of strength on April 9. But such knowledge was literally unbearable—it left the Confederates too vulnerable to recrimination
and despair. Lee would not let his guard down, in quite the same way as he
had in his letter to Jefferson Davis, ever again. Instead, he would demand
of himself and his lieutenants strict fealty to the "overwhelming numbers
and resources" interpretation of Confederate defeat. In the summer of
1865, he reached out to them, requesting that they furnish him the
"necessary data" to establish definitively the "effective strength" of the
Army of Northern Virginia; this was the "only tribute" that could be paid
to the "worth of its noble officers and soldiers." His men—especially Taylor, Long, and Gordon—would rise to the challenge and churn out
speeches, articles, and memoirs designed to banish the specter of Confederate failure and to enshrine the sentiments expressed in the Farewell Address. The Confederates' "constancy and devotion" was their keynote. Lee
"surrendered at Appomattox eight thousand starving men to the com-
bined force of two great armies whose chiefs had long despaired to con-
quer it by skill or daring, and who had worn it away by weight of numbers
and brutal exchange of many lives for one," as Taylor emphatically put it.
There could be no shame in such a defeat.[52]

Neither Lee nor Grant was present at Appomattox to witness the April
12, 1865, stacking-of-arms ceremony. That morning, having obtained a
certificate of his parole, Lee rode to Richmond, accompanied by Taylor,
Venable, and Marshall; Grant had left Appomattox on the afternoon of
April 10, bound for Washington, D.C.[53]

The basic parameters of the ceremony were set by the six commissioners
who met on April 10, but the details were entrusted to Joshua L. Chamberlain of the Fifth Corps. Most of the Union army, including Sheridan's
cavalry, had departed on April 10 and 11, while the First Division of the
Fifth Corps stayed behind to receive the surrendered arms and flags of the
Confederate infantry. On the morning of April 12, Confederate infantry
regiments led by Gordon's Second Corps—some 21,000 to 22,000 men in
all—filed past the victorious Union troops along the stage road and stacked
their arms and delivered their tattered battle flags. In Long's account, "not
a sound of exultation arose from the Army of the Potomac," for "when it
was seen how small was the number that had so long opposed their proud

array," the Union men "accorded the meed of honor where honor was due."
Gordon noted that in their "worn-out shoes and ragged uniforms," his tattered band "challenged the admiration" of Chamberlain's men—and
Chamberlain rose to the challenge by ordering the Union soldiers to go to
right shoulder shift, offering a marching salute to the Confederates. This
was a "fitting tribute to Southern chivalry," thought Gordon.[54]

An April 13, 1865, account by Chamberlain, in a letter to his sister,
struck a different note. Of the Confederates, he had this to say: "Poor fellows. I pitied them from the bottom of my heart." Chamberlain's emphasis
was not on "Southern chivalry" but on the skill and daring of the Northern
army in achieving its "crowning triumphs." "We captured the enemy by the
thousands & carried their positions by a dash," he wrote. Chamberlain
took special pride in the fact that his brigade was a "remnant" of the "old
5th corps, veterans of thirty battles." In his postwar memoir, Chamberlain
developed the theme. He referred to the Confederates at the surrender ceremony as "the last remnant of the arms and colors of that great army which
ours had been created to confront." But he noted, pointedly, "We were
remnants also": "veterans, and replaced veterans; cut to pieces, cut down,
consolidated . . . made nearer by blood shed." The noble manhood and
righteousness of the Union cause—not the "overwhelming numbers and
resources" of the Union war machine—had won the war. "It was our glory
only that the victory we had won was for country," Chamberlain attested,
and "for the well-being of others." Among those others were the surrendered Confederates themselves, who had been "fatally wrong in striking at
the old flag." Chamberlain, in short, was as determined as his fellow Union
commanders to claim the moral high ground at Appomattox. "Whoever
had misled these men, we had not," he said of his proud Union remnant.
The challenge facing Northern soldiers in the aftermath of the surrender,
Chamberlain reckoned, was to lead the errant rebels back home.[55]

Did Appomattox signify the triumph of right over wrong or of might
over right? As the news of the surrender rifled through the two armies, the
rank-and-file soldiers struggled to make sense of the dizzying events that
had brought U. S. Grant face to face with Robert E. Lee—and they joined
the battle over just what sort of peace the two men had wrought.

4

The Armies

Although they lacked direct access to Grant and Lee and to their strategic and tactical calculations, the Union and Confederate soldiers who fought the Appomattox campaign were keenly aware, as aware as the men in the two generals' inner circles, of the political nature of the surrender and of the high stakes involved in interpreting it. In their letters, diaries, and memoirs, these men parsed the difficult distinction between the idea that the Confederates had been defeated and the competing idea that they had been overwhelmed; the former put the emphasis on Union soldiers' skill, and the latter on their sheer numbers. In the eyes of Union men, the surrender marked the providential triumph of their democratic republic and its hardy citizen-soldiers over the arrogant slaveholders' oligarchy and the deluded masses it had led to the slaughter. Grant's army inflicted on the rebels a punishing defeat; his turn to mercy was the crowning proof of the Union's moral superiority. The surrender had yet another level of meaning for the African American troops who fought in Grant's legions. They viewed the decisive role of United States Colored Troops (USCT) regiments in blocking Lee's escape route as the crowning proof of their own fitness for citizenship. They embraced Grant's magnanimous terms as a means to promote racial harmony and to dispel the long-standing charge that the demise of slavery would bring race war.

While Union troops elaborated narratives of vindication, Confederate troops rallied around the sentiments expressed in Lee's Farewell Address and drew out its premises. The Yankee army, mercenary in its very nature, had vastly outnumbered the Confederates and had practiced a barbarous form of warfare befitting the ruthlessness of Northern society. This counternarrative found expression among Confederate soldiers in wildly inflated estimates of the strength of the Federal forces and in prophecies that divine retribution might still await Grant's hordes. But the "overwhelming numbers" interpretation could not keep at bay troubling questions about the Southern army's condition, performance, and morale in the final campaign. Lee, all his men agreed, bore no blame whatsoever for their defeat. But had they in the end failed him? Had the politicians, Jefferson Davis, and his embattled administration failed them all? Nor could the dominant understanding of the surrender terms among Confederates—that Grant's leniency honored and protected them—keep at bay fears that Yankee retribution might be at hand.

"And now on their sin has the punishment fallen. Petersburg and Richmond in our hands, Lee fleeing from the wrath to come, on every side men falling off from the cause like leaves in autumn, ignominy, ruin, misery behind and before, on the right hand and the left." This, according to the two Union officers, Major R. C. Eden and Captain C. H. McCreery, who edited the soldiers' newspaper *Grant's Petersburg Progress*, was "the situation" on April 5, 1865. From their vantage point in occupied Petersburg, it seemed the Confederacy was in its "convulsive death-throes." Grant's final triumph was imminent, they were sure—so sure that they felt moved to reflect on the nature of the peace. "Now is the time to show magnanimity," the two editors insisted, "for we can afford to do so." "Exulting over a fallen foe adds no laurels to a visitor's crown"; the "bitter despondency" of the Confederates was punishment enough.[1]

The whirlwind of events in the days that followed, from the Sailor's Creek battles to the surrender conference, proved these men to be astute judges of the tactical state-of-play and of the mood in the Federal army in the last days of the retreat. The Union soldiers who chased Lee across the Virginia countryside to Appomattox did constant battle with their own hunger and fatigue, but they were buoyed by the knowledge that the "ragged half fed Johnies" in the rebel army were worse off, and that, as cavalry Lieutenant Samuel Cormany put it on April 6, 1865, the "wild adventurous work of crushing the Southern Cause" would soon be crowned with success.[2]

Cormany, a devout evangelical from rural Pennsylvania, was an ordinary soldier who left behind an extraordinarily rich diary, spanning the eve of the war to its dramatic closing scenes. In his account, it was the Union army's prowess that made its victory inevitable. The Confederates, although diminished, fought with desperate resolve—and thus Union men had to muster every ounce of their own skill and strength. "But for our long experience we would have been badly used up," Cormany wrote of the hard fighting on April 7. The final battle at Appomattox brought forth the best of the men: with "steady tread" and "deadly aim" they rendered Lee's escape hopeless. "Our men knew no faltering," Cormany proudly noted in his diary entry for April 9, 1865.

Yet, however strong the Union soldiers' expectations of victory, the news of the surrender—when it came at last—overwhelmed them. The appearance of white flags of truce along the battle line seemed to Cormany surreal. "Oh what a lull! What a wondering Why?—Flags of Truce meet—What's up?" Union soldiers outside of Grant's circle of key commanders and staff officers had nothing but rumors to go on and little knew how close to victory they were. With the news came release: "Next Comes the Cry, LEE SURRENDERS!," Cormany wrote. "'Ye Gods!' What cheering comes along in waves. . . . Hats and caps uplifted on the points of Sabers are whirled and waved overhead—and with tearful voices—Scores of overjoyed men exclaim 'Now I can go home to Wife Babies Mother Sister Sweetheart, and our Country is forever safe.'"[3]

Union soldiers at Appomattox registered their surprise and joy in a wide variety of ways. Some found that at this surpassing moment, words failed them. In a letter to his father, Major Farnham Lyon of the 7th Michigan Cavalry wrote of April 9, "to say it was the happiest day of my life would not half express it." Infantryman David Lane, another Michigan volunteer, confided to his diary upon hearing official news of the surrender, "I cannot write! I cannot talk; only my glad heart cries 'Hosanna! Hosanna in the Highest; in the Highest!'"[4] Some professed disbelief. "We can hardly realize the fact of the Surrender, after fighting LEE's army for nearly three years," wrote Sergeant Jacob J. Zorn, a sturdy yeoman from Pennsylvania, in his diary on the night of April 9. Two weeks later, Colonel Stephen Minot Weld, the Harvard-educated scion of an elite Boston family, made the same point, though more evocatively, in a letter to his sister: "To tell the truth, we none of us realize even yet that [Lee] has actually surrendered. I had a sort of impression that we should fight him all our lives. He was like a ghost to children, something that haunted us so long that we could not realize that he and his army were really out of existence to us. It will take me some months to be conscious of this fact." Indeed, this feeling of disbelief lingered and is attested to in soldiers' memoirs as well as their initial reactions. "We would hardly believe it," wrote George H. Allen of the 4th Rhode Island Volunteers in his postwar reminiscence of the surrender. "No more to face the storm of death upon the battle-field. The dogs of war were chained at last."[5]

Many soldiers were determined to somehow capture the moment—not only to bear witness to the stirring events that had transpired but also to interpret them. Their diary entries, letters, and memoirs, taken together, constitute a counternarrative to the overwhelming numbers and resources interpretation of the war's end. Union soldiers insisted that it was strategic savvy and fortitude that won the day. John L. Smith, a corporal in the 118th Pennsylvania infantry, wrote to his mother in Philadelphia a detailed account of the surrender that was by turns jaunty and solemn: "Our generals meant 'biz' this time; never gave the Rebs a moment's rest; went for them and made them fight," he crowed. Smith also described his Union comrades-in-arms as starving and "nearly bare-footed," thanks to the hard marching that had put his unit far ahead of their supply trains and to Grant's decision to give over Union rations to the defeated Confederates. The Union men had grappled, too, with a special kind of fear, born of the very nearness of success: "It seemed to me every one was more scared than ever" on the last day of fighting, Smith confided to his mother, "from the fact that we knew the war was nearly over, and we did not want to be killed at the end of the war." His letters home bristled with pride at the men's ability to overcome such fear. Infantryman Henry Miner, for his part, wrote breathlessly to his parents in New York that the war hung in the balance during the retreat: "If Genl. Grant had been two hours later he would not have caught Lee." The rebels, in their headlong flight, left behind the debris of defeat—caissons, wagons, payrolls, ammunition, and bodies. They had had "no time to bury the dead" strewn along their line of march, so relentless was the Union pursuit.[6]

On April 10, Major Charles Mattocks of the 17th Maine, whose bravery leading a charge at Sailor's Creek had earned him a Medal of Honor, wrote his mother that the Appomattox campaign had "afforded ample chances for the ambitious to 'show their hands,'"—and that he and his fellow officers had "their full share of the danger as well as the glory." He could not resist the opportunity to get in a dig at those who had missed out, and at those, his mother included, who had doubted that victory would come: "I presume every one will now regret that they were not at the 'wake.' Now do you think I was foolish to hurry away? I would not have missed these ten days for all the world." Captain Henry C. Matrau of Michigan, who had snuck away from home at age 16 to enlist in 1861 and who served for the duration of the war with Wisconsin's famed "Iron Brigade," had many moments of doubt and despair, which he confided in heart-wrenching letters back home. He had been so traumatized by the carnage of Gettysburg that it had been weeks before he could put pen to paper to describe the hellish scene for his parents. But on April 10, 1865, he limbered up his pen with pride and glee. After explaining to his parents how Grant's forces surrounded Lee's army, he asked, pointedly, "Where are the men now who said that the army of the Potomac has never accomplished anything?" The taste of vindication was sweet.[7]

"I would not have missed these ten days for all the world": Union soldiers at Appomattox Court House. (Library of Congress)

In a similar vein, Major Holman S. Melcher of the 20th Maine, a hero of the fabled charge at Little Round Top during the battle of Gettysburg, wrote his brother that it required "almost superhuman efforts" for Union soldiers to endure the "sleepless nights, weary marches and terrible conflicts" of the Appomattox campaign. At the moment of "jubilee," Melcher noted, "stern officers who have never failed on the bloody field of battle, wept like children, for joy."

In the minds of soldiers such as Melcher, there was no contradiction in attributing victory both to "superhuman effort" and to divine Providence. "Thanks! And praise to Almighty God, for the great thing He has done for us, in saving our country," he wrote, expressing the widely shared conviction among the Union troops that Providence had, in the end, rewarded the righteous. Two core convictions among Union troops were reaffirmed for them at the moment of victory: that courage would be decisive on the battlefield, and that courage was linked to godliness. The first conviction reflected a Victorian cultural consensus, among Northerners and Southerners alike, that courage was the essence of manliness and war its ultimate test. The second reflected the equally pervasive view that courage was the emblem of moral purity and of divine favor. This belief-system had motivated young men on both sides to enlist in 1861 in what they were sure would be a short and glorious war. The war's duration, its carnage, its expanding scope, the seemingly senseless slaughter in a train of indecisive battles—all this had sorely tested these convictions, and some soldiers on each side had openly abjured them and fought on not in the name of courage and moral purity but instead out of fealty to their comrades or simply to survive. But, as Union reactions to the surrender demonstrate, faith in the decisiveness and righteousness of courage was not simply a belief that one might profess or reject, but instead a kind of cultural reserve, that victory itself could sustain and renew.[8]

For Union soldiers at Appomattox, there seemed to be something providential in the very physical setting for the surrender. Many of them noted, with satisfaction, that at the moment of final victory they had Lee nearly surrounded—how fitting it seemed that the defeated Confederates, massed on the low ground, "laid in a valley" while the triumphant Union soldiers lined the hills of the "great natural amphitheater" sweeping around the town of Appomattox. A "strange Providence" was surely at work, army chaplain A. O. Roe of the Fifth Corps surmised, because the surrender terms were signed in the home of a man, Wilmer McLean, who had owned a house on *"the battle-ground of Manassas, on which the first great victory was won."* "How wondrous the Divine retribution!" The most stirring sign of divine favor was to be found in the providential timing of the surrender, on Palm Sunday. "It was the universal expression" among the Union soldiers, wrote Roe, that the surrender was a "blessed Sabbath's work."[9]

Union soldiers naturally took special pride in the fact that the "blessed Sabbath" marked the demise of none other than the fabled Army of Northern Virginia. But they differed sharply in their assessments of what exactly Lee and his army represented. Some simply emphasized the status of Lee's troops as the Confederacy's elite fighting force. "What a glorious victory," wrote John H. Westervelt of the 1st New York Volunteer Engineer Corps, in a daily journal that he sent in installments to his 13-year-old son. "The best army the rebels had in the field [is] in our hands together with their ablest general as well as the highest in rank." Most Union soldiers were quick to acknowledge the bravery and skill of their defeated foe. This was in keeping with what the historian Gerald F. Linderman calls a "fundamental assumption" of the Victorian cult of courage: "One's achievements in war were enhanced by the worth of the enemy." If Lee was worthy, then Grant was worthier still; if the Confederates fought bravely, how much more admirable then was the superior bravery of the boys in blue.[10]

For some, however, Lee represented the very worst of Southern society. Private John W. Haley of the 17th Maine, the author of one of the classic field diaries of the war, used his April 9, 1865, entry to register a searing indictment of Lee and of the South. "General Lee has the reputation of being very humane, and yet to gratify ambition he witnessed all this suffering and waited for Grant to admonish him of its folly and ask for its cessation." The rebel soldiers, Haley believed, were the dupes of their leaders and had been "toted around half-starved and half-clad, with no reasonable hope of victory." Lee's willingness to sacrifice these soldiers reflected the brute arrogance of Southern slave society: "Perhaps such a course does not seem inhuman," Haley editorialized, "to people who have been accustomed to buying and selling human flesh the way we in the

North do cattle and hogs." Haley was no abolitionist. He was contemptuous of all who were not true "*Yankees*": blacks, secessionists, Irish immigrants, and Northern Copperheads. But he reserved his strongest ire for
the "miserable Rebel devils" whose folly and treachery had cost so many
lives. For Haley, the Confederate soldiers were not deserving of clemency.
He resented being ordered by his officers to treat the Confederates as
"erring brothers" rather than as a "foreign foe"; he noted, archly, "The fact
that they are not foreigners is not due to any lack of effort on their part."[11]

Haley's assessment of the Southern cause tapped a deep vein in the
ideology of the Republican Party: the conviction that a slaveholder oligarchy held the nonslaveholding white Southern majority in their thrall.
It reflected a practice that cut against the grain of the Victorian valoriza-
tion of courage—the demonization of the enemy as godless and beyond
redemption. As the historian George Rable has explained, from the war's
outset, the Union and Confederacy mobilized religion against each
other; each side claimed that it alone fought a "just and holy war." On the
Union side, "loyalty to nation and loyalty to God became one and the
same." Just war arguments emphasized that secession represented law-
lessness, the South had been the aggressor, and slavery polluted the land
and "offended the Almighty." On the Confederate side, just war arguments cast Northern society as mired in greed, materialism, infidelity,
and hypocrisy. For Union soldiers such as John Haley, the surrender at
last settled the score: how sweet it was that, he noted with caustic sarcasm, that "high-toned Southerners" were forced to surrender to "mean,
craven-spirited Yankees."[12]

Haley's rejection of Grant's lenient terms put him outside the mainstream of soldier opinion. Most Union troops embraced the policy of
magnanimity. They did so in part in deference to their officers, who
enforced the policy as Grant's will. During the April 12 stacking-of-
arms ceremony, soldiers in the 118th Pennsylvania taunted Confederate
General John Wise, who had been Virginia governor at the time of John
Brown's raid in 1859, with the jeer, "Who hung John Brown! Who hung
John Brown!" When their officers reproached them "very sharply," John
L. Smith wrote, they quickly desisted and fell into line.[13]

More important than such deference to authority was the abiding
belief that in so thoroughly defeating the rebels, the Federal army had

meted out sufficient punishment to the South and accomplished its great object of putting the nation back together. Many Union soldiers felt that the Confederates were so desperately beaten that they actually welcomed the surrender. Smith marveled at the "ragged and lousy" state of the Confederate soldiers and at their war weariness; he was bemused when one rebel soldier at the stacking-of-arms ceremony leaned over and said wryly, "Good-bye, gun; I am darned glad to get rid of you." "They are tired of this war and cant See any use of carrying it on any longer," wrote Jacob Zorn of the rebels, while army surgeon Henry J. Millard of Massachusetts sent word to his sister Hattie that the Confederate army was in a "very disorganised and demoralized condition, and were glad enough to give up the ship." Massachusetts cavalryman Stanton P. Allen had seen evidence of Confederate desperation scrawled on the canvas covers of the army wagons that were abandoned along the line of retreat: "We all can't whip you all without something to eat," one such piece of graffiti read. In Allen's estimation, the rations the Union provided to the surrendered Confederates helped account for why the rebels "accepted the inevitable with better grace then could have been expected." After all, "when you put food into a starving man's mouth the chances favor his smothering his hatred."[14]

Union soldiers reckoned that magnanimity was the best means to secure the redemption and reconstruction of the South. Brevet Major General Alvin C. Voris of the 67th Ohio, a staunch believer in the Republicans' "free soil" principles, was certain that the heroic campaign that had "annihilate[d] the army of Gen Lee" had also left the Confederacy itself a "*broken* concern": "Their supplies are gone, munitions of war captured, their soldiers thoroughly demoralized, the inhabitants discouraged with an utter prostration of business and no public treasure," he wrote in his April 13 diary entry. A show of kindness by the triumphant Union would, he reasoned, demonstrate "that right not might rules" and that it was the superior moral character of the North—its commitment to "free institutions" and to "personal enterprise"—that won the war.[15]

In a series of letters to his wife, Mary, written in the immediate wake of the surrender, Hallock Armstrong, an army chaplain stationed at Petersburg, took his own measure of Confederate defeat. The war had rendered the South a "charnel house," he explained to her. The South had "suffered enough"; all that was left was to "forgive and forget." Armstrong shared the view that elite slaveholders like Lee had led the common folk of the South astray, and he believed that the Union's mission was "to disenthrall just such men." Victorious Northerners, if animated by the spirit of forgiveness, could lift up the South's "ignorant and degraded" poor whites and "open up before them a brighter future for themselves and their children." His fellow chaplain, A. O. Roe, agreed, arguing that if the Union would forgive, and scorn revenge, the masses of defeated rebels would realize they had misjudged Northerners and would "turn the torrent of their indignation against the guilty authors of their own woes"—namely, rebel leaders such as Davis and Lee. Roe felt this view was shared by "every intelligent man" in the Union army, and he hoped that as the Union government formulated its reconstruction policies the "voice of the army [would] be heard." Lieutenant Colonel Elisha Hunt Rhodes succinctly captured this consensus when he observed in his diary entry for April 10: "I think General Grant's way of managing affairs will help on the peace that must come."[16]

As word of Lee's surrender spread outward from Appomattox to Federal troops stationed across the South, Union soldiers responded with "wild exultation." On April 12, the news reached Sherman's forces in North Carolina. Captain Augustus Ricks of the 104th Ohio Infantry, who had the happy duty of carrying the tidings of the surrender through the ranks of the Army of the Ohio, captures the boyish glee with which soldiers reacted: they commenced "pounding each other with knapsacks, waving blankets on the points of their bayonets, pounding canteens with belt buckles. . . . playing foot-ball with haversacks, jumping at leap-frog," and generally making a "pandemonium of sounds and a circus of tumbling and vaulting." Sergeant Alexander G. Downing of the 11th Iowa Infantry in the Army of the Tennessee noted in his diary that his "whole brigade commenced singing songs—'John Brown's body lies a-mouldering in the grave, As we go marching on!" Fired by Grant's victory, Sherman's men anticipated the "speedy close of the rebellion," as Sergeant Bluffton Miller of the 75th Indiana, put it.[17]

All Union soldiers, no matter where they were stationed, could take rightful pride in the triumph in Virginia. But those who were there, at Appomattox, had a special pride of place. "To be an Eye Witness to such an important event," Henry J. Millard wrote his sister, was a "blessed privilege."

Elisha Hunt Rhodes perhaps put it even better: "Such a scene only happens once in centuries."[18]

Union soldiers' awareness of the epochal importance of the surrender translated not only into eloquent reflections on the moment but also into a seemingly more down-to-earth impulse: a mania for relics. In this, as in their embrace of Grant's terms, the rank and file followed the lead of their officers. As soon as the surrender conference in the McLean house was over, the Union commanders there began angling for the precious mementos of the occasion. General Ord procured the marble-topped table at which Lee had sat, while Sheridan claimed the table on which Grant drafted the surrender terms; he then offered it as a gift to Libbie Custer, in tribute to her "gallant husband." George Sharpe seized the candlesticks, while an aide-de-camp of Sheridan's, Lieutenant Colonel Thomas W. C. Moore, took home a rag doll belonging to McLean's daughter Lulu—and dubbed it "Silent Witness." While the evidence suggests that Sheridan and Ord bought the tables from McLean, it is unclear whether the other relics were purchased or purloined. In some accounts, McLean eagerly sold the items, but this claim was disputed by his family. Some relics were discreetly tucked away. Horace Porter, who during the conference had lent Lee a pencil with which to go over Grant's draft of the surrender terms, kept it as a treasured souvenir; Ely Parker kept one of the three manifold order-book copies of the surrender terms, written in his own hand.[19]

Those not privy to the surrender conference took whatever was left in the McLean house when the principal officers were done. "Cane bottomed chairs were ruthlessly cut to pieces; the cane splits broken into pieces a few inches long, and parceled out among those who swarmed around. Haircloth upholstery was cut from chairs, and sofas were also cut into strips and parches and carried away," recalled *New York Herald* correspondent Sylvanus Cadwallader, who was there to record the scene. No item was too small to have value. Major Farnham Lyon, for example, wrote his father proudly: "I enclose a few sprigs, etc. taken from the room the capitulation was made in ... also a paper which I took off the table. I think it was used as a cover at the time." Cavalryman Alanson M. Randol and some of his comrades rode over to the Court House after the surrender "in search of some memento of the occasion." Finding that "everything had been appropriated," they asked Wilmer McLean to autograph their diaries and paid him a dollar per signature. McLean "thus received quite a golden harvest," Randol mused.[20]

Union soldiers also fell eagerly, as did Confederates, upon Sweeney's apple orchard, where Lee had rested along the stage road on April 9, and where he had received Babcock's summons. They swarmed the orchard, cutting down "Lee's" tree and carving its limbs into countless souvenir chunks and splinters. "I have some of the apple tree that Lee sat under when he was waiting to surrender," John L. Smith crowed to his mother. By the afternoon of the ninth, Union men were "paying $5.00 and $10.00 for chips." When the tree was gone, enterprising soldiers commenced "digging for [its] roots."[21]

Very soon rumors surfaced that Lee had met Grant under a tree in the orchard and even that the surrender had taken place there. Southern soldiers, possessing nothing but worthless Confederate currency, and eager to make cash for the long trip home, began to sell "small pieces of Bark which they say is taken from the tree under which LEE and GRANT met," wrote Jacob Zorn in his diary. Zorn initially opted to procure a different souvenir—a "Surgeons Pocket Medicine case with small bottles filled with medicine"—but the apple tree story so intrigued him that he went to the orchard on April 11 to see it. He found Union men, who were no less entrepreneurial than Confederate ones, hacking at the trunk and roots of a tree there. He inquired whether this was *the* tree where Lee and Grant met or merely a tree that was "close by" to the original one—and he got a noncommittal answer. "Close by" was good enough for Zorn: "For a relick I concluded to take a chip from this apple tree, large enough to make a picture case wherin I intend to have the Photographs of Gen's GRANT & LEE." Many other soldiers likewise determined that it was better to have some ersatz relics than none at all; one Union man plucked some thorns from a locust tree near the surrender site "to weave into a wreath."[22]

The frenzy for relics was captured in a sketch by Alfred Waud, one of the premiere illustrators of the war. Waud had covered the major battles in Virginia for the popular New York-based periodical *Harper's Weekly* and had proven fearless in his determination to render meticulously accurate depictions, even if doing so brought him dangerously close to the front. At Appomattox, he again was in the right place at the right time. He waited patiently outside the McLean house during the surrender conference and sketched a proud but somber Lee as he rode away from the site. That sketch makes a striking contrast with Waud's depiction of the surrender's aftermath. He chose to record the image of troops hacking away at the tree under which Lee and Grant allegedly met and the faint outlines of men milling at the scene clutching their "trophies," as Waud's caption put it, show that a process of bargaining over the surrender's spoils was already well under way.[23]

Relics not only served as treasures and commodities but were also pressed into service to conjure, for the public, the meanings of April 9, 1865. The symbolic value of the surrender artifacts is dramatized in striking photographs of General Ord taken by Mathew Brady in Richmond on April 20. Ord was by then posted in Richmond as commanding general of the Department of Virginia—and his headquarters was none other than Jefferson Davis's mansion, the former White House of the Confederacy. Brady had arrived in Richmond on April 7 to record a series of images of the war-torn rebel capital. He turned his lens on sites such as the Confederate War Department in ruins; Libby prison, where Union officers had languished; and St. John's Church, where Patrick Henry had delivered his famous "Give me liberty or give me death!" oration. Remaining in Richmond after the surrender, he rendered portraits of Union heroes who had brought the rebels to heel. Together, Brady's images—which were converted for commercial sale

Waud's sketch of soldiers cutting up the apple tree for trophies. (Library of Congress)

into collectible photographs, stereographs (crudely three-dimensional pictures), and cartes de visite—offered the Northern public a panoramic view of the Confederacy's demise and the Union's triumph.[24]

The treatment of Ord is particularly revealing. He was photographed with his wife and young daughter at the White House of the Confederacy, with the marble-topped table at which Lee had surrendered—and which Ord had carried off from the McLean house—prominently in view. In one image, Ord looms as fierce protector over the two females, with the surrender table visible to their right. In the second, he and his wife flank their young daughter, who rests her head upon Ord's shoulder; the marble-table top in the background literally connects the mother and daughter. The parents' expression is thoughtful, determined, and wary. Ord, like countless other Northern men, was sustained during the war by visions of home. Indeed, Grant said admiringly of Ord: "This man recovered from near-mortal wounds by concentrating his thoughts upon his wife and small daughter." By situating the surrender table in the Ord family tableaux, and situating that tableaux at the Davis mansion, the Brady portraits offered visual testimony that Lee's capitulation had made possible the reunion of Northern families and suggested that if Northerners vigilantly safeguarded the peace, they could effect the reunion of the national family.[25]

Artifacts of Appomattox long retained their talismanic properties. Horace Porter took to the lecture circuit after the war with a "graphic," insider's account of the surrender and relics served as his props. For example, at a presentation for Brooklyn schoolchildren in 1894, Porter "held up in sight of his audience, one after another, a piece of the flag of truce sent by Gen. Lee to Gen. Grant, a slice of the famous apple tree, and the identical pencil with which Lee had corrected the draft of the surrender." He also exhibited photos of the tables used by Lee and Grant and arranged the classroom to look like the McLean parlor had on April 9, 1865.[26]

Few Northern soldiers could boast the prominence of Porter or his flair for self-promotion. But the Union veterans of Appomattox could surely understand the impulse to brandish one's cherished relics. They were, more than anything, badges of honor—physical proof that these men had taken part in the climactic clash of the war.

To the victor go the spoils: Ord and family with the surrender table. (Library of Congress)

No soldiers took greater pride in the surrender than the African Americans who fought in the Appomattox campaign. Six regiments of the USCT played a key role in the last day's fighting; one other waited in the wings. These regiments had just been reassigned from the Twenty-fifth Army Corps of Ord's Army of the James to its Twenty-fourth Corps. The Twenty-fifth Corps, the brainchild of Ord's predecessor, General Benjamin Butler, had the distinction of being the only corps consisting solely of African-American regiments; white officers commanded the black troops. In the last stages of the Appomattox campaign, the Twenty-fifth Corps had been split up, and two of its prime brigades, under Colonel Ulysses Doubleday and Colonel William W. Woodward, were attached to Gibbon's Twenty-fourth Army Corps to fight alongside the white troops there. Doubleday's brigade was folded into the First Division, under Brigadier

General Robert S. Foster, and Woodward's brigade joined the Second Division, under Brevet Major General John W. Turner.[27]

On April 9, Doubleday's brigade went into action first. Three of its regiments—the 8th, 41st, and 45th USCT (a fourth, the 127th, was posted to the rear)—clashed with Confederate cavalry on Foster's left flank in the edge of the woods parallel to the stage road. These units then hung back while Woodward's brigade, consisting of the 29th, 31st, and 116th USCT, moved forward to take their place along the Union's main battle line, between Foster's and Turner's white brigades, astride the stage road. These were the units that blocked Lee's escape route and convinced the Confederate high command of the hopelessness of their break-out strategy. When they heard confirmation of Lee's surrender, the black troops' "exultation knew no bounds." "They shouted, danced and sang" and "embraced each other" with exuberant joy, a white Union private observed.[28]

The seven black regiments at Appomattox, numbering 2,000 men in all, were a microcosm of black life in America. They included ex-slaves trained at Kentucky's Camp Nelson and free blacks trained at Philadelphia's Camp William Penn. They included men who would become race leaders in the postwar era, such as the renowned scholar George Washington Williams; the influential AME minister William Yeocum; South Carolina judge and legislator William J. Whipper; and Baptist editor William J. Simmons, who was the journalistic mentor to none other than Ida B. Wells. Filling out the ranks were men more obscure but no less fascinating—such as William H. Costley, whose mother, Nance, had been freed in an 1841 Illinois court case argued by an up-and-coming lawyer named Abraham Lincoln.[29]

For all these soldiers, regardless of their backgrounds, their presence on the battlefield was the culmination of a long struggle. The Federal army had initially turned away black volunteers, on the grounds that African American men did not possess the attributes of patriotism and courage and that their enlistment would alienate conservative Northerners, particularly Unionists in the border states; even after the Union, midway through the war, endorsed emancipation and black enlistment, it granted to black troops only a second-class status within the ranks and shunted them into noncombat roles under white officers. Black troops kept faith, though, that the war was their "golden moment," as a circular distributed among USCT recruits put it. "Our manhood has been denied, our citizenship blotted out, our souls seared and burned. . . . If we love our country, if we love our families, our children, our homes, we must strike *now* while the country calls." When blacks finally got the chance to fight, they showed their mettle at dozens of engagements, such as the famous charge on Fort Wagner in the summer of 1863. Indeed the USCT regiments at Appomattox had seen considerable action. The 8th USCT, for example, survived a bloody initiation into combat at Olustee, Florida, in February of 1864; joined in the grueling warfare of the Overland campaign in Virginia; and manned the trenches through the siege of Petersburg, entering that city in triumph when it fell on April 2. They were given a "most cheering and hearty welcome from the colored inhabitants of the city, whom their presence had made free," noted one of their white officers in his report on the campaign.[30]

African American soldiers were keenly aware that even after proving their courage, their march toward equality could still be turned back, so long as powerful Confederate armies were in the field. The Confederate government viewed all black Union soldiers as so many rebellious slaves, and "left it to state authorities either to return captured [soldiers] to owners or execute them as insurrectionaries." Indeed, Olustee and Petersburg were sites of atrocities committed by Confederates against surrendering black troops. Black soldiers were aware too that many white Northerners viewed their enlistment as a social experiment—testing the capacity of blacks for citizenship—and that some of those whites hoped and expected that the experiment would, in the end, fail.[31]

Given this context, black soldiers quickly seized on the USCT's critical role in Lee's surrender as a vindication. As William McCoslin of the 29th Regiment USCT put it in a May 1865 letter, "We the colored soldiers, have fairly won our rights by loyalty and bravery." He was echoed by a soldier in the 41st USCT, who in a letter to the black newspaper the *Christian Recorder* noted proudly that African American soldiers had displayed "remarkable courage and bravery" in the "capturing of Lee's army." Thomas Morris Chester, a Harrisburg, Pennsylvania, native who had earned a post as the first black war correspondent for a major daily paper (the *Philadelphia Press*), was at the front during the surrender, embedded with the

This USCT banner encapsulates black soldiers' hopes: "Let soldiers in war be citizens in peace." (Library of Congress)

Army of the James; he too, reveled in the fact that USCT regiments had participated in the "vigorous campaign" that gave "Lee's forces as trophies to the Union army."[32]

Many of these men's white officers and comrades-in-arms shared the conviction that the USCT's role in the last battle had been decisive. Luman Tenney of Sheridan's cavalry recounted the scene for his mother and sisters:

> The morning of the 9th came. The Cavalry was being pushed back rapidly towards the station. The boys were falling, scores of them—why was it with victory so near?—when over the hill a dark column was espied coming down the road in close column at quick time. What a relief from the awful suspense! What cared we for the color or race of those men so they brought relief to us. We saw courage and determination in their coal-black faces.

His fellow cavalryman Captain Stephen Tripp described the USCT troops as a "beautiful sight," while Samuel Cormany thought them "Fine fellows." General Foster, whose division had absorbed Doubleday's brigade, praised the black soldiers for driving back the rebel flank attack in the rear of Foster's column and for "being among those who struck the last blow against the Army of Northern Virginia." In the after-action reports of the USCT's leaders, African American men-at-arms were folded into a grand narrative in which the Federal army's fortitude, not its overwhelming numbers, won the day. C. P. Heichhold, the Surgeon-in-Chief of the black troops, marveled at how the men held up during the retreat: "In an experience of more than three years I never witnessed greater powers of endurance. There was no straggling, and the men were constantly in the best of spirits." Colonel Woodward, whose brigade had joined Turner's division, likewise praised the "good conduct" of the men "during a period of severe marching and reduction of rations, amounting to almost absolute destitution." In the minds of these white men, the "experiment" of black enlistment had been a resounding success.[33]

African Americans' crucial role in the last major engagement of the war would remain a point of pride. George Washington Williams, the preeminent black historian of the late nineteenth century, would note in his landmark *History of the Negro Race in America* (1883) that at Appomattox, in the "last hour of the Slave-holders' Rebellion," the "brilliant fighting" of black troops had ensured the salvation of the Union. Williams had been there, in the USCT ranks, at the surrender, at the tender age of 15. In the postwar period, he would lead an altogether remarkable life as a soldier, legislator, minister, and scholar. Williams's work would take him across the country and across the Atlantic in the cause of research and reform; his informal audience with King Leopold II in the Belgian Congo resulted in the publication of a scathing critique, Williams's *Open Letter to His Serene Majesty Leopold II* (1890), of the human rights violations of that colonial regime. Through it all, Williams's memories of Lee's surrender remained a vivid source of inspiration. He would, his biographer John Hope Franklin explains, long "rejoice that he was involved in the final battles of the Civil War."[34]

Like white Union soldiers, African Americans gloried in the "superior military tactics and masterly genius of our noble, persevering commander, *General Grant!*," as one USCT soldier put it. The fact that black soldiers in Grant's legions had defeated *Lee* lent additional symbolic meaning to "the surrender." Lee and his Army of Northern Virginia typified in the eyes of the USCT the haughty slaveholding elite and its pretense of racial superiority. According to Thomas Morris Chester, the Confederate capitulation was especially sweet because it was a rebuke to the "F.F.V.'s" or "first families of Virginia"—whom he wryly dubbed, after the surrender, the "Fleet-Footed Virginians." This view was echoed by veterans such as Joseph T. Wilson, author of an influential military history, *The Black Phalanx* (1887). Only after USCT troops had proven their mettle elsewhere, Wilson noted, were they allowed to fight in the critical Virginia theater; by defeating the "flower" of Confederate manhood at Appomattox, the USCT had answered unequivocally the question of whether black soldiers were the equals of the white master class.[35]

In short, men such as Williams and Wilson made and then sustained the bold claim that in defeating Lee's army, African American troops had dealt a death blow to all that the army stood for. This Appomattox narrative highlighted black agency in two overlapping registers, national and millennial. Black soldiers were agents of the state: they were, Williams wrote, the "muscle and sinew of the Republic." But they were also the agents of

Providence. For writers such as Williams, Appomattox was the grand culmination of an epic and indeed providential story—the long struggle
against slavery—that featured a panoply of freedom fighters, from Crispus
Attucks, to Toussaint L'Ouverture, to Nat Turner, to the regiments that
"fired the last shots" at Lee. It was no accident that the black soldier became
the "determinative factor in the problem of war," Williams wrote. "In the
Universe of God there are no accidents."[36]

In the eyes of black troops, the fate of the Union was still uncertain on
April 9, 1865, and their own agency tipped the scales. They insisted not
only that the Union army's victory emanated from its superior morality
and courage and manhood but also that black troops in particular exemplified how military prowess was animated by moral purpose.

African Americans soldiers' interpretation of the surrender incorporated the themes of not only racial pride and liberation but also of
clemency: they attempted to inscribe a civil rights message into the
magnanimous terms of the surrender. Emphasizing the promise of Appomattox, black veterans depicted the freedpeople, and black soldiers in particular, as agents of national healing. Williams's 1888 *History of the Negro
Troops in the War of the Rebellion* praised black soldiers for treating the
vanquished Confederates with "quiet dignity and Christian humility." He
wrote:

> After the Confederate army had been paroled the Negro troops
> cheerfully and cordially divided their rations with the late enemy,
> and welcomed them at their campfires on the march back to
> Petersburg. The sweet gospel of forgiveness was expressed in the
> Negro soldiers' intercourse with ex-rebel soldiers, who freely
> mingled with the black conquerors. It was a spectacle of magna-
> nimity never before witnessed.[37]

As Williams explained, the black soldier had "first swept away the bitter
prejudice of the Northern army," then "convinced the Southern soldier
that he was his equal in arms," and then proved himself to be a merciful
conqueror. The alliance of white and black Union troops, and their shared
impulse of magnanimity toward the South, made possible a new narrative
of cross-racial unity; that narrative, of which Williams was the principal

author, arrayed the black race, in defiance of long-standing prejudice, with the forces of order and progress and civilization.[38]

The ideal of cross-racial unity had long been an animating idea of the abolitionist movement. African Americans elaborated in the early nineteenth century their own narrative of an "unfulfilled" Union, an imagined community dedicated to the principle of the "universal brotherhood of man." Black leaders from Richard Allen and James Forten to David Walker to Frederick Douglass invoked this unfulfilled Union to refute anti-abolitionist claims that emancipation would open a Pandora's box of racial recrimination and social chaos. But abolitionists were unable, as sectional tensions escalated, to dispel the pervasive fears among whites that any disruption of the racial caste system would embolden slaves to seek vengeance against their masters. Indeed, secessionists cannily played on that fear, arguing that abolition and race war were inseparable.[39]

This antebellum linkage of emancipation and retribution is essential to understanding why the Union was so slow to enlist black troops during the war, why the Confederacy was so quick to label black soldiers as insurrectionists, and why the presence of black troops at the moment of peacemaking, on April 9, 1865, was so rife with meaning. For the victors, the Appomattox surrender repudiated, in a way that no other event could, the long-standing charge that emancipationists were disunionists, who sought war, chaos, and vengeance.

USCT veterans were celebrated by African Americans in the postwar period as both proven warriors and Christian gentlemen, models of courage and of self-restraint. The story of William J. Simmons is a case in point. Simmons was born a slave in Charleston, South Carolina, in 1849. He joined the Union army in 1864, at age 15, and was present, as a member of the 41st USCT, at Appomattox on April 9, 1865. After the war, Simmons rose to prominence as pastor of the First Baptist Church of Lexington, Kentucky, and then president of State University in Louisville; he often discoursed on the topic of "true masculinity," and he penned an influential race history on that topic, entitled *Men of Mark: Eminent, Progressive, and Rising* (1887). Simmons was widely regarded, as an 1890 eulogy by a fellow Baptist pastor explained, as a shining model of black masculinity: of a "heroic indomitable spirit" and of "Christian self-control and patience and magnanimity."[40]

In short, the USCT's courage had redeemed the country from slavery; the purpose of its clemency was to redeem the country from racial hatred. Black magnanimity at Appomattox was the exercise of moral authority— a conscious effort by men like Williams and Simmons, as purposeful as Grant's own act of clemency to Lee, to break the cycle of violence that slaveholders had so long perpetuated.

The aspirations of black soldiers for the surrender are given voice in the correspondence of William P. Woodlin, a musician in the 8th USCT. Hailing from New York, Woodlin joined the army in Syracuse in August of 1863. After training at Camp William Penn in Philadelphia, he and his fellow recruits were sent south to take part in the Petersburg siege. Woodlin's role as a member of the regimental band was to raise the morale of his comrades-in-arms as they endured the grinding warfare of the siege and the hard marching and fighting of the retreat. Woodlin sustained his own morale with a vision of the peace. Even as the USCT pursued Lee across the Virginia countryside, he raised money among the black troops for the cause of black education. Two weeks after the surrender, he sent a sum of $241 to the black newspaper the *Christian Recorder*, an organ of the AME church. The money was for Wilberforce University in Ohio, the nation's first college for African Americans, established in 1856 with AME support, on the line of the Underground Railroad. Woodlin proudly wrote the editors of the *Recorder* that the contribution was "collected on the march after General Lee, from Petersburg to Appomattox Court-house, and some of it the day after his surrender." The soldiers, he explained, were acutely aware that "great changes" were "rapidly moulding the public mind," and they wanted to show their commitment, in this moment of triumph, to the "intellectual improvement" of their people. Their eyes were fixed not on the bitter past but on the hopeful "days to come."[41]

"Our gallant and hitherto invincible army of Northern Va. has been overcome by mere brute forces of numbers, and the long desired and dearly purchased prize is at last in their grasp." So wrote an anonymous Confederate signalman on April 3, 1865, in his diary of the retreat to Appomattox. The loss of Richmond and Petersburg struck him as fatal blows to his cause, but equally ominous was his own gnawing hunger. "Footsore and weary and O, so hungry" were the "utterly worn out" men who tried to elude Grant's grasp, and with each passing day and night they grew more wretched; by April 8, the diarist noted that he had only a morsel of "raw meat to eat." Yet, when word of the surrender reached this soldier's unit as it approached the front, he and his comrades simply could not believe it. "Of course we consider[ed] it a hoax a first," he wrote in his entry for April 9. Only when "party after party" passed them "repeating the same story" did reality sink in: Lee, "surrounded by overwhelming numbers," as the signalman again put it, had been compelled to surrender.[42]

Such a counterpoint—in which soldiers acknowledged the depleted state of Lee's army and yet were utterly shocked at the news of its capitulation—runs through Confederate first-hand accounts of Appomattox. Confederate surgeon Henry Augustine Minor, for example, bemoaned the "half naked, hungry and weary state" of troops during the retreat. But when he received news of the surrender, he was "shocked beyond expression." His colleague, Dr. Hodijah Baylies Meade, had seen "innumerable & unmistakable signs" of the Confederate demise but he, too, was "greatly shocked" to learn of Lee's defeat. Like so many other Confederates, he had "implicit confidence" in Lee: "I believed[d] he would deliver us in a way we knew not of," Meade later confessed.[43]

Like Lee's lieutenants, the Southern army's junior officers and rank and file felt a strong compulsion to establish that they had faced insurmountable odds in the last fight. Confederate troops at Appomattox generally agreed that Lee's army threw a mere 8,000 infantrymen into battle on the morning of April 9. But in their confusion and despair, they showed a propensity, from the start, to give credence to swirling rumors about the immense size of the Federal army. John Walters of the Norfolk Light Artillery Blues wrote on April 9 that, while the Confederates "numbered only about eight thousand muskets," the "enemy's army" was "over one hundred and twenty thousand strong." Assistant Surgeon Robert Poole Myers of the 16th Georgia Infantry recorded in his diary on April 9 that "Genl. Lee was forced to surrender the Army of Northern Virginia he being surrounded by 200,000 Union troops." Southern soldiers reached for words and images to correspond to these numbers: "We were but a little band, standing there in the soft spring light of that Sabbath morn; THEY were as the sands upon the sea shore, or as the leaves upon the forest trees," wrote W. S. White of the Richmond Howitzers in his journal. Of Grant and his strategy of attrition, Randolph H. McKim, chaplain for the 2nd Virginia Cavalry, wrote, "When the lion is caught in the net, it does not require the skill of a mighty hunter to slay him." A postwar champion of the over-whelming numbers creed, he would insist in his recollections of the retreat that Lee had "outgeneralled" Grant to the last.[44]

Like McKim, most Southern troops were loathe to concede to the enemy any courage and skill. Instead, they portrayed the Yankees as a fun-damentally unworthy foe. The April 9 diary entry of Captain Henry A. Chambers of the 49th North Carolina fumed: "These worthless fellows whom we have so often whipped, whose cowardly backs we have so often seen, have at last by sheer force of numbers, numbers swelled by contribu-tions from almost every race and color on the face of the globe, have com-pelled us to come to this." "We were surrendering to men who fled before us at Manassas, Fredericksburg and Chancellorsville," Confederate vet-eran W. R. Houghton would later write, conjuring up the agony of the surrender. Distraught Confederates "broke their swords and rifles; some cursed the day of their birth; others laughed hysterically, like men gone mad from a sudden frenzy." In their reckoning, the Yankee army had grown baser even as it grew larger over the course of the war, its ranks filled by "foreigners of every nationality" and "regiments of our former slaves," as artilleryman Edward A. Moore contemptuously put it. Major Edward M. Boykin of the 7th South Carolina Cavalry estimated that the Federal army numbered 150,000 at the end and "varied in its nationality"; its "recruiting stations were all over the world," beacons for immigrants lured by the "almighty American dollar."[45]

In short, the Confederate soldiers who surrendered at Appomattox an-ticipated as well as echoed the major themes of Lee's Farewell Address. They made explicit what Lee only implied—namely, the social and racial inferiority of those to whom the Confederates were surrendering, and the baseness of the North's hard-war tactics. Claims of Northern barbarity and Southern righteousness were the twin pillars of a culture of invinci-bility that had sustained Confederate soldiers, Lee's men especially, over the course of the war. "Overwhelming legions of Yankees trampling crops, wrecking railroads, burning homes, freeing slaves, stealing valuables, and leveling cities actualized white southerners' greatest fears of the enemy," historian Jason Phillips has written; the Union's hard-war policies confirmed Southern men's image of the Yankees as ruthless cowards and of themselves as paragons of virtue. In the aftermath of the surrender, these same arguments about why the Yankees should not and would not win served to explain, so diehard rebels insisted, why they had won. Northern "hell-hounds," Henry A. Chambers wrote, "burned our houses desecrated our altars, plundered our wealth, waged unrelenting warfare upon the aged, the weak, and helpless." The crude Yankees had not fought fair, and the moral superiority of the Confederates was uncompromised.[46]

"The South went down in defeat, but with glory," to quote the pithy formulation of Colonel Herman H. Perry. Perry's account of the surrender underscores just how quickly Lee's address took on iconic status. As soon as the address was promulgated, Perry "sat down and copied it on a piece of Confederate paper, using a bass-drum head for a desk." "I then carried this copy to General Lee, and asked him to sign it for me." On the back of the document, Perry wrote of Lee, "Tears were in his eyes at the time he wrote his name." Along with Perry's parole, his copy of Lee's address was the "best authority" that the surrender was honorable. John E. Roller, a Virginia Military Institute graduate from the Shenandoah Valley serving as an officer in the Confederate States Engineers, also turned the address into a tangible artifact: "I took the precaution to get a couple of sheets of paper and on these I had one of my orderly sergeants to inscribe General Lee's farewell address, and below I took the signatures of all the officers and men who were still with us. . . . I thought it due to the men who had served to the close of the war, that they should have the fact preserved."[47]

However comforting and fortifying, Lee's address could not banish from the minds of his soldiers the specter of failure. Roller's reference to the "men who were still with us" betrays his own sense—one shared by most of the soldiers who left detailed accounts of the surrender—that the depleted state of the Confederate army demanded an explanation. Hunger, of course, had taken a terrible toll. "We tried to eke out what we had," Roller wrote; "parched corn" and the "roots of the sassafras" were the woeful "delicacies on the Confederate menu." But something more had gnawed at the vitals of the army: fear and despair. Over the course of the retreat, Roller explains, dread of capture had worn on the spirits of the

Lee's Farewell Address became an enduring symbol of Southern honor.
(Library of Congress)

men. In the aftermath of the Sailor's Creek debacle, which had left so many Confederates in Federal hands, Roller witnessed Lee "begging the men to rally and form again." Many simply passed to the rear and disappeared. "I tried to stop some of these myself by telling them that they were poor soldiers indeed who would not rally when General Lee asked them, but such appeals went unheeded," Roller lamented. George P. Clarke, a foot soldier who had done a turn in a Federal prison after Gettysburg, was among those who were dispossessed and unnerved by Sailor's Creek. Most of his regiment was taken prisoner, and so Clarke, exhausted and starving, clung to the wagon trains that snaked their way to the front. Others scoured the countryside for food or went home. Giles B. Cooke, a staff officer of Lee's who was wounded by an exploding shell at Sailor's Creek, was among those who stayed with the army until the bitter end and who puzzled over what had become of Lee's legions over the course of the retreat. His calculations, recorded in his diary on April 9, are faulty but revealing. In Cooke's view, Lee surrendered about 7,000 infantrymen that morning. He continued: "We left Petersburg last Sunday with 30,000 infy. . . . the diff between 30,000 and 7,000=23,000." How did he account for the difference? Many had been killed or wounded, but not all. "Our men straggled awfully," he wrote.[48]

Confederate commentators differed in their estimation of whether those who straggled and deserted should be objects of sympathy or of scorn. George Shreve of Fairfax, Virginia, a sergeant in the Stuart Horse Artillery, was inclined toward charity. As his mounted company overtook and passed through one of the Confederate infantry divisions, the tired foot soldiers "accosted" the artillerymen with the following words: "You fellers can do all the fighting you want; we've had enough; we've done our share; we've quit; no more fighting for us." Shreve knew it to be a grim omen that "such brave veterans, who had proved their bravery on so many fields," should now falter. He would not judge them: they "knew more than we, and were justified in their decision." George Cary Eggleston, for his part, believed that Confederate desertions began en masse at the very moment that Davis and his cabinet abandoned Richmond. With the administration itself in flight, he asked, "What were the men to do?" Deserters had simply "followed the example of the government."[49]

Eggleston's assessment reveals the propensity of some Southern soldiers to lay blame at the feet of Jefferson Davis and his administration. A Virginia planter with a literary bent, Eggleston made a name for himself after the war as a writer who romanticized the "old regime" of antebellum plantation society while excoriating the wartime regime of Davis for its "cumbrous inefficiency." Poor administrative appointments and "red tape" accounted, in his view, for the fact that Confederate troops were chronically underfed and poorly supplied. Such an interpretation has found much support among modern scholars of the Confederacy, who have amassed evidence of mismanagement by Davis appointees such as Commissary General for Subsistence Lucius B. Northrop. For the soldiers, the case against the government did more than explain their hunger. To blame the politicians was to exonerate the fighting men—"The Rebels are all very bitter against Jeff Davis," wrote Union soldier John L. Smith, of the mood at Appomattox, "but they love Gen. Lee."[50]

Many others could not see fit to exonerate the army en masse. Confederate chaplain William Edward Wiatt, a Baptist preacher from a prominent family in Virginia's tidewater region, was not inclined to be charitable. He wrote on April 9: "Only 8,000 muskets were for action this morning; I suppose at least 25 or 30,000 men deserted before reaching this place." Those men, he reckoned, had lost heart after the fall of Richmond and had broken faith with the dauntless core who remained in arms. "Oh! if the spirit of '61 & '62 had been possessed by our troops," Wiatt wailed, bemoaning the precipitous decline in Confederate morale. General Walker of Gordon's corps was harsher still. On the evening of April 9, he made a speech to his command that offered a "most scathing rebuke" to the skulkers and stragglers. Artilleryman John Walters transcribed part of the speech in his diary: "This morning, I led into battle seven hundred good and true men," Walker thundered. "This afternoon, my muster rolls showed me fifteen hundred. Where were you all when the stern voice of battle pointed out to every man his place and post of honor? Where were you? Sulking cowards! You noble men of the seven hundred, go home with the consciousness that if the cause failed, it was from no fault of yours." It was with this address ringing in his ears that Walters, on April 10, transcribed Lee's Farewell Address—with its own reference to the "true" men's "consciousness of duty faithfully performed"—into his diary.[51]

Perhaps no account of the surrender better captures the Confederate soldiers' mixed feelings of pride and recrimination, defiance and despair, than the lengthy letter Captain Franklin Potts of Mecklenburg County, Virginia, wrote on his way home from Appomattox. A paymaster in Longstreet's command, Potts crafted the letter for his brother, a minister in Canada. On the one hand, Potts affirmed the sentiments of the Farewell Address. The "glorious" Lee, whom the men had "loved as a father," was "forced to surrender by overwhelming numbers"; the Army of Northern Virginia had faced a force that exceeded it "more than four to one." On the other, Potts acknowledged that many had lost their will to fight. Conjuring the moment in which Lee returned to the apple orchard after the surrender, to be met by his stalwart troops, Potts wrote: "Oh, had all the men in our armies been such as those who shed salt tears in that orchard that bitter morning, we [would have] never been reduced to the extremity we then found ourselves in." "No one is to blame for the catastrophe but ourselves," Potts concluded. "Surely our sins must have been great when God withheld his blessings from us."[52]

As Potts's invocation of Confederate sins suggests, Southern soldiers looked to religion to make sense of their defeat. They prayed for consolation, believing, as one artilleryman put it, that "this deep well of sorrow, suffering and affliction must contain some pure clean waters of comfort, of resignation and of hope." He ended his war diary with the wish: "God grant that I may never see another war, with all its horrors, blood and desolation." J. C. Painter, another artilleryman, juxtaposed excerpts of poems (such as Robert Burns's "To a Mouse," with its couplet on the "best laid plans o' mice & men") and psalms in his pocket diary's account of the surrender. "Mark the perfect man, and behold the upright," he quoted from Psalm 37:37, "for the end of that man is peace."[53]

Hope for a reversal of fortunes, however, ran deeper than resignation. Many of the Confederates at Appomattox clung to the idea that God, however He might chastise his chosen people, would someday deliver them. Such a conviction was the most comforting answer to a pervasive question: had all the suffering been in vain? In his April 9 diary entry, William Wiatt plaintively asked, "Has God forsaken us?" only to answer "I, for one, can't believe it; God, I verily believe, has humbled us to exalt us; I believe He will, yet, in His good way & time grant unto us deliverance &

prosperity & honor." That night, he noted, the men in his regiment sung the hymn "God moves in mysterious ways." Samuel Pickens of Alabama's Greensboro Guards, in a similar call-and-response, wrote on April 12, "Oh! can it be possible that after all sacrifices made—immolation of so many noble heroes it is not to end in our favor?" To his own question he answered, "God forbid! . . . still if it is thy will, O Lord, deliver us out of the hands of our too powerful enemies and bless us with Independence & Peace!" Henry Chambers, the soldier who had derided the Yankees as "those worthless fellows we have so often whipped," hoped that "some terrible retribution" might yet fall upon the Northerners for waging "so unjust, so barbarous a warfare!"[54]

In short, providential theology was "flexible enough," as the historian George Rable has explained, to accommodate defeat: the Lord's will was inscrutable; his chosen people must suffer; He might still furnish earthly victory, in his own appointed time; and "final victory would not come on this earth anyway." Snatching moral victory from military defeat, such a theology blended seamlessly with the sentiments of the Farewell Address. As Royall W. Figg, an artilleryman in Lee's army, saw it, might could triumph over right in the short term but not in the long. "The right never fails!" he wrote in his reminiscences. "It is as indestructible as God! Every labor performed with noble motive has its sure reward."[55]

Confederate hopes that their sacrifices would be rewarded were awkwardly intertwined with their fears of earthly punishment. Over the course of the retreat, Lee's men had been haunted by visions of what retributions Grant might exact. Grant was "by no means regarded as a man of mercy," cannoneer Edward A. Moore noted, with a touch of understatement. "That we should be subjected to abhorrent humiliation was conceived as a matter of course," he continued, conjuring up the image of Confederate soldiers being "paraded through Northern cities for the benefit of jeering crowds." In Moore's account, the announcement of Grant's lenient terms—granting key "privileges," such as the retention of horses—flooded the Southern soldiers with relief. Thus those soldiers began their long journeys home "buoyed with the consciousness that we had fought a good fight . . . and that the cause for which we had undergone it all was not one we *thought* was right but that we *knew* was right." The honorable surrender terms "restored our souls," as Moore put it.[56]

Many soldiers rallied around the emerging Southern orthodoxy, accepting the idea that Grant's terms were both a gesture of respect to the Confederate troops and a blueprint for the peace that was to follow. "Never in all history was a captured army treated with so much respect," surgeon Henry Augustine Minor claimed in his account of the surrender. Henry Kyd Douglas, commander of the Army of Northern Virginia's "Light Brigade," agreed: Grant's "soldierly and chivalric" treatment of the Confederates and his "quiet courtesy" set the tone for the entire Union army's treatment of its foes.[57]

Many others were not so sure. Infantryman John Bell Vincent captured such soldiers' feelings of foreboding when he wrote twice, in his diary entries of April 11 and April 12, that the Confederate troops were "in suspense," awaiting some sign of their "final destiny." The stacking-of-arms ceremony, which officers like Gordon chose to interpret as a "tribute to Southern chivalry," did nothing to dispel Vincent's unease about the status of the surrendered troops. Giles B. Cooke, for his part, ended his wartime diary, on April 13, with this mournful declaration: "I am now a citizen-slave and what will become of me and the people of our South land God only knows—." The comportment of the victorious Union soldiers betrayed, to the more perceptive Confederate commentators, the Yankees' determination to convert Confederates to a new orthodoxy, one centered on the sanctity of the Union. Confederate surgeon Hodijah Baylies Meade noted that while some of those Union soldiers who visited the Confederate camps after the surrender were inclined to show "little kindnesses" to the defeated Southerners, others "with more zeal than discretion," sought to teach the rebels a lesson. "Inspired by the extensive field for proselytism now opened them, [they] addressed themselves to the task of converting us from our damnable heresies: and to this purpose diligently obstructed us with facts, while they violently assailed us with arguments." Moreover, rumors circulated that the Radical Republicans were already, at the very moment Confederates were being paroled, calling for retribution. While awaiting his parole, Samuel Pickens anxiously noted in his diary that "Beast Butler"—the Union General Benjamin Butler, long a symbol of the Union's hard-war strategy—had made a speech insisting that Davis and the ringleaders of the Confederacy be rounded up and hanged.[58]

Looking back on the aftermath of the surrender, George Cary Egg-leston would write, "It is difficult to comprehend, and impossible to describe, the state of uncertainty in which we lived at this time." Thanks to Grant, Confederates might have avoided the fate of being paraded in humiliation through "jeering crowds" of Northerners. But they still faced weary journeys home to devastated communities that would soon begin to grapple with the very same questions—What had gone wrong? Had God forsaken them? Who was to blame? Who was among the blameless?—that already preoccupied the men of Lee's army. The jour-ney itself could prove humiliating. Lacking rations and "a cent of money that would buy food or clothing," infantryman James Birdsong wrote of his trip home to Petersburg that he and his comrades "had to beg" civil-ians for sustenance. Frank Potts, on his way home, described himself to his brother as a "subjugated rebel, who has no nation, no rights and no greenbacks."[59]

It is little wonder, then, that in the midst of this uncertainty, Confed-erate soldiers clung to their parole certificates as their most treasured artifacts of the surrender. The certificates were, in the first instance, tickets home, rather than to the prison camps in which many captured Southern soldiers, including those taken at Sailor's Creek, still lan-guished. Lee's men waited impatiently for the documents to roll off the presses for four days at Appomattox, as no one would undertake his journey without his certificate. John Walters, for example, was frus-trated that the cavalrymen got their paroles first, leaving artillerists, like him, to cool their heels; infantrymen came last, as they participated in the stacking-of-arms ceremony on April 12. Paroles represented, too, Grant's terms and the prospect that the terms would be widely hon-ored. Whatever their assessment of the genuineness of or motives behind the Yankees' seeming generosity, the Southern soldiers at Appo-mattox hoped against hope that the parole certificates might not only gain them access to Federal rations and transportation but also confer a measure of protection and immunity. Most important, the parole certif-icates symbolized the "consciousness of duty faithfully performed," as Lee's address had put it. They embodied the Southern soldiers' pride in having served in the most fabled Confederate army and having served in its final campaign.[60]

Roughly the size of a blank check, the printed parole passes were uniform in their wording. Each read "THE BEARER_____of Co.___, a Paroled Prisoner of the Army of Northern Virginia, has permission to go to his home, and there remain undisturbed." They were nearly uniform in design (three separate plates were used to print them, each furnishing a different ornamental design on the left margin of the pass). Some handwritten paroles survive, in which officers copied the terms and tried to approximate the design of the printed versions. That the paroles were treasured objects is evident from the physical condition of those still preserved. "The parole passes show signs of use and wear," John Coski, historian of the Museum of the Confederacy has written. "Soldiers obviously carried them, sweated on them, handled them, folded and unfolded them often." In time, as the remaining Confederate armies in the field capitulated, Southern soldiers on other fronts would receive parole certificates that were modeled on the ones issued at Appomattox. But no passes could match the enduring prestige of the Appomattox paroles. In time, they came to symbolize not just the consciousness of duty performed but also the case for duty performed—the case that the bearer had not skulked, straggled, or deserted, and had not doubted or despaired. The paroles served to prove that the Southern soldiers who came under Grant's terms, and under Lee's too, were among the stalwarts he honored in his Farewell Address. They became emblems of a particularly stoic and heroic kind of service. In his early nineties as he prepared his memoirs, Edgar Warfield, who had served in Lee's army as a private, wrote of his parole certificate, "I still have it. I have carefully preserved it, valuing it as a priceless relic, as it furnishes official proof that I was present with the army to the last." Abner Crump Hopkins, chaplain to John Brown Gordon's Second Corps, concluded his memoir by juxtaposing his parole pass and Lee's address. They told the same edifying story, while keeping an altogether more troubling story from view. As Southern soldiers trudged home in the aftermath of the surrender, they had little way of knowing which story those on the home front would choose to embrace.[61]

PART TWO

HOME FRONT

‖ 5 ‖

Tidings of Peace

At 4:30 p.m. on April 9, 1865, Grant telegraphed Secretary of War Edwin M. Stanton in Washington, D.C., with the news from Appomattox: "Gen. Lee surrendered the Army of Northern Va this afternoon upon terms proposed by myself. The accompanying correspondence shows the conditions fully." Stanton telegraphed back, "Thanks be to Almighty God for the great victory with which he has this day crowned you and the gallant army under your command."[1]

As soon as the news from Appomattox flashed across the wires, Northerners prepared to battle over just what the peace really meant. Abolitionists claimed Grant's terms for the cause of black freedom and for racial equality; moderate Republicans and War Democrats claimed the terms for the supremacy of the Union and for a cautious approach to Reconstruction; and Copperheads claimed the terms as a rebuke to Radical Republicans and as tribute to Southern honor. They all embraced the principle of magnanimity—but they offered sharply divergent interpretations of the political ends it should serve. There was no unified Northern vision of what the peace should bring.

Lincoln received the news as he returned to Washington, D.C., from Virginia. Since March 24, he had been based at the Federal army's nerve center at City Point. There he had consulted with his high command, toured hospitals, and anxiously awaited telegraphs from the Richmond–Petersburg front and from the route of retreat. On March 28, he had met with Grant aboard the *River Queen* and voiced his desire for a generous peace; on April 4, he had visited the fallen rebel of capital of Richmond and received from the city's African American population a hero's welcome.

As he began his trip back to Washington on April 7, Lincoln knew that Grant's crowning triumph was at hand.[2]

The confirmation he received on the evening of April 9 filled Lincoln with joy. "Our hearts beat with exultation at the victories," Stanton would recall of Lincoln's mood. The city around them exploded in a frenzy of celebration. As dawn broke on the morning of April 10, batteries fired salutes, rattling and cracking windowpanes; flags and transparencies were affixed to government buildings and private residences alike; and streams of citizens—taking advantage of the fact that many government offices and businesses declared the day a holiday—converged on the White House to congratulate their heroic leader. Clerks from the Treasury Department, for example, marched in procession singing the "Star Spangled Banner" and "Rally Round the Flag, Boys," while some 2,000 workmen from the Navy Yard, headed by a band, formed their own line of march, "huzzaing" and firing a howitzer along the way. Soon, the scene in front of the executive mansion was one of joyous delirium. The band played patriotic airs while the ever-growing crowd sung gleefully along. They called and called again for the president. Finally he appeared, "calm amid the tumult," as one reporter put it. Lincoln declared himself "greatly rejoiced" at the crowd's unrestrained enthusiasm, and he promised them that he would offer some remarks on the occasion of the surrender very soon. In the meantime, he joked, "I propose closing up this interview by the band performing a particular tune which I shall name." The tune was "Dixie." The Confederates, he noted, had "attempted to appropriate it," but, Lincoln declared with a flourish, on April 9 the Union "had fairly captured it." The crowd cheered with delight at this image, and the band struck up "Dixie," followed by "Yankee Doodle." Lincoln asked the crowd to offer up three cheers to "General Grant and all under his command."[3]

In the early evening, Lincoln appeared again at the White House window and pledged that the next night, on April 11, he would "endeavor to say something" formal. He joked that he needed time to prepare his comments, lest he misspeak on such a momentous occasion. "Everything I say, you know, goes into print," he wryly observed, eliciting laughter and applause from the crowd. They knew that Lincoln had withstood, over the past four years, the relentless scrutiny and carping criticism of the press and that he might now, at last, point to victory as his vindication.[4]

Lincoln's speech of April 11, 1865, would be his last public address, and it has been interpreted as a window into how he would have handled post-war Reconstruction had he lived. But in the moment it was delivered, the speech was Lincoln's first formal public address after the surrender. Along with Grant and Lee's correspondence, the surrender terms, and Lee's Farewell Address, Lincoln's April 11 speech is an essential artifact of Appomattox.

Lincoln delivered his address before the concourse of serenaders who thronged the White House grounds, in a city aglow with bonfires and illuminations. Reading from his carefully crafted text, Lincoln began by expressing his "gladness of heart" at the "surrender of the principal insurgent army"; it had cleared the way, he hoped, for a "righteous and speedy peace." He next thanked the Union army. "To Gen. Grant, his skillful officers, and brave men, all belongs."[5]

Then Lincoln pivoted toward the hard road ahead. "By these recent successes the re-inauguration of the national authority—reconstruction—which has had a large share of thought from the first, is pressed much more closely upon our attention. It is fraught with great difficulty." The rest of his speech would grapple with the challenges of Reconstruction. First he reiterated a central premise of the Union war effort. The Confederacy was not an independent nation that the Union could "treat with"; instead, the peace would have to harmonize "disorganized and discordant elements." That last phrase conjured the volatility of the moment, one in which Jefferson Davis was still on the run, several Confederate armies were still in the field, and the experiment of wartime Reconstruction was under way in Union-occupied areas of the South. Next Lincoln turned to the most important of those experiments: the Reconstruction of Louisiana. He had been "much censured" for his policies. At issue was Lincoln's Ten Percent Plan, which he had promulgated in his December 1863 Proclamation of Amnesty and Pardon. It laid out the steps for the readmission of errant states to the Union, stipulating that when 10 percent of those who had voted in the 1860 election in a given state took an oath of allegiance to the Union, that vanguard could elect delegates to a new constitutional convention, write a new constitution (which must recognize emancipation), and send representatives to Congress. All those who took the oath would receive amnesty and pardon and the restoration of their property rights, except the right to hold slaves. High-ranking Confederate officials could not simply take the oath but were also required to apply for pardons; Lincoln signaled that he would use his power to pardon liberally. His aim with the Ten Percent Plan, as the historian Richard Carwardine has explained, was "to offer generous terms as a bait to waverers to give up the rebellion."[6]

Louisiana, where the Federals established a stronghold after the fall of New Orleans in 1862, seemed a promising test case for a policy of amnesty that would draw Southerners back into the Union. New Orleans was the base of an unusually strong core of prewar Unionists, but despite the relatively promising conditions, the experiment was soon dubbed by Radical Republicans a failure in the making. They worried that the Ten Percent Plan set too low a bar—that it did not insist strictly enough on loyalty to the Union—and that it was, by its very nature, undemocratic. Moreover, developments on the ground were discouraging. Louisiana's military governor, Nathaniel Banks, instituted a contractual labor system in the place of slavery, one that fell far short of "free labor"—ex-slaves were pressured into working for their former masters or for new landlords on their old plantations—and held elections that brought to power conservative loyalists intent on blunting the changes of emancipation, rather than radicals who embraced black freedom. Most galling, the conservative loyalists were deaf to the appeals of New Orleans' free black activists and their call for black suffrage.

Radical Republicans had offered a counterstroke in the Wade-Davis bill of July 1864. It raised the bar: 50 percent, not 10 percent, of the state's electorate must take an "iron-clad" oath of allegiance, foreswearing that they had ever supported the Confederacy, before that state could be readmitted. Many supporters of the bill were also vocal advocates of black suffrage, on the grounds of both idealism and pragmatism: the vote would reward blacks for their iron-clad Unionism, and blacks in turn would reward the Republicans with their votes, helping to secure the party's power in the region. Lincoln pocket-vetoed the bill and "held back from what the radicals wanted, namely the federal imposition of black suffrage on the South as a non-negotiable condition of reconstruction." The Radicals' simmering discontent was a backdrop to Lincoln's April 11 speech.[7]

Lincoln answered them by protesting that the Ten Percent Plan was merely one good option, not an overarching and irrevocable policy; that Congress had enthusiastically endorsed the plan; and that the Louisiana experiment had done more good than harm. The new constitution of the state had duly upheld emancipation, which was the groundwork for future progress. He dismissed as a "pernicious abstraction" the old debate over whether the seceded states were technically still in the Union (such a position emphasized the illegality of secession) or out of it (such a position opened the way for a radical reorganization of the states and their possible reversion to territorial status). Here Lincoln gestured to the profound implications of Lee's surrender. With the back of the rebellion now broken, the old debate was irrelevant. The way was cleared to bring the states into their "proper practical relation" to the Union. "Finding themselves safely at home," Lincoln said of the Southern states, "it would be utterly immaterial whether they had ever been abroad."[8]

But what was that "practical proper relation"? One in which a loyal core—consisting both of those Southerners who had long rejected and those who had recently repudiated the political and social doctrines of the secessionists—would hold the balance of power. Lincoln conceded that it would be better to have the Louisiana government rest on a broader constituency than the 12,000 white voters who made up the loyal core. Signaling that he had moved toward the Radical Republican position on the issue of black citizenship, Lincoln, for the first time, publicly endorsed black suffrage, saying he would prefer that the vote were conferred "on the very intelligent, and on those who serve our cause as soldiers." It may be that his recent experiences, as well as political logic, informed this position. In his weeks at City Point, and during his visits to occupied Petersburg and Richmond, he had seen USCT regiments at work and heard of their vital role in the fall of the rebel strongholds. The nation must, Lincoln insisted, send a strong message of support to those Unionists in Louisiana, white and black, on whom the future depended—to nerve them to "fight" for the principles of Union and of "perpetual freedom." In short, the Louisiana experiment had just begun, and a great deal was riding on its success. Lincoln closed by promising to make "some new announcement to the people of the South" about how the work of Reconstruction would proceed.[9]

Why had Lincoln chosen, in his first address after Appomattox, to mark the surrender in this way? Scholars have long analyzed the silences in Lincoln's oratory—the lack of narrative detail in his Gettysburg Address and the absence of triumphalism in his Second Inaugural Address—and here, too, the silences are revealing.[10] Lincoln made no reference whatsoever in his April 11 speech to Grant's terms. Instead, he implicitly upheld the crucial distinction between the military and civil realms. Grant had fulfilled his limited mandate and secured the capitulation of Lee's troops; Lincoln and the Congress would take up, in earnest and with new urgency, the question of how best to "re-inaugurate" national authority. As he had in his Second Inaugural, Lincoln again refrained from reveling in victory and instead emphasized the work still to be done.

Lincoln's April 11 address was, nonetheless, very much a victory speech, marking victories both military and political. He delivered a clear message to his detractors: there was to be no turning back. To Radical Republicans, who condemned his Reconstruction plan as too lenient, he announced that there would be no turning back on the road to reconciliation. To antiwar Copperheads, who condemned his emancipation policy as punitive, he announced that there would be no turning back on the road to freedom. To Southerners, he announced that he expected, as his condition for reconciliation, their full commitment to the Union and to freedom. In Lincoln's eyes, Grant's victory made it possible for the nation to move forward.

Would this be the consensus view? There were already signs of trouble. Even among the victors, there was little clarity about what would happen next. In the North, the news of the surrender was contested by the partisan press. Newspapers and journals represented positions along the Northern political spectrum and reflected the agendas of political parties, reform societies, religious denominations, and of factions therein. At one end of that spectrum were abolitionist and Radical Republican newspapers, which cast the war as a struggle to remove the moral blot of slavery from American society. They pushed Lincoln toward his policy of emancipation and advocated for black citizenship. They spoke for the "progressives" of their day: reform-minded Americans who espoused a particularly Victorian ethos of progress in which the material and technological advancement of society should go hand-in-hand with moral improvement, and in which the unfolding of history would carry America to higher stages of "civilization."[11] In the middle of the political spectrum were mainstream Republican sheets, which defended emancipation as a military necessity but had not accepted the necessity of black citizenship, and pro-war Democratic newspapers that were often critical of Lincoln's methods but fully committed to Northern victory. Moderate newspapers, Republican and War Democrat alike, put the emphasis on saving the Union and on the theme of patriotic loyalty.

At the far end of the political spectrum, in stark contrast to the pro-war sheets, were the newspapers of the Peace Democrats, or Copperheads. Their antiwar rhetoric was centered on the fantasy that the Union could return to the antebellum status quo, if only the Lincoln administration would abandon its reckless and unconstitutional crusade against slavery and negotiate a peace satisfactory to the South, one guaranteeing slavery's perpetuity. Venomous in their hatred of Lincoln and openly sympathetic to the South, the Copperheads seemed, at times, "willing to trade victory for peace."[12]

In the vanguard among abolitionists was Horace Greeley, the irascible chief of the nation's leading antislavery paper, the *New York Tribune*. The minute he received the dispatch announcing Lee's capitulation, he set to work drafting a series of editorials on the nature and implications of the surrender. The first of these, printed on the morning of April 10, began "Lee has surrendered! Three words only, but how much they mean!" How much indeed. Lee's surrender signified, Greeley told his readers, a vindication of the principle of human equality and thus a fulfillment of the American Revolution. Treason had been "suppressed and punished"; the "strong arms, and stout hearts, and wise heads" of the Union, and the "masterly generalship" of Grant had won the day. On April 11, Greeley elaborated on these themes in a lead column entitled "Magnanimity in Triumph." He argued that there should be no reprisals against the Confederates, for trials and executions would make martyrs of the fallen Confederates. He declared that blacks, including newly freed slaves, were "on the side of Clemency—of Humanity" and were thus ready to exercise the full prerogatives of citizenship. On the following day, Greeley folded Lincoln's

April 11 speech into this analysis; he found the "tenor and spirit" of the speech to be "kindly and reassuring."[13]

Greeley's clearest articulation of the rationale for leniency came on April 13, in a column entitled "Peace—Punishment." In this piece, Greeley alluded to his status as a pariah in the South, a status he had earned by popularizing the "free soil" creed before the war and by pushing relentlessly for emancipation, in advance of Lincoln, once the war began. Why would such a crusader call for clemency? Because magnanimity was, in Greeley's view, the means to achieve a sacred purpose: "To secure the assent of the South to Emancipation." Only by making kindness their policy could victorious Northerners prove that a "civilization based on Free Labor is of a higher and humaner type than that based on Slavery." In a letter to his former neighbor Rebekah M. Whipple, written on April 13, Greeley further noted, "I want as many rebels as possible to live to see the South rejuvenated and transformed by the influence of free labor." He confided his view that "our great triumph is God's answer to the prayer of the colored people" for their liberation. What fitter fate for the likes of Davis and Lee than to bear witness to the unfolding social revolution?[14]

Abolitionists for magnanimity: Horace Greeley of the *New York Tribune*. (Library of Congress)

In the slip stream of the mighty *Tribune* were a host of Radical Republican and abolitionist journals, each making its own case for magnanimity in triumph. They attributed Grant's triumph to his army's superior skill and courage and argued that such skill and courage flowed directly from the righteous principles of free society. The *National Anti-Slavery Standard*, for example, the official organ of the American Anti-Slavery Society, crowed that the war "taught the nation its strength in men and money, and yet more in ideas." "We put our faith in Gen. Grant, who knew better than we can know what strength for mischief yet remained in Lee's arm, and are content to believe that his mercy was well-judged as well as abounding," the editors proclaimed. The rebels would face no reprisals but instead be "punished by freedom, education, prosperity, wealth, security, and peace."[15]

While Grant embodied the moral virtue of free society, Lee embodied the immorality of the South. An article in the *Christian Recorder*, the organ of the AME Church, insisted that it "was no mere game of chance" by which Lee was "so beautifully checkmated." "It was a problem requiring the most consummate skill for its solution. On the one side was a cool, determined and skillful General, conscious of the final victory, and fighting for his country's honor. On the other a desperate and oath-breaking leader, seeking individual renown, even when mindful of the utter hopelessness of his espoused cause." As early as April 10, newspapers were reprinting the entire exchange of letters between Lee and Grant. Some took special note of Lee's suggestion, on April 8, that he and Grant might negotiate a peace, and they praised Grant for resisting such unmanly "special pleading" and for insisting simply on surrender. As an editorial in the *Independent*, an abolitionist paper edited by the charismatic reformer Theodore Tilton, said of Lee, "This last campaign ought to convince his most idolatrous admirers of his immeasurable inferiority to Grant in every way."[16]

In lockstep with Greeley's *Tribune*, progressive newspapers saw black citizenship as the fruits of Grant's victory. "How marvelously the connection between right and might has been illustrated in this war!" exclaimed William Lloyd Garrison in the pages of the pioneering abolitionist paper the *Liberator*. The "God-defying Confederacy, founded upon human bondage" had been crushed. In Garrison's view, mercy should temper Northerners' judgment of the traitors—but only if those traitors left slavery for dead and accepted the march toward black citizenship. "Let there be no concession to caste, no shadow of compromise concerning the equal rights of the colored race," he concluded. The *Christian Advocate and Journal*, for its part, argued that "expediency and right" alike pointed to the enfranchisement of the freed people; they had been integral, as soldiers, to the Union triumph and would be the key to ensuring that a "loyal population" dominated the postwar South. The black newspaper the *Anglo-African* covered an Appomattox victory parade in Cincinnati in which joyous "colored citizens" had marched under banners proclaiming, "All men are born equal." Its correspondent plaintively asked: "Have we not won for ourselves a place in the ranks of mankind?"[17]

These sentiments were echoed by African Americans across the North. Joshua McCarter Simpson, a composer of antislavery ballads, gave them voice in a song entitled "Let the Banner Proudly Wave. Written after the Surrender of Lee." "We can now sing," the lyrics proclaimed, that "Old Slavery is dead." Simpson highlighted the contributions of both Northern and Southern blacks to the Union victory:

> We've stood and fought like demons,
>   Upon the battle field;
> Both slaves and Northern freeman
>   Have faced the glowing steel.
> Our blood beneath this banner
>   Has mingled with the whites,
> And 'neath its folds we now demand
>   Our just and equal rights.[18]

Moderate newspapers, which had staked out a middle ground between the abolitionist and Copperhead extremes, viewed black freedom as secondary to the overarching goal achieved by the surrender: the salvation of the "glorious Union." Leading the way among moderate Republicans was Henry J. Raymond, editor of the *New York Times*. The *Times* generally supported the policies of the Lincoln administration; Raymond had helped orchestrate Lincoln's reelection in 1864. Fancying himself a watchdog against the threat that Lincoln might drift toward abolitionist radicalism,

Raymond rejected Greeley's equation of Appomattox with the prospect of black citizenship and instead defended Grant's magnanimity as the means to liberate the white South: to redeem the white Southern masses from their thralldom to the "slave power" and speed the advent of "order and fraternity." The *Times* praised Lincoln for his April 11 speech: Lincoln would gauge the temper of the South before committing to a policy.[19]

Rivaling both the *Tribune* and *Times* in popularity was James Bennett's *New York Herald*. Bennett had walked a fine line over the course of the war. The *Herald*, trumpeting its independence from the political parties, strongly supported the Union—but frequently excoriated Lincoln for his conduct of the war effort, deeming his emancipation proclamation unnecessary and unconstitutional. Only when Lincoln's reelection seemed certain did the paper belatedly support the president. Northerners, Lincoln included, were willing to abide Bennett's mercurial disposition as a political commentator because his *Herald* unquestionably offered up unparalleled coverage—detailed and up to date—of military developments in the field. With a team of experienced correspondents, such as Sylvanus Cadwallader, sending out a steady stream of dispatches from the front, the *Herald* had thrilled Northern readers with its accounts of Grant's pursuit of Lee. In its accounts of the surrender, Grant's terms were the extension of his brilliant military tactics: by offering a soft peace to end his hard war, Grant had disarmed Lee's legions of both their "physical and moral weapons of resistance."[20]

For Bennett, as for Raymond, Grant's terms were the means to bring the errant states as quickly as possible back into the national family. The *Herald* saw in Lincoln's April 11 speech a strong defense of wartime Reconstruction in Louisiana and the prospect of a "liberal, easy, comprehensive" peace. Indeed, moderate newspapers generally fused Grant's terms and Lincoln's lenient cautious Reconstruction policies. The editor of the *Franklin Repository* (Pennsylvania), Alexander McClure, for example, read Lincoln's April 11 speech as a rebuke to the radical critics of the Ten Percent Plan who called for more stringent Reconstruction terms and for political equality for blacks. Lincoln, he was sure, would move with the "utmost caution" on the race question and would use magnanimity to "induce the deluded people of the South to throw off the yoke of treason."[21]

As a rule, moderate newspapers joined progressive ones in emphatically rejecting the overwhelming numbers interpretation of Confederate defeat and claimed instead that Grant had waged a campaign for the ages. As the *Philadelphia Inquirer* put it, when Grant assumed command of the federal forces in March of 1864, Southerners wrote off his prior string of victories by sneering that "GRANT has never met ROBERT E. LEE." "Well, he has met ROBERT E. LEE face to face," the paper gleefully asserted on April 11, and Lee was "unequal to the shock." The *Philadelphia Press*, for its part, lauded the "indomitable will and genius" of Grant and declared grandiosely that "to the surrender of LEE ... there is no parallel, to our knowledge, supplied by history." Grant compared favorably, it suggested, to Napoleon and Wellington. Adding the name of Frederick the Great to the list of Grant's historic peers, the misleadingly named *St. Louis Democrat* (a pro-Lincoln Republican paper) relished the Union's defeat of the allegedly "invincible" Army of Northern Virginia. Grant's legions, it averred, had broken the spirit of Lee's vaunted legions; the Federals "fought better than ever" even as rebel morale decayed.[22]

Having outgeneraled Lee, Grant then "summarily disposed" of Lee's bid to negotiate a peace and instead forced the rebel chief to surrender on the Union's terms. Lee's "weakness" was evident in his correspondence with Grant, as was his duplicity in seeming to stand down even as he planned his final break-out attempt. Grant's "little notes to Lee," by contrast, were considered by Republicans to be the "most effective epistles" imaginable. The *New Haven Palladium*, in its April 10 issue, opined of Grant: "His pen, if not mightier than his sword, brings down his game with deadly certainty." His terms were a tribute to Northern, not Southern, manliness and chivalry. "As for saving their honor," the *Sacramento Daily Union* wrote of the defeated rebels, "after the original desertion of the national flag they had none to lose. They obtained a show of liberal terms only because their conquerer desired to spare the lives of better men" (namely, Union ones). In an article entitled "The End," the *Philadelphia Press* concisely summed up the dominant Northern understanding of the war: "Right has triumphed over Wrong."[23]

The Copperheads flatly rejected that conclusion. Fiercely opposed to Lincoln's policies of emancipation and conscription, newspapers such as the *New York World* and *New York Daily News* accused the Lincoln administration of wantonly sacrificing white men for the shibboleth of racial equality and of needlessly prolonging a war that should have ended much sooner in a negotiated settlement. The Copperheads' antipathy to the Lincoln administration suffused their coverage of the Appomattox campaign and the surrender. As the scholar Andrew S. Coopersmith has noted in his study of Civil War newspapers, the "Copperheads denied that the Union had won any kind of moral victory over the rebels; Northerners had triumphed not because they were better or more deserving of success than Southerners, but only because they were more powerful." Editors such as Manton Marble of the *World* (who had drifted from the War Democrat into the Peace Democrat ranks) and Benjamin Wood of the *News* (the brother of New York's Copperhead mayor, Fernando Wood) were unabashed admirers of Lee, and their take on the surrender had more in common with the accounts of Lee's lieutenants than with the accounts by Grant's. The *World*, for example, asserted that Lee's comportment in the days leading up to the surrender entitled him to "all the respect which justly attends the frank and magnanimous abandonment of a struggle become visibly hopeless." Lee, not only Grant, had displayed magnanimity. Why had the struggle become hopeless? Not because of the moral rectitude of Lincoln and Grant and their armies. "In their valor, their endurance, their martial skill and their faith in the justice of the cause," Southerners were, the *World* maintained, "equal to the North." The Confederacy was "subdued by overwhelming numbers."[24]

In the minds of men such as Marble and Woods, Grant's terms were a repudiation of the Republican Party's vengeful wartime policies. With the war effectively over, the "plea of military necessity" could no longer be invoked to defend Lincoln's radical measures of emancipation, conscription, suppression of dissent, and enlargement of federal power. The Copperhead press focused on the costs of the war and on the threat of a radical resurgence. The *Harrisburg Patriot & Union*, for example, lamented that the war had steeped the country in misery and given credence to the "anti-slavery dogmas and anti-democratic heresies of the dominant party." Claiming that the "Abolition party" was already calling for violent retribution against the defeated Confederates, Copperheads predicted that those Radical Republicans—the likes of Charles Sumner,

Thaddeus Stevens, and Ben Wade—who had opposed Lincoln's lenient Ten Percent Plan would try to undermine Grant's "humane and magnanimous settlement." Moreover, Copperhead papers were critical of Lincoln's April 11 speech, viewing it as a "partisan manifesto"—a departure from rather than an endorsement of Grant's terms. In short, the Copperhead press appropriated Appomattox, symbolically, as a bulwark against change.[25]

As progressives, moderates, and conservatives tailored the theme of magnanimity to their respective political agendas, they opened a debate over how far up the Confederate hierarchy Grant's leniency should extend. While Copperheads charged that antislavery radicals were bent on vengeance against the leading rebels, this was simply not true. There was no clear correspondence between support for black citizenship and calls for vengeance against the Southern elite. On the contrary, there were prominent abolitionist editors who made the case for mercy, and moderates who, while skeptical about racial equality, demanded that an example be made of the Confederate chieftains. For example, the Radical Republican Greeley argued that all rebels, even the leadership class, should come under the umbrella of Grant's generosity; mercy was the best way to redeem them from sin and to induce them to atone for their treason. Henry Raymond, by contrast, was not willing to go so far. "All this talk about 'magnanimity in triumph' is excellent in its place," an April 12 editorial in the *Times* stipulated, referring to Greeley's piece. "But when it comes to include the pardon of every rebel leader, of JEFF. DAVIS himself, we demur, we protest." Upholding the Republican Party doctrine that a "slave power conspiracy"—an evil cabal of Southern leaders and their Northern lackeys who had deluded the Southern masses—orchestrated the rebellion, Raymond and the *Times* demanded that the "arch-traitor" Davis (who was still on the run) be hunted down and held accountable. This was the only way to neutralize fully the threat of the conspiracy. It was not enough that the Union had won moral vindication, Raymond insisted: "Authority still needs to be vindicated." The North had to maintain a distinction between the "criminal instigators of the rebellion" and the "mistaken men" who were "dragged by the resistless influence of social ties" into warring against the federal government. In Raymond's eyes, Radical Republicans, like Copperheads, bore the taint of disloyalty, and only moderates could be trusted to safeguard the Union's victory.[26]

While Greeley and Raymond argued over whether magnanimity could effect the redemption of Confederate elite, some moderate Democratic papers joined ranks with the Copperheads in proclaiming the utter blamelessness of Lee and the rebel leadership. The Washington, D.C. *Constitutional Union* editorialized on April 11 that the noble Lee, that "great Captain," had elicited Grant's magnanimity by his "spotless virtue" and the "heroic valor and generous fortitude" of his Army of Northern Virginia. Lee should be allowed to go back to his "ancestral acres" at Arlington, Virginia (which had been occupied by Union forces) and should thenceforward "be protected in his home from molestation." In a similar vein, the *Brooklyn Daily Eagle* observed admiringly that Lee, the "soul of military strength and genius and chivalric endurance," had earned his honorable peace and had secured a "general amnesty" that covered the

Holding Davis accountable: Henry Raymond of the *New York Times*. (Library of Congress)

entire Confederacy. Lee was one with his men and "made no stipulations for himself" that he had "not secured for the humblest drummer boy in the army." Summing up the Copperhead case for leniency to the Confederates, the *New York World* insisted that the North and South should not stand in relation as "conquerer and conquered." Instead the *World* offered this prescription for the peace: "Let perfect equality between the sections be established, let the sovereignty of the States be acknowledged." The old order could—must—be restored.[27]

The editorials and columns that Northern papers churned out in the first days after the surrender were aimed at the party faithful, designed to insure that, when the initial celebrations were over, they would hew to interpretations consistent with their political affiliations and reject the arguments of their political rivals. Would party lines hold?

In the first flush of victory, Northerners were overwhelmed by emotions of joy and relief. Word of the surrender had reached New York City via telegraph dispatches from the War Department at 11:00 p.m. on April 9, 1865. In the hours that followed, the news circulated quickly, rousing New Yorkers from their beds. Northern diarist Maria Lydia Daly noted that at midnight a newspaper boy called out "Surrender of Lee's army, ten cents and no mistake." His breathless report brought hosannas of joy to Daly's lips. George Templeton Strong, a wealthy New York lawyer who had served as an officer of the U.S. Sanitary Commission and had helped recruit and supply a Union regiment, was roused early from his bed on the morning of April 10 by his son John, "who was hallooing all over the house, hurrahing for Grant . . . [and] making well-meant efforts to chant 'John Brown' and 'The Red, White, and Blue.'" As daylight dawned, the public began to celebrate in ways ranging from gleeful to solemn. Teachers read schoolchildren the news and dismissed them early; militiamen fired cannons and churches rang their bells; a "sudden eruption" of flags bedecked the streets and buildings; and plans were made for a "grand te deum" to be sung as part of a special thanksgiving service at Trinity Church the following day.[28]

Such scenes were played out across the North. Sophia Stockett Sellman of Annapolis "couldn't help from laughing" when she heard the news of Lee's surrender on the morning of April 10, while her children, for their part, "commenced hurrahing." Caroline Cowles Clarke of Canadaigua, a small town in upstate New York, gave herself over to her community's reckless revelry. Beginning at 7:00 a.m. on April 10, men and women began "running through the streets wild with excitement"; everyone had a bell or gong or horn in hand, and she gleefully waded into the crowd, a flag in one hand and a bell in the other, determined to "make all the noise" she could. The Andrews family of Hudson, Wisconsin, celebrated the surrender by inserting the names of two soldier brothers into a joyful song: "The boys will shout, the girls will all turn out, when Jimmie and Charlie come marching home." For Northerners, the most elemental meaning of Appomattox was that soldiers would at last be reunited with their loved ones. The order from the War Department on April 13 "to stop all drafting and recruiting in the Northern states" promised to banish from Northern homes the specter of suffering and death.[29]

Soon, amidst the celebrations, the impulse to analyze events kicked in. Daly, a pro-war Democrat, evinced her hope in her April 10 diary entry that Grant's terms would dispel the "animosity" that had "so long reigned" and that God would "change the hearts of our so long vindictive foes." She preferred to extend Grant's amnesty to the Confederate leadership; it was better to "let Jeff Davis go" than to "make him a martyr." Strong found "the correspondence between Grant and Lee in the morning papers at the breakfast table" on April 10. It seemed to him that "Lee made a decent show of coyness" in the exchange, but that Grant had seen right through it. Strong confessed to his diary that day that his "first thought was that Grant had been too liberal." Further reflection convinced Strong that Grant had gotten it right. His terms would be a "fountain of cold water on whatever pugnacity and chivalry might yet survive" in the Confederacy. Sidney George Fisher, an elite Philadelphian and moderate Republican, recorded the "great news" of the surrender in his April 10 diary entry but turned to its political implications on the following day. His April 11, 1865, diary entry expressed his disgust at the opportunism of radical abolitionists, who were, in his view, recklessly exploiting the moment to push their "absurd" plan of black suffrage. The lust for "party victory," he lamented, seemed to overwhelm the commitment to social order.[30]

The power of partisanship to cloud the North's moment of victory is dramatized by an incident in Portsmouth, New Hampshire, that transpired the day after the surrender. A crowd of nearly 2,000 citizens—among them a host of sailors and shipyard workers—attacked the offices of the Copperhead paper the *States and Union* and threatened to lynch its editor, Joshua Lane Foster. Foster had made himself a public enemy among Lincoln's supporters by directing torrents of hateful rhetoric toward the president, the Republican Party, African Americans, and even the Union army; he had tried to foment opposition to the draft and emancipation and to Lincoln's reelection. A small-scale draft riot had broken out in the city in the aftermath of the massively destructive New York City draft riot of July 1863. On April 10, 1865, the crowd that teemed outside Foster's office demanded that he make amends and mark the surrender by hanging an American flag from his window. Foster reportedly told them, "Go to Hell!" Angry at Foster's unwillingness "to perform this act of loyalty," and by some accounts inebriated, the rioters broke into his offices and smashed his printing press to pieces. The provost marshal finally appeared and quelled the crowd but by then the damage was done. Foster was livid and vowed revenge. The coverage in the Republican press was entirely unsympathetic to him. While disavowing, perfunctorily, the mob's resort to violence, Republican sheets opined that Foster, a "skunk" who was "devoid of principle," had courted his fate and "richly deserve[d] it." His Copperhead newspaper was "in politics the counterpart of the Secesh journals of Charleston and Richmond," the editors of the *Portsmouth Journal* insisted. If he had only "possessed as much shrewdness as traitorism," and seen fit to celebrate the surrender with his townsmen, Foster could have prevented the mobbing.[31]

This incident, though unusual, is revealing of the uncertain mood of the North as it assimilated the news from Appomattox. Amidst the parades, illuminations, and fireworks, Northern celebrations of Appomattox often featured public denunciations of the Copperheads by local Republican leaders and private expressions of resentment against such Northern "traitors" by staunch loyalists. Sergeant James Henry Avery, who had served in the 5th Michigan Cavalry Regiment under Custer, was convalescing at a hospital in Frederick, Maryland, after bouts of dysentery when he heard the news of Lee's surrender. "Cannons boomed, flags were displayed, the streets were decorated, and the soldiers who were able to walk, marched in procession, those not able to walk, but who could ride, were carried in vehicles of some kind. In this way, the column moved until late at night, through brilliantly lighted streets, where all kinds of mottoes were displayed," he reported. Not everyone was in a mood to celebrate, however: "We moved through dark streets where we could occasionally see a scowling face, as dark as the street. Those were the copperheaded sneaks hiding themselves in the darkness."[32]

Loyalists were just as contemptuous of those Copperheads who experienced, at the moment of victory, a last minute conversion to a pro-war position as they were of those who clung to an antiwar one. It was unseemly that so many Copperheads suddenly applied to the Republican Union League for admission, Strong wrote in his diary on April 11; they claimed, conveniently, that they had been "uncompromising Union [men] from the first." Strong added, with sarcasm: "What a pity we had not known this a year ago; we should have been saved much uneasiness."[33]

The most biting mockery of the Copperheads came from the pen of humorist David Ross Locke, who created the fictional character of Petroleum Vesuvius Nasby to lampoon the disloyalty of the antiwar Democrats. The Nasby character's "letters," vitriolic and crude, were published in Northern newspapers to the amusement of loyal readers for whom "the sharp pinch of humor" mitigated "the dull pain of war." Locke, the historian Jon Grinspan explains, "caricatured Nasby as an ignorant pontificator, a virulent racist, and a drunken, thieving hypocrite"; Nasby avoided book learning, lest it turn him into an abolitionist, and deserted the Union for the Confederacy, only to return when he realized that Confederate uniforms were nothing more than "holes with rags around 'em."[34]

The Nasby character weighed in on the major developments of the war, including Lee's surrender to Grant. In a letter dated "*April the* 10th, 1865," Nasby, writing from New Jersey, expresses his shock and dismay at the news from Appomattox. Nasby "survived the defeet ov Micklellan. . . . the loss uv Atlanty. . . . the fall uv Richmond," he notes, because he "still hed faith" in "that grate and good man, Lee." After each setback, Nasby had turned to the "Ablishnists" and shook his fist with the warning, "Wait, and yoo'll see"—Lee was not losing ground, just "consentratin" his forces for a final blow against Lincoln and his minions.

The surrender at last dispelled Nasby's fantasy. He wrote:

> This ends the chapter. The Confederasy hez at last consentratid
> its last consentrate. It's ded. It's gathered up its feet, sed its last
> words, and deceest. And with it the Dimokrasy hez likewise given
> up the ghost. It may survive this, but I can't see how. We staked
> our political fortune on it; we went our bottom dollar on it; it's
> gone up, and we ditto. Linkin will serve his term out—the tax on
> whiskey won't be repeeled—our leaders will die off uv chagrin,
> and delirium tremens and inability to live so long out uv offis.[35]

This prognostication was Locke's fantasy and rhetorical revenge—if there
was an ounce of decency in the disloyal Northern Democrats, they too
would concede defeat and leave the field.

Grant's terms raised the question of not only how much mercy Northerners might show Southerners but also of how much mercy they would
show each other.

6

Victory and Martyrdom

Abraham Lincoln had spent Good Friday, April 14, in high spirits; it seemed to observers that a great weight had been lifted from his shoulders. In a cabinet meeting that morning, he had learned from General Grant, there to report on the events at Appomattox, that the surrender of Johnston's Confederate army in the Carolinas was imminent; the last dominoes were falling. Lincoln had reiterated at that meeting his desire that the country transcend "feelings of hate and vindictiveness." He would countenance "no persecution, no bloody work, after the war was over." As for the leaders of the rebellion, Lincoln expressed his hope that their fate would be exile—that they could be frightened out of the country and left to languish in isolation without the honor of martyrdom. After the cabinet meeting, the president and his wife, Mary Todd Lincoln, had gone on a cheerful carriage ride, eaten dinner at home, and then proceeded to Ford's Theatre for a welcome evening of entertainment.[1]

But a trap had been laid. Lincoln, attended by only two bodyguards despite his having received numerous death threats over the course of the war, was set upon in the president's box at Ford's Theatre by John Wilkes Booth, who delivered a point-blank shot from his Derringer pistol to the back of Lincoln's head. Booth then leapt to the stage, hissing out the state motto of Virginia—*Sic semper tyrannis*—and disappeared into the night. News of Booth's attack on Lincoln reached the Northern public around 10:30 p.m. that night. Booth's co-conspirator Lewis Paine had attempted to assassinate Secretary of State William Seward, attacking him in his home, but had failed. On Saturday the 15th, Northerners learned that

Lincoln, who never recovered consciousness, had passed away, Booth's
bullet lodged in his brain.

One need only to tally the number of published books on Lincoln and
on Appomattox to conclude that, in modern-day scholarship and popular
histories, the assassination of the president on April 14, 1865, utterly
eclipses the surrender. Those books contend that Lincoln's death marked
a turning point. Northern public opinion was revolutionized: joy turned
to grief and magnanimity to vengeance.[2] Such a view captures Northerners' anger at Booth's deed but fails to capture their determination to hold
on to victory. Northerners coped with the tragedy of Lincoln's death by
clinging to the triumph—Lincoln's triumph—at Appomattox. In a call-
and-response that played out in public forums, churches especially, across
the Union, some Northerners cried out for stern retribution against the
South for Booth's deed, while others answered that the spirit of magnanimity must prevail. Both arguments mobilized images of Appomattox—
of the Union's victory, of Lee's surrender, and of the terms of the peace. In
the eyes of the Northern public, the surrender and the assassination were
inextricably linked. The impulse to see mercy as a source of moral authority remained powerful among Northerners.

Six days after the mobbing of Copperhead editor Joshua Lane Foster, the
citizens of Portsmouth, New Hampshire, gathered in their churches to
hear eulogies for their late president. The minister of the South Parish
church, James De Normandie, delivered a sermon on Sunday morning,
April 16, entitled "The Lord Reigneth." Conjuring the atmosphere of
sorrow and dread that had fallen on the city, he asked "What mean these
anxious inquiries, these mute looks, this hope against hope for some denial of our sad news, these mutterings of vengeance, these streets lined
with black, the air filled with murmurings, the very heavens joining in our
tears?" Why had Lincoln been murdered, and who was responsible? The
answer, thought De Normandie, was clear: Booth was "only an instrument
of others," an agent of the "slave power conspiracy" that had brought the
war. Indeed, De Normandie condemned as guilty of the assassination all
the "supporters of slavery for the last two hundred years." But he reserved
his special wrath for the wartime Copperheads. "Every man who has withheld his word of support or sympathy for this nation struggling for a

broader freedom," De Normandie intoned, "helped murder our President." And yet, De Normandie vouched to his parishioners that he harbored "not a single feeling of revenge." "I call for no vengeance," he declared, making a crucial distinction, "but we must demand punishment."[3]

De Normandie gave voice to the widespread consensus among Northerners that Booth was "merely a tool" in a broader Confederate plot. In the days after Lincoln's death, the nature of that plot and of Booth's precise motivations were the subject of rampant speculation. Swirling rumors connected Booth directly to Jefferson Davis and to Confederate operatives in Canada; such rumors gained credence when those in charge of bringing Booth to heel, Secretary of War Stanton and Judge Advocate General Joseph Holt of the Bureau of Military Justice, publicly proclaimed in early May that Booth was an agent of Davis's fugitive regime.[4]

At the time De Normandie delivered his call for punishment, Northerners did not yet know that Booth had been in the audience when Lincoln gave his April 11, 1865, speech on Reconstruction, endorsing limited black suffrage. Enraged at the prospect of black citizenship, Booth had vowed at that very moment, "Now, by God, I'll put him through. That is the last speech he will ever make." Booth's ardent secessionism and commitment to white supremacy—typical of many in his native Maryland who identified with the South—had mixed, in a lethal blend, with his delusions of grandeur and his persecution complex. He had taken aim on April 14 at the prospect of racial equality. As Lincoln's biographer Michael Burlingame has put it: "Lincoln was not murdered because he had issued the Emancipation Proclamation or because he endorsed the Thirteenth Amendment. He was killed because he endorsed the enfranchisement of blacks, and therefore Lincoln should be considered a martyr to black citizenship rights, as much as Martin Luther King Jr., or Medgar Evers, or Viola Liuzzo, or Micky Schwerner, or James Reeb, or James Cheney, or Andrew Goodman, or any of the others who were killed in the 1960s as they championed the civil rights movement."[5]

Such an assessment eloquently captures the enduring meaning of Lincoln's legacy, but in the immediate aftermath of the assassination, that legacy still hung in the balance. Many Northerners mourned Lincoln as a martyr to emancipation, and some mourned him as a martyr to black civil rights. Nearly all mourned Lincoln as a conqueror and peacemaker, a martyr to the Union itself.

Northerners assumed, rightly, that Booth was distraught over Lee's surrender. As the *New York Herald* editorialized on April 16, Booth and his
conspirators were "fanatical zealots, crazed by the ruin which has overtaken the cause of treason, and the destruction and extinction of their
bogus confederacy." Northerners saw the assassination as a base bid to rob
the Union of the victory that its commander-in-chief, with Grant's army
as his instrument, had just won at Appomattox: to turn back the clock and
to plunge the country once again into hatred, bloodshed, and chaos.
Booth's long-standing desire to aid the rebellion became, after the surrender of Lee, "a desperate determination to avenge its downfall," as
Henry Raymond of the *New York Times* put it. The assassination was, the
Rev. Richard H. Steele proclaimed in a sermon entitled "Victory and
Mourning," a "cowardly effort of defeated and disappointed men." Northern commentators likened the assassination, in a pervasive metaphor, to
the "expiring sting" of a snake or dragon or scorpion, "venomous and vindictive even in its death throes." How, then, could Northerners mete out
justice to the guilty without being drawn into the vortex of vengeance and
thus betraying the magnanimous spirit of Lincoln's peace?[6]

Within the Union ranks, filial grief mingled with rage. "Everyone
seems to feel as though his Father had been assassinated," wrote John
F. L. Hartwell, a veteran of the Appomattox campaign, to his wife in upstate
New York. Wilbur Fisk, stationed at City Point, Virginia, too wrote those
at home that the men-in-arms felt they "had lost a father." The soldiers
vented their rage rhetorically in "terrible oaths and imprecations . . . uttered
through clenched teeth against the vile perpetrators," wrote one Union artilleryman. Holman Melcher of the 20th Maine Infantry noted that
Booth's crime aroused among the troops "an intense feeling of hatred . . .
against the Southern people." Soldiers attributed the crime to the bitter
"resentments" of the Confederates against their conquerors and to the
"fiendish spirit" of slavery. "We felt that the rebs were trying to gain by
murder what they had lost on the battle field, or at least be revenged for
their loss by taking the life of the President," Michigan cavalryman James
Henry Avery explained in his journal. Some Union soldiers suspected that
the fingerprints of Northern Copperheads were on the crime: Taylor
Peirce, with the 22nd Iowa Volunteer Infantry in North Carolina, wrote his
wife, Catherine, on April 17, 1865, that the assassination "had its inception

in the north among the traitors and Cowards." The Copperheads, he avowed, "would stop at nothing to carry out their ends."[7]

Yet the soldiers knew that they must abide by the terms of the recent surrender and strive, "as civilized men and gentlemen," to keep their "feelings of hatred in subjection," as Holman Melcher put it. The Union men who had just secured the Appomattox victory made no "open demonstration" of their anger and instead "remained calm," observed Ellis Spear, an officer in the 20th Maine. "It was fortunate that the war had been practically finished," he added, for if the assassination had come before the surrender, with Lee's army still a threat, no such restraint would have been possible. Stanton P. Allen of Sheridan's cavalry similarly noted that when the Union troops "recovered from the first shock of the dreadful calamity," they "were ready to exonerate the men who had laid down their arms at Appomattox from any complicity in the plot that struck down the noble Lincoln at the very moment that the glorious sun of peace was rising." They were enjoined to show forbearance by army chaplains such as the Reverend Jacob Post, who in a sermon preached in the Union army camp at Harrison's Landing, Virginia, on April 23 declared, "Let us, above all things, not give full scope to our passions and hatred towards the people of the South, but rather carry out the intentions of our late President to pursue a humane and conciliatory policy." As "Christian soldiers" the men should know that "God alone is capable of judging."[8]

White soldiers were especially struck by the restraint of African American troops. James Shaw, a brigade commander in the Twenty-fifth Army Corps, bore witness to that restraint in his published reminiscences. He and his USCT brigade received the news of the assassination as they were moving along the central Virginia countryside, from Appomattox to Petersburg, in the days after the surrender. "The fields on either side of us were full of paroled rebels going home," wrote Shaw, but the black troops, though they "looked on Lincoln as little short of a God," did not exact retribution on the Confederates in their midst. Indeed, "not a word or threat or insult did we hear." Shaw felt that the black soldiers would have been justified, under the circumstances, in tearing the rebels "limb from limb." Instead, they paid tribute to Lincoln, as most white soldiers did, by upholding the fragile peace.[9]

Among Northern civilians, the assassination brought forth "an out-pouring of grief not seen before or since in the nation's history." Countless Northerners gathered to hear sermons preached to their martyred presi-dent; an estimated seven million (one in every four Americans) watched his funeral train over the course of its 13-day trip to Springfield, Illinois, and over one million paid respect to his remains as he lay in state in the cities the train passed through. "Many observers," historian John C. Neff has noted, "were especially sensitive to the grief of black Americans." African American mourners thronged the streets of the nation's capital along the route of Lincoln's funeral train; a regiment of black soldiers, from the 22nd USCT, led the procession. Free black communities across the North held meetings to mourn and honor Lincoln. For example, on April 16, the "colored citizens" of Bloomington, Indiana, met in the AME Church, and passed a resolution: "[We] do hereby express our grief, and mingle our tears with the great *loyal and liberty-loving* masses of the American people . . . we, as colored American citizens have lost a *tried friend*—A GREAT DELIVERER—A REAL BENEFACTOR."[10]

White and black alike, Northerners mourned Lincoln as the man who had saved the Union—as the "captain," in the words of Walt Whitman's immortal poem on the assassination, who had brought his ship through a terrible storm and anchored it "safe and sound, its voyage closed and done." Whitman conjured Northerners' joy at the surrender and their gratitude to their commander-in-chief.

> O Captain! my Captain! rise up and hear the bells;
> Rise up—for you the flag is flung—for you the bugle trills,
> For you bouquets and ribboned wreaths—for you the shores
>   a-crowding
> For you they call, the swaying mass, their eager faces turning

And he conjured their shock, and trauma:

> Here Captain! dear father!
> This arm beneath your head!
> It is some dream that on the deck
>   You've fallen cold and dead.

While Whitman's language is inimitable, his sentiments were pervasive. In their commentary on the assassination, Northerners lingered over the moment of victory even as they wrestled with the recent tragedy. Invoking Appomattox, a memorial sermon by the Reverend J. E. Rankin, an ardent antislavery reformer and future president of Howard University, said of Lincoln, "He saw Treason vacating her capital and strongholds, in the vain attempt to flee inland to the mountains, ensnared on every hand, and, finally, surrendering her sword, and sending her disarmed minions to proclaim at their homes their final discouragement and discomfiture. This was the vision that blessed the gaze of Abraham Lincoln; and all this success and prosperity and freedom was henceforth forever to be associated with his own name."[11]

Lincoln, the martyr, victorious, in an 1866 engraving. (Library of Congress)

Why, then, had God permitted Lincoln to be struck down in his hour of triumph? On this question, Northerners were divided. Sermons constitute an especially revealing window into their agonized debate. Many, including Rankin, believed that Lincoln's death was providential—ordained not only to preserve the Union but also to make possible fitting retribution for the rebellion. In their view, Lincoln had been too good and kindly for the work of punishing the leading traitors. His successor, Vice President Andrew Johnson, was the man for that job: the Joshua to Lincoln's Moses, in a common biblical analogy. Johnson, a Tennessean with humble roots, had been chosen as Lincoln's running mate in 1864 to represent Southern Unionism and the fusion of War Democrats with Republicans into a "Union" party; here was an exemplary white Southern yeoman who had not been duped by the "slave power conspiracy." Johnson's intense antipathy to the slave power seemed evident in his tough talk. He proclaimed in a speech in Washington, D.C., on April 3, after the fall of Richmond and Petersburg, that "treason must be made odious and traitors must be punished and impoverished."[12]

Northerners frequently avowed that Booth had unwittingly killed the South's "best friend" and that Johnson would not show Lincoln's forbearance. Rankin disavowed the "mawkish sentimentalism" that had prevailed since the surrender and insisted that "treason of such long standing, so intelligent, so persistent, so destructive, so infernal, as that of the leading spirits in the South ought not to be forgiven by this people." He was echoed in countless other sermons. Again and again Northern ministers suggested that Lincoln had been ideally suited to achieving victory but was perhaps poorly suited to safeguarding it. "There was a danger that the late President, by reason of his kindness of heart, would not be equal to the retributive work which was soon to be required of him; that pardoning the very arch-rebels themselves he would fail to place upon the crime of treason its appropriate stigma," the Reverend C. B. Crane opined; the Reverend Frank L. Robbins of Philadelphia's Greenhill Presbyterian Church, in a similar formulation, speculated that "possibly, had [Lincoln] survived, his disposition would have inclined him to a too lenient policy towards the leaders of this atrocious rebellion." For these Northerners, the assassination proved that the South was as yet unrepentant. "The juncture at which the event occurred is significant," intoned the Reverend Marvin

R. Vincent, an antislavery Presbyterian from Troy, New York: "It was the spirit of the *conquered* South that smote down the President." "The hatred of free institutions, and the spirit of revenge and malice," he lamented, "have not died out with the military power of the rebellion."[13]

A decidedly more pointed version of this argument was offered by the Reverend Thomas Tousey of the Presbyterian Church in Palmyra, New York, whose April 19 memorial discourse lamented that Northerners had already, in the days since April 9, begun to lose a "just appreciation" of the "awful crimes of the rebellion." Alluding to the Copperheads' sympathetic disposition toward the surrendered rebels and to the debate over Appomattox that had raged in the Northern press, he reflected that "it seemed doubtful whether Gen. GRANT or Gen. LEE was to be the hero of our times." Tousey would countenance no clemency to "traitors with their hands reeking in patriot gore." He concluded his sermon by proclaiming, "God bless ANDREW JOHNSON and preserve him to carry out to the

In this 1865 print in remembrance of Lincoln, Jefferson Davis, flanked by Lee and Booth, spurns the president's offer of reconciliation. (Library of Congress)

fullest extent the policy thus indicated!" He was echoed by a fellow New
York Presbyterian, Reverend Henry Fowler, whose funeral sermon asked,
"Is Robert E. Lee to be cheered by Americans, because as a Virginia aris-
tocrat he fought desperately against his country? Is treason only a difference of political sentiments? What lessons have we to learn? The President,
living, teaches us mercy, and we listen with consent to amnesty and
re-construction; but the President murdered, teaches us retribution, and
we swear above his open grave, extermination against treason and its
plotters."[14]

In a similar vein, a Presbyterian minister, whose sermon was published
in the New York newspaper the *Evangelist*, insisted that Lee as well as
Davis must bear the blame for Booth's deed. "I have been surprised at
certain apologetic opinions, which I have heard expressed. . . . in regard to
this chief of rebel generals," he noted. Lee was a "gentleman," but he was
also a "thorough-paced traitor." "Were I going to select two men, one
from civilians and the other from the army, to be executed for treason,"
the minister concluded, "I would take Jefferson Davis and Robert E. Lee."
The Reverend Samuel T. Spear, for his part, agreed: the only fit punishment for Davis and Lee was to "hang them by the neck till they are dead."
Stronger still in his condemnation of Lee was the Reverend Gilbert
Haven of Boston, an ardent advocate of emancipation and of racial
equality. He declared from the pulpit that "Booth is but a babe in iniquity
compared with Lee." How was it, he asked, that the rebel chief was allowed
to "dwell among us unharmed, almost in honor"? Lee was the guiltiest of
all the rebels: it was he who, in brutal warfare, "attempted to assassinate
the nation."[15]

In the press as well as from the pulpit, some Northerners expressed
regret that Grant's terms at Appomattox had covered Southern officers as
well as enlisted men. As the progressive, antislavery Methodist journal
Zion's Herald of New York editorialized, "all talk of Lee's 'magnanimity,'
and of clemency to the rebel leaders, is hushed"; it was time for "stern
justice" for those "incarnate fiends" who had brought "four mourning,
blood dripping years." The assassination laid a new sin at the table of the
South: that of ingratitude. A Kansas newspaper declaimed that Booth's
deed, coming on the heels of Lincoln's clemency, showed "Southern rebels
to be possessed of less gratitude than wild beasts of prey." These views

found echo among private citizens. Northerners confided to their letters and diaries their hope that Johnson would teach the rebels a lesson—"that they may be made to regret the whole affair, from the firing on Sumter to the murder of our President," as Andrew Evans of Brown County, Ohio, wrote his soldier son on April 23, 1865. The eminent abolitionist Lydia Maria Child wrote her best friend Sarah Shaw, the mother of Robert Gould Shaw, the white colonel of the African American 54th Massachusetts Infantry, that while the assassination "shocked and distressed" her, she soon saw it as "only another of the wonderful manifestations of Providence. The kind-hearted Abraham, was certainly in danger of making too easy terms with the rebels. Perhaps he has been removed, that he might not defeat his own work."[16]

Other civilians, however, were wary of the shift in the public mood, fearing, as Emma Yarnell of Philadelphia put it, that with Johnson at the helm, "indignation should carry us too far in visiting upon the whole South the crime of the few." Leading Copperheads took up this theme as a centerpiece of their coverage of the assassination. They worried that calls for vengeance would drown out the rhetoric of magnanimity and that vengeance might be visited on all those, Southern and Northern, perceived as disloyal. Marcus "Brick" Pomeroy was among those Copperheads who made an abrupt about-face. His *La Crosse Daily Democrat* (Wisconsin), which during the election campaign of 1864 had dubbed Lincoln the "Widow Maker of the 19th Century," printed mourning bands and praised the late president as a "man of genius—a lover of his country." Copperhead journals such as the *New York News* claimed that they could divine Lincoln's intentions and that he was, on the eve of his death, "about to publish a proclamation of general amnesty so conciliatory in its tone and so honorable in its conditions, that it would have been acceptable to a large portion of the South as well as to the conservative people in the North." Radicals, they charged, were poised to exploit Lincoln's death to make a policy of their "savage vindictiveness."[17]

Not all Copperheads could stay on message. A small minority of antiwar Democrats openly rejoiced at Lincoln's assassination, seeing it, as Booth intended, as the just reward for a tyrant and oppressor. In a self-fulfilling prophecy, those who voiced such opinions brought the wrath of the loyal public down upon themselves. "Treasonable utterances were liable to land the speaker in prison," the historian Thomas R. Turner has observed—or worse. The North witnessed a wave of mob violence and reprisals against people who expressed their approval of the assassination and the targeting of some who were wrongly suspected of treasonable views. For example, as Turner notes, the townspeople of Westminster, Maryland, killed Joseph Shaw, editor of the local Democratic paper, for "disrespectful" language about Lincoln. Even where they were not attacked, Copperheads were put on notice as many Northern communities passed resolutions like this one from Camden, New Jersey: "The presence of rebel sympathizers *shall no longer be tolerated in our midst.*"[18]

The assassination, in short, undermined the case that clemency should extend up the Confederate chain of command and intensified the antipathy of loyal Northerners to the Copperheads. But it did not dispel the image of Lincoln as both the architect and guarantor of the peace. While some Northerners demanded retribution, others defended the principle of mercy.

Reminding her audience that the purpose of Northern magnanimity was to change Southern hearts and minds, celebrated spiritualist Emma Hardinge, in a funeral oration she delivered to more than 3,000 people at the Cooper Institute in New York on April 16, 1865, praised Lincoln for "returning good for evil, dispensing blessings for curses, and conquering foes more surely with his generous acts of mercy than all the armies of the earth could do with sword and cannon." She looked forward to the day when "all other blood-stained memories [would be] wiped away, and all other stormy passages of this tempestuous time be obliterated in the triumph of that Christ-like spirit which opened its arms of welcome to the fallen and penitent General Robert E. Lee."[19]

Again and again, Northern ministers argued, in a counterpoint to calls for retribution, that Grant's generous terms had emanated directly from Lincoln's affectionate heart, and that Lincoln's spirit must guide the nation still. A. D. Mayo, pastor of a Cincinnati church, hoped that Northerners would "not give way now to the voice of wrath and pagan vengeance," but instead "live and act in [Lincoln's] lofty spirit," so that "all men in this broad land shall finally gather about his feet in unity." Calling for "justice, not vengeance," the Reverend Herrick Johnson, an eminent Presbyterian theologian and author, argued that a "reckless dealing out of retribution" would only "lift the conspirators in the eyes of mankind . . . into the welcome elevation of heroic martyrs." He pleaded: "Let the grave of ABRAHAM LINCOLN be unpolluted by the blood of Americans slaughtered for revenge."[20]

Ministers often spoke of the battle that raged within their own hearts between the impulses of mercy and vengeance, and of how Lincoln had summoned the better angels of their nature. In the late president "was vindicated the greatness of real goodness and the goodness of real greatness," declared the Reverend Phillips Brooks, the rector of Philadelphia's Church of the Holy Trinity, and a popular champion of the Union cause and of emancipation. Lincoln's character was the "true result of our free life and institutions," he continued, and the antithesis of the "brutal, barbarous, and treacherous" Southern character. Brooks vented that "every false citizen at home" who had labored against the war effort was "brother to him who did this deed" of assassination. He recoiled from the prospect of revenge, guided by the image of Lincoln "standing with his hand reached out to feed the South with Mercy and the North with Charity." The "commander-in-chief is with his army now," united with his fallen soldiers "in victory and peace," intoned the essayist Josiah Holland in his eulogy in Springfield, Massachusetts. He observed with wonder that "all the insults heaped upon [Lincoln] by the foes of the government and the haters of his principles . . . never seemed to generate in him a feeling of revenge." Holland banished the "thoughts of vengeance" that simmered inside him, he explained, by feeling the presence of Lincoln's "kindly spirit, the magnetism of those kindly eyes, appealing to me to forbear."[21]

In the resilient idea of the "slave power conspiracy," Northerners found a rationale for urging the harsh punishment of Booth and his accomplices while preserving the policy of clemency toward Southern soldiers and civilians. The Reverend C. M. Butler of Philadelphia sketched out the "lessons" of recent events in his April 19 funeral address. Northerners must see the assassination as an indictment of slaveholding society, of secession, and of the Confederacy. Booth's deed stripped from the Southern rebellion the "masks of honorableness and worth." But they must also strive to imitate Lincoln's "own noble forbearance and magnanimity in dealing with the misled and misinformed masses." The Reverend Richard

Eddy, a Philadelphia Universalist and wartime chaplain of the 60th New York Volunteer Infantry, insisted that Northerners should dissociate the names of Davis and Lee from "anything that can appeal to American pride and honor." Justice demands, he said, that "they go into the catalogue of the enemies of man." He, too, quoting directly from Lincoln's Second Inaugural, with its call for malice toward none and charity for all, disavowed "wild and furious retaliation."[22]

Fittingly, the most powerful invocation of Lincoln's abiding spirit was offered by the pastor who had ministered to the president over the course of the war: Reverend Phineas Densmore Gurley of the New York Avenue Presbyterian Church in Washington, D.C. On April 19, Gurley pronounced an oration over Lincoln's coffin in the East Room of the White House for an audience of some 600 mourners, among them Grant and Andrew Johnson. Lincoln's body was then conveyed in formal procession down Pennsylvania Avenue to the Capitol Rotunda, where he lay in state. Gurley said of Lincoln:

> The cause survives his fall and must survive it. The light of its brightening prospects flashes cheeringly today athwart the gloom occasioned by his death, and the language of God's united providences is telling us that though the friends of liberty die, liberty itself is immortal. There is no assassin strong enough and no weapon deadly enough to quench its inextinguishable life, or arrest its onward march to the conquest and empire of the world. This is our confidence and this is our consolation, as we weep and mourn to-day. Though our beloved President is slain, our beloved country is saved, and so we sing of mercy as well as of judgment. Tears of gratitude mingle with those of sorrow, while there is also the dawning of a brighter, happier day upon our stricken and weary land. God be praised that our fallen Chief lived long enough to see the day dawn, and the day star of joy and peace arise upon the nation. He saw it, and he was glad.

Although many who eulogized Lincoln invoked the president's ringing Second Inaugural Address, no one captured its providential view of the war better than Gurley. He spoke repeatedly in his funeral sermon of mercy: not only of the mercy Lincoln had shown the South, but also of the mercy the Almighty had shown Lincoln and his countrymen in guiding them to their "final triumph." In Gurley's view, Northerners' anger must be tempered and their passions subdued by their own humility in the face of the "overruling providence of God." Mercy, Gurley explained, was the "best hope [Lincoln] had for himself and for his country."[23]

For these ministers, no less than for those whose keynote was vengeance, the assassination discredited the emerging view—one taken by the Copperheads as well as white Southerners—that the Appomattox terms somehow represented an acknowledgment of the bravery and decency of Lee and the defeated Confederates. Booth's heinous crime should "sever the rebellion from the respect and sympathy of the world," as the eloquent Holland put it. The assassination did not, however, vitiate Lincoln's generous policy or Grant's terms. Rather, for many Northerners, it strengthened the argument that the offer of magnanimity to the mass of deluded Southerners—a policy that demanded and then rewarded true penitence on the part of the South—was the ultimate sign of the North's moral superiority. Indeed, even those ministers who called fervently for the punishment of Lee and Davis, as accomplices in Booth's crime, often drew a sharp line between the slaveholding "oligarchs" and the millions of white yeomen who were merely the "tools" of Confederate elite. The question remained: Must the leaders of the rebellion be silenced in order for the masses to be disenthralled? Or could those leaders be converted and then guide the masses toward the light of repentance and reunion?[24]

Northerners' varied efforts to answer these questions, after the assassination, pointed out just how malleable the concept of magnanimity could be. The abolitionist Wendell Phillips—as uncompromising an advocate for emancipation and black civil rights as could be found among white reformers—declared in his oration on the death of the president that Americans must reject the siren song of vengeance. Mass punishment of the rebels would "sink our civilization to the level of Southern barbarism. It would forfeit our very right to supersede the Southern system, which right is based on ours being better than theirs. . . . [and] degrade us to the level of Davis and Lee." Phillips would not consign any Southerners, not even "the bloodiest and guiltiest of all, Robert Lee," to the gallows; nothing was gained by making martyrs of them. Instead, he called for the banishment of Confederate ringleaders, confiscation of the planters' great estates and the redistribution of their property to loyal whites and blacks, and the extension of the franchise to African American men. These measures, directed against the slaveholding elite, would destroy the spirit of "caste" in Southern society. Phillips knew perfectly well that this was a radical agenda, one that Confederates and Copperheads viewed as brutally punitive. In Phillips's view, so terrible were the sins of treason and slaveholding that any punishment for the leading Confederates short of capital punishment should rightly be considered merciful, a sign of the mighty North's forbearance, confidence, and decency.[25]

Across the spectrum of opinion on the issue of retribution and clemency, Northerners clung to Grant's victory as a source of solace in their grief. Newspapers interspersed coverage of the 12-day manhunt for Booth, his death at the hands of his Federal pursuers on April 26, and of the transfer of power to Johnson with articles on the Appomattox campaign—articles that lingered over its sweet and edifying details, that gloried in the prowess of Grant and his legions, and that upheld the dominant Republican interpretation of the surrender over the Copperhead one. The *Connecticut Herald* of April 22, for example, featured an article entitled "Rebel Honor" that took Lee to task for dissembling in his correspondence with Grant and for trying to "extricate his army by crawling off in the night." How glorious it was, the paper noted, that the "inevitable Sheridan stopped him again and blocked this highly 'honorable' proceeding." On that same day, the *National Anti-Slavery Standard* juxtaposed on its front page articles entitled "The Character of Mr. Lincoln" and "Lee's Surrender: Details of the Event from an Eyewitness." The *Central Press* of Bellefonte, Pennsylvania, for its part, featured a long editorial entitled "Grant's Victory" in its April 28, 1865, issue, which weighed in on the "overwhelming numbers" debate. The article took issue with the specious claim that Lee had surrendered only 8,000 men to Grant's force of more than 100,000, and instead noted that Grant, in an "extraordinary feat of generalship," had whittled Lee's force of more than 60,000 to 27,000 over the course of the retreat. "Obviously, Lee's losses all through the campaign are to be counted as the successive trophies of the victor," the editor noted, "and it might even be said that the fewer troops Lee had to surrender on the 9th of April so much greater was the triumph of Grant."[26]

Celebrations of the Appomattox victory that had been in the planning stages before the assassination went forward, though marked by a tone of somber determination. For example, African Americans in Philadelphia met at the Third Methodist Episcopal Church on April 18 to "give thanks to Almighty God for the triumph of Freedom in our land"; they mourned the death of their Great Emancipator and expressed their gratitude that such a "sagacious statesman" had been "selected" by the Almighty to lead the nation through its "ordeal of fire and blood." Four days later, Philadelphia blacks gathered again to celebrate the contributions of the USCT to the nation's victory. One of the city's leading black activists, Octavius Catto, paid tribute to the nearly 200,000 black soldiers who fought in the war and who now trusted a "redeemed country for the full recognition of their manhood." At the conclusion of the meeting, "cheers were given for the Union, [and] Abraham Lincoln." The message of such meetings was clear: the Union's victory and its redemption from slavery were indelible.[27]

Grant's Appomattox terms again made the headlines when General Joseph Johnston surrendered to General William T. Sherman at Durham Station, North Carolina, on April 26, 1865. Sherman and Johnston had negotiated an agreement on April 18 that seemed to recognize the Southern state governments, extend amnesty to all Confederates, and even restore the property and political rights of the rebels. Sherman had been manipulated by Johnston who, acting at the behest of Jefferson Davis and his cabinet, was trying to impose a series of favorable conditions on his inevitable surrender. This accord was promptly rejected by President Andrew Johnson, Stanton and the cabinet, and Grant himself as contravening Lincoln's explicit orders that military commanders not negotiate political settlements and as contrary to the letter and spirit of both Lincoln's December 1863 Proclamation of Amnesty and Reconstruction and of Grant's terms to Lee. Grant was dispatched to North Carolina to carry word of the administration's displeasure directly to Sherman and to enjoin the wayward general to secure a new peace in line with the Grant's April 9 terms. When Jefferson Davis learned that the Union cabinet had nullified the Johnston-Sherman pact, he ordered Johnston to resume fighting. Johnston, knowing full well he was cornered, wisely refused. On April 26, Sherman and Johnston signed a new surrender accord, in keeping with the Appomattox model, and Davis and his cabinet continued their flight southwest.[28]

The imbroglio sparked a heated debate in the press; Stanton made no secret of his distrust for Sherman, and Sherman struggled to defend his public reputation. In the eyes of some critics of the initial accord, Sherman had, in effect, promised the rebels that "they were still to be permitted to *hold their slaves* in spite of the Emancipation Proclamation," as one of the many negative press accounts of "Sherman's fiasco" put it. The *National Anti-Slavery Standard*, published in New York City, called the April 18 accord a "virtual surrender" of all the Union had been fighting for. It attributed Sherman's behavior to his long-standing "disinclination towards the Anti-Slavery policy of the government." Sherman defended himself by noting that tensions were at a fever pitch on April 18, because news of Lincoln's assassination was fresh in the minds of Northern and Southern troops alike. His terms, he asserted, were calculated to keep passions in check and to prevent Johnston's army from dispersing and doing "infinite mischief." He believed he had co-opted Johnston into urging the surrender of the last rogue rebels forces. Sherman also protested that his initial terms were consistent with Grant's terms and with Lincoln's wishes for a restoration of the Union. Democratic papers in the North rushed to Sherman's defense, lambasting Radicals for impeaching Sherman's loyalty while upholding the notion that Grant's terms to Lee had in fact pardoned the Confederates. Sherman's leniency, in their view, was consistent with that of Lincoln and Grant.[29]

The Johnson administration's prompt and emphatic efforts to bring Sherman in line confirmed to some their belief that the new president would hold the rebels accountable. More than anything, Sherman's blunder strengthened the dominant Republican interpretation of Appomattox and the reputation of Grant. By proposing a peace that the Republican administration deemed too lenient, Sherman pointed out the limits of Grant's terms: the Appomattox terms had not, Republicans insisted, conferred political amnesty on all Confederates, had not recognized the state governments, and had not restored the old order. Grant, Republican newspapers pointed out, had made a strictly military calculation in offering the Appomattox terms—to "secure the speedy close of the war without the further effusion of blood"—and events, such as Johnston's fall, had "vindicated the practical wisdom of Grant's military policy." The fact that Grant was called on to secure the final settlement of April 26 only reinforced his image in the North as "The Capturer of Armies," to quote a *New York Times* article of May 5, 1865. Tracing Grant's chain of battlefield successes, the article credited him with bringing to heel the four great armies of "BUCKNER, PEMBERTON, LEE and JOHNSTON." "The whole South is now at his feet," it concluded, "its great armies 'melted into thin air.'" With the surrender of General Richard Taylor's army in Alabama on May 4, the capture of Jefferson Davis on May 10, and General Edmund Kirby Smith's capitulation in Texas on May 26, the last dominoes fell.[30]

For Northerners, then, Lincoln's death came in the midst of a prolonged moment of victory, and they cherished that moment, even as they mourned the martyred president. Their impulse to cling to Appomattox was rendered in powerful visual form by the North's preeminent political illustrator Thomas Nast. Nast, in the pages of the popular periodical *Harper's Weekly*, had advanced the cause of emancipation over the course of the war with illustrations pointedly depicting the evils of slavery, the righteousness of emancipation, and the treachery of antiwar Democrats. With the war over, he offered poignant testimony to its meaning in an illustration titled "Palm Sunday," published in the May 20, 1865, issue of *Harper's*. In two adjoined tableaux, he presented images of Christ's entry into Jerusalem and of Lee's surrender to Grant. The first image tapped the Northern public's association of Christ with Lincoln; this association, the historian Richard Nelson Current has written, "was everywhere at once, spontaneous, like an obvious truth." The adjoining image of Appomattox showed Grant holding out the hand of fellowship to Lee. But these images, in this case, did not speak for themselves. Nast anchored the insets with captions that explicitly spelled out the meaning of Grant's clemency. "We Hold Out the Olive Branch to Our Erring and Misguided Brethren of the Southern States, and Pledge to All of Them Who Are Loyal a Hearty Welcome to All the Benefits of a Free Republic," read one, stipulating that Southerners must repudiate their discredited doctrines to be welcomed back into the national fold. "Honor the Illustrious Dead. And Heartily Sympathize with the Sufferings of our Gallant Heroes and Their Families" read the other, reminding readers that the moral high ground was the province of the victors. In the bottom center of the image, heavenly hosts heralded the Union victory. To celebrate Appomattox was, for Northerners like Nast, to insist that Booth had ultimately failed: he could not undo the work of Lincoln and of Grant and of the Union army's gallant heroes.[31]

Northerners' determination to savor their victory was best dramatized by the Grand Review—the magnificent parade of Union soldiers, 150,000 strong, down Pennsylvania Avenue in Washington, D.C., on May 23 and 24. The Army of the Potomac was in the vanguard on the first day, while Sherman's armies were featured on the second; it took nearly seven hours on each day for the immense column of soldiers to cover the parade route. Gone was the mourning black that had bedecked the city after the assassination. Flags, banners, and bunting, in red, white and blue, again graced federal buildings and residences as they had on April 10. Added now to the kaleidoscope of colors were battle flags "thickly covered with names and dates of battle-fields where victories were won by these proud veterans," as one newspaper correspondent described it. "The flagstaffs were decorated with flowers, and very many bouquets hung from the muzzles

Thomas Nast's "Palm Sunday": reunion as vindication. (Library of Congress)

of muskets." The new president and his cabinet, along with Grant, Sherman, and an assemblage of other dignitaries, watched the proceedings from a reviewing stand near the executive mansion. An estimated 50,000 to 100,000 visitors thronged the capital to join the city's residents in witnessing the spectacle. "Packed several people deep along most of the route, the crowd included men and women, black and white, young and old—many dressed up as for a formal occasion," the historian Gary Gallagher has noted. To these spectators, the "marching men personified a diverse citizenry brought together in a mighty and successful enterprise."[32]

The marching men were awed by the scene. It was "the grandest sight I ever saw," wrote one veteran, Abial Hall Edwards of the 29th Maine, to his "dear friend" and future wife Anna Conant on May 26, 1865. Edwards was thrilled to get a "good view" of Johnson and Grant and to see the Capitol bedecked in a giant banner proclaiming, "The Only National Debt We Never Can Pay Is the Debt We Owe Our Brave Soldiers." "Our welcome will be long remembered," he added, for "every soldier there felt himself honored." In Edwards's view, the joyous events did not belong to Johnson, or to Grant and Sherman, or even to the Union veterans. "There was but

"Every soldier there felt himself honored": The Grand Review of May 1865. (Library of Congress)

one thing to mar our pleasure," he explained to Anna—"that was the thought that our beloved President A. Lincoln should have lived to see this which his hard work has done for us."[33]

For many Americans, the best way to honor Lincoln's victory in war was to defend his peace settlement. Most prominent among them was Grant, whom Lincoln had invited to join him that evening of April 14 at Ford's Theatre; Grant did not accept the invitation because he and his wife, Julia, had plans to visit their children in New Jersey. Grant learned of the assassination while stopping over in Philadelphia and quickly headed back to the capital. "It would be impossible for me to describe the feeling that overcame me," he would later write of the terrible moment, saying of Lincoln, "I knew his goodness of heart, his generosity, his yielding disposition, his desire to have everybody happy." Grant felt the peace—Lincoln's peace—was in danger. "I knew also the feeling that Mr. Johnson had expressed in speeches and conversation against the Southern people, and I feared that his course towards them would be such as to repel, and make them unwilling citizens; and if they became such they would remain so for a long while." Johnson would indeed betray Lincoln's legacy. But in April of 1865, Grant could not yet fathom the nature and scope of that betrayal.[34]

7

Defeat and Liberation

Northern civilians' reactions to the surrender paint a picture of a society deeply divided on the eve of Reconstruction. Southerners, too, were divided. Confederate civilians lionized Lee in defeat. They believed that he had commanded Grant's respect at Appomattox, and they embraced Lee's Farewell Address as an explanation for the Confederate army's demise. But they were less willing than Lee and his lieutenants to view the surrender terms as a sort of promissory note guaranteeing Northern leniency and less willing than the Southern rank and file to consider the possibility that the Confederate war effort had in any way fallen short. Engulfed in grief, Confederate civilians did not believe themselves to have been spared humiliation by Grant. Their reactions to Lincoln's assassination would reveal the depths of their bitterness.

If the Confederacy is not equated with the South, and the support of black Southerners and a significant minority number of white ones for the Union is taken into consideration, the question of "Southern" reactions to Appomattox becomes even more complex. White Southern Unionists considered Grant's victory their vindication, and they grappled with the question of how much magnanimity they could afford to show the traitors in their midst. Freedpeople, in their accounts of the surrender, elaborated the theme, so prominent in black veterans' accounts, of Appomattox as a freedom day. USCT soldiers provided the perspective of the liberators; former slaves testified to the experience of being liberated.

"Last night, (it seems strange that we have lived to speak or write of it,) between nine and ten o'clock, as some of the ladies of the house were

collected in our room, we were startled by the rapid firing of cannon,"
wrote Judith W. McGuire in her diary on April 10, 1865. McGuire was an
elite Virginian whose family had fled Union-occupied Alexandria, Virginia, early in the war and taken refuge in Richmond—only to face the
specter of occupation again, when the Confederate capital fell into Federal hands. The cascade of cannon fire she heard at first gave McGuire
hope—"bright thoughts of the return of our army darted through my
brain," she wrote—but she quickly realized that the firing she heard was
"too regular" to be the din of battle. "What do those guns mean?" she
called out to passers-by on the street. "A voice answered, as if from a broken heart: 'They say that General Lee has surrendered.'" The cannonade
was the "dreadful salute" of the Union army to Grant's victory.[1]

McGuire was incredulous. "We cannot believe it, but my heart became
dull and heavy, and every nerve and muscle of my frame seemed heavy
too." At daybreak on the morning of April 10 and at noon, Federal 100-
gun salutes again jarred McGuire's body and soul. Even then, she could
not bring herself to assimilate the grim news from Appomattox. She
remained in a state of agonized disbelief until Thursday, April 13, when,
finally, she accepted that the surrender was a fact not a rumor. That day,
she inscribed the words in her diary, "General Lee surrendered on Sunday
last, the 9th of April." Of the mood in Richmond, McGuire observed,
"The calmness of despair is written on every countenance." Countless
others in the Confederate capital were pitched into suspended animation
by the news of the surrender. Sallie Brock Putnam, a Richmond native of
the "genteel" class, recalled in her memoirs how the reverberations of
Yankee cannons announced Lee's defeat, leaving her fellow Richmonders
stunned: "In the speechless agony of woe, in the mute eloquence of
despair, we moved about, little more than breathing automatons, and were
slow to receive all the dreadful truth, and slower still to say: 'Thy will be
done, oh Lord!'"[2]

The dislocations of four years of grinding warfare left the Southern
press in shambles. Editors and printers had gone to serve in the army;
basic supplies, like paper and lead typefaces, had become prohibitively
expensive; distribution lines had been cut; and Yankee occupation had
shut down many Confederate newspapers. Thus news of the surrender
spread outward from Virginia and across the South in fits and starts.

Reaping the whirlwind: Richmond in ruins in the spring of 1865. (Library of Congress)

As McGuire and Putnam had, those in Union-occupied areas absorbed the shock of the surrender amidst the celebrations of the victorious occupiers. For James Rumley, a county clerk in Beaufort, North Carolina, the news from Appomattox was reported on April 12 by a Federal 100-gun salute at nearby Fort Macon—but he felt it was "too astounding to believe without confirmation." By April 14, he had come to accept the reality of Lee's defeat. His diary entry for that day noted that an illumination of the town had been ordered by the Federals to mark the surrender. "The friends of the Confederacy are pale with despair, and their countenances give 'signs of woe, that all is lost,'" Rumley wrote, quoting John Milton's *Paradise Lost*. As a general rule, those in the Upper South learned of Lee's capitulation before those in the Deep South did; newspapers in the cotton states typically did not announce Lee's surrender until the third week of April, and on the Confederacy's frontier periphery, in Texas, the news did not arrive until early May. But there were many exceptions to the rule: proximity to the Union army and to cities and towns, as well as access to telegraph and newspaper offices and to railway lines were all factors in how quickly Southerners heard the tidings from Appomattox.[3]

Though Confederate civilians learned of the surrender in a variety of ways, a clear pattern is evident in their written reactions. With near perfect unanimity, they insisted that Lee had achieved a moral victory in the face of defeat and that the North's overwhelming numbers and resources had decided the Confederacy's fate. It is fitting that one of the most cogent expressions of this view was penned by Robert E. Lee's wife, Mary Custis Lee. An April 23 letter to her cousin Mary Custis offered a heroic account of her husband's comportment at Appomattox:

> I want you all to know that when Gen'l Lee surrendered, he had only 8 thousand 7 hundred muskets; that the enemy by their own account had nearly 80 thousand men well provisioned & equipped, while ours had been out 7 days with only 2 days rations; that they were fighting by day & marching all night without even time to parch their corn, their only food for several days; that even in this exhausted state they drove back the hosts of the enemy, but could not follow up their advantage; that had Grant demanded *unconditional* surrender, they had determined to sell their lives as dearly as possible & cut their way thro' his encircling hosts; but the conditions he offered were so honorable, that Gen'l Lee decided it was wrong to sacrifice the lives of these brave men when no object would be gained by it. . . . The cruel policy of the enemy has accomplished its work too well. They have achieved by *starvation* what they could never win by their valor.[4]

In short, the bravery of Lee and his bereft, outnumbered men, in the face of Grant's teeming hosts, had won the Confederates an honorable surrender.

Such a view proved an irresistible consolation to Confederate civilians. Elite Southern women, who had the time, tools, and education to put their thoughts on paper, left behind an extensive record of their reactions to the surrender, a record that bespeaks their deep investment in the Confederate cause. Margaret Junkin Preston of Lexington, Virginia, the South's most eminent female poet, heard the news of the surrender on April 10. "We are struck dumb with astonishment!" she confided to her diary, adding the lament: "Why then all these four years of suffering—of separations—of horror—of blood—of havoc—of awful bereavement! Why these ruined homes—these broken family circles—these scenes of terror that must scathe the brain of those who witnessed them till their dying day!" She

answered these haunting questions in her postwar poetry, which emphasized the theme of honor in defeat. In her poem "Virginia Capta," published in 1866 but dated "April 9, 1865," Preston cast her native state as an
"unconquered captive" who must with "majestic, silent grace" maintain
her "regal bearing still." In a second poem on Confederate defeat, entitled
"Acceptation," Preston urged Southerners to take solace in a "proud consciousness of quenchless powers" and "a Past whose memory makes us
thrill." Lee, in Preston's view, embodied just such a spirit of acceptation; he
faced the "inevitable fiat of war with princely nobility, [and] with exalted
self-respect." When he yielded his sword, the "whole heart of the South
broke itself over him in love, pride, and benediction."[5]

Confederate civilians expressed their reverence for Lee in their accounts of the surrender scene, imagining it as an enactment of Lee's superiority to Grant. Emma Holmes, whose Charleston family had taken
refuge in Camden, South Carolina, learned of Lee's surrender on April 20.
In early May, she recorded in her diary this wishful account of Lee's
meeting with Grant and of the dialogue between the two men: "Gen. Lee
& his army were treated with greatest respect by the Yankees: Grant would
not receive his sword, saying Lee was too brave a man who had been overpowered by disparity of numbers, not conquered. He asked Lee how
many muskets all told he had had all winter around Petersburg & Richmond. 32,000 said Lee. If anyone else had told me so, rejoined Grant, I
would have said it was false, but it is *you* and I believe it. I had 120,000
infantry, 10,000 cavalry & 20,000 artillery." Her fantasy extended to the
soldiers on both sides. The Yankee officers, she wrote, cheered as loudly
for Lee as for Grant. Southern soldiers remained proudly defiant, and
Northern ones cowered before them: "Our men laid down their arms,
cursing their enemies from the depths of bitterly wrung hearts, to their
faces. The Yankees answered not a word, &, when they afterwards mingled
among our men, they did not even utter a single insulting word. They
feared the lion even in chains."[6]

Holmes's account closely mirrors one that circulated in Confederate
newspapers in late April, in which Grant says to Lee at the McLean house,
"Gen. Lee, keep that sword. You have won it by your gallantry. You have
not been whipped, but overpowered, and I cannot receive it as a token
of surrender from so brave a man." Just how overpowered? Southern

newspapers typically asserted that Lee's 8,000 effectives faced a Federal force of 200,000 men and they editorialized on the moral implications of that disparity. According to an April 26 piece in the *Edgefield Advertiser* of South Carolina, Lee "proved his lofty heroism and high moral courage by refusing to sacrifice [his men] to 200,000 butchers." The rumor mill churned out still higher estimates of Federal strength. Kate Cumming of Alabama, who had served the Confederate cause tirelessly as a hospital matron with the Army of Tennessee, estimated Grant's force at 250,000 in her diary entry of April 17, while Judith McGuire referred in her April 13 entry to how Grant's "hundreds of thousands" of men had overrun Lee's "little band." Grace Brown Elmore of South Carolina invoked that same image in her April 27 diary entry, stating that the "little band" had yielded to an army "twenty times" its size. Whatever the exact figure they offered, Confederate commentators asserted that Lee had confronted insurmountable odds, much worse than those he faced earlier in the war.[7]

Confederate civilians were more hesitant than soldiers to acknowledge the toll that desertion and straggling had taken on Lee's army or to consider the possibility that the army had lost its fighting spirit in the last days of the retreat. The April 7 diary entry of Mary Washington (Cabell) Early of Lynchburg reported the rumors that "demoralization, desertion & straggling" were "rife" among Lee's troops. But such rumors did not figure in her explanation for Confederate defeat. "Lee and his army have surrendered!!!!," she wrote on April 9. "Without provisions, without ammunition, hemmed in between Grant & Sherman, they could do nothing else." She praised the "firm & manly" comportment of the Southern troops and wrote of Lee: "Dear noble old man I love & revere him now more than ever." A few Confederate editors gave voice to the troubling charge that "the responsibility for the alarming desertion from Lee's army . . . rests mainly upon the people at home"—that despondency on the home front had sapped the morale of the soldiers—but such expressions of doubt were drowned out by the chorus of voices affirming that Lee and his men "had done all they could do to sustain the honor of their country," as the *Southern Watchman*, of Athens, Georgia, put it.[8]

References to the Yankees' overwhelming numbers were not new. The Southern press had featured the phrase in its coverage of the war since the spring of 1861. Early on, press reports denied that the Union would muster as many men as it hoped and denied that Yankee numbers would be decisive. But by the winter of 1862, Southern newspapers frequently professed anxiety about the "overwhelming numbers" of Federal troops and used such fears to motivate Southern enlistment. The onset of Grant's Overland campaign in the spring of 1864 sparked claims that the Union was determined to win through the exercise of brute force alone, and in the last year of the war the Southern press repeatedly insisted that Grant's way of war was fundamentally illegitimate; should the Confederates bow to his overwhelming numbers, there would be no shame in defeat. In short, Southern civilians had been primed to accept the idea that this was a war of might against right; Lee's Farewell Address sanctified that explanation for the South's defeat. "Not till we had seen General Lee's farewell to his army, printed on a slip from the *Danville Register* office, and read in household circles with tears and sobs—not till then did we finally and fairly give up the Southern cause, and feel that it was indeed lost" wrote Cornelia Phillips Spencer in her 1866 memoir of the war's denouement in North Carolina. Lee's address converted the theory that the Yankees' numbers and resources would prevail into a "dismal fact."[9]

When it came to assessing the surrender terms, unanimity among Confederates on the home front broke down. Some were hopeful that the terms would be the blueprint for a soft peace. For example, John B. Jones, a clerk in the Secretary of War's office in Richmond, speculated on April 11 that "from the tone of the leading Northern papers, we have reason to believe President Lincoln will call Congress together, and proclaim an amnesty." For many, the restoration of the Union on any terms—even one premised on Northern respect for Lee and his army—was simply unacceptable. While they attributed great dignity to Lee, Confederate civilians felt robbed by defeat of their own dignity. Their diaries and letters testify to the deep sense of humiliation they felt upon hearing of the surrender. Diarist Cornelia Peake McDonald, a refugee in Lexington, Virginia, wrote of how she and her family absorbed the news from Appomattox: "Grief and despair took possession of my heart, with a sense of humiliation that till then I did not know I could feel. The distress of the children was as great as mine; their poor little faces showed all the grief and shame that was in their hearts, and each went about sad and dejected as if it was a personal matter." As refugees and soldiers streamed back into the city, she observed that some were "happy at the thought of being released from danger, hunger, and weariness." "By far the greatest number, however," she added, "seemed to regard peace as a dire misfortune." Eliza Rhea Anderson Fain of East Tennessee watched as paroled soldiers returned to her home state in late April; a group of them left with her family a copy of Lee's Farewell Address, prompting Fain to observe in her diary that the noble Confederates were "overpowered but not defeated, . . . might for the time overpowering right." The soldiers' reports that they had been "treated respectfully by the Yankees since the surrender" could not dispel Fain's "fearful foreboding of evil" and her sense that the South could never again "link her political destiny" to the North.[10]

Confederate civilians were, on the whole, more distrustful than Confederate soldiers were of Grant's motives and intentions. Many regarded the conciliatory surrender terms as a transparent bid to lure Southerners into accepting renewed subjugation. Emma LeConte of Columbia, South Carolina, a fervent Confederate with a keen intellect and acid pen, wrote in her diary in late April, "I used to dream about peace, to pray for it, but this is worse than war. What is such peace to us? . . . It is too horrible. What I most fear is a conciliatory policy from the North, that they will offer to let us come back as before. Oh no, no! . . . Let them oppress and tyrannize, but let us take no favors of them." Sarah Fowler Morgan Dawson, who produced a massive diary of life in wartime Baton Rouge and New Orleans, was equally defiant. She learned of Lee's surrender on April 13. To those around her who seemed to welcome the return of "blessed Peace," she had this to say: "Never! Let a great earthquake swallow us up first! Let us leave our land and emigrate to any desert spot of the earth, rather than return to the Union, even as it Was!" Mary Early conceded that Grant's terms were "free & liberal" and that he had "treated Lee & his army with the utmost consideration." But the terms did nothing to reconcile her to the peace: "I believe I would rather have Virginia a French province than have her back in the Union," she wrote on April 17.[11]

Others feared that there would be no restoration because the Yankees were incapable of genuine magnanimity. Thomas S. Bocock of Appomattox County, Virginia, speaker of the house of the Confederate Congress, represented the views of such Southerners when he wrote of the surrender: "I trust very little to the clemency of our conquerors. They are bitter, intolerant, and exacting." Grace Elmore's diary entry on the surrender described the Yankees as a "faithless, avaricious, cruel and wicked people," whose hands were red with Southern blood and "hearts black with hatred." The hearts of defeated Southerners were, in her view, "boiling with rage." Confiding to her diary her heart's rage, Lucy Buck of Virginia's war-torn Shenandoah Valley wrote, "Our dearest hopes dashed—our fondest dreams dispelled—we and our brave ones who had struggled, bled and suffered—slaves and to such a tyrant."[12]

Newspaper commentary on the surrender terms ran the gamut from resignation to defiance and reflected the political fault lines within the Confederate South. Anti-administration Confederates—those who were critical of the Davis government's prosecution of the war, particularly of the conscription policy—had found a champion in North Carolina's William W. Holden, editor of the Raleigh newspaper the *North Carolina Standard*. Appealing to the war weariness of North Carolinians, Holden began arguing in 1863 that a negotiated peace could bring an honorable end to the grueling conflict and restore the key elements of the old order: peace would preserve the slave system, while a prolongation of the war would surely obliterate what remained of it. He lost his bid to capture the governor's chair as leader of a Peace Party in 1864 to another vociferous critic of Davis's, Zebulon Vance, who "steadfastly vowed to fight the war to its conclusion." Holden experienced Lee's surrender as a kind of bittersweet vindication, and he urged his fellow Southerners to accept Grant's terms as the means to effect restoration. The April 27, 1865, issue of the *North Carolina Standard* expressed Holden's hope that "every thoughtful and reasonable war man" would follow Lee's example and deem further resistance to the Yankees to be futile: "In the name of God and humanity let the conflict cease, and let the bow of reconciliation, now spanning the heavens, be regarded as a sign of endless peace and brotherhood."[13]

On the other end of the spectrum of Confederate opinion, historian Andrew Coopersmith has noted in his study of the Civil War press, were newspapers in Texas. That state had been "spared the devastation suffered by other states in the Confederacy" and "responded to the loss of Lee's army with a virulent determination to fill the breach." Thus the *Houston Tri-Weekly Telegraph*, announcing on May 10 that "disaster" had struck the

Army of Northern Virginia and that Lee was a "prisoner of war," editorialized that there was "no reason for yielding, even to a momentary panic, still less for giving way to manly despair." Texas might still "redeem the cause of the Confederacy from its present perils."[14]

In between these extremes were Southern newspapers, scattered across the region, which registered first disbelief and then defiance in more glum and tentative tones. For most Southern editors, neither the image of peaceful restoration nor that of heroic redemption rang true. So they worked with what they had: they reprinted Lee's correspondence with Grant and his Farewell Address; invoked the mysterious workings of Providence; conjured the impossible odds Confederates had faced; and expressed inchoate longings for an elusive victory that was, somehow, still possible. In this spirit, the *Augusta Constitutionalist* vowed on April 21 that the gloomy news from Appomattox did not necessitate "the folding of the hands of the people in mute despair" but should instead nerve Southerners to "more determined and united action." An editorial on Lee's surrender in the *Edgefield Advertiser* (South Carolina), entitled "Chaos," captured both the uncertainty of the moment and the depth of Confederate civilians' will to believe. "What is to be done? We know not. But let our people dismiss the idea that we are going to pass under the Yankee yoke. Nothing of the sort is going to take place." The Almighty would make things right: "Man's extremity is God's opportunity."[15]

Even as Confederates groped through the chaos of defeat, anti-Confederate Southerners claimed Grant's victory, and God's favor, as their own. In Union-occupied Little Rock, Arkansas, the seat of a loyalist legislature pursuing Reconstruction under Lincoln's Ten Percent Plan, the announcement of Lee's surrender brought a "storm of applause" in the State House and touched off "days of hilarious rejoicing" among the town's Unionists. In Union-occupied Nashville, Tennessee, newly elected Governor William G. Brownlow, long the voice of loyalists in his state, marked the surrender by issuing a proclamation that designated May 4 as a day of "thanksgiving prayer to Almighty God." In his capacity as editor of the *Knoxville Whig and Rebel Ventilator*, he rejoiced that the "greatest army and General of the so-called Confederacy" had been "defeated and scattered" and made to surrender to Grant "upon his own terms." He attributed the Union victory to the blessings of Providence and to the "devotion" of Grant's officers and men. In Loudoun County, in northern Virginia, Quaker minister Samuel M. Janney "received the gratifying intelligence of Lee's surrender" and rejoiced at the "termination of this desolating and destructive war, caused by the love of power and gain on the part of slaveholders." Speaking on behalf of the "loyal citizens" of Virginia, Janney wrote, "Our emotions cannot be expressed, but will be remembered by us as long as memory endures."[16]

While such testimony abounds, the extent of Southern Unionism has proven difficult for scholars to measure. At issue is the sometimes tenuous distinction between anti-administration Southerners, who registered protests of one kind or another against the way the Confederate government conducted the war, and true Unionists, who worked for and welcomed Northern victory. Northerners had hoped that the great mass of Southern whites who did not own slaves might be induced—by their resentments of the slaveholding elite, by the Union's show of might, and by war weariness—to furnish legions of converts to the free soil creed. But that hope had run aground. Confederate nationalism proved powerful and resilient, both among those who embraced secession enthusiastically and among those who accepted it reluctantly. To be sure, disillusionment and dissent took a toll on the Confederate war effort—most clearly measurable in the rates of desertion—but as historian Aaron Sheehan-Dean has noted, expressions of discontent by white Southerners did not translate into a wholesale repudiation of the Confederacy or an embrace of the Union. Instead, "Confederate identity, like that in most fledgling nations, drew great strength from its opposition to the North, and the people who built that identity drew effectively on their rivalry with the Union to mask internal dissent and conflict." Close to 15 percent of Confederate soldiers deserted—meaning that roughly 85 percent did not. War weariness did not yield significant Unionism.[17]

Lincoln's own Ten Percent Plan for Reconstruction, in which a loyal core of 10 percent of the electorate would reconstitute the Southern state governments, had represented an implicit admission that only a small number of Southern whites could be induced to pledge allegiance to the Union; even so, Radical Republicans charged, as part of their critique of the plan, that opportunistic Confederates would find it all too easy to pose as loyal Unionists in order to regain power. Indeed, opportunism could serve as a survival strategy. White Southerners sometimes professed Unionism and masked their Confederate loyalty in order to coexist with the occupying army. As historian Judkin Browning has put it, "Many of those who did profess Union sentiments believed in a conditional form of Unionism; this is, they would be Unionists provided that they were returning to the Union of 1860."[18]

However murky the line between dissent, opportunism, and true loyalty could be, it is clear that "unconditional" Unionists—those Southerners who had never accepted secession and never renounced the United States—lent decisive aid to the Union war effort. In *The South vs. the South*, historian William Freehling has shown that the slave states furnished 450,000 troops to the Union army: 200,000 came from the border South states (Kentucky, Maryland, Delaware, and Missouri) that had not seceded; 150,000 were African Americans, predominantly former slaves; and 100,000 were whites from the Confederate states. African American resistance to the Confederacy was the beating heart of Southern Unionism; slaves fled farms and plantations by the hundreds of thousands to seek refuge with the Union army and contributed to the Union victory not only as soldiers but also as nurses, spies, scouts, teachers, and day laborers. For them, the Union's success at arms was synonymous with freedom. The motivations of white Southern "unconditional" Unionists were so varied as to defy generalization. Some had Northern roots or family ties to the North, but most did not; many advocated the economic development of the South, along the lines proposed by the Whig Party, but some (such as Andrew Johnson) were Jacksonian Democrats; many were antislaveholder rather than antislavery and resented the political power of the secessionist elite, but some actively supported abolition. Strong pockets of Unionism were found in the mountainous, "upcountry" regions of the South, where plantation slavery had not firmly taken root, such as East Tennessee, the stomping grounds of Brownlow. Unionist "undergrounds" persisted even in Confederate strongholds such as Atlanta; indeed, a Richmond espionage cell, led by spymaster Elizabeth Van Lew, furnished Grant with vital military intelligence in the last year of the war.[19]

For unconditional Unionists (and for some erstwhile ones, too), Grant's was an army of "deliverers," as Van Lew put it, effecting the liberation of the South from the secessionists' tyranny. But there were divisions within the Unionist ranks over the issue of clemency and punishment. Conservative loyalists from the South's social elite, who were tied by kinship and commerce with Confederate leaders, "sought to minimize the war's permanent impact on patterns of power and wealth," Robert Tracy McKenzie, author of a study of wartime Knoxville, Tennessee, has argued. Unionists of a more populist bent, such as Brownlow, called for the harsh proscription, including the disfranchisement and confiscation of property, of leading secessionists, as a way of leveling the invidious social distinctions of the slave system. In Brownlow's view, true Unionism was restricted to the white laboring classes, who had suffered under the slaveholders' regime.[20]

Not all white Unionists saw things this way. In Van Lew's eyes, those who risked the most for the Union victory and yearned the most for liberation were the slaves. With the fall of the Confederacy, "the chains, the shackles fell from thousands of captives, and thousands of arms fell powerless to wield the Christianizing lash. Civilization advanced a century. Justice, truth, humanity were vindicated," Van Lew wrote in April 1865. Just what the moment of deliverance meant, the slaves "feel but cannot tell you," she continued. "When eternity shall unknot the records of time, you will see written for them by the Almighty their unpenned stories, then to be read before a listening universe."[21]

Southern blacks celebrated Lee's surrender as a day of jubilee: with the most powerful Confederate army defeated and the slaveholders' republic in ruins, slaves could finally realize the promise of the 1863 Emancipation Proclamation. They knew implicitly that emancipation was not a moment but a process and that its consummation depended on the success of the Union army. Confederate victories kept freedom at bay; Union ones inexorably eroded the power of slaveholders and brought freedom into view.[22]

Because of white scrutiny, material deprivation, and Southern laws criminalizing black literacy, slaves could not record and leave behind "in the moment" literary accounts of the surrender as whites did. So postwar memoirs and interviews conducted with former slaves during the New Deal serve as a window into how African Americans in the South interpreted Appomattox. Virginia slaves were the first to hear the tidings of the surrender and to fathom the significance of the event. The Reverend Peter Randolph's memoir *From Slave Cabin to Pulpit* described Lee's surrender as the day on which the slaves in his native Virginia became free; by congregating where Union soldiers were quartered, he observed, these slaves could at last "see what freedom meant." Booker T. Washington, in his classic autobiography *Up From Slavery*, remembers how "when the war closed, the day of freedom came" to southwestern Virginia; the sight of Confederate soldiers who had deserted Lee's army or been paroled by Grant dramatized for the slaves—as much as a U.S. officer's belated reading of the Emancipation Proclamation did—that the April surrender brought the long-awaited moment of deliverance.[23]

Samuel Spottford Clement was a slave on a Southside, Virginia, farm, close enough to Appomattox to hear the "boom of the cannon and the crack of the musketry" from the fighting on April 8. "The old field hands

"The day of freedom came": Booker T. Washington. (Library of Congress)

prayed in concert that the Yankees might win the fight," he recalled in memoirs. On April 12, Clement's master, a Mr. Ward, ordered the slaves to gather together and then solemnly informed them of their freedom. Ward raised a newspaper to his face and read: "General Lee to-day has surrendered to General Grant. General Grant had six months rations while General Lee had only three day's rations for his starving troops. So the Southern Confederacy is now at an end and all negroes are free." Ward's wife stood by his side, crying. Such scenes, repeated again and again in the aftermath of Appomattox, were profoundly embittering for Southern slaveholders, who regarded the surrender as the omen of a long-dreaded social revolution. Henri Garidel, who had fled Union-occupied New Orleans in 1863 and taken a post as a War Department clerk in Richmond, learned of Lee's capitulation from the Federal 100-gun salutes and from the "shouts of joy of the Negroes," which made "Richmond tremble as much as the cannons." The surrender brought a new order. "The Negroes are refusing to work," he despondently observed in his diary on April 11. As Letitia Burwell, an elite white Virginian, wrote in her memoir of plantation life, with "the surrender at Appomattox, . . . negro slavery ended forever." "All was ruin around us," she continued. "Tobacco factories burned down, sugar and cotton plantations [were] destroyed. The negroes fled from these desolated places." In the eyes of Confederates, the advent of emancipation compounded the abject misery of defeat.[24]

Federal Writers' Project interviews echo the published reminiscences of African Americans who were slaves in Virginia. Charley Mitchell, remembering his boyhood in Lynchburg, told an interviewer in 1937 that after the surrender slaves in the area were summoned to the city's fairgrounds to hear the news of their emancipation announced. Joseph Holmes recalled seeing General Grant's legions on the march though the Virginia countryside; after the Yankees came through, and after "de Surrender," Holmes's mistress told him he was free. William Harrison, a native of Richmond, got an early taste of war when his master enlisted in the Confederate army and brought Harrison along with him as his body servant; after the master was captured at Bull's Gap, Tennessee, in November of 1864, Harrison joined the Union army. More than 100 years old at the time of his WPA interview, he recalled his service as a USCT soldier, "I was with General Grant when Lee surrendered at Appomattox. That was freedom." Fanny Berry, for her part, remembered that slaves in Pamplin (Appomattox County), Virginia, burst into spontaneous song when they learned that Lee, his escape blocked by the USCT, had raised the white flag—for they at that moment "knew dat dey were free."[25]

As news of the surrender traveled throughout the South, slaves far away from the events at Appomattox, too, experienced Grant's final triumph as the end of their enslavement. Wesley John Gaines, in his 1897 book *The Negro and the White Man*, describes the "beautiful and enrapturing" moment when he "heard the first tidings proclaiming liberty to the captive":

> I was ploughing in the fields of Southern Georgia. The whole universe seemed to be exulting in the unrestraint of the liberty wherewith God has made all things free, save my bound and fettered soul, which dared not claim its birthright and kinship with God's world of freedom. . . . Suddenly the news was announced that the war had ended and that slavery was dead. The last battle had been fought, and the tragedy that closed at Appomattox had left the tyrant who had reigned for centuries slain upon the gory field. In a moment the pent-up tears flooded my cheeks and the psalm of thanksgiving arose to my lips. 'I am free,' I cried. . . . Oh! The rapture of that hour![26]

Ruby Lorraine Radford, who interviewed 30 Georgia slaves for the Federal Writers' Project, concluded that "although the Emancipation Proclamation was delivered on January 1st, 1863, it was not until Lee's final surrender that most of the negroes knew they were free." This was a recurring theme in former slaves' reminiscences. For example, James H. Johnson of South Carolina lamented that after "President Lincoln's freedom proclamation in 1863," the "status quo of slavery kept right on as it had." It was only when "General Lee surrendered," he observed in his WPA interview, that "we learned we were free."[27]

For some former slaves, the date of Lee's surrender structured their very sense of time and of history. Eliza Washington told her WPA interviewer, S. S. Taylor, "The first thing I remember was living with my mother about six miles from Scott's Crossing in Arkansas, about the year 1866. I know it was 1866 because it was the year after the surrender, and we know the surrender was in 1865. I know the dates after 1866. You don't know nothin' when you don't know dates." For Della Harris of Petersburg, too, the passage of time came into focus in 1865. "I don't know just how old I is," she told Susie Byrd in 1937. But Harris remembered with certainty: "I was 13 years old at de time of Lee's surrender." Among the earliest memories of Easter Jones of Georgia was that her brother was born the Sunday that Lee surrendered and that he was named, after the fallen Confederate capital, Richmond. Fannie Dorum of Arkansas, 94 years old when she was interviewed, began by observing that "I was here in slavery time. The third year of the surrender (1868), I married—married Burton Dorum"; for Dorum, the surrender brought the consciousness and the prerogatives, such as legal marriage, of freedom. When Lucy Redman Crawford turned 100 years of age in 1939, the *Pittsburgh Courier* featured a story explaining how she had endured slavery in Virginia and built a new life in the North. "Her mind is clear and she has a very retentive memory," the reporter noted, adding that she dated almost every milestone in her life from the time of the surrender.[28]

Just as Appomattox persisted in the memory of many ex-slaves, it was an enduring presence on the commemorative calendar of the freedpeople. The same premise that underlay the reminiscences—that Lee's surrender fulfilled the promise of Lincoln's proclamation—animated the anniversary celebrations. "Surrender Day" festivities began in southern Virginia as early as 1866. Blacks in Mecklenburg County, on the border with North Carolina, commemorated April 9 because, as they saw it, "If Lee had never been beaten . . . the [emancipation] proclamation would have been to no avail."[29]

Black remembrance of Appomattox as a freedom day incorporated the theme of magnanimity as well as of liberation. Judging by the WPA interviews, it was not just the Union victory that gave the moment lasting resonance but also the comportment of Lee and Grant. Eliza Washington remembered that "General Lee said there wasn't any use doing any more fighting," while "General Grant let all the rebels keep their guns. He didn't take nothin' away from them." Ellis Bennett noted that Lee's surrender came with the promise that "he warn't takin up no arm gainst 'is country no mo." In Cornelius Garner's vivid account, "Grant had Lee all bottled up. Lee couldn' go back, he couldn' go forward, an' he couldn' go sideways.

Grant gave him five minutes to surrender. He surrendered too." Grant, Garner noted, made only one demand of the defeated rebels: that they go home and be "good citizens."[30]

For Southern Unionists, the assassination of Lincoln was irrevocable proof of the rebels' incapacity for citizenship and of the need to place political power in the reconstructed South firmly in the hands of those who had kept faith with the United States all along. Amherst Stone, a transplanted Vermonter who had been an anchor of Atlanta's Unionist underground, delivered a memorial address for Lincoln in Union-occupied Savannah on April 22. Blaming the leadership of the Confederacy for the assassination, he insisted that henceforth "magnanimity would have to be earned." "No indefinite negative love of the government will do," he proclaimed, chiding those white Southerners who might dare to posture as loyal. "It must be earnest and sincere; and if there are those who hate the Government, I would advise them to seek some other country more congenial to their own feelings." In Tennessee, William G. Brownlow editorialized in his newspaper that there were "tens of thousands in the South" who had the "heart and will" to commit assassination. "History will look in vain for such a causeless rebellion, and yet one in which the actors were animated by such bitter and murderous passions," he declared, with a warning— "That spirit moves them still."[31]

There is ample evidence of such a bitter spirit in Southern civilians' commentary on the assassination. Emma LeConte began her diary entry for April 21 by exclaiming, "Hurrah! Old Abe Lincoln has been assassinated!" "It may be abstractly wrong to be so jubilant," she continued, "but I just can't help it. . . . Our hated enemy has met the just reward of his life." Mary Chesnut, the elite South Carolinian who kept the war's most extensive diary of life on the home front, declared on April 22: "The death of Lincoln I call a warning to tyrants." That same day, Charlotte S. J. Ravenel, another South Carolinian diarist, wrote, "Today's news is very cheering; it is that both Lincoln and Seward have been assassinated." Caroline Jones of Augusta, Georgia, too, took comfort from the assassination: thanks to Booth's deed, Lincoln could not "raise his diabolical howl of triumph" over the South. Looking back at this moment in his memoir, John S. Wise, the Confederate lieutenant who had carried the news of Lee's surrender to

Jefferson Davis, confessed that Booth's act was regarded by Confederates as "a sort of retributive justice":

> For four years we had been fighting. In that struggle, all we loved had been lost. Lincoln incarnated to us the idea of oppression and conquest. We had seen his face over the coffins of our brothers and relatives and friends, in the flames of Richmond, in the disaster at Appomattox. . . . We were desperate and vindictive, and whosoever denies it forgets or is false. We greeted his death in a spirit of reckless hate, and hailed it as bringing agony and bitterness to those who were the cause of our own agony and bitterness. To us, Lincoln was an inhuman monster, Grant a butcher, and Sherman a fiend.[32]

For many Southerners, this spirit of reckless hate soon gave way to the sober realization that Lincoln's assassination would call forth from Northerners their own brand of retributive justice. When Cornelia McDonald first heard of Lincoln's death, she thought "it was just what he deserved." But a "little reflection" made her see that the assassination was a calamity. "Now no mercy was to be expected from a nation of infuriated fanatics whose idol of clay had been cast down." Mary Chesnut drew the same conclusion: the assassination would bring upon the South "worse miseries." Such an assessment rested on the widely held view that Andrew Johnson was a man primed to lash out against defeated Confederates; as the *Shreveport News* put it, Lincoln, though a "despicable despot," was "without any doubt, a much better man than the one who has succeeded him in the Presidential chair of the United States."[33]

Some Southern newspapers were reticent on the subject of the assassination, as they operated in the shadow of the Union conquest. But Texas papers, Coopersmith has reported, openly gloried in Lincoln's death and cast Booth as a hero. The *Houston Tri-Weekly Telegraph*, for example, argued that Lincoln's purported magnanimity had been conditioned on Southerners' willingness to bend, meekly and submissively, before the North. Booth was to be hailed for bravely rejecting such a fate: "Let despotism and whoever may be its minions beware the deserved fate of tyrants," the paper offered as an epigram for the assassination. Keenly

aware of the political danger in such a position, anti-administration Confederates who had argued for a negotiated peace distanced themselves
from Booth and from his defenders; the *North Carolina Standard*, for example, expressed its "profound grief" at the assassination and its hope for
continued mercy: "We pray God that [Lincoln's] untimely and cruel death
may not add to the miseries of our afflicted State."[34]

Whatever their political calculations, Confederates could not easily
dispel the lingering sense that assassination was beyond the pale of human
civilization, of the laws of war, and of Southern honor. The *Shreveport
News* editorialized that had Lincoln died while the war was raging, and by
any means other than assassination, Southerners could have rightfully
rejoiced. But "feelings and principles revolt alike," it insisted, at so "infamous and cowardly" a crime as Booth's. Sarah Morgan of Baton Rouge
put it most poignantly. She shuddered "with horror, wonder, pity and
fear" at the news of the assassination and at her own temptation to be
"grateful for a fellow-creature's death." Booth's deed raised a terrible question: "Where does patriotism end, and murder begin?" Morgan knew implicitly that the South's fate hinged on how President Andrew Johnson
and his government answered the question of whether the likes of Davis
and Lee would be classed with Booth as criminals.[35]

Andrew Johnson's handling of the dispute over Sherman's armistice
with Joe Johnston was a discouraging sign. In rejecting Sherman's terms
and insisting on the application of Grant's, the new president seemed to
signal that there would be no ready restoration of political rights to Southerners. An editorial on the Johnston surrender in the *Nashville Daily Union*
asked, "Now that adversity has overtaken the South; now that we have
become a people overpowered in a contest long, bloody, and fearful . . .
what becomes our duty?" Would Southerners "yield to despair?" The
writer answered an emphatic "No!" Southerners would accept defeat but
not a verdict of guilt: "Nothing have we to paliate or deny," the writer
insisted, and "nothing to beseech mercy for."[36]

This was the conviction at the heart of the most popular literary artifact
of Appomattox among Confederates, Abraham Joseph Ryan's poem "The
Conquered Banner." Ryan was a native of Maryland, where his father had
worked as a plantation overseer. A devout Catholic and ardent supporter
of slavery and Southern rights, Ryan cultivated a career as a priest and

poet; after sojourns in hostile territory, in New York, Missouri, and Illi-nois, he finally settled, in 1863, in Tennessee, where he served as an itin-erant chaplain, bringing "spiritual solace" to that embattled state's "increasingly war-weary soldiers and citizens."

He would later recall the moment at which he wrote his most famous poem:

> It was night when news of the surrender of Lee came. I was in my room in a house where many of the regiment of which I was chap-lain were quartered, when an old comrade came to me and said: "All is lost—General Lee has surrendered." I knew by his whit-ened face that the news was true. Then a thousand thoughts came rushing through my brain. That banner was conquered, but the story must be told. . . . I looked around for a piece of paper to give expression to the thoughts that cried out within me. All I could find was a piece of wrapping paper. . . . I seized this piece of paper and wrote "The Conquered Banner."[37]

Ryan's poem captured perfectly the profound sadness and exhaustion that overwhelmed Confederates as they realized that the cause was lost; it captured too their conviction that Lee had, in the end, no choice but to surrender. It begins:

> Furl that Banner, for 'tis weary;
> Round its staff 'tis drooping dreary;
>   Furl it, fold it—it is best;
> For there's not a man to wave it,
> And there's not a sword to save it,
> And there's no one left to lave it
> In the blood which heroes gave it;
> And its foes now scorn and brave it;
>   Furl it, hide it—let it rest!

After developing this theme for three more stanzas, Ryan then shifts to sacralizing the Confederate flag as the enduring symbol of Southern ideals and calls on Southerners to proclaim and perpetuate those ideals:

For, though conquered, they adore it—
Love the cold, dead hands that bore it!
Weep for those who fell before it!
Pardon those who trail and tore it,
    Now who furl and fold it so!

Furl that Banner! True, 'tis gory,
Yet 'tis wreathed around with glory,
And 'twill live in song and story
    Though its folds are in the dust!
For its fame on brightest pages,
Penned by poets and by sages,
Shall go sounding down the ages—
    Furl its folds though now we must.

Ryan's modern biographers have analyzed how the poem's word choice and metrical structure echo both Ralph Waldo Emerson's 1837 "Concord Hymn" and Edgar Allan Poe's "The Raven" (1850), and how it likens, in images that would have resonated powerfully with Ryan's readers, the Confederate banner to the body of Christ. The poem, scholars Donald Robert Beagle and Bryan Albin Giezma have observed, doubled as a Christian hymn. "The Conquered Banner" suggested that "there will be a redemption" for Confederates.[38]

Published in June in 1865 under the penname "Moina," the poem "swiftly penetrated popular consciousness across the South." It rivaled Lee's Farewell Address as the supreme expression of the idea that Confederates, even in defeat, occupied the moral high ground and had no cause for shame and nothing to atone for. Revealingly, the poem initially appeared not in a Southern newspaper or journal, but in the New York *Freeman's Journal and Catholic Register*, one of the most incendiary anti-abolition Copperhead papers in the North. Ryan had come across the paper while he was a seminary student in upstate New York and found in its editor, James McMaster, a journalistic mentor. In 1866, McMaster would republish "The Conquered Banner" over Ryan's name.[39]

The fact that a Northern newspaper published "The Conquered Banner" serves as a stark reminder that the battle over the meaning of Appomattox

The promise of redemption: Father Abraham Joseph Ryan's "The Conquered Banner." (Library of Congress)

did not simply pit South against North or even Confederacy against Union. Instead it pitted those who opposed a thoroughgoing transformation of the South (diehard Confederates and white Northern Democratic Confederate sympathizers) against those who demanded such a transformation (Northern Republicans and Southern Unionists, black and white). Within these camps, fierce debates had already taken shape, in the month after the surrender, over what sort of changes—social, political, and moral—might come to the South. Between these two camps were countless Northerners and Southerners who were neutral, agnostic, or undecided on the issue of Reconstruction and who could not discern in the surrender a clear road map for the future.

There had been no moment, however brief, in which Southerners had mourned, in unison, for their lost cause, and no moment in which Northerners had, in unison, rejoiced. Nor was there any moment of shared reconciliation or of agreement to bury the hatchet. As the spring of 1865 turned to summer, Americans, in their joy and grief, regret and exultation, uncertainty and confusion, looked to their leaders for guidance. They looked to the new president, Andrew Johnson. But they looked also to Lee and to Grant to explain what the surrender meant. The heroes of Appomattox would now be drawn, reluctantly, into the vortex of postwar politics.

PART THREE

AFTERMATH

The Trials of Robert E. Lee

"The people look first to you in their trying difficulties—no one has their confidence as you have. Your counsel would produce an effect like that of oil on troubled waters." So wrote General Richard S. Ewell, formerly commander of the Second Corps of the Army of Northern Virginia, to Robert E. Lee on April 17, 1865. Ewell was a prisoner of war, en route to Fort Warren in Boston Harbor: he had fallen into Federal hands at Sailor's Creek and was therefore unable to claim the probationary freedom that came with an Appomattox parole. He would spend the spring and summer lobbying the Federal authorities, with the help of his formidable wife, Lizinka, for his release on the grounds that he was ready—and indeed had been for some time—to accept Confederate defeat and pledge allegiance to the victorious Union. Finally in July of 1865, Ewell was paroled, by President Andrew Johnson, and headed south to settle on his wife's farmlands in Tennessee.[1]

In the immediate aftermath of the surrender and assassination, Ewell sought, in reaching out to Lee, both to ascertain the General's views and to influence them. He laid out the abject situation of his and Lee's native Virginia: the state was "overwhelmed by the vast power & resources of the US government after having borne the brunt of a war, not of her own seeking"; her landscape was ravaged by the "repeated tread of hostile armies." What were defeated Southerners to do? Ewell's advice for Lee was this: "It ought to be recommended to them to accept the past, to make the best of the present, & future, & to yield quietly and with dignity to the U.S. authorities."[2]

Lee has enjoyed a modern-day reputation for exerting precisely the kind of leadership that Ewell urged on him: for counseling Southerners, by deed and word, to "accept the situation."[3] But to attribute to Lee a posture of dignified resignation is to miss the nuances and dissonance in his postwar exercise of leadership. In the year after the surrender, Lee was not unanimously regarded, in the North or South, as a symbol of reunion or a model of resignation. Instead, he was a profoundly polarizing figure. Defeat was an ongoing trial for Lee—and the public was determined to make him the test case in the difficult project of determining whether Confederates could bring themselves to embrace the victorious Union.

Heading east from Appomattox, Lee entered Richmond, accompanied by five members of his staff, on April 15. As he approached his family residence on East Franklin Street between 7th and 8th streets, a "great crowd rushed to see him, and set up a loud cheering, to which he replied simply by raising his hat." Lee obliged the crowd by shaking some hands and then he slipped into his house "as quietly and unostentatiously as possible."[4]

Over the next few weeks, Lee and his family jealously guarded his privacy. But Lee did choose, on two occasions that April, to drop this reserve and present himself, as it were, to the public. The photographer Mathew Brady, during the same Richmond visit during which he had photographed General Ord with a table from the McLean house, called on Lee and persuaded him to pose, in his uniform, for a series of photographs. Brady would later claim that the two men were already acquainted, having met during the Mexican War; whether that was true, Lee surely knew that Brady was the nation's most celebrated photographer. According to Brady, Lee received him with the "utmost affability and cordiality of manner."[5]

The photographs taken on April 20 are among the most revealing portraits of Lee. Brady took six different negatives of the General, posed at the back door of his Richmond home. Two of the negatives feature Lee's son, General Custis Lee, and trusted aide, Colonel Walter Taylor, at his side. In the other images, Lee is alone. The photographs allow many different readings. Some see defiance blazing in Lee's eyes, particularly in the images of him standing, his gaze directed right at the camera. But it might also be said that those eyes convey, more than anything, his profound exhaustion. The images of Lee sitting, his face in profile, perhaps capture a tinge of vanity—understandable in a man whom contemporaries had described as a near perfect specimen of male beauty.[6]

Lee, photographed by Mathew Brady, in the aftermath of defeat. (Library of Congress)

The Southern press pronounced the photographs "admirable," to quote the *Richmond Whig*. But some Northern commentators, when they learned that Lee had sat for a series of pictures, mocked the entire exercise as unseemly and even pathetic. Thus the *Providence Journal* (Rhode Island) in late April offered a bitingly satiric account of the Brady session, suggesting that each of Lee's six poses represented a phase of Lee's wartime treachery. First Lee had posed in a "meditative" mood—recalling his attitude as he contemplated resigning from the U.S. army in April of 1861. Next he posed in a "sneaking mood," slinking, in ignominy, away from Washington, D.C., toward the Confederate capital in Richmond; then he adopted a "dignified attitude," receiving his commission as a rebel general. Fourth, Lee was photographed in a "chivalric mood," the article noted with caustic sarcasm, signifying how he stood by while Union prisoners starved in notorious Confederate prison camps. Next Lee posed in "sub-mission," recalling his posture before Grant at Appomattox. Finally, Lee posed in triumph, reflecting on the hero's welcome he received as he entered Richmond after the surrender. The message of the parody, which was reprinted in newspapers across New England, was clear: Lee was a guilty, unrepentant traitor, dangerous still, and certainly not the image of Southern chivalry or resignation.[7]

Lee's second effort to publicly define his postwar image proved even more controversial than his photo session with Brady. On April 24, 1865, Lee agreed to be interviewed by a reporter, Thomas M. Cook, for the *New York Herald*, a pro-war Democrat paper that endorsed Grant's terms and a cautious approach to Reconstruction. In the ensuing newspaper article, published in the *Herald* on April 29 under the heading "The Rebellion: View of Genl. Robert E. Lee," Cook would claim that he was motivated to meet with Lee by the "new complications growing out of the murder of President Lincoln." Regarding what Southern leaders thought of Booth's terrible deed, Lee told Cook what many Northerners, eager to uphold a policy of magnanimity, wanted to hear: he viewed the assassination as a deplorable crime, "beyond execration." To Cook's palpable surprise, Lee proved willing to address a broad range of other topics, from secession to emancipation to the recent surrender itself.[8]

Cook's lengthy account of the interview begins on a deferential note. He describes Lee as the very image of the chivalry, the "nobility" even, of elite Virginians. Cook found that the "vigor and animation and ability of ripe manhood" were "prominently conspicuous" in Lee's bearing; the general in no way conveyed "an impression of decay or old age." Cook confessed at the outset that he intended to present Lee's "political views" to the public. Lee at first demurred—"I am a paroled prisoner," he told Cook, not a politician. But when prompted by Cook, Lee was expansive in his answers. Cook began by asking about secession and about Lee's famous pledge, from the eve of the war, that save in defense of his native state, Lee would never again raise his sword. Lee obligingly portrayed himself to Cook as a reluctant secessionist—someone who clung to the Union until secession was a fait accompli and then chose the Confederacy because his state allegiance to Virginia demanded that he do so. This image of Lee accords well with what we know from other sources: Lee had indeed agonized over secession and his dilemma had played out, in the spring of 1861, as a public drama, with Unionists and secessionists alike courting him—and secessionists winning him over, in the eleventh hour.[9]

Cook then turned to the subject of the surrender and the peace. Lee claimed, according to Cook, that the South had long been anxious for peace and had waited only for "some word or expression of compromise or conciliation from the North." The demise of slavery was no obstacle to peace, as the "best men" of the South had "long been anxious" to do away with the peculiar institution and fully accepted the reality of emancipation. In a move that struck Cook as bizarre, Lee volunteered the following observation: "The South was never more than half in earnest in this war." Cook was at a loss to "translate this remark or elucidate it." He nonetheless tried. Perhaps Lee meant that the South was "most heartily sick of the war, and anxious to get back to the Union and to peace." Southerners had, Cook went on in his gloss on Lee's comment, left the Union in a "moment of passion" but had now come to their senses. Indeed for Cook, the most striking feature of his conversation with Lee was that the rebel General, "strange as it may appear, talked throughout as a citizen of the United States." Lee "frequently alluded to the country, and expressed most earnestly his solicitude for its restoration to peace and tranquility."[10]

What can be made of this? How reliable an interlocutor was Cook? It may well be that Cook, in this portion of the interview, heard what he wanted to hear. He confesses in his published account that he at times relied on "inference" to make sense of the conversation—and many Northerners were eager to infer that Southerners were anxious for peace. What of Lee? Could he really have said the things that Cook attributes to him? Lee may well have implied that the South desired peace long before the North did—this was standard anti-Republican cant, part and parcel of the charge that Lincoln needlessly prolonged the war in order to effect a social revolution in the South. Lee might well have said that the "best men" welcomed emancipation—this was a form of anti-abolition cant that was part and parcel of the old "necessary evil" defense of slavery; it implied that Southerners would have voluntarily devised a gradual way to end slavery if fanatical abolitionists had not steered the country off of its moderate course. However ludicrous this rationalization sounded to abolitionists, it was not uncommon among Virginians of Lee's social class and generation. But could Lee have really said that the South was never more than half in earnest during the war? This seems uncharacteristic from a man whose Farewell Address praised Southerners' unflagging devotion. Lee's wartime letters had privately lamented that as the war ground on, too few recruits stepped forward to fill his army's decimated ranks; too few Southerners, it seemed to him, were willing to make the necessary sacrifices. But it is highly unlikely that at this moment, in the wake of defeat, Lee was acknowledging dissent and disillusionment within the South, or that he would *publicly* indict his fellow Southerners for a lack of commitment to the cause. It is more likely that Lee meant to allude here to the psychological undercurrent with which even the most devoted Confederates had had to grapple: the desire to close the war, on honorable terms, before what was left of their antebellum world was ground into the dust. On this subject, Cook may have read Lee right.[11]

If, then, Lee said all these things, what did he intend? According to one modern biographer, he saw the interview as an opportunity to "say something that would be conciliatory without being apologetic"; the main message of the interview was that every Confederate should "forget the war and take a constructive role in the peace." According to another biographer, Lee's interview was a naive and clumsy effort "not only to justify himself but to argue away the threat of retribution."[12] But the notion that Lee was naive is belied by the key passage in the interview. Even as he offered professions of goodwill, Lee also issued a warning to Northerners. The peace, he argued, was conditional—and Southerners would hold Northerners to the observance of the conditions. Lee put special emphasis on the following point: "Should arbitrary or vindictive or revengeful policies be adopted, the end was not yet." The South still had "sources of strength," which "harsh measures" on the part of the North would "call into action." Lee warned that the "South could protract the struggle for an indefinite period." If "extermination, confiscation and general annihilation" were the North's policy, Southerners would renew the fight and "give their lives as dearly as possible."[13]

Lee went on to explicitly reject the idea—one so resonant in the North—that the political leaders of the South bore a special stigma of guilt for dragging the deluded masses into war. It would not be just, Lee told Cook, to hold Jefferson Davis accountable for the war: Davis's "acts were the acts of the whole people, and the acts of the whole people were his acts." Northerners could not drive a wedge between the elite and the masses and could not displace their vengeance onto the Southern leadership. Instead, knowing that Confederates might still present a united front, they must extend a general amnesty to all Southerners. The fate of the peace was contingent not on Southern repentance and compliance but on the willingness of good, conservative Northerners to seize the political reins and to uphold the lenient spirit of Grant's terms. Lee, in effect, proposed that the Appomattox terms were a contract by which the North must abide.[14]

In a sense, such a rendering of Lee's comments may have suited Cook's purposes. Moderate Northerners already warned that if the Union's policies were too punitive, the Southern fighting spirit might be revived. However intent Cook may have been on presenting his own narrative to the public, Lee's own political views come through, strongly and unmistakably, in the April 29 interview. Lee's insistence that the Appomattox surrender was conditional—that the terms were a contract binding the North to good behavior—would prove to be politically potent in ways that Cook could not possibly imagine.

Lee's interview with Cook escalated a fierce debate in the North, one that had taken shape in the days after the assassination, over whether the rebel general was a fearsome villain or a tragic hero. Lee's words and behavior proved as open to interpretation as his photograph. On one side of the debate were those in the antislavery and Radical Republican press, and some moderates too, who believed that Lee represented the worst of the South— that Lee was, in his own way, as wily and deceitful a politician as Jefferson Davis. Some of these critics were sure Lee should be punished for his treason; others would be satisfied with evidence that he had truly repented of his crimes. On the other side were Democrats, and some conservative Republicans, who insisted that Lee represented the best of the South, possessing a soldier's courage, honesty, and decency. Lee was dragged reluctantly into war and always yearned for peace, even as he proved himself the most gifted general in the war. Among his defenders, some believed that Lee was genuinely repentant and others that he had nothing to apologize for.

Interestingly, Lee's critics considered his Farewell Address his first foray into politics and the bellwether of his views on Reconstruction. They interpreted the address not as a salve to Southern soldiers but instead as an effort to manipulate public opinion, one that foreshadowed the defiant warning he issued in his interview with Cook. An article in the *New York Evening Post*, edited by Radical Republican William Cullen Bryant, excoriated Lee for his references to the Confederates' "devotion to their country" and their satisfaction in "duty faithfully performed." That Lee dared to congratulate the rebels at the moment of defeat was nothing less than a "slap in the face to loyal soldiers." Lee had chosen to "blurt out his treason, and to use his influence over the army which he had surrendered, to rouse them to new rebellion and justify future insurrection." An editorial entitled "Northern Humiliation and Southern Spirit," in the New York *Anglo-African*, reprinted the Farewell Address in its entirety and observed, "There is not a single word or breath of humiliation or confession in the above.... There is nothing of the honest soldier, but there is of the reckless, bloodthirsty murderer." "The whole South has taken the type of its spirit from R. E. Lee," the editorial continued: proud, impetuous, and resistant to change. Such an indictment was not limited to radical journals. *Harper's Weekly*, a New York-based periodical with mainstream popularity and a moderate Republican tilt, offered its own gloss on the Farewell Address in a May 13 article entitled "The Rebel Chiefs." It, too, took issue with Lee's language: "The duty of which he speaks is armed resistance to the constitutional government of his country. Its faithful performance is the slaughter upon many fields of men spotlessly true to their own government." Lee was no apolitical soldier; he was and remained a ringleader of the rebellion.[15]

Such negative portrayals of Lee often raised the specter of suffering Union prisoners of war, who languished in Confederate prisons so close to Lee's Richmond headquarters and to his home that he "might have heard their dismal groans," the *New York Evening Post* charged. The *New York Times* added: "There is a special stain on General Lee's reputation which no military skill or personal courage can wash away. We allude to *his treatment of his prisoners*." Lee must have know that Union men were "perishing by the tens of thousands" in prison camps such as the notorious Andersonville. How could this *"magnanimous, Christian* soldier" have done nothing to end such atrocities?[16]

For many Northerners, the single most damning of Lee's sins was the original sin of his Confederate career: breaking his soldier's oath to defend the United States. While his defenders viewed Lee's initial ambivalence toward secession as an exonerating factor—he had been propelled by a strong sense of duty to his family and state, not by ideology, to take up arms—his detractors thought that Lee's latter-day professions of his ambivalence about secession were a cowardly ruse to dodge accountability for the war. Incredulous at the eagerness of some to "canonize" Lee as a "household god," one Colorado paper sternly reminded its readers that Lee had "openly and wantonly violated a solemn oath to protect and defend his country." This fact alone established that Lee was a traitor, and in the eyes of Lee's detractors, he had done nothing since the surrender to earn the trust of the North. Instead, Lee had, as a Cleveland, Ohio, paper put it, dissipated the "lenient disposition at first manifested toward him" by "boldly avowing himself a thorough and unrepentant rebel."[17]

In a June 4 article entitled "The Paroled Rebel Soldiers and the General Amnesty," the *New York Times* offered a penetrating overview of where the debates over Lee stood at the beginning of the summer of 1865. Copperhead papers claimed that Grant's terms—particularly the clause stipulating that parolees would "not be disturbed by United States authority so long as they observe their parole"—conferred political immunity on Lee and protected him from being tried for treason. The *Times* countered that only the president could confer civil immunity and offer pardon and amnesty. Alluding to Lee's recent *Herald* interview, the article fumed: "He still persists in declaring that he has not committed treason—that he drew his sword only to defend Virginia against an unconstitutional invasion, in obedience to a prime allegiance to his native State." There was only one way to resolve the debate: "by an arraignment, a trial and a sentence."[18]

As Lee made the difficult transition to life as a civilian, President Andrew Johnson formulated his plan for securing the fragile peace and restoring the shattered Union. Johnson did so in a power vacuum: Congress was out of session when he took office in April 1865 and not due to reconvene until December 1865. At first Johnson seemed to make good on his promise to deal sternly with traitors. On May 1, he issued a document consigning the eight people arrested as conspirators in the Lincoln assassination to trial by a military commission rather than a civil court; at the end of June he would approve the sentences handed down by that commission, including the executions of four of those convicted. On May 2, 1865, Johnson put a bounty of $100,000 on Jefferson Davis's head, and when Union soldiers captured the fugitive Confederate president in Georgia on May 10, Johnson had him imprisoned, at Fort Monroe in Virginia, to await an uncertain fate.[19]

Johnson seemed to change course when, on May 29, he formally proclaimed his Reconstruction policy. His Amnesty Proclamation required Confederates to take an oath of allegiance to the U.S. government as the condition for the restoration of their individual political and property rights. There were fourteen categories of exemptions to this rule; for example, high-ranking Confederate civil and military officials and members of the antebellum elite (those who owned $20,000 or more in taxable property) would have to apply directly to the president for their pardons. His biographer Paul Bergeron has noted that Johnson believed that his Amnesty Proclamation represented a "proper middle ground between universal forgiveness and universal punishment." But in practice, the new president soon abdicated that middle ground. He proved susceptible to the entreaties of his former foes and granted them pardons gladly, issuing at least 15,000 to individual rebels over the course of his time in office.[20]

At the same moment he inaugurated his amnesty policy, Johnson also laid out the procedure by which the errant rebel states would be readmitted to the Union. His test case was North Carolina. On May 29, he appointed William W. Holden, the wartime critic of the Davis administration who had led his state's Peace Party, as provisional governor. Holden was given the authority to fill a raft of appointive offices and to hold elections for a state convention. That convention would in turn meet and take the required steps for readmission: it would overturn the state's secession ordinance, endorse abolition and the Thirteenth Amendment, and repudiate the Confederate debt. Johnson's key stipulation was that the electorate of North Carolina would consist of those who had taken the oath of allegiance and who had also been eligible to vote in 1861, under the state's prewar constitution. Johnson's North Carolina proclamation was thus a rejection of the proposal advanced by Radical Republicans in Congress, such as Charles Sumner and Thaddeus Stevens, that the Federal government should insist on black suffrage as a precondition for the readmission of Southern states to the Union. The North Carolina

The offer of amnesty: Andrew Johnson. (Library of Congress)

plan was to be the blueprint for the reestablishment of state governments across the South.[21]

Johnson's May 29 proclamations initiated a period of "self-reconstruction" in the South, during which provisional governors appointed thousands of former rebels to political office and in which the new Southern state governments proscribed the rights of the freedpeople, to push them into a state of subordination as close as possible to slavery. Retooling the old "slave codes," the new Black Codes, which took shape by the end of 1865, were designed to extract the labor power of African Americans and to enforce white supremacy. As they required freedpeople to carry papers proving that they were gainfully employed and passes permitting them to travel, lest they be arrested for vagrancy, the Black Codes compelled African Americans to sign annual labor contracts with white employers, who were typically their former masters. The codes made it a crime to act "insolent" or "insulting" to whites; permitted white judges to seize and apprentice out to whites any black children whose families who did not meet white approval; levied regressive and punitive taxes on black property, including such vital rural assets as dogs and guns; and increased the penalties for crimes such as larceny and trespassing. As Eric Foner has noted, "The entire complex of labor regulations and criminal laws was enforced by an all-white police and judicial system," and by white patrollers, "often composed of Confederate veterans still wearing their grey uniforms."[22]

Historians have offered a variety of explanations why Johnson so quickly abandoned his tough talk against the "slave power conspiracy" and settled into a policy of appeasement. They have cited Johnson's virulent racism, his pleasure in having the favored planter class come before him on bended knee, his Jacksonian belief in the supremacy of the executive branch and attendant suspicion of Congress, his Southerner's commitment to states' rights and his desire to build a new electoral constituency for a presidential bid in 1868. There was a strong ideological connection between these factors. Johnson's animus against the planter aristocracy was real, as was his support for the abolition of slavery. Paradoxically, his racism linked these two positions. Johnson believed that the greatest achievement of the war was "emancipating the white man," by which he meant not only disenthralling the nonslaveholding yeomen from the dominance of the planter class but also breaking the back of an unholy alliance—between Southern white elites and their black slaves—that had kept the white farmer down. As he put it to a delegation of Charlestonians in June of 1865, revealing the depths of his resentments, "The negro in South Carolina that belonged to a man who owned from one to five hundred slaves, thought himself better than the white man who owned none. He felt himself the white man's superior." If African American men were granted the vote, Johnson continued, the elite planters would control the black vote as they had once controlled black bodies, and the middling white man would continue to be marginalized. As president, Johnson on occasion paid lip service to the possibility that some educated blacks might merit the franchise, within the constraints of literacy and property requirements. But such empty rhetoric collapsed under the weight of

Johnson's fear that black enfranchisement would promote race competition and even race war, and his conviction that only the states, and not the federal government, could confer the vote. Johnson's vision was of a South in which the old planter elite would share power with their natural allies, the white yeomen, and in which blacks, though nominally free, would be relegated to peasant status and second-class citizenship, at best. For such a vision to come to pass, the Southern states must be able to govern their own affairs, with minimal interference from the federal government.[23]

Some Americans, particularly those from Johnson's social milieu, could clearly see this political vision at work in his early pronouncements and acts as president. For example, a Tennessee associate of Johnson's, John W. Gorham of Clarksville, wrote the president approvingly on June 3, invoking their shared commitment to preserving "a *white* Mans Government in America." "The People of this Country was frightened when they first learned that you was the President," he noted, "but those of us that knew you best and had bin your life long Political Friends assured them that you would not adopt the Radical but the Constitutional Polacy in which I see that I was not mistaken." This constituent was gratified that Johnson's May 29 proclamations upheld "True Democratic Principles"; he assured Johnson "the White People will sustain you." James Rumley of Beaufort, North Carolina, too, took the May proclamations as proof that Johnson knew "too much of the mental incapacity of the negro, and too much of southern sentiments, even among Union men, to attempt to force the bitter cup of negro suffrage down the throats of his conquered and afflicted countrymen."[24]

But to many others, Johnson's intentions were ambiguous; it was not yet clear, in the late spring and early summer of 1865, whose interests he might still be persuaded to serve. Thus, his voluminous correspondence contains not only letters of support and applications for pardons from former rebels but also a wide range of conflicting appeals, warnings, and threats from across the political spectrum. Committees of African American leaders in North Carolina, Virginia, Kentucky, and South Carolina petitioned Johnson for suffrage. They invoked their natural rights, their rock-ribbed Unionism, their contributions to the Northern victory, and the patent unfairness of allowing former rebels to vote while denying the franchise to the loyal. "It seems to us that men who are willing on the field of danger to carry the muskets of republics, in the days of peace ought to be permitted to carry its ballots," stated a North Carolina petition; "we cannot understand the justice of denying the elective franchise to men who have been fighting for the country, while it is freely given to men who have just returned from four years fighting against it." As the summer of 1865 unfolded, such petitions increasingly invoked the new assaults on their fragile freedom: "unrepentant rebels," explained a committee of Richmond blacks, had reimposed the "old negro laws" on free blacks, enforcing a pass system and wantonly arresting and harassing innocent citizens.[25]

A smattering of white Southern Unionists wrote Johnson with their own appeals for black suffrage, and these were grounded in political expediency. If loyal black Unionists were not enfranchised, warned a Tennessee Unionist in May, presciently, "rebels will re-elect rebels." Prominent Northern Republicans wrote Johnson to sound their own alarms: they urged him not to set Reconstruction policy before consulting Congress first; condemned the "morbid tenderness" toward the leading rebels among many Northerners; warned that many Southerners who pretended to be good Union men were rebels in disguise; and cautioned Johnson not to let the old Southern elite planters be his "masters."[26]

From the opposite end of the political spectrum came advice of an altogether different kind: threats that Johnson should not dare punish or harm the leaders of the Confederacy. In mid-May, four days after Jefferson Davis fell into the hands of his Federal pursuers, Johnson was sent such a threat from a defiant Confederate, under the pen name "Pro Patria et Preside" (for country and president). Calling Davis the "*servant of the people*" and pledging their continued devotion to him, the anonymous writer hissed, "You dare not hang that man! Do so, and YOUR LIFE SHALL BE THE FORFEIT." Two weeks later, an anonymous "Southern man" wrote Johnson, warning: "Sir *I swear* by all that is honorable beneath the skies that if any of our *Great Captains* are made to suffer any severe penalty, that *I will be one* of a *host* that will neither rest day or night until your life pays the penalty of such a monstrous crime." Having heard a rumor that Lee was arrested by the Federal authorities, the writer held up the Appomattox terms as a shield: "When Genl. Lee the patriot the Soldier & the high toned Gentleman Surrendered to Genl. Grant, he did it on condition that he nor his men were to be molested by the US authorities." This interpretation was soon put to the test. On June 7, 1865, a Federal grand jury in Norfolk, Virginia, handed down an indictment of treason for Robert E. Lee.[27]

The state of Virginia's own idiosyncratic process of Reconstruction was already well under way. During the war, Virginia Unionists, based in the town of Wheeling in the west and in Union-occupied Alexandria in the east, had engineered the creation of West Virginia as an independent state and had then established a "Restored government" in Alexandria under Governor Francis H. Pierpont. The loyalist government aligned itself with Lincoln and, in 1864, passed a new antislavery constitution; needless to say, the Pierpont forces exercised authority only in areas of the state that were in the firm control of the Union army. After Lee's surrender, the Restored government moved to Richmond and was endorsed by President Johnson, who recognized its legitimacy in a May 9, 1865, executive order. Like Johnson, Pierpont proved "exceptionally liberal and conciliatory toward the ex-Confederates," explains historian Richard Lowe, believing the rebels had "learned their lesson at Appomattox." In June 1865, the Restored legislature renewed the voting rights of white adult males who would take the amnesty oath or who received presidential pardon, as stipulated in Johnson's May 29 proclamations, and called for October 1865 statewide elections and for a referendum on whether high-ranking Confederate officials would be disqualified from holding office in the new order.[28]

Pierpont's lenient course appalled Virginia's emerging Republican Party and instigated protests from African Americans and their white Unionist allies. How could the governor let the vote be "restored to thousands of white voters, who were but recently in arms against the national authority" and deny it to blacks, the "most faithful friends of that Union"? So asked the June 1865 "Address from the Colored Citizens of Norfolk, Va., to the People of the United States." The address was the work of an impressive collection of black leaders, who had come to prominence during the Union occupation of Norfolk, which dated back to 1862. They included Dr. Thomas Bayne, a former slave and agent of the Underground Railroad; John M. Brown, pastor of the city's AME Church; and Joseph T. Wilson, a veteran of the 54th Massachusetts Infantry of the USCT. These astute men exposed not only the moral bankruptcy of denying blacks the vote but also the political illogic. Once the black population was fully counted in the tallies that determined congressional representation (instead of partially counted, as slaves had been, following the controversial three-fifths compromise of the federal Constitution), white Southerners might "find themselves, after defeat, more powerful than ever"—unless black votes, for the Republican Party and for the Union, could secure power to the righteous victors in the war. This appeal went unheeded, and in the coming months, the dystopian scenario that the "Address from the Colored Citizens" had conjured came to pass. With local elections in Virginia starting as early as July 1865, the all-white electorate soon filled city and county offices with former Confederates.[29]

In the vanguard of the anti-Pierpont forces was the Virginia Republicans' most controversial standard bearer, John C. Underwood. A transplanted New Yorker, Underwood had settled in northern Virginia before the war and gained notoriety as an outspoken champion of free labor. In recognition of his central role in establishing a Republican Party beachhead in Virginia, Underwood was, in 1863, appointed to a federal judgeship in which he presided over the Union-controlled "eastern district" of the state. With great relish, Underwood used the court to confiscate rebel property, an "apt punishment" for traitors. It was Underwood who handed down the June 1865 indictment of Lee. Underwood's position on the surrender, as he articulated it in his charge to the grand jury, was that "the terms of parole agreed upon with General Lee" were a "mere military arrangement" that could have "no influence upon civil rights or the status of the persons interested." In other words, Appomattox paroles did not immunize their bearers against prosecution.[30]

Underwood represented a powerful group of Republicans, led by Judge Advocate General Joseph Holt, Secretary of War Edwin Stanton, Attorney General James Speed, and the influential theorist of the laws of war, Francis Lieber, who believed that the United States "had expressly reserved the right of a sovereign in a civil war to resort to treason prosecutions at war's end." Lee's indictment came as part of a wave of arrests of prominent Confederate leaders, civil and military; they included the Confederate president and vice president, cabinet officials, governors, justices, legislators, and military officers. Advocates of stern retribution were confident that Northern public opinion would favor the prosecution of the Confederate political and military elite: that Northerners deemed the Confederate leadership guilty of treason, of war crimes, and of complicity in Lincoln's assassination, and that they feared the Republic would never be truly safe, and secession thoroughly discredited, so long as the arch rebels were still at large. In Lee's case, there seemed to be ample evidence that the public's wrath had been stoked by the brazen attempts of his defenders to argue, preemptively, that he was legally immune from charges of treason, and by Lee's own protestations of his innocence. "President Johnson owes it to the country to see that Gen. Robert E. Lee is tried for treason," a June editorial in the *San Francisco Bulletin* declaimed, precisely because "the rebel chieftain persists in denying that he is guilty of that crime." Invoking Lee's claim that he took up arms only out of fealty to his native Virginia, the *Bulletin* insisted that to punish Lee was to establish, once and for all, the supremacy of national allegiance over state allegiance.[31]

In Virginia, the Lee indictment became a touchstone in the political battle between those who favored Johnson and Pierpont's exculpatory policies and those, like Underwood, who insisted that truly loyal Unionists, white and black, should govern the state. The conservative *Petersburg News*, in a June 10 editorial, excoriated Underwood as an "imported" abolitionist lackey who harbored sentiments "obnoxious to the people" of Virginia. "For violence, blasphemy and unfounded aspersion of a chivalrous people," the editorial continued, Underwood's indictment of Lee defied comparison. Moreover, the indictment ran counter to the purported spirit of Appomattox, where Grant had not only pardoned Lee but "exhaust[ed] the etiquette of conventional respect" in his deferential dealings with the rebel chief, and where the soldiers of the "great Army of the Potomac" had doffed their hats in homage to the "genius, courage and chivalry" of their Southern foes. The *News* reassured its readers that it had heard no word of sympathy for the prosecution and that the good people of Norfolk were indignant at Underwood's "foul deed." In a pointed counterargument, the independent *Norfolk Post* defended Underwood, condemned the "malign spirit" of the *News*, and advised that unreconstructed rebels should choose "repentance" rather than reviving "sectional bitterness and animosity."[32]

In the midst of this acrimony, Lee acted quietly and decisively to secure immunity for himself and to advance his interpretation of the surrender terms as conditional—namely, as imposing conditions pertaining to the respectful treatment of Southerners that Northerners were bound to obey. On June 13, 1865, he wrote U. S. Grant from Richmond:

> Upon reading the Presidents proclamation of the 29th Ulto: I came to Richmond to ascertain what was proper or required of me to do; when I learned that with others, I was to be indicted for treason by the Grand Jury at Norfolk. I had supposed that the officers & men of the Army of N. Va. were, by the terms of their surrender, protected by the U.S. Government from molestation so long as they conformed to its conditions.
>
> I am ready to meet any charges that may be preferred against me, and do not wish to avoid trial; but if I am correct as to the protection granted by my parole, and am not to be prosecuted, I desire to comply with the provisions of the President's proclamation, and therefore enclose the required application, which I request in that event may be acted upon.

He signed the letter "I am with great respect yr. obdt. svt. R. E. Lee." Lee also wrote President Johnson, explaining that as he was excluded from the amnesty provisions by virtue of his high office and social position, he was applying to Johnson for the "benefits, & full restoration of all rights & privileges" that a presidential pardon could confer.[33]

The very same day, June 7, that Lee's indictment was handed down in Virginia, Grant received a hero's welcome in New York City, where he had traveled to attend a rally, the ostensible purpose of which was to celebrate Johnson's presidency. For the thousands of New Yorkers who thronged Grant, seeking to shake the great man's hand or get his autograph, Johnson was an afterthought; the speakers at the evening banquet at Cooper Union dutifully praised the president, but the masses who filled the hall chanted "Grant—Grant—Grant." They called for a speech, and Grant obliged, but he could muster only a heartfelt "thank you." The patience and good grace with which he endured what was for him a trying scene—he shook so

Grant salutes his adoring crowd in New York City, June 1865. (Library of Congress)

many hands his own right hand turned red and swollen—only endeared Grant further to the adoring crowds, as did his reticence. "The General doesn't talk," one of Grant's admirers observed. "He fights."[34]

Grant could not long remain above the political fray. Lee's letter forced him into a confrontation with the president. On June 16, Grant wrote to Secretary of War Stanton:

> In my opinion the officers and men paroled at Appomattox C.H. and since upon the same terms given to Lee, can not be tried for treason so long as they observe the terms of their parole. This is my understanding. Good faith as well as true policy dictates that we should observe the conditions of that convention. Bad faith on the part of the Governm't or a construction of that convention subjecting officers to trial for treason, would produce a feeling of insecurity in the minds of all paroled officers and men. If so disposed they might even regard such an infraction of terms, by the Government as an entire release from all obligation on their part.

I will state further that the terms granted by me met with the
hearty approval of the President at the time, and of the country
generally. The action of Judge Underwood in Norfolk has already
had an injurious effect, and I would ask that he be ordered to
quash all indictments found against paroled prisoners of war, and
to desist from further prosecution of them.

Over the course of the next four days, Grant pressed this interpretation on
Johnson, and when the president, who viewed Lee as an "arch-traitor,"
equivocated, Grant resorted to a threat of his own: he would resign his
army post if Johnson moved forward with a treason trial for Lee. On June
20, the president relented, and Attorney General James Speed duly
instructed the U.S. district attorney to drop the case against Lee.[35]

Did Grant at this crucial moment accede to Lee's interpretation of
the surrender terms? Was this a second "finest hour" for the two men,
second only to their Appomattox meeting? The answer to both questions is no. Although their interests in a sense converged, Lee's and
Grant's interpretations of the surrender terms remained fundamentally
divergent and their understanding of each other clouded and imperfect.
Lee yearned for "restoration." He repeatedly gave voice to this desire in
his correspondence with his fellow Southerners in the summer and fall
of 1865. "All should unite in honest efforts to obliterate the grevious
[sic] effects of war, & to restore the blessings of peace," he wrote to
John Letcher, the wartime governor of Virginia; in the same letter, Lee
applauded the "conciliatory manner" in which President Johnson had
chosen to treat the South. Lee did not wish for the restoration of slavery,
but he did hope to turn back the clock to an imagined era of racial order
and deference, in which those whites in power recognized the incapacity of blacks for citizenship—a time before, as he saw it, abolitionism
had brought the pall of racial malaise to the South and had imbued
blacks with false hopes. Lee hoped that Johnson's policy of conciliation
would restore to white Southerners the "bright hopes and prospects
of the past" and would restore, too, the political prestige and power of
the region. The "protection" afforded to Confederates by Grant's terms
was the vehicle by which Southerners would return to "prosperity &
influence."[36]

In October of 1865, Lee took two more crucial steps on his personal road to restoration: he signed an amnesty oath, and he assumed the presidency of Washington College in Lexington, Virginia. The oath, in which Lee swore to "protect and defend the Constitution" and to "abide by and faithfully support all laws and proclamations which have been made during the existing rebellion with reference to the emancipation of slaves," was a requirement for receiving Johnson's pardon, one Lee had neglected to provide in his June 13, 1865, application. Thanks to a subterfuge, the October amnesty oath never reached its intended audience. Secretary of State William Seward, upon receiving the document, bestowed it as a souvenir to a friend, and it went missing among the State Department's files until it turned up in the recesses of the National Archives in 1970. In 1975, President Gerald Ford conferred a formal pardon, and restored citizenship, on Lee. The gesture was largely symbolic, because Johnson had in December 1868 issued a blanket amnesty proclamation that covered all former Confederates, including those in excepted classes to which Lee belonged; the modern "pardon" was an effort to set the clock back to 1865 and correct the government's malfeasance in the matter of Lee's initial application.[37]

While some former Confederates criticized Lee for taking the oath in 1865, on the grounds that an innocent man should not stoop to ask forgiveness, most white Southerners implicitly understood that Lee's pardon application was a means to the end of restoring his influence—and the political voice of his fellow Confederates. As one Virginian put it to a Northern reporter who was visiting Richmond in July 1865, Lee hoped in applying for his pardon to set an example for the "high-toned young men of the South": to show that the salvation of the country would depend on their "participating in the rights of citizenship." Lee had not bowed down and begged for mercy; instead, his pardon application had "avowed his unchanging devotion to his former principles." Lee's own liminal citizenship status and the public's scrutiny of his every move were very much on his mind as he contemplated the offer to head Washington College. Lee had written the trustees of the college in late August, expressing his concern that as a man excluded from Johnson's May 29, 1865, amnesty proclamation, and as an "object of censure to a portion of the country," he might draw a "feeling of hostility" to the college. He was duly reassured by them that his services would be of great benefit to their institution, and he accepted the new post. It is a mark of how intense Northern scrutiny was that even this seemingly apolitical move was fodder for debate over Lee. Some newspapers saw Lee's position as college president as a good platform for his "earnest striving to bring about the old state of peace." But a few Northern commentators saw something nefarious at work. The *Boston Daily Advertiser*, for example, thought it unseemly and ominous that Southerners viewed "military service against the government" as a sound "qualification for office"—even that of college president. In Lee's investiture it read "a clear protest against the result of the war" and even a measure of "cool defiance." The rebel chieftain was not "a safe instructor of youth."[38]

A letter Lee wrote to General P. G. T. Beauregard, the Confederacy's "Little Napoleon," in October of 1865 is perhaps the most revealing window into Lee's mindset in the immediate aftermath of Appomattox. Lee's embrace of his role as college president represented an investment in the future, and his determination, as he put it to Beauregard, to be "of some benefit to the noble youth of our country." But Lee's self-image and sense of duty remained firmly rooted in the past. Thus, he began his letter by enlisting Beauregard's aid in a project Lee considered vital to the prospects for restoration: writing the "true" history of the bravery and devotion of the Confederate army during the war. Such a history would establish beyond doubt that Southerners had fought against overwhelming odds. Lee ended his letter by reaching further into history for proof of the moral rectitude of the Southern cause, all the way back to the example of George Washington. "True patriotism," he explained, sometimes compels men to take seemingly contradictory stands. Washington himself "at one time fought against the French, under Braddock, in the service of the King of Great Britain; at another he fought with the French, at Yorktown, under the orders of the Continental Congress of America, against him." He had "not been branded by the world with reproach for this" but instead applauded and rightly so—for in each instance, Washington's "desire to do right" was "precisely the same." Lee here implicitly made the case that there was no ethical inconsistency in his own behavior. He had fought for the United States; he had fought against it; he now sought its protection and restoration. All along, he desired to do right.[39]

U. S. Grant soundly rejected this powerful rationalization. On the face of it, Grant's June 16 letter on Lee's behalf seems to endorse the idea, popular among Confederates and Copperheads, that the Appomattox terms conferred a blanket political immunity on Confederates. But a careful reading of the sources suggests otherwise. Grant had no compunction about urging the arrest of the "obnoxious political leaders" of the Confederacy, including the likes of Virginia Governor John Letcher, as he explained in a May 4, 1865, letter to Major General Henry W. Halleck; it was the political leaders of the Confederacy who bore the greatest burden of guilt and responsibility for the war. Grant implicitly acknowledges in his June 16 letter to Stanton that his Appomattox terms were a military convention, applying to the Southern army alone, that the Federal civil authorities must construe; he asks in the letter that his terms be construed as Lincoln intended, as an act of magnanimity calculated to change Southern hearts and minds. He had already made this understanding of the purposes of the terms clear—if a man of Lee's prestige could be made to accept Federal authority, the Southern people would "be guided to a great extent by his example," as Grant put it, again in a letter to Halleck. If, on the other hand, Lee was persecuted, the fighting spirit of the South might be revived, and the prospects for reunion would dissolve.[40]

A few prominent Northerners took Grant to task for having unwittingly, in wording the surrender terms as he did, provided Lee with a "loophole" by which he might "escape the clutches of the law," as the newspaper editor and former Assistant Secretary of War Charles A. Dana put it. In Dana's view, Grant should have shown more "lawyer cunning and less magnanimity . . . towards a cruel and unscrupulous foe." But most Northerners were inclined to acknowledge the merit in Grant's calculations. Indeed, although Grant's paroles applied only to soldiers, his rationale for leniency became a central argument in the broader case against treason trials for Confederate leaders. Despite the rash of new treason indictments in the wake of the war, "treating the rebels as criminals proved to be a step too far," as John Fabian Witt has succinctly put it. The Northern public's weariness of blood-letting; its belief that wartime suffering had been fit punishment for the Confederates; its memory of Lincoln's lenience; its fear that executions would turn those targeted into martyrs; and its sense that the United States had granted the Confederates de facto

belligerent status during the war and must therefore treat Southerners as
defeated enemies rather than criminals—all of these factors counteracted
the impulse for vengeance. Moreover, the massive scale of the rebellion
vitiated the case for retribution. How would Federal authorities distin-
guish between leaders and followers of the rebellion? Once executions
started, where would they end?[41]

This constellation of attitudes was consistent with Grant's view, embodied in his Appomattox terms, that magnanimity was the policy best calculated to discredit Confederate ideology, and that it was an emblem of
Northern moral authority. The case for magnanimity proved both resilient and popular; it had defenders not only among Democrats and moderate Republicans but also among prominent abolitionists and Radical
Republicans such as Horace Greeley, Congressman Thaddeus Stevens,
Senator Charles Sumner, and Chief Justice of the Supreme Court Salmon
Chase. The radical abolitionist Gerrit Smith summed up the case in a June
1865 speech, insisting "that the government has neither the legal nor the
moral right to try the rebels, and that the way to a sure and enduring peace
lies not through perfidy and vengeance but through justice and love." The
South was guilty of treason—but the "safety of the North" depended on
its silencing "the clamor for blood." What Smith wanted for the South was
not punishment but rather "change": for Southerners to be "born again,"
free of "caste spirit."[42]

On June 20, the same day that the indictment against Lee was dropped,
Grant elaborated on the theme of sin and repentance in a detailed report
on the final campaigns of the war he prepared for Secretary of War
Stanton. In a series of key passages that Grant drafted and then crossed
out, perhaps thinking them a digression from his military narrative, he
addressed the fraught question of Lee's guilt. Lee's offenses against the
"dignity of the Nation" were great, Grant wrote—"but there should always
be some atonement sufficient for every offence." Grant did not believe
Lee to be morally blameless. Instead, the terms made it possible for Lee to
atone for his sins and to call on the South to atone. The terms were the
means to two ends: capitulation and repentance. If Lee had believed that
his capitulation would lead to a treason trial, Grant wrote Stanton, alluding to the recent Underwood affair, the Appomattox surrender would
have never taken place. And Lee's example *had* guided the Confederate

men-at-arms, just as Grant calculated it would: "The surrender of Lee's Army was followed by the surrender of all others of the enemy in rapid succession," Grant noted proudly, closing out his account of the war. Grant was deeply invested in the idea that Lee had seen the error of his ways and that his bid for pardon and protection signaled a commitment to the Union victorious.[43]

Even as he praised Lee's "manly course" at Appomattox, Grant maintained the moral high ground. His June 20 report abjured Lee's conviction—a lynchpin of Lee's efforts to restore Southern prestige and power—that Confederate soldiers had proven themselves the equals of Northern ones. The unsurpassed "endurance and bravery" of the Union armies, Grant wrote, in a paean to the free labor system, could "only be engendered by long training and institutions that gives to each individual a consciousness of his own manhood and equal importance and rights with all others in the state." Grant asked, pointedly, "What other Nation can boast of Armies composed of such material?"[44]

At virtually the same moment that Grant wrote this account, he received from some admirers a portrait of George Washington, "created by arranging the words of the Declaration of Independence." On June 22, he wrote a thank you note for the gift, telling the bearers, "I will prize this very highly and will have it framed to hand down to my children." In the eyes of most Northerners, and of Southern Unionists, it was Grant and not Lee who wore the mantle of Washington. It was Grant for whom a grateful Congress had, in 1864, revived the rank of lieutenant general, which only Washington had held, and Grant whom Northerners, alienated by President Johnson's policies, increasingly regarded as the nation's best hope in peace as he had been in war.[45]

As the partisan struggle over Reconstruction sharpened, so too did the debate over whether there was room, in the story of Appomattox, for two heroes or only one.

‖ 9 ‖

The Promise Betrayed

On July 28, 1865, Carl Schurz, a Union general and leading Radical Republican, sent Andrew Johnson his assessment of the political atmosphere in the defeated South: "I think a large majority are ready to 'return to their allegiance' *as far as the mere restoration of the political machinery of the Government is concerned*, especially as this restoration would place their internal affairs again under their immediate control." Schurz had volunteered his advice and services to Johnson and had undertaken a fact-finding mission for the president in the form of a late summer and early fall "grand tour" of the South. But Schurz's facts, and his interpretation of them, proved inconvenient for the president. White Southerners would welcome reunion on their terms, Schurz found, but resist change. Their tenuous acceptance of emancipation was quickly being undermined by their "traditional impressions and prejudices": while they could not restore slavery, they would mobilize their economic, political, and legal power; their social prestige; and their penchant for violent coercion to "keep the negroes down." Schurz implored the president to use the military force of the federal government to protect the freedpeople and to insist that "federal offices should be filled with *real* union men wherever any such can be found." In Schurz's view, Johnson's lenient Reconstruction policies were breeding recalcitrance, not repentance, among former Confederates.[1]

A few months later, Abial Edwards, stationed with the Union occupying force in Darlington, South Carolina, wrote home to Maine with the following lament: "the President is fast yielding inch by inch all we have gained in our years of toil & strife & the very worst that were fighting against [us] are having all the rights of citizenship accorded to them but that they may once more turn against the old victorious Red White & Blue." "I think my self it is best to be magnanimous to our conquered foe," he continued. "But not so much so that a few years hence that the serpent (Traitors) will once more become gigantic in size & cause us all the sorrows of the last few years."[2]

Schurz and Edwards gave voice to an emerging view of the surrender as a golden moment lost. In the year after Appomattox, Americans across the spectrum of opinion on Reconstruction would argue that their political opponents had betrayed the magnanimous spirit of the surrender. For Republicans, Andrew Johnson was the arch-betrayer, for capitulating to Lee's idea that peace must bring the restoration of power to elite Southerners. For Lee and his followers, the Radical Republicans were the arch-betrayers, for pushing an agenda of race equality and black suffrage that contravened the promise in the parole terms that Southerners would "not be disturbed." For African Americans, whites in both the South and the North—the Confederates who sought to reimpose the racial caste system and the conservative Northerners who once again submitted to the South's will—betrayed the promise of a peace built on justice.

Dissatisfied with Schurz's report and seeking counterevidence, Johnson in November of 1865 dispatched a second prominent Union general—one whom he expected to draw the right conclusions—on a Southern grand tour. That general was none other than U. S. Grant. The fact that he chose Grant for this assignment and that Grant accepted it seems, on the face of it, evidence that the two men had forged an alliance in the wake of their June clash over Lee's indictment. Johnson had come to see Grant as his "most prestigious advisor" and had tapped Grant's "instinctive deference," that of a soldier to his commander-in-chief.[3] On November 27, Grant dutifully embarked on a tour through Virginia, the Carolinas, Georgia, and Tennessee. Along the way, he spoke with prominent Southern politicians, such as William W. Holden of North Carolina; with Union commanders keeping the peace in the South, such as General Daniel E. Sickles; with Freedmen's Bureau officials; with newspaper reporters; with Southern Unionists; and even with former Confederate General John B. Gordon. At each stop, Grant and his traveling party were cheered by crowds of African American admirers.[4]

Grant returned to Washington, D.C., and one week later submitted his report to the president. "I am satisfied that the mass of thinking men of the south accept the present situation of affairs in good faith," Grant told Johnson. Southerners were "anxious to return to self-government," he continued, and "in earnest in wishing to do what they think is required by the government." This was exactly what Johnson wanted to hear: it meant, so he believed, that his policies were working, his authority well established, and restoration proceeding apace. Johnson held up the report as proof, too, that Grant was firmly in his camp. The principal audience for this claim was the recently convened 39th Congress, which locked horns with Johnson over the seating of the congressional delegations that "restored" governments had elected under Johnson's plan. Those delegations included dozens of prominent Confederates—not only generals but also political leaders such as the former Confederate Vice President Alexander H. Stephens. Johnson wanted them recognized, to close the book on Reconstruction; Congress's refusal to seat these representatives, along with its establishing a Joint Committee on Reconstruction to conduct its own investigation into conditions in the South, served the president notice that he was in for a fight.[5]

Grant, the object of adulation among Northerners and the general-in-chief of the Union armies keeping peace in the South, was a great prize in this fight. Moderate and Radical Republicans in the Congress were as eager as Johnson to claim Grant as their man. Historian Eric Foner has cogently broken down the differences between the two Republican camps. Moderate Republicans, whose leaders included Lyman Trumbull and William Pitt Fessenden in the Senate and James G. Blaine and John A. Bingham in the House, favored "leaving Johnson's governments in place but adding federal protections of the freedpeople's rights"; they were ambivalent about black suffrage. The Radicals, led by Charles Sumner, Benjamin Wade, and Henry Wilson in the Senate and Thaddeus Stevens and George Julian in the House, "embraced the wartime expansion of national authority" and believed that the Southern states could be "treated by Congress as conquered provinces." Some advocated the confiscation and redistribution of Southern plantations to furnish land to the freedpeople, but most Radicals rejected this as too extreme and a dangerous precedent. The core of the Radical program was black suffrage: only the ballot could ensure that blacks would be given a "perfectly fair chance." At this stage, the moderates outnumbered the Radicals in Congress.[6]

Johnson felt fully confident of Grant's support in December of 1865—but he should not have. Grant was a moderate Republican, whose own keen sense of fairness, along with his determination to win, had compelled him, during the war, to champion emancipation and black enlistment. Grant's report of his grand tour was no simple endorsement of Johnson's policies. Instead, the hero of Appomattox was beginning to stake his own claim in the Reconstruction debates, one that would soon prove incompatible with Johnson's. Grant's report noted that some Southerners were not yet ready to yield in obedience to federal authority; argued for the "absolute necessity" of maintaining the Freedmen's Bureau, the federal agency created to oversee the transition of former slaves to freedom; and insisted that a strong military presence was necessary to keep the peace in the South. "The white and black mutually require the protection of the general government," Grant told the president. In the summer of 1865, Grant had been somewhat naive in his "optimism about the regeneracy of Southern loyalty," historian Brooks Simpson explains—but in the winter of 1865–66, having been greeted on his tour by crowds of hopeful African Americans and having seen ominous signs among Southern whites of the persistence of racism, Grant "began to emphasize justice for the freedmen and loyal whites as an essential part of the peace settlement."[7] The political education of U. S. Grant—a process that would pit the Union general against both Johnson and Lee—was under way.

"The patriotism and virtue of General Robert E. Lee stand unquestioned today by all parties whose reputation for intelligence and candor renders their opinion desirable," declared C. Chauncey Burr, in his New York-based Copperhead journal, the *Old Guard*, in January of 1866. The *Old Guard* (which during the war had vilified Grant as a "butcher" and "death's head") held up Lee as a beacon of patriotism and Radical Republicans, Secretary of War Stanton, in particular, as the true rebels: "The Union, as it was established by our father, was dear to General Lee, as it was to everybody in the land, except the *negro-equalizing* revolutionists now in power. They *were* and *are* the real foes to the Union." As a courtesy, Burr sent a copy of the article to Lee in Lexington, Virginia, and Lee wrote Burr in return to express his thanks and approval. "I am glad to know that the intelligent and respectable people at the North are true and conservative in their opinions," Lee declared. "All that the South has ever wanted, was that the Union, as established by our forefathers, should be preserved." If Northerners, too, could "unite in advocating that policy which will soonest restore the country"—namely, Johnson's policy—then, Lee averred hopefully, "there can be no contention between the two sections."[8]

Lee's reference to the "intelligent and respectable people" of the North, like Grant's reference to the "mass of thinking men" of the South, evinced their desire to position themselves in the political mainstream. Each man longed to see, and tried to furnish, evidence that his interpretation of Appomattox had gained credence among his former enemies. But for Grant, such evidence proved increasingly elusive. The account of his campaigns against Lee that Grant had sent to the War Department in June was published in pamphlet form in the winter of 1865, for dissemination to the public. The Southern press did not hesitate to critique the report. The *Charleston Daily News* charged that it was rife with errors and misinformation. Countering Grant's analysis of Union strategy and his emphasis on his men's bravery, the *News* argued that it was "fortune," and not "genius" that had rewarded the conquerors with victory: Grant was fortunate to have "immense power in his hands." He had brought "brute force," on a "gigantic scale," to bear upon the Confederates. The "handful" of men who surrendered at Appomattox had done so not because they had been "maneuvered into a position which made resistance a military folly, but because they had been reduced to a number which made it a physical impossibility." The defeated Confederates appreciated the "moderation" of Grant's surrender terms. "More he cannot ask from the Southern people, who, with one heart, have awarded the hero's crown to another, and who abide with confidence the confirmation which they expect present and future generations to give their verdict," the article concluded.[9]

More discouraging still for Grant were reports that poured in from the South—not only from the likes of Schurz but also from Grant's own commanders, posted with the occupation force in the former Confederacy—of violence against blacks. Such reports prompted moderate Republican Senator Lyman Trumbull, chairman of the Senate Judiciary Committee, to propose a bill that would extend the life of the Freedmen's Bureau. He went further still, crafting a civil rights bill that would invalidate the Black Codes, the punitive laws constricting African Americans. Trumbull's bill, Eric Foner has explained, "for the first time offered a legislative definition of American citizenship." It guaranteed the right of national citizens, defined as those born in the United States, to make contracts, bring lawsuits, hold property, and claim the "full and equal benefit" of the laws protecting persons and property. Although the bill did not broach the subject of black suffrage, it was nonetheless revolutionary: "No longer could states enact laws such as the Black Codes declaring certain actions crimes for black persons but not white."[10]

Grant supported Trumbull's bills and took an initiative of his own. On January 3, 1866, he issued General Orders No. 3, directing commanders in the South to protect Freedmen's Bureau agents, Southern Unionists, and the freedpeople from persecution. Former Confederates howled that this was an unlawful imposition of martial law, but Grant stood his ground. He knew that the presence of African American troops in the occupying force was especially objectionable to white Southerners, but while he was willing to redeploy some black troops, he was not willing to withdraw them from the South altogether.[11]

The ensuing congressional debates over the Civil Rights bill revealed that the contending sides were every bit as determined to claim the Appomattox terms for their respective causes as they were to claim Grant the man. Republican champions of the Civil Rights bill argued that Grant's victory at Appomattox had brought on a "golden moment," as Radical Republican Senator Henry Wilson put it. In May of 1865 the rebels "were prostrate at the feet of the nation, completely conquered and subjugated"; they "could then have been molded at the nation's will." Wilson quoted a popular poem by John Greenleaf Whittier, the New Englander known as "freedom's poet" for his ardent support of abolition. Entitled "To the Thirty-Ninth Congress," the poem argued both for clemency toward the former rebels and for suffrage for the former slaves: Southerners would get their forgiveness if they would take "their hands off the negro's throat." In Wilson's view, if Andrew Johnson had seized that golden moment and granted the freedmen the ballot and civil rights, "sectional controversies would have perished forever, the representatives of the rebellious States would ere have filled these vacant chairs, and the heavens would be raining their choicest blessings upon the nation for a deed so wise and so just." Now the moment had passed. "The poor freedmen" were "trembling with apprehension, everywhere subject to indignity, insult, outrage, and murder," while the "blended voices of unrepentant rebels and rebel sympathizers and apologists mingling in full chorus" demanded "the restoration to these vacant chairs of the 'natural leaders' of the South."[12]

John Martin Broomall, a Pennsylvania Republican, offered on behalf of the Civil Rights bill his own lament. Make no mistake about it, he warned his colleagues, new political battle lines had been drawn. "The northern party corresponding with the loyal men of the South ask that the legitimate results of Grant's victory shall be carried out," he asserted, on behalf of the Republicans, while "the northern party corresponding with the rebels of the South ask that things should be considered as if Lee had been the conquerer, or at least as if there had been a drawn battle, without victory on either side." Broomall, like Wilson, had favored the policy of magnanimity. "I am willing to make forgiveness the rule and punishment the exception," he noted, adding that he was even willing to pardon Lee and Davis. But, he continued, "There is a point beyond which I will neither be forced nor persuaded. I will never consent that the Government shall desert its allies in the South and surrender their rights and interests to the enemy, and in this I will make no distinction of caste or color either among friends or foes." This was a recurring refrain among supporters of the bill. Congressman William Windom of Minnesota had this to say to the bill's Democratic opponents: "I am willing to carry my magnanimity to the verge of justice. . . . but when you advise me to sacrifice those who have stood by us during the war in order to conciliate unrepentant rebels whose hearts still burn with ill-suppressed hatred to the Government, I scorn your counsel."[13]

The idea that Johnson had squandered a "golden moment" appealed to both moderate and Radical Republicans beyond the halls of Congress. "Here was the opportunity for a statesman to grasp," Whitelaw Reid, a former war correspondent for the *Cincinnati Gazette,* wrote of conditions in the South in the spring of 1865. His tour of the region persuaded him that "the National government could at that time have prescribed no conditions for the return of the Rebel States which they would not have promptly accepted. . . . The people wanted civil government and a settlement. They asked no terms, made no conditions." The Southern "body politic was as wax," but under Johnson, the "plastic moment" was "suffered to pass." By the start of the new year, "The reaction had set in." White Southerners "now began to talk of their rights, and to argue constitutional points; as if traitors had rights, or treason was entitled to constitutional protection." The hope that the Southern masses would forsake their old, failed leaders had run aground, Reid noted. They remained devoted to Davis, Beauregard, and Johnston, and especially to Lee, whom they "everywhere reverenced."[14]

Sidney Andrews, a correspondent for the *Boston Daily Advertiser* and *Chicago Tribune*, saw the same spirit of recalcitrance in his tour of the Carolinas and of Georgia in the fall of 1865. He had hoped that the "Northern idea of right and wrong, justice and injustice, humanity and inhumanity" would take root after the surrender, but he found instead white Southerners' hostility to black freedom and citizenship unabated; they would accept emancipation as a "concession" to the North only if that concession brought "the full restoration" of political rights to ex-Confederates. "We are thoroughly whipped," one Charlestonian told Andrews, "and now we want you to quit reproaching us" and "let us back into the Union." The white Southerners Andrews met did not think Grant "much of a soldier," but Lee "they all considered the greatest man of the age."[15]

That reverence for Lee was evident, a third Northerner who published a Southern travelogue revealed, in white Southerners' frequent, even relentless, allusions to the "overwhelming numbers" theory of Southern defeat. John Richard Dennett, a correspondent for the new progressive journal the *Nation*, traveled the Southern states in the year after the war and marveled at how often he heard former Confederates declaim that Lee at Appomattox had faced Grant's army of 150,000 with only "a handful of men," and that the Union hordes consisted of "mercenaries from Europe and Yankees and Negroes outnumbering General Lee's army in the proportion of five to one." One fellow Northerner whom Dennett met in his travels explained in the spring of 1866 that he had been converted from a conservative to radical position on Reconstruction after encountering so many recalcitrant rebels:

I came out with the kindliest feelings for these people down here. I wanted to see it made easy; we had whipped them, and I wanted

it to rest there. I thought the South wanted it to end there. But I
was tremendously mistaken. They hate us and despise all belonging to us. . . . They won't even allow that we won our own battles. "We were overpowered by numbers," they say; "of course we
couldn't fight all Europe." They've said that to me more than fifty
times within the last few weeks. And they say that they are the gentlemen; we are amalgamationists, mudsills, vandals, and so forth.

For Dennett, such testimony was proof that the North had missed the
chance to reap "the fruits of war." Dennett saw for himself how the overwhelming numbers theory was wielded as a political tool: by denying the
legitimacy of the Yankees' military victory, white Southerners denied
Northerners the right to impose their political will in the region.[16]

Nonetheless, Northern commentators writing in the "Southern tour"
genre clung to the idea that the war might still yield its fruits, if only
Northerners would reward and give voice to those Southerners who had
steadfastly supported the Union. J. T. Trowbridge, a prolific antislavery
novelist and editor in Walt Whitman's social circle, undertook his own
tour of the South in the summer and fall of 1865 and prepared his findings
for publication while the Civil Rights bill was debated in Congress. In
Trowbridge's view, "At the close of the war, the South was ready to accept
any terms which the victorious government might have seen fit to enforce.
The ground was thoroughly broken; it was fresh from the harrow; and
there was the time for the sowing of the new seed, before delay had given
encouragement and opportunity to the old rank weeds." Trowbridge
defended magnanimity to the rebels, provided it was coupled with repentance on their part and justice for the freedmen. "Let peace, founded upon
true principles, be the only retribution we demand," he declared; such a
policy would permit the "current . . . of progressive ideas" to flow into the
South. The passage of a Civil Rights bill and of universal suffrage could
undo the damage Johnson had wrought.[17]

The idea that the achievement of a real and lasting peace must be contingent on the grant of citizenship to African Americans was also developed in the black press. An editorial in the *Christian Recorder* entitled "Is
Peace Secured?" answered the question in the negative, lamenting the
"desperate efforts made by Southern politicians with pardons fresh from

the hands of the President, to resume control of the several State governments, solely with a view to oppress the freemen and all truly loyal citizens." The Southern elite and their Copperhead allies still held the
"common people" of the South in their grasp, and such domination was
"utterly destructive to prosperity and national harmony." Only when the
"dictates of an enlightened, progressive humanity" prevailed—permitting
the Southern masses to shake off their "social degradation" and blacks to
enjoy "perfect freedom"—would the nation enjoy the "blessings of true
peace." A March 31, 1866, letter to the *Christian Recorder* signed "Ruth
G—" offered a powerful articulation of the argument that the nation
should not abjure black citizenship in the name of conciliation. "Rebellion, though humbled, defeated even, lives. . . . Can the sacrifice of the
negro satisfy its appetite? Never. Offer up the negro, and secession, grown
strong from its having counted on the offering, will turn and demand the
nation's life anew." Johnson's veto of the Civil Rights bill was a warning
and a setback, Ruth G— lamented. But she did not despair. For in the "moral
heroism" and "refined and elevated patriotism" of the USCT troops she
read the promise of the triumph of "Liberty and Equality."[18]

Opponents of the Civil Rights bill, who included some conservative Republicans as well as Democrats, countered such arguments with their own
invocation of a golden moment. In their view, Johnson's clemency had
made it possible for the nation to sow the seeds of goodwill that Grant and
Lee had planted at Appomattox. Pennsylvania Senator Edgar Cowan told
his colleagues that Southerners were firmly back in the national fold. If the
United States was threatened by a foreign government, "nine out of every
ten" Southerners, he claimed, would "stand by the flag." The bill's critics also
resorted to race-baiting tactics, drawing up dystopian scenarios in which its
passage would lead to race competition and race mixing. According to Andrew Jackson Rogers, a New Jersey Democrat, "If you pass this bill you will
allow the negroes of this country to compete for the high office of President
of the United States"—no "civilized" country on earth gave rights to such
"barbarians." Moreover, he insisted, the proposed bill was an unconstitutional abrogation of states' rights and would invalidate the host of laws that
Northern states had passed in the antebellum era to deny blacks full civil
rights. Senator Reverdy Johnson of Maryland amplified this theme, noting

anxiously that the bill would overturn laws, such as the one on the books in his native state that forbade interracial marriage. "We made the war to restore the dominion of the laws," as Senator Cowan put it, not to extend the principle of racial equality. It was Republican agitation, rather than Johnson's clemency, that threatened to dispel the golden moment of victory and reunion.[19]

This argument resonated broadly throughout the South, where former Confederates elaborated the idea that Grant's terms were a covenant that the South had upheld and that Northern Radicals, in pushing for black civil rights, had betrayed. According to a February 21, 1866, editorial in the *Valley Virginian*, the Southern people had "honestly submitted to the arbitrament of the sword. They were willing to give the North all it won in the fight and they have performed their part of the contract." It went further still: "Nothing the Southern people endured during the war adds so much to their honor and glory, as the honorable manner in which they have carried out the pledges made to Grant at Appomattox." Thanks to the Radicals, Southerners were "threatened with new penalties and forced to live in a constant state of uncertainty and doubt"; they had faith in Johnson but had come to fear that the mass of Northern people might be swayed by his enemies. Explicitly rejecting the Republican article of faith that the Southern masses had during the war been duped by "scheming politicians," the editorial asserted the unity of the Southern people and the impossibility, for the Republicans, of a divide-and-conquer political strategy. The only hope for a lasting peace lay in the resurgence of "conservative sentiment" in the North. Johnson's policy, the *Valley Virginian* insisted, was consistent with Grant's terms and embodied the true spirit of Appomattox.[20]

This case was pressed in the winter of 1866 by what had arguably been the most influential Southern rights journal of the antebellum era, the New Orleans-based *De Bow's Review*. Before the war, its prolific editor, J. D. B. De Bow, positioned himself in the vanguard of the secessionist movement, with a cascade of editorials and articles defending slavery, urging the reopening of the African slave trade, and calling for Southern economic development and independence from the North. After a hiatus during the war, the journal was relaunched in January of 1866, with its old subtitle (*Agricultural, Commercial, Industrial Progress and Resources*) changed to reflect its new focus: *Devoted to the Restoration of the Southern*

States and the Development of the Wealth and Resources of the Country. The journal took up the banner of Johnsonian Reconstruction, claiming that the president's "magnanimous and forbearing spirit" would "speedily restore to the United States all that it has lost by the war." The contributors to *De Bow's* revived a rhetorical tactic they had perfected before the war: obscuring the political middle ground by claiming that all Northern Republicans were radical abolitionists in disguise. As the Honorable W. W. Boyce, a former congressman from South Carolina, explained, the country in 1866 had a stark choice between two policies: "One, the policy of repression; the other, the policy of conciliation." The leading Republicans, Radicals all, he suggested, favored repressive measures such as the confiscation of Southern property, the disfranchisement of all Confederates, and capital punishment of all rebel leaders. Fortunately, he continued, the heroic Andrew Johnson stood in their way. In Boyce's view, Southerners should not be surprised that Johnson had proved to be their friend—he was a "follower of the Jackson school," committed to the idea that the federal government should not encroach on the "powers and privileges" that the Constitution had vested in the states. *De Bow's* mobilized a second time-tested rhetorical tactic: conjuring frightful images of what would happen if the Northern radicals had their way. The policy of repression, Boyce warned, would not only alienate white Northerners and Southerners—it would also pit Southern whites and blacks against each other in "violent discord" and plunge the region into chaos and anarchy.[21]

Even as contributors to *De Bow's* fell in line behind Johnson, they tried to claim both Grant and Lee for the policy of conciliation. De Bow himself editorialized in the February 1866 issue that Grant at Appomattox "paid a tribute" to Southern pride and valor; in April, the journal selectively quoted Grant's December 1865 letter to Johnson (the passage on how the "thinking men of the South . . . accept the present situation") as proof that Grant believed Johnson's policy of conciliation to be a splendid success. But for De Bow, the biggest prize was not Grant but Lee. Leaving nothing to chance, the editor wrote to Lee on December 29, 1865, asking for his blessing. De Bow could hardly contain his glee when he received a response. On January 20, Lee wrote, "I am happy to learn by your letter of the 29th ult. From New Orleans that you have re-established your valuable REVIEW upon a large and liberal basis, and trust you will be able, by your ability, to aid in the restoration of the South." Lee pledged: "You will have my hearty co-operation." De Bow printed the letter in the March 1866 issue of the journal, as part of an editorial on how Southerners must "sustain the arms of the Conservatives" in the North. Lee's endorsement was key: it boded well, De Bow averred, "to have God-speed in our labors, of such a man."[22]

Ironically, both sides—those who believed that Johnson and the ex-rebels had betrayed the spirit of Appomattox and those who believed that the Radical Republicans had done so—found support in Lee's testimony before the congressional Joint Committee on Reconstruction. Lee was called as a witness on February 17, 1866. The Joint Committee consisted of six senators and nine representatives; of the 15, a dozen were staunch Republicans. Over the course of the winter and spring of 1866, it conducted interviews with 144 witnesses. Most were Northerners, typically army officers or Freedmen's Bureau officials; 57 were white Southerners, Unionist and Confederate; and eight were African Americans. As historian John Hope Franklin has explained, the "Joint Committee was a natural forum for airing all the shortcomings of the President's reconstruction policies and justifying the need for a congressional program." It interviewed Lee to gauge the disposition of former Confederates toward the federal government.[23]

The first substantive question Lee was asked was about the "state of feeling" among former Confederates in Virginia. "As far as I have heard any one express an opinion," Lee responded, "they are for co-operating with President Johnson in his policy." When asked to elaborate, Lee continued: "His policy in regard to the restoration of the whole country. I have heard persons with whom I have conversed express great confidence in the wisdom of his policy of restoration, and they seem to look forward to it as a hope of restoration." Lee's reflexive use of the word "restoration," three times, piqued the committee, and they pressed him: did Southerners support Johnson out of a desire for "peace and good feeling in the country," Congressman Henry Blow, a Missouri Republican, asked Lee, "or from the probability of their regaining political power"? Lee answered, cagily, "So far as I know the desire of the people of the south, it is for the restoration of the civil government, and they look upon the policy of President Johnson as the one which would most clearly and most surely re-establish it." Blow would not let the question go—when his turn next came to interrogate Lee, he asked again—did Southerners want peace or to regain their lost power? This time Lee answered that he was not inclined to separate the two points. Southern states sought to have their equality with Northern ones restored; the North should be generous because it was the best way of regaining the "good opinion" of the South.[24]

Throughout the interview, Lee proved calm and collected, resolute but not bitter. He did not concede an inch. When asked about race relations, he repeated the argument he had made in his April 1865 interview with the *Herald*—he had always favored *gradual* emancipation. Blacks, he averred, were "not as capable of acquiring knowledge" as whites; they were an "amiable, social race" who liked their "ease and comfort." They were, he insisted, being well treated in the postwar South by their former masters. When asked whether former Confederates would fight for the United States in a foreign war, Lee was noncommittal, saying, "So far as I know the feeling of the people of Virginia, they wish for peace." When asked whether secession was tantamount to treason, Lee repeated his mantra about state allegiance: "The act of Virginia, in withdrawing herself from the United States, carried me along as a citizen of Virginia." When asked if he had any knowledge of the "cruelties practiced towards the Union prisoners at Libby prison and Belle Isle" in Richmond, Lee denied any knowledge and responsibility. "I never knew that any cruelty was practiced," he stated, to the stunned disbelief of his Republican examiners, "and I have no reason to believe that it was practiced."[25]

Lee's testimony contradicted that offered by most of the committee's other witnesses. Loyalist Southerners, white and black, along with their Northern allies, presented the committee with a "dreary recital of inhumanity," as John Hope Franklin has explained: hundreds of pages of testimony describing the hostility of former Confederates to the Union, the threats and abuse directed at Federal soldiers and Freedmen's Bureau officials, and the suffering and vulnerability of the freedpeople. The Reverend William Thornton of Elizabeth City, Virginia, one of the African American witnesses, testified that a couple he knew "received thirty-nine lashes" for going to a religious meeting, "according to the old law of Virginia, as if they had been slaves" (he alluded to an antebellum law that forbade blacks to attend religious meetings without white permission and supervision). When Daniel Norton of Yorktown was asked, "In the case of the removal of the military force from among you, and also of the Freedmen's Bureau, what would the whites do with you?," he replied that he and his fellow African Americans "would be in danger of being hunted and killed." Thomas Bayne of Norfolk added, "It is not uncommon to hear threats such as this: we will kill one negro, at least, for every rebel soldier killed by them."[26]

Lee, on February 17, 1866, looked his questioners in the eye—the very same men who heard the searing testimony of African witnesses William Thornton, Daniel Norton, and Thomas Bayne—and denied the reality of violence against blacks in the postwar South. Is it possible that Lee, in relative seclusion at Washington College, did not know about the extent of white ill-will and violence toward blacks? Scholars have long debated Lee's views on slavery and race, and a strong consensus has emerged that Lee was very much a man of his time and place, who, despite paying lip service to gradual emancipation, was thoroughly committed to white supremacy. He sold slaves, thus separating families; inflicted corporal punishment on them; and even, as his army invaded Pennsylvania during the Gettysburg campaign, captured Northern free blacks to have them transported South and sold as slaves. Lee's professed distaste for vigilante violence—a stance that informed his rejection of guerrilla warfare as an option for the defeated Confederacy—is also a matter of the public record. Lee's defenders have frequently noted that he formally prohibited and condemned acts of racial violence by Washington College students against Lexington's black population. In one incident that is central to Lee lore, he prevented the lynching of an African American man who got into a scuffle with a student after failing to step into the gutter when the student's mother walked down the street. Such stories, of course, cut both ways: they reveal that Lee was all too aware that Southern communities, even his beloved Lexington, were seething cauldrons of racial tension and recrimination.[27]

In telling the Joint Committee of the "kind feelings" whites in Virginia had for blacks, Lee revived the prewar Southern fantasy of "paternalism," the idea that masters had been the kindly custodians of their black wards, extending them care in exchange for their submission. Its postwar corollary was the fantasy that only the Southern elite could steward the freedpeople through a transition—not to equality but to a new form of benign subordination as a class of perpetual serfs. After the war as before, paternalism was an ideological bulwark against Yankee "interference" in the South and a shield for Southerners against charges of moral wrong-doing. Although Lee dissembled and defied them, he, no less than the other witnesses, confirmed for the Republicans on the Joint Committee their central conclusion. "The evidence of intense hostility to the federal Union, and an equally intense love of the late Confederacy, nurtured by the war, is decisive," the majority report of the Joint Committee read. They found Lee to be utterly lacking in repentance and took him to be represen-tative of his fellow Confederates. There had been a golden moment—the Confederate South was "in a state of utter exhaustion" at the close of the war—but Johnsonian policies had revived the Southern temper, and the ex-rebels now brazenly sought "to participate in making laws for their conquerors."[28]

The Republican press drew the same conclusion when the Joint Committee's findings were made public in the spring of 1866. In a March 30, 1866, article entitled "Gen. Lee's Testimony," the *Chicago Tribune* attributed to Lee a series of "important admissions": that Vir-ginians still put state allegiance before their allegiance to the Union; that they did not believe themselves guilty of treason; that "colored men would not be allowed to vote in Virginia"; and that "the rebels endorse Andrew Johnson's policy." The article mocked Lee for playing the political innocent and completely discounted his claim that the South had accepted the verdict of the war. Lee revealed that South-erners still regarded secessionism as "the highest form of patriotism." Some of Lee's critics worried that these "admissions" came at too high a price: by asking Lee to testify at all, the Joint Committee had given him a political platform and a new means by which to embolden Southern-ers in their bid for power. "Is the evidence of this perjured traitor to be held up as trustworthy before the American people?" asked the *National Anti-Slavery Standard*. Why should Lee be permitted to parade himself as an honest man, the editors continued, "as if his opinion was of any worth ... as if he had any right to show himself in the presence of loyal and Christian men?" Lee's lies should not have been intermingled with the testimony of the truth-tellers.[29]

While Lee confirmed Republicans in their fear that a golden moment for reunion on the North's terms was slipping away, supporters of Johnson drew an entirely different conclusion from Lee's testimony. In their eyes, restoration was nearing completion and could be consummated if only Republicans desisted from pushing their radical agenda. In accounts of Lee's interview by Northern conservatives, he was a victim, being needlessly hounded by the "radical fools" on the "so-called Reconstruction (?) Committee." The Joint Committee came in for mockery as well as criticism; a correspondent for the Cincinnati *Commercial* drew up a parody of the "suppressed" parts of Lee's interview. In it, Lee was asked a ludicrous series of questions, such as "What kind of shirts did you wear during the war?," and "Is it true that the women of the South wear Jeff. Davis' picture in their bosoms?," and "Which side do you sleep on?" The message here was that Lee had been disrespected by the Joint Committee; it had trifled with him and should have known better.[30]

The most inventive defense of Lee came from the pen of Herman Melville. The author of *Moby Dick* was an ardent War Democrat; like many Democrats in his native New York City, he was highly critical of the Lincoln administration and openly admiring of Lincoln's antagonist in the 1864 election, General George McClellan. Melville was committed to Union victory but also to a rapid reunion, on the premise that Southerners were not sinners or criminals but "honestly-erring men," who had acquitted themselves honorably in the war, and that the North's "triumph was won not more by skill and bravery than by superior resources and crushing numbers," as he put it. The Appomattox surrender captured Melville's imagination, and he commemorated it in *Battles-Pieces*, his 1866 collection of war poems. In "The Surrender at Appomattox (April, 1865)," he praised the humane way that Grant and Lee, the "warring eagles," folded their wings; he saw in their comportment a "glad token" for all humankind. Melville was more overtly political in a poem entitled, "Rebel Color-bearers at Shiloh. A plea against the vindictive cry raised by civilians shortly after the surrender at Appomattox." Its final stanza read:

> The life in the veins of Treason lags,
> Her daring color-bearers drop their flags,
> And yield. Now shall we fire?
> Can poor spite be?
> Shall nobleness in victory less aspire
> Than in reverse? Spare Spleen her ire,
> And think how Grant met Lee.

The rebels had behaved nobly in defeat and the Union, following Grant's lead, must be generous in victory.[31]

This message was amplified in "Lee in the Capitol (April, 1866)," the most extensive of Melville's poetic treatments of the surrender. For dramatic effect, Melville set Lee's congressional interview in April 1866, the one-year anniversary of Appomattox, rather than in February. The poem begins by setting the stage. Lee, "hard pressed by numbers," capitulates to Grant and accepts his fate, acquiescing in the "asserted laws" of the Union. He soon becomes a "quiet seminary's head" (a reference to his position at Washington College) and looks forward to a life in seclusion. This solemn reverie is broken when Lee is summoned to Washington by "missives from the Senators" invoking "reasons of state." Lee embarks on a mournful and tense journey from his home in Lexington, Virginia, to the capital, past "blackened homes" and his own ancestral estate of Arlington, which he had forfeited, by choosing war, to the Union. As the Capitol dome comes into view, Lee speaks directly to the reader; as literary scholar Stanton Garner puts it in a recent book on Melville's Civil War, he becomes a Melville character:

> So be it! They await me now
> Who wrought this stinging overthrow;
> They wait me; not as on the day
> Of Pope's impelled retreat in disarray—
> By me impelled—when toward yon Dome
> The clouds of war came rolling home

Lee thus alludes to hopeful days, when his Army of Northern Virginia had threatened Washington, D.C.; the tables are now turned, and Lee represents "power made powerless and brought low." To underscore this point, Melville invokes the May 23 Grand Review, when "Grant and Sherman shone in blue"; Lee passes along the very streets that had hosted the victor's pageant.

However humbling his trip to Washington, D.C., once Lee meets the Joint Committee, the tables are turned again, with Lee resuming the moral high ground while his intimidated inquisitors look on in wonder. Alluding to Lee's family connections (though marriage) to the father of the country, Melville tells us of Lee:

> The meeting follows. In his mien
> The victor and the vanquished both are seen—
> All that he is, and what he late had been.
> Awhile, with curious eyes they scan
> The Chief who led the invasion's van—
> Allied by family to one,
> Founder of the Arch the Invader warred upon:
> Who looks at Lee must think of Washington;[32]

The committee then asks its questions, the central one of which is, "Does the sad South still cherish hate?" Lee's answers are "Briefly straightforward, coldly clear." In closing, the congressmen ask him one last time to speak his mind, to reveal something. He struggles with his conscience, but he knows he must speak, "for the brave, Who else no voice or proxy have." And so Lee says:

> My word is given—it ties my sword;
> Even were banners still abroad,
> Never could I strive in arms again
> While you, as fit, that pledge retain.
> Our cause I followed, stood in field and gate—
> All's over now, and now I follow Fate. . . .
> . . . How shall I speak? The South would fain
> Feel peace, have quiet law again—
> Replant the trees for homestead-shade.
>   You ask if she recants: she yields.

Lee warns the committee. "Push not your triumph; do not urge / Submissiveness beyond the verge." Southerners had fought for home and heart, for "kith and kin." Lee asks: "Was this the unforgivable sin?" And instructs: "These noble spirits are yet yours to win."[33]

Melville's invented dialogue is a remarkable exegesis of Lee's actual recorded interview; he read between the lines. In having Lee say that the South yields but does not recant, Melville went straight to the heart of the conflict over the Appomattox terms: was it enough, to yield? Melville captured the essence of Lee's wishful concept of restoration—the reinscription of "quiet law"—and also echoed the argument that Radicals betrayed the spirit of Grant's terms. Melville wanted the reader to believe that "Lee might have lived out his life in chastened peace had not the Senate summoned him," Stanton Garner noted, but the summons rekindled Lee's "pride of conquest." Melville's portrait of Lee thus served a partisan purpose: to promote Andrew Johnson's Reconstruction policies.[34]

The most revealing defense of Lee came from the pages of the *Richmond Examiner*, and from its combative editors, the arch secessionists H. Rives Pollard and Edward A. Pollard. Long in the habit of denigrating Jefferson Davis's leadership and elevating that of Lee, the *Examiner* held up Lee's testimony as a political beacon for Southerners to follow through the dark days ahead. "The words that fall from the lips of such a man as General LEE must be heard with great respect. He has shown himself a great and good man through a testing ordeal," the *Examiner*'s analysis began. It then praised Lee for having taken a strong stand. In his meeting with his congressional inquisitors, he had demonstrated "the proper idea of the colored man's intellect" and fully endorsed Johnson's policies as "wise and humane." The *Examiner* noted that Lee professed to keep his distance from politics but chalked up Lee's disavowals to modesty: "We may be assured that in what he says may be found the matured results of a clear mind, working on a sufficient fund of fact." The editors predicted that the Lee interview would "tend to do much good." The bulk of the Joint Committee's report, the Pollards insisted, was slander intended to "blacken the character of the Southern people and to furnish a pretext for the denial of their constitutional rights." Who better to defend Southern character than Lee?[35]

The *Examiner* editors trumpeted the influence of Lee's interview because they knew perfectly well just how important an ideological claim

Lee had staked. Lee's testimony before the Joint Committee not only lent his prestige to Johnson's policies, it fortified white Southerners, as Lee's Farewell Address had, conviction that they were blameless.[36]

Strikingly, on the very same day, February 17, 1866, that Lee testified before the Joint Committee, Grant demanded that the *Richmond Examiner* offices be seized and its publication suppressed. Grant was keenly aware that the paper had published a series of articles, accusing Union officials and soldiers of malfeasance and corruption, intended to "increase the ill feeling existing towards the Government of the United States by the discontented portion of the Southern people." He felt that it was in "the best interests of the whole people, North and South"—and within the purview of martial law—to silence the kind of "inflammatory" speech that would undermine the fragile peace. H. Rives Pollard protested Grant's decision and prevailed directly upon President Johnson, who in turn ordered that the newspaper be permitted to resume publication on the condition that it cultivate "friendly relations" between North and South. Grant continued to monitor the content of the *Examiner* and again threatened Pollard with suppression when the *Examiner* published a "malicious slander" accusing a Union general in Virginia of bigamy. Pollard, a skilled escape artist, published a retraction of the article, but the damage was done— and ongoing.[37]

The *Examiner* imbroglio was a learning experience for Grant. It impressed upon him how far Johnson had veered toward the Confederates and Copperheads, and it illustrated the cagey ruthlessness of those Southerners bent on restoration. The starkest evidence of that ruthlessness came in the form of reports Grant received from the field. On March 14, 1866, he forwarded to Johnson information he gleaned on interracial violence from the military's Department of Alabama. The report revealed in the form of tabulated statistics that whites had committed 53 acts of assault and battery against blacks, and blacks 10 against whites; whites had murdered 14 blacks, and blacks had murdered one white. Lest Johnson not get the message, Grant did the math, noting that the "assault and battery excess committed by whites" was 43 and the "murder excess by Whites" was 13. Grant held up the statistics as a window into "the feeling and condition of society in Alabama." But as Lee's testimony had shown, white Southerners were masters at veiling violence toward blacks, obscuring it behind the screen of paternalist ideology. When that did not work, they justified violence in the name of self-defense, casting blacks as the aggressors. Johnson, for all his professed antipathy to the old planter aristocracy, was fluent in this discourse of denial and well aware of its political potency. It dawned on Grant, slowly but inexorably, that this president only saw what he wanted to see.[38]

Even as he confronted evidence of Johnson's bad judgment, of white Southern defiance, and of the freedpeople's proscription, Grant remained committed to the broad application of his parole policy. In March of 1866, Grant intervened, as he had for Lee the previous summer, on behalf of two prominent Confederates who faced arrest at the hands of Federal authorities. These two men, General George E. Pickett and General Bradley T. Johnson, were charged with violations of the laws of war: Pickett for ordering the execution of some deserters who claimed to be Union men seeking refuge behind Federal lines, and Johnson for ordering the burning of Chambersburg, Pennsylvania, and for commanding the Confederate prison camp at Salisbury, North Carolina. Both claimed that their actions were commensurate with the rules and customs of war, and that the surrender terms accorded to Lee and to Johnston protected them from federal molestation; Pickett and his supporters had worn Grant down with an incessant lobbying campaign for his aid. Grant, in support of each man's bid for immunity from prosecution, deemed their acts, though harsh, to be within the bounds of legal warfare.[39]

Grant's position on the laws of war was in keeping with an emerging consensus in the North. The Lincoln administration's wartime efforts to define the laws of war, embodied in the Lieber Code of 1863, had resulted in the rigorous prosecution by military commissions of Southern guerrillas and of noncombatants who had committed disloyal acts, such as blockade running, evading military service, or encouraging desertion. In the war's aftermath, military commissions tried dozens of Confederates for war crimes—and some, most notably Henry Wirz, commandant of the notorious Andersonville Prison camp, and Champ Ferguson, a Tennessee guerrilla charged with the murder of Unionist civilians and black soldiers, were sent to their deaths. But the Lieber Code had also advanced a capacious understanding of what soldiers in conventional forces might do in the name of military necessity; such an understanding had helped to justify the Union's "hard war" strategy. However much Grant may have disapproved of actions such as Pickett's execution of deserters, he believed that Pickett had been guided by the dictates of military necessity and had exercised his "belligerent rights." Most important, Grant held that to make an example of Pickett was to invite Southern accusations of Northern bad faith.[40]

Determined though Grant was to hold his ground, Northerners found it increasingly difficult, as indictments against the rebels fell by the wayside, to push back against the prevailing Southern interpretation of what magnanimity meant: namely the view that Confederate soldiers had earned, through their matchless valor, the promise of honorable treatment. The case of Admiral Raphael Semmes is instructive. Semmes had commanded the Confederacy's most infamous commerce raider, the CSS *Alabama*, which preyed upon U.S. merchant ships on the Atlantic and Indian oceans. As Richmond was falling in early April of 1865, Semmes had scuttled his fleet and headed inland; he was among those paroled in North Carolina with Joseph Johnston's army. Semmes was arrested by Federal authorities in December of 1865, on charges of treason, piracy, and the abuse of Union prisoners. Widely loathed in the North as a fiendish brigand, Semmes was a perfect target: even Johnson was enthusiastic about making an example of Semmes, as a way to counter radical Republican charges that the president had totally knuckled under to Southern interests.[41]

But Semmes proved canny in his defense, and the case against him soon fell apart; after three months in prison, he was set free. Semmes's defense invoked, again and again, those key words in Grant's terms (and then Johnston's): the stipulation that Confederates were "not to be disturbed" if they upheld their paroles. Northern commentators regarded it as cynical and hypocritical for Semmes—a man known for his lawless and unconventional tactics—to now seek the protection of military convention. But they had to concede that the terms could be construed to "imply a bargain," as the *US Army and Navy Journal* put it, whereby "no past action through the war should be 'disturbed' by the review and censure of the United States." To go back on that bargain was to risk attenuating the North's moral authority. In Semmes's eyes, the bargain in no way enjoined upon him repentance; in the ensuing years, he would be a vocal defender of Confederate pride and critic of Reconstruction.[42]

Emboldened by the sense that he was successfully building a constituency among Northern Democrats as well as among former rebels, and convinced that the Radicals were the traitors who now threatened the peace, Johnson vetoed the Civil Rights bill on March 27, 1866. His veto message claimed that Congress had no authority to legislate on the South until the Southern representatives were seated and that the bill both discriminated against whites and promoted interracial marriage. The conservative Southern press concluded that in this key battle the Republicans had been "*ignominiously* defeated, and *driven from the field*." "All that is necessary for the South is to continue to *hold up the President's hands*, and wage unceasing and *bitter war* against the Republican Congress," editorialized the *Norfolk Post*. John Dennett, who was visiting Vicksburg, Mississippi, as part of his Southern tour, witnessed a meeting there that had been called "to endorse the President's recent veto message." The speakers reminded their audience that all the Northern Democrats needed was the "active cooperation" of Southerners in order to "hurl the Radicals from power"; they "represented the South as being cruelly injured, insulted, and oppressed, and the North as her wanton oppressor." Johnson's veto, along with his quashing the bill to extend the Freedmen's Bureau, obviated the hope of any cooperation between the president and Congress. A week later, on April 2, Johnson followed up by declaring the war to be officially over. This was no mere claim of "mission accomplished" but another effort to advance Johnson's policy of restoration; as historian Brooks Simpson explains, the "proclamation cast doubt on the continued legitimacy of martial law throughout the South" and undermined the military authority of Grant and his commanders as they tried to keep the peace there.[43]

Faced with Johnson's intransigence, Republicans closed ranks. Speaking on behalf of his Civil Rights bill, Senator Trumbull declared that "the right of American citizenship means something": in exchange for allegiance, citizens, black and white, deserved protection. The black press elaborated this case, with an emphasis on the wartime sacrifices of African American troops. "With garments all dyed in blood—our own heart's blood, shed to save the nation's life; with hands still fettered by the vilest prejudice, and our rights denied by the most sweeping persecution . . . we come to ask for protection—simply for *protection*," a correspondent to the *Christian Recorder* wrote, in an article entitled "A Word on the Veto."

Republicans declared Johnson to be a traitor to the party and to the Union—a Copperhead "undraped, unmasked," prone to "alcoholic rowdyism" (a reference to Johnson appearing to be inebriated on the day of Lincoln's inaugural in March of 1865). His vetoes served the nefarious purpose of "awakening the old defiant, insolent spirit which the events of the war had humbled and silenced, and which might have been exorcised forever," an April 1866 article in the *New Englander and Yale Review* stated.[44]

Images of Appomattox—of Grant and Lee, war and peace, victory and surrender, sin and atonement—suffused the Northern defense of the bill. "The lessons taught by the war—precious lessons, like those coming from the blood of martyrs," the antislavery *Independent* lamented in its April 5 issue, "have, one by one, been rejected and denounced" by Johnson. "Thank heaven," the article continued, that "Congress refuses to surrender all that the war purchased, to please an ambitious, prejudiced, deceitful President." Significantly, the very same issue of the newspaper featured an article entitled "Gen. Lee a Woman-Whipper" that would soon captivate the attention of the antislavery press. The article told the harrowing story of Wesley Norris, a former slave of Lee's. The context for Norris's testimony was a long simmering controversy over Lee's disposition of the estate of his father-in-law, George Washington Parke Custis. When he died in 1857, Custis left behind a will that both named Lee executor of estate and directed that once the estate's considerable debts had been paid down, its slaves were to be freed. Lee, to set the books in order, had sold off many of the slaves and alienated the others by instituting a harsh regime of work and discipline and by delaying their manumission, in seeming contravention of their old master's last wishes. In the spring of 1859, three of these slaves, Wesley and Mary Norris and George Parks, escaped and headed north, only to be captured in Maryland and returned to Virginia to face the fate of a grisly punishment. With Lee looking on, the three, Mary Norris included, were stripped to the waist and whipped.[45]

As historian Elizabeth Brown Pryor has noted, the story of the slaves' flight, capture, and punishment was picked up by some abolitionist newspapers in 1859 and recounted secondhand, with some embellishment— much to Lee's consternation. Not until April of 1866 was the press able to offer a firsthand account, that of Wesley Norris, a government employee who worked in the national cemetery that had been established in 1864 on the Arlington estate. Norris described in excruciating detail how Lee had vented his wrath on the captured fugitives, promising to give them a lesson they "never would forget"; as Lee's overseer wielded the lash, Lee had enjoined him to "lay it on well." "Not satisfied with simply lacerating our naked flesh," Norris went on, "Gen. Lee ordered the overseer to thoroughly wash our backs with brine." Pryor, through careful cross-referencing, has argued for the veracity of Norris's story. In her view, Norris, then a free man, had no ulterior motive—"nothing to hide, gain, or fear"—in confiding to the newspapers after the war. One might also argue, without calling into doubt Norris's credibility, that the timing of the *Independent*'s article was no accident. His firsthand account appeared at the very moment when the Northern public was assimilating Lee's recently published testimony before the Joint Committee and at the very moment when the fate of the Civil Rights bill hung in the balance. The two were connected: the case for the bill depended on exposing as lies the stories of a placid, stable South that Lee and other restorationists wove. The editors of the *Independent*—and perhaps Norris too—addressed themselves directly "to the admirers of Gen. Robert E. Lee," as the article began, to discredit his recent testimony and to bolster the case that the white South had reverted to its old ways.[46]

Even as they scorned Johnson's and Lee's ethos of restoration, Republican commentators invoked the promise of Appomattox and of Grant's magnanimity. They rejected the conservative charge that the party, led by fanatical Radicals, was bent on retribution. All that was required of the Confederate South, wrote Presbyterian clergyman George L. Prentiss in an April 1866 analysis of "The Political Situation," was a "frank and manly acknowledgment of error." If Confederates would only say, "Father, I have sinned against Heaven," averred Prentiss, then even the "hardest 'Radicals'" would be "willing to forget the past." What the Civil Rights bill's supporters wanted was magnanimity with justice—and this, they insisted, is what the hero of Appomattox stood for. Kansas Republican Sidney Clarke, speaking in the House of Representatives, warned that the "pestilent politicians of rebel States, aided by their more pestilent northern allies," sought to "win at the ballot-box what they failed to achieve on the battlefield." They hated "not only those who defeated them, but the principles and purposes which animated the victors." But Northerners would stand by those principles and purposes. Citing Grant's December 1865 report to Johnson, with its finding that the freedmen required the protection of the federal government, Clarke expressed his faith that "having led us to victory in war," Grant might lead the Union to a "still greater victory in peace."[47]

On April 6, the Senate overrode the president's veto, 33 to 15; three days later, on April 9, 1866, the House cast the two-thirds vote needed to uphold the bill. The House galleries erupted into "tumultuous applause ... lasting for several minutes and participated in by ladies as well as gentleman, black as well as white," the *National Anti-Slavery Standard* reported. Among the African American women witnessing the scene was the prolific poet, author, and abolitionist Frances Ellen Watkins Harper. When the bill's passage was announced, she "covered her face, and wept" tears of joy. This was the "first time in American history," Eric Foner explains, that "Congress enacted a major piece of legislation over a President's veto"— and the fact that the bill passed on the one-year anniversary of Lee's surrender at Appomattox was rife with symbolism. The bill represented, according to an editorial in the New York-based *Zion's Herald*, progress as inevitable as the victory over Lee of the "*inevitable Grant.*" The next step, the author hoped, was the extension to the freedmen of the ballot. The African American press held up the bill as proof that white prejudice could be broken down and the promise of the Union's victory fulfilled: "The nation is learning the lesson," declared an April 21, 1866, editorial in the *Christian Recorder*, "that God has unalterably decreed that the elevation of the colored man in this country is the *sine qua non* of the elevation of this nation to the highest point of national greatness." Frederick Douglass, the greatest of all abolitionists, agreed: the Civil Rights bill was a step in the right direction, but the logical next step was the franchise. Only black votes could secure the North "the rightful reward of victory over treason," namely "a solid nation, entirely delivered from all contradictions and social antagonisms."[48]

Ominously, Southern backers of Johnson used the occasion of the Civil Rights bill's passage to glean a very different lesson. In his 1866 tome *The Lost Cause; A New Southern History of the War of the Confederates*, Edward A. Pollard excoriated Congress, seeing in the bill a blueprint for the white South's subjugation:

What is known as the Civil Rights Bill (passed over the President's veto) has not only established negro equality, but has practically abolished, on one subject of jurisdiction at least, State laws and State courts. In short, the extreme Black Republican party at Washington has sought to disfranchise the whole Southern people, to force negro suffrage upon the South, to prevent the South from being represented in Congress so as to perpetuate the power of the Radicals, and afford them the means of governing the Southern states as conquered and subjugated territories.[49]

Southerners, Pollard insisted, rallying the Confederate faithful, conceded military defeat but could not be compelled to change their hearts and minds or to forsake their principles:

The war properly decided only what was put in issue: the restoration of the Union and the excision of slavery; and to these two conditions the South submits. But the war did not decide negro equality; it did not decide negro suffrage; it did not decide States Rights, although it might have exploded their abuse; it did not decide the orthodoxy of the Democratic party; it did not decide the right of a people to show dignity in misfortune, and to maintain self-respect in the face of adversity. And these things which the war did not decide, the Southern people still cling to, still claim, and still assert in them their rights and views.

Lest his readers mistake his message, Pollard posed a chilling question: "*Has the past war merely laid the foundation of another?* The pregnant lesson of human experience is that few nations have had their first civil war without having their second." The South now welcomed a "war of ideas," for there were still "noble victories to be won, memorable services to be performed, and grand results to be achieved."[50]

Among those who assumed the mantle of leadership in the war of ideas was the irrepressible North Carolina poet Mary Bayard Clarke. An elite Southern lady who through literature found a political voice, Clarke achieved new prominence in the year after the war by submitting a series of essays critical of Republican Reconstruction to conservative journals such as the Copperhead *Old Guard*. Lee and his wife, Mary Custis, were old acquaintances of Clarke's and admirers of her work. Clarke took it upon herself to parse the surrender and Lee's comportment in defeat and to derive from both a code of conduct for Southern men and women. In an April 1866 essay, she wrote of the defeated Confederates:

> As men of honor should, they contended to the last for what they believed to be their rights; failing, they yielded, and being men of honor, will abide by their terms of surrender. More than this an honorable enemy should not desire. It is idle to attempt to force them to say and feel they were wrong. They were right.[51]

Later that summer, Clarke would elaborate, explaining in an essay directed at white Southern women that they must walk a fine line in the presence of the occupying force of Yankees. Outright defiance and overt rudeness would have political repercussions. If you "turn up your nose" at the local Freedmen's Bureau official, she cautioned, "he will decide the next case that a negro brings before him against the white man." Better to register one's discontent in a "genteel, lady-like way." Southerners must, she went on, give the impression of compliance while at the same time conceding nothing to their Yankee tormentors. The master of this balancing act was, of course, Lee. "Oh, my noble and patriotic country-women! Look up to, and follow the example of our great and glorious General, Robert E. Lee. . . . Let him be your guide in defeat as he was your star in the hour of triumph," Clarke urged. Lee had not "sullied his fame" with discourtesy toward his opponents. But neither had he "stooped his grandly proud head one hair's breadth since he surrendered to Gen. Grant."[52]

In the postwar South, as during the antebellum era, the veneer of elite gentility overlay a system of brutal racial repression. Ideas were marshaled as weapons in a protracted campaign of vigilante violence that white Southerners perpetrated to secure peace on their own terms. Only a few weeks after the passage of the Civil Rights bill, tragic events in Memphis, Tennessee, dramatized the scope and toll of that violence and the need to offer additional protections for black citizenship. On May 1, 1866, a white mob, led by city policemen, began a wave of attacks against African Americans in South Memphis. The violence would stretch out over three terror-filled days. The precipitating incident was a clash between recently discharged black Union soldiers and white policemen at a festive gathering of African Americans on South Street when the police tried to suppress the blacks' celebration of emancipation and Union. In the midst of false rumors that the black troops were staging an "uprising," white civilians poured into South Memphis, setting fire to shanties, schools, and churches; pillaging stores and residences; sexually assaulting black women; and murdering at least 46 freed people. As historian Hannah Rosen explains, the context for the mob violence was white fear and resentment at the prospect of "social equality" between the races—a prospect heralded in the passage of the Civil Rights bill, in the "relative freedom" of movement and expression that blacks in Memphis had achieved since the war's end, and in the presence of black soldiers in the army of occupation. Firing a volley in the "war of ideas" that Pollard had called for, Memphis whites justified the riot by representing black troops as lawless and domineering and black women as lewd and disorderly. What was needed, these whites insisted, was "a restoration of the old order of things."[53]

General George Stoneman, the Union commander in Memphis, ordered the rioters to stand down and then charged a military commission to gather testimony from black witnesses to the tragedy. A congressional committee conducted its own investigation, interviewing some 66 freed people. In the end, "no rioters were arrested or charged with any crimes," but, Rosen notes, the African American witnesses, particularly women who had the courage to speak out about the sexual assaults they had suffered, nonetheless shaped the public debate on Reconstruction. The congressional committee's final report, widely distributed across the North, condemned the "licentious brutality" of the mob and described black women as respectable and blameless victims of "fiends in human shape."[54]

Grant read these reports with a heavy heart, concluding that the scenes of "murder, arson, rape & robbery" in Memphis had victimized innocent "unresisting negroes" and "stamp[ed] lasting disgrace upon the civil authorities that permitted them." The events confirmed Grant's conviction that a military force was still required in the South to "give a feeling of security to the people." His plea that the instigators be arrested fell on deaf ears in Washington. Grant increasingly felt, as his biographer Jean Edward Smith has put it, that the "Union victory was slipping away."[55]

He gave vent to this gnawing fear in an interview he granted, on May 12, 1866, to the editor of the Lewiston Falls (Maine) *Journal*. A transcript of their conversation was published in the May 24 issue of the *New York Times* and then republished in the *Chicago Tribune*; because it quoted Grant directly and is consistent with other sources from the period, the interview is considered by Grant's modern biographers to be an accurate reflection of his views at this crucial moment. Grant, dressed in a plain black suit, puffed out wreaths of cigar smoke as he talked. The conversation turned first to the Virginia theater in 1864 and 1865. Grant took issue with a recently published "history" of the war, William Swinton's *Campaigns of the Army of the Potomac*, which claimed that Grant had "lost many lives uselessly" in his Overland campaign and should have moved by water down the coast to the Peninsula, as McClellan had. Grant thought this view naive. There was no easy way to defeat the rebels—"Fighting, hard knocks only, could have accomplished the work."[56]

When asked if he was surprised by how quickly the rebellion collapsed in 1865, Grant revealed that he had expected the Confederates to "hold

This Thomas Nast image, titled "Slavery is Dead (?)" laments the persistence of antiblack violence in the wake of the 1866 Civil Rights bill. (Library of Congress)

out another season." Next, in a passage that reveals as starkly as any other his understanding of the legacy of Appomattox, Grant offered that perhaps it would have been better if the rebels had held out—for then the Union army would have had the chance to impose the "blighting effects of war" on those sections of the South that had been spared destruction and to bring the Southern people "to a realizing sense of the enormity of their crime and the necessity of a thorough repentance." The conviction at the heart of Grant's terms remained unchanged: war had been the South's punishment, peace its chance for atonement. But the promised atonement had not come. So Grant now thoroughly embraced the "golden moment" critique of Johnson's leniency. Southerners, he told his interviewer, were "much less disposed now to bring themselves to the proper frame of mind than they were one year since," when the victory was new; "now they regard themselves as masters of the situation."[57]

Grant took to task Robert E. Lee, who was, in his view, "behaving badly." "He is conducting himself very differently from what I had reason, from what he said at the time of surrender, to suppose he would. No man at the South is capable of exercising a tenth part of the influence for good that he is, but instead of using it he is setting an example of forced acquiescence so grudging and pernicious in its effects as to be hardly realized." Such an assessment strongly suggests that Grant had read Lee's testimony before the Joint Committee and perhaps his *New York Herald* interview, too. But it raises the question: how exactly had Grant hoped Lee would behave? Grant offered a clue when, in this interview, he praised the comportment of Generals Joseph Johnston and Richard Taylor; these men were urging Southerners to "throw aside their old prejudices and conform their course to the changed conditions of things." Neither man, as it turned out, would stand by Grant or the Republican Congress in the long term. But in the coming years, a few prominent rebel leaders—Appomattox veterans Longstreet and Mahone and the famed "partisan ranger" of Northern Virginia Colonel John Mosby— would embrace the Republican Party, as Grant hoped the "thinking men" of the South might. Longstreet proved the most eloquent in explaining his conversion. As he put it in an 1867 letter endorsing the "practical reconstruction" of the South and urging Southerners to accept black civil rights:

It is fair to assume that the strongest laws are those established by
the sword. The ideas that divided political parties before the
war—upon the rights of the States—were thoroughly discussed
by our wisest statesmen, and eventually appealed to the arbitrament of the sword. The decision was in favor of the North, so her
construction becomes the law, and should be so accepted.

Longstreet confessed that like most Southerners, he had "naturally acqui-
esced" in the principles of the Democratic Party, but he noted that those
principles were "put to the test in the war and there lost." "As there is
nothing left to take hold of except prejudice, which cannot be worked for
good for any one, it seems proper and right that we should seek some
standing which may encourage hope for the future." The most powerful
grounds he could give for accepting the new order, Longstreet would add
in his memoir, were "the obligations under which we were placed by the
terms of our paroles."[58]

While Grant was not naive enough to have expected these words to
come from Lee's mouth, he would surely have liked for Lee to evince
some of the deference, gratitude, and repentance, some of the good faith
and good sense, found in Longstreet's letter. Longstreet paid a heavy price
for his conversion, as did Mahone and Mosby. These men were dubbed
traitors to the Confederacy by Southern Democrats and took on pariah
status among many white Southerners. Indeed, when Longstreet reached
out to Lee for support, his old mentor rebuffed him, writing, "I cannot
think the course pursued by the dominant political party best for the
interests of the country, and therefore cannot say so, or give my approval."[59]

If Longstreet's conversion represented an alternative to Lee's posture of
"forced acquiescence," the behavior of Henry A. Wise, another of Lee's
Appomattox generals, raised the spectre of open defiance. In May of 1866,
Wise gave a pair of speeches in Richmond and in Alexandria, Virginia,
that ridiculed the Union government and "scoffed at mercy." If the tables
had been turned and Grant's men had surrendered, Wise would "have
favored stripping them naked," he declaimed. "Pardon! They might have
appealed for pardon, but I would have seen them damned before I would
have granted it." Embracing the label of "traitor" and rejecting that of
"prisoner," Wise flaunted the freedom that Grant's parole conferred on

Accepting the new order: James Longstreet, Confederate turned Republican.
(Library of Congress)

him, boasting that no one had the authority to dictate his movements. He added, with a flourish: "I have the profound satisfaction of saying that I fought until we won the privilege of being paroled."[60]

The Northern press took notice of these speeches and expressed its disapproval—nowhere more congently than in the *Army and Navy Journal*, the official gazette of the Union military forces. In a lead story entitled "A Page from History," published on May 19, 1866, the *Journal's* editors sought to set the record straight. Conceding that unrepentant Confederates "consider it very weak and stupid of our Government to act as it does" in extending its mercy, the *Journal* countered, "the Government does not ask the opinion of such as WISE, and has its own motives for treating him beyond his deserts." Rejecting Wise's claim that "the parole granted at Appomattox Court-House was one extorted by the army which surrendered," the *Journal* recounted the heroic campaign in which Grant's "relentless pursuers" had tracked down Lee; the exchange of letters in which Lee tried in vain to deny the hopelessness of his cause; and Lee's last failed attempt to break through the Union's cavalry front. "At the very moment of annihilation, GRANT stayed the uplifted arm," the *Journal* insisted, adding with sarcasm and indignation, "and that is the way the conquered enemy 'extorted' the privilege of parole!" The "magnanimity of GRANT appears the greater the more thoroughly one examines the final facts," the article concluded.[61]

Was Lee's standing among Southerners so exalted—as Grant imagined it to be—that he could have, had he so chosen, reconciled the likes of Wise to the "changed condition of things"? The question was moot. Lee had chosen, in the year since the surrender, to play a nervy game. No one could deny that he had, technically, upheld the terms of his parole. But Grant had wanted more. He had hoped, at Appomattox, that the military men might teach the politicians a lesson or two, that is, he and Lee together would show the world how soldiers win, and lose, with courage and candor. Instead, Lee spoke to his followers in code, encouraging them to denigrate the Union victory as a mere show of force, to resist change in the name of restoration, and to obscure Southern violence behind the veil of genteel paternalism. Grant resented the influence of Lee's overwhelming numbers creed and the dishonest practice of accounting for Confederate defeat by "magnifying the number of Union troops," and "belittling" the number of Confederate ones; that numbers game replicated the tactics of the Peace Democrats, who, during the war, had routinely "magnified rebel successes and belittled those of the Union army." To Grant's profound disappointment, Lee forfeited a measure of his soldier's honor and cast himself into the company of those arch cowards, the Copperheads. It was for such "mischief-makers at the North" that Grant reserved his special ire. They were guilty, he declared in his May 1866 interview, of "making the late rebels believe that they are just as much entitled to rule as ever."[62]

As the curtain fell on the first anniversary of Appomattox, Grant was chastened but not despairing. He still believed that the golden moment might be recaptured. The "large majority of the Southern people would smother their resentments and become good citizens," he told the *Journal* editor, hopefully, if only the Copperhead fifth column could be neutralized.

Despite his growing alienation from Johnson, Grant had not yet fully given up on, or publicly broken, with the president. Johnson, for his part, had not given up the hope that he might still manipulate the general into his corner. But Grant's eyes were wide open. With influential Republicans already suggesting that the hero of Appomattox must lead the party in peace as he had led the army in war, Grant was coming to see that "fighting, and hard knocks only"—this time in the teeming arena of politics—could accomplish the work he had begun on April 9, 1865.[63]

Epilogue

The Apple Tree

"I never have been so tired of anything before as I have been with the political stump speeches of Mr. Johnson from Washington to this place. I look upon them as a National disgrace." So wrote Grant to his wife, Julia, from St. Louis, Missouri, in September 1866, in a sharp critique of Johnson's "Swing Round the Circle"—the ill-fated goodwill tour of Northern cities that Johnson undertook in the late summer and early fall in order to drum up support for his agenda of restoration. Provoked by hecklers, Johnson repeatedly lashed out at the crowds that gathered to hear him, hissing that he was as prepared to "fight traitors at the North" as he had been to fight Southern traitors. Northern traitors were, in his eyes, all those who supported black civil rights. Grant, who had been pressured by the administration into accompanying the president, could barely disguise his contempt for the sputtering spectacle that Johnson had become.[1]

The politically disastrous "swing" was a taste of things to come. In 1867 and 1868, Johnson's reckless policies and erratic behavior pushed moderate Republicans into an alliance with Radical ones, and together they would pursue and nearly effect Johnson's impeachment; demand that the Southern states meet stringent new requirements for readmission to the Union; pass the Fourteenth Amendment, protecting black citizenship; and preside over an unprecedented experiment in interracial democracy in the former Confederate states, as the newly enfranchised freedmen formed a governing coalition with white Southern Unionists and Northern Republican transplants to the South. Conservative defenders of Johnson, sharpening arguments they had made against the 1866 Civil Rights Act, would again turn to Appomattox, as a political touchstone, in their battle against the "military bill," the 1867 Reconstruction Act that established temporary military rule in the South. Grant's terms had explicitly permitted Lee's men to "return to their homes and remain unmolested and undisturbed," the *Valley Virginian* reminded its readers, adding, pointedly, "The Military bill violates that pledge, for it 'molests and disturbs us.'" Republicans, too, would turn to Appomattox in their defense of the bill. The rebels, declared Senator Jacob M. Howard of Michigan in February of 1867, "are our prisoners of war to-day, having been captured and paroled, sent home upon their *parole d'honneur.*" These prisoners had broken their pledge and had usurped the very power that they forfeited in the war. The military bill was a means, well within federal authority and the spirit of the Appomattox, to "suppress insurrection, disorder and violence, and to punish or cause to be punished all disturbers of the peace."[2]

In the summer of 1867, Grant was asked to account definitively for the meaning of the surrender terms by the House Judiciary Committee considering the impeachment of Johnson. Distancing himself from the president, Grant reiterated that his terms were a purely military convention that protected the lives of surrendered soldiers so long as they observed their paroles; denied that he had ever seen fit to advise Johnson on political matters or to "inaugurate any policy" of general amnesty and pardon; lamented that a golden moment of "fine feeling" in the South had been squandered by the president's policies; and affirmed that the authority to establish civil governments in the South lay with Congress. The Democratic press tried in vain to salvage the notion that Grant's views placed him in Johnson's camp, while the Republican press crowed that Grant had offered to the Judiciary Committee a "perfectly simple and manly" endorsement of Congressional Reconstruction. In Grant's eyes, Johnson had not only bolstered the power of unrepentant rebels and endangered the freedmen, he had undercut the capacity of the military to keep the peace and to protect the lives and property of loyal citizens—and so as Congress drafted its Reconstruction measures, Grant "worked openly with Republicans to develop provisions that reinforced military authority." Grant came to see Congressional Reconstruction as the means to secure the gains of the Union's victory at Appomattox.[3]

With his embrace of the congressional program, Grant would move to center stage as the man designated to unseat Johnson, while Lee would move to the wings, where he disavowed any political ambitions even as he studiously made known his political opinions. Grant won the election of 1868, as the candidate who stood for "*both* sectional harmony *and* the guarantee of the freedpeople's newly gained political and economic freedoms," to quote his biographer Joan Waugh. Lee, who, along with two dozen former Confederate generals and politicians, had recently endorsed a treatise, the "White Sulphur Manifesto," which condemned the military bill and called anew for "restoration," considered Grant's election a tragedy. Lee wrote to his cousin: "I grieve for posterity, for American principle & American liberty. Our boasted self Govt. is fast becoming the jeer & laughing stock of the world."[4]

In peace as in war, Grant and Lee were enemies—still. Had they ever been anything else? Even as the two men intervened in postwar politics, a myth of Appomattox began to take shape: this was the myth of the meeting at the McLean house as a "gentlemen's agreement"—a sublime moment of selflessness on the part of two great leaders, who rose above their hatreds and resentments, and, for the good of the nation they both loved, ceased, as they agreed to the surrender terms, to be enemies. The wellspring of this myth was American exceptionalism, the idea that America had broken free of the bonds of history and was not destined to experience the interminable miseries and rivalries of the Old World. The civil way in which Americans ended their Civil War, so this argument went, proved that Americans were distinct and superior. The argument was present, in public discourse on the surrender, from the start. The very same newspapers that contended over the precise meaning of the terms promised that the "world will be surprised by the rapidity, the certainty, wherewith our country will return to the days of peace and industry, and with the immense expansion of our National energies," as Horace Greeley put it on April 13, 1865. The United States would neither repeat the pattern of bloody reprisals furnished by the English Civil Wars and the French Revolution, nor would it give its rival powers the satisfaction of seeing its energies sapped by disunion and backlash. From the start, Americans could hear this argument about the surrender repeated back to them in international coverage of the Appomattox. "It is difficult for a foreign spectator of the great event," wrote a correspondent of the London *Times* on April 25, 1865, "to decide to which of the two Generals the highest meed of praise should be accorded for true nobility of character"; there was no elation or humiliation visible in the comportment of Lee and Grant—only states-manship. Perhaps the United States was destined, after all, to become a real nation, like England and France, and perhaps it would prove "greater than either," the correspondent mused.[5]

In the aftermath of the war, this exceptionalist view proved more com-patible with the program of restoration than with that of reconstruction. "Other nations celebrate the repressing of a rebellion by turning upon the conquered fire and sword, the rack, the bullet, and the gibbet," proclaimed an editorial in the New York journal the *Round Table* in April of 1866. "We had no corps of hangmen stalking in the trail of our victorious legions. We had no Sepoy atrocities, Jamaica massacres, or Arab tortures," it contin-ued. "We restored the southern people their rights as fast as they could take them . . . and the Union became whole and harmonious."[6]

The myth of Appomattox as a moment that transcended politics was given powerful visual representation in a series of postwar prints that depicted Lee surrendering to Grant in an apple orchard. The image had its origins in the fact that Lee had sat in an apple orchard as he awaited Grant's reply to the proposal that they meet in the village of Appomattox Court House; it gained credence as word spread that Lee and Grant had met a second time, on horseback, on April 10, 1865, and as soldiers trafficked in relics that they gathered when they felled the orchard. In 1866 and 1867, Northern printmakers would blend these facts and rumors into "imagined scenes of the purported apple orchard peace conference." These scenes lifted the surrender from its "mundane surroundings" and lent grandeur to proceedings that had been, on the face of it, "formal and unemotional." In their particulars, the prints imbued the two generals with dignity and ci-vility and elevated Lee to the status of a worthy foe and an icon of reunion: "By depicting him unbowed before Grant, the printmakers demonstrated that reunion could be accomplished without subjugation," Mark E. Neely Jr., Harold Holzer, and Gabor S. Boritt noted in *The Confederate Image: Prints of the Lost Cause*. While Southerners did not contribute to the prolif-eration of orchard scenes, they did circulate the apple tree lore in their news-papers and reminiscences. The *Edgefield Advertiser* of January 10, 1866,

"Capitulation & Surrender" (1885), one of the many postwar prints in the "orchard peace conference" genre. (Library of Congress)

for example, featured an account of the last Confederate soldier still convalescing at Richmond's Fair Grounds Hospital. He had been wounded on April 9, 1865, "within a few yards of the famous apple tree under which General Grant and Lee signed the articles of surrender."[7]

However comforting it was, the pastoral fantasy of the orchard meeting could not hold sway. Images of Lee and Grant extending the hand of fellowship beneath the boughs competed with images of Jefferson Davis "hanging from a sour apple tree," as a popular Union ballad, commemorating Davis's capture by Federal forces and urging his punishment, had it. Indeed, Davis became the focal point of Northern scorn; rumors that he had been captured in May 1865 wearing his wife's raincoat and shawl were translated into visual images of him bedecked in hoopskirts, the "Belle of Richmond."[8]

As the struggle over Reconstruction escalated, the Appomattox apple tree became a symbolic prize. It was a fixture of Grant's 1868 presidential campaign imagery, as the party faithful were rallied with a song that proclaimed:

In this 1865 print, Jeff Davis in a hoop skirt hangs from a sour apple tree
while his accomplices (Lee and Booth among them) await their turn.
(Library of Congress)

> So, boys, a final bumper,
>   While we all in chorus chant,
> For next President we nominate
>   Our own Ulysses Grant.
> And if asked what State he hails from,
>   This our sole reply shall be,
> From near Appomattox Court-House,
>   And its famous apple tree
> For 'twas there to our Ulysses
>   That Lee gave up the fight
> Now boys, to Grant for President
>   And God defend the right.[9]

The tree figured prominently in African American remembrances of
Appomattox, as black commentators positioned USCT troops at the center of the narrative of Grant's triumph. "Lee surrendered at Appomattox
under the shade of the old apple tree," intoned the Reverend G. V. Clark at
a meeting of a black literary association in Memphis, Tennessee, "leaving
our brave black heroes covered with glory and crowned with imperishable
laurels." "A race with such indomitable courage," he assured his listeners,

"must have under God a future, inspiring and glorious." T. Thomas Fortune, editor of the influential *New York Age*, struck a similar note in an 1890 address to the National Afro-American League. He paid homage to the black veterans of the Civil War, who "*came from Appomattox and its famous apple tree*" and who "like their white comrades went back to their homes after the toils of war and mingled in the pursuits of peace." Their comportment had vindicated "the right of every man born on this soil to be free indeed."[10]

But the opponents of black civil rights would not cede so powerful an image to their enemies. The apple tree materialized, too, in conservative attacks on Grant, on Radical Reconstruction, and on racial equality. An article in the Democratic *Brooklyn Daily Eagle*, published on the tenth anniversary of the surrender, looked back on Grant's "vengeful Administration" and concluded that "a blight came upon the apple tree of Appomattox. The blossom withered, and the promised fruit when it came turned to ashes on the lips." The Democrats alone had "kept the promise of that crowning hour"; Grant, seduced by ambition, had proved a traitor to his own purposes.[11]

In the South, conservative Democrats seized Appomattox as a symbol and held it hostage. "If the programme which our people saw set on foot at Appomattox Court-House had been carried out—if our people had been met in the spirit which we believe existed there among the officers and soldiers, from General Grant on down—we would have had no disturbance in the South, and we would long since have had a very different state of things in this country," John Brown Gordon, one of the heroes of Lee's final campaigns, told a congressional committee in 1872. The committee was charged with investigating the depredations of the Ku Klux Klan in the South. While black rhetoric invoked Appomattox to signify a righteous peace, white Southerners used it to call forth violence. Gordon, who headed Georgia's Klan and represented the state in Congress, credited Lee's army and Grant's with sheathing the "sword of vengeance" and indicted Southern blacks, whom he regarded as criminal and insurrectionary, for unsheathing it. He declared in the U.S. Senate in 1875 that "deluded, ignorant negroes . . . with arms to murder and hearts for plunder" perpetrated "crimes not to be described on this floor," which left white men no choice but to resort to violence in self-defense. In Gordon's view, blacks had no place whatsoever in the "fraternity" of "once opposing soldiers" who had tried to "inaugurate an era of peace."[12]

The tragic implications of this ideology are starkly illustrated by the WPA reminiscence of Lucinda Elder. Elder was born into slavery near Concord Depot, Virginia. After the war, her master, John Caldwell, announced to his slaves that they were free but could continue to work for him, for wages. Lucinda's family accepted this offer. Some years later, she was hired to work as a nursemaid for the family of one Will Jones.

One day Jones announced to the family that they were going to Appomattox to spend the day and that Lucinda and the children could come too. The significance of the site was well known to Lucinda. "Course, I was tickled mos' to pieces," she told her WPA interviewer, at the prospect of this trip. But Jones had not told her why they were going to Appomattox.

John Brown Gordon, who blamed radical Northerners for breaking the Appomattox covenant. (Library of Congress)

The purpose of the Jones family outing was to witness a lynching—"to see a nigger hung," in Elder's words. She was told he was being punished because he had "kilt a man." "I never saw so many people 'fore, as the number there to see him hang," she recalled. "I jes' shut my eyes." But the macabre lesson was not over. After the lynching, Jones took the family to what he claimed was the famous apple tree of Appomattox lore. Elder described it as a "big tree that had all de bark strip off it and de branches strip off." Jones turned to her and said "Lucinda, dis de tree where Gen. Lee surrendered." She put her two hands on the tree. She would never ever, as long as she lived, she told her interviewer, forget that one day.[13] Whatever Jones's intentions in orchestrating this grim excursion, the message was clear: the South had not surrendered white supremacy at Appomattox.

How then did the myth of Appomattox as a gentlemen's agreement come to triumph over such images of competition and conflict, of repression and woe? One might argue that it never fully did—and that Americans' efforts to remember and memorialize Appomattox have been dissonant. Evidence abounds that white Americans closed ranks in the late nineteenth century around a cult of reconciliation, celebrating the manly valor of all Civil War soldiers, blue and gray; pushing to the side the fraught issue of racial justice; justifying the overthrow of Radical Reconstruction by ex-Confederate "redeemers," in the name of order and stability; and romanticizing the South's doomed but noble "Lost Cause." Selective images of Appomattox, such as the Union army's sharing of rations with the Confederates (which did take place) and Grant's return of Lee's sword (which, like the apple orchard surrender, never actually happened), became staples of the reconciliationist lore of the surrender. Veterans of Appomattox, John Brown Gordon most prominently, wrote memoirs that seemed to be simple celebrations of the fraternal spirit both armies had shown on April 9, 1865.[14]

But as historian Caroline Janney has demonstrated, Appomattox also resisted commemoration. Confederate veterans and their descendants doggedly opposed efforts to erect a peace monument at the site, for the pain and shame of the surrender lingered. However well Appomattox served as a political touchstone, however much of their power had been

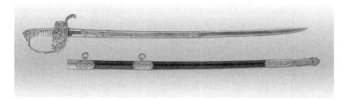

Lee's ceremonial sword, which, according to a stubborn legend, he offered to Grant at Appomattox only to have Grant refuse it. (Museum of the Confederacy, Richmond, Virginia, photograph by Alan Thompson)

restored, April 9, 1865, still signified the finality of Confederate military defeat and the looming "tragic era" of Radical Reconstruction. It was easier to commemorate Gettysburg, with all its many "might have beens." Not until 1950—after decades of planning, debate, fundraising, and historical restoration—was a National Park Service site at Appomattox officially dedicated.[15]

African Americans commemorated Appomattox for decades after the war. So deeply did the case for USCT heroism at Appomattox resonate that the epigram "the last guns fired at Lee's army were in the hands of Negro soldiers"—which captured a symbolic truth if not a literal one— became a recurring motif in black public discourse, invoked in the name of uplift and social justice. At an 1885 Philadelphia meeting to promote education, AME church officials called on African Americans to vanquish the foe of illiteracy by showing the same courage as the heroic black soldier who "fired the last gun at Lee's army." And it was not only men who seized this epigram. Leila Amos Pendleton, an eminent educator, clubwoman, and race historian, invoked the "last shots" in her textbook, *A Narrative of the Negro*. Animated by the "highest sentiments of courage and patriotism," as Pendleton put it, USCT soldiers had "won for themselves lasting glory."[16]

The image of Appomattox as the dawn of freedom found frequent expression in African American culture, in the North as well as the South. Frances Ellen Watkins Harper gave it voice in her acclaimed novel *Iola Leroy*, set in the Civil War and published in 1892. She wrote: "On the ninth day of April, 1865, General Lee surrendered to General Grant. The lost cause went down in blood and tears, and on the brows of a ransomed people God poured the chrism of a new era, and they stood a race newly

anointed with freedom." That sentiment was commemorated annually in
black churches. On April 9, 1914, the black congregation of Philadelphia's
Miller Memorial Baptist Church gathered to celebrate "the Emancipation
of the Ethiopians from American slavery, by the surrender of General
Robert E. Lee to General U. S. Grant at Appomattox."[17]

The notion that Appomattox heralded racial reconciliation found its
most enduring expression in Chicago's Appomattox Club, a civic organization established in 1900 by the city's black political leadership. Deeming Lee's surrender an "epoch making event," the club held an annual
"monster celebration" to mark the Appomattox anniversary and to renew
the hope that "millions of white and black men" might "bridge the chasm
of political, social and economic prejudice and in universal brotherhood
shake hands as did Grant and Lee." In addition to memorializing the surrender, the club held an annual memorial service in honor of two heroes
of the antislavery cause, Abraham Lincoln and Frederick Douglass. For
this organization, reunion was premised not on forgetting emancipation
but on remembering it.[18]

In the first decades of the twentieth century, an alternative, more somber interpretation of the surrender began to gain currency among black
opinion makers. Some commentators insisted that Lee and the South had
never accepted defeat; Grant had been too lenient, and thus the spirit of
Southern defiance had survived the surrender intact. Decrying "lynching,
disfranchising, intimidation, and the present effort of eliminating almost
wholly Negro education," a writer in the Baltimore *Afro-American* lamented in 1902 that white Southerners had revived an argument over
black inferiority that "we imagined we had won at Appomattox." In 1912,
with the "Lost Cause" mythos at a peak of popularity, an article in the
Pittsburgh Courier lamented that "southern thought is conquering the
entire country on the race question." The article quoted a poem called
"Appomattox," by the black poet Charles Dinkins, in which Lee addresses
his defeated army with the following charge:

> When falls the sword, the better way
> Becomes the soldier's part to play
> The south will whip the north some day
> With ink and pen

Lee's prophecy, the article noted, had come to pass: the unrepentant South had struck down the doctrine of social equality and "revolutionized the sentiment, doctrines and practices of the north." In this interpretive mode, the surrender was not a golden moment that might be recaptured, but instead an inherently tragic moment—a catalyst to and harbinger of the South's resurgence.[19]

Such laments testify to the waning of a once proud tradition—of the "fondly cherished" belief, as one black journalist put it, that Appomattox had consigned the regime of racial subordination to "the things of the past." While there were many factors regarding the fading of Appomattox from black public discourse, it was ultimately the "long absence of any real freedom," historian Mitch Kachun has cogently observed, that caused the demise of emancipation day celebrations.[20]

Recently, the gentlemen's agreement myth has been revived as part of an impulse to detach the noble intentions of Lee and Grant from the political turmoil that followed in the wake of the surrender. In Philip Glass's acclaimed opera *Appomattox* (2007), scenes of postwar strife—of decades of antiblack violence and of the long struggle for civil rights—intrude upon Grant's and Lee's selfless exercise of statesmanship; in Jay Winik's bestseller, *April 1865: The Month that Saved America* (2001), the two generals' comportment on April 9 instantiates a new America, a nation "for the first time, largely whole, looking as much to the future as to the past." Although the keynote of one treatment is tragedy and of the other is triumph, both pay homage to the genius of Lee and Grant and lament leaders of such caliber passing from the scene.[21]

This book has argued that we should see Lee's and Grant's genius and evaluate their leadership in a different light. Their great, enduring achievement was to end the war. No matter how irresistible it was, and is, to use metaphors of combat to describe postwar politics, those metaphors should not be pushed too far: Appomattox ended the massive bloodletting of two contending armies. Southerners and Northerners alike, who had absorbed shocking casualty rates and death tolls, drew a line, on April 9, between war and peace, and so must we.

However compelling and comforting the image of a gentlemen's agreement may be, it does not begin to capture the complex legacy of the surrender. From the very start, the peace was uneasy, fragile, and fraught. Lee did not passively accept the verdict of defeat. Instead he maintained that the "judgment of reason" had been "displaced by the arbitrament of war," and that reason, synonymous with conservative politics, must be made to prevail again. For Lee the peace was an opportunity for the country to restore the equilibrium between the North and South, and between the federal government and the states; to restore the best men of the South to positions of political leadership; and to restore the virtues of the founding era. "As long as virtue was dominant in the Republic, so long was the happiness of the people secure," he wrote nostalgically to a fellow Confederate veteran in the fall of 1865. As Lee encountered Northern hostility and resistance to this interpretation of the war's meaning, he dug in his heels and became more entrenched ideologically. No longer was he willing, after the war as he had been on the eve of secession, to decry Southern extremism as well as Northern. Lee had come to firmly believe that "THE ONLY DIFFICULTY IN THE WAY OF AN AMICABLE ADJUSTMENT WAS WITH THE REPUBLICAN PARTY," as he stridently put it to Sir John Dahlberg Acton, a pro-Confederate British politician and historian, in December 1866. Lee symbolized a South committed to peace, but unbowed and unrepentant, and determined to protect itself against Northern interference.[22]

Grant symbolized a Union righteous and vindicated, committed to instructing Southerners in a new moral order. Thanks to his magnanimity, he believed, the South would benefit even more than the North from the Union victory: white Southerners would be disenthralled from the autocratic social system that had degraded them and welcomed back to the republican fold. Grant considered his position so eminently reasonable that he was caught off guard by the resistance he encountered, both from Confederates and Copperheads who refused to yield their principles, and from freedpeople, white Southern Unionists, and northern Radicals, who insisted that the Union could not safeguard its victory without granting African Americans a political voice. Confronted with the "foolhardiness of the President and the blindness of the Southern people to their own interest," Grant adapted: "[I] gradually worked up to the point where, with the majority of the people, I favored immediate enfranchisement" for blacks, he wrote in his memoir. This was the only way to neutralize the "political party in the North which had sympathized with the rebellion" and to dispel the ex-Confederates' pretension that "they would be able to control the nation . . . and were entitled to do so."[23]

It is impossible to reconcile Lee's and Grant's interpretations of the surrender, because they represented two positions in a perennial debate in American political life: Did the nation's best days lie in its past or in its future? In his memoirs Grant would write of the Civil War, "We are better off now than we would have been without it, and have made more rapid progress than we otherwise should have made." In his view, there was no point in nostalgia, and no point in trying to fix in amber the principles of the founding generation. The nineteenth century had brought transformative change—"steam to propel vessels against both wind and current . . . machinery to do all manner of work . . . the instantaneous transmission of messages around the world by means of electricity." The "immaterial" world had changed as much as the "material" one. The triumph of the Union had consigned the moral blight of secession and slavery to the past. The war was "worth all it cost."[24]

This ethos of progress held no charm for Lee. Even as Grant, in the late 1860s, braved the shoals of political office, Lee found a safe harbor among his students, his admirers, and his books. Lee dreamed of writing a definitive account of his campaigns, in which a band of honorable heroes would ride forth again to strike at Northern tyranny and power. "I want that the world shall know what my poor boys, with their small numbers and scant resources, succeeded in accomplishing." He prepared and published a biographical sketch of his father, the Revolutionary war hero Light Horse Harry Lee. He found solace in works of history: the *Iliad*, the *Meditations of Marcus Aurelius*, Goldsmith's *History of Rome*, Macaulay's *History of England*, Ramsey's *History of the American Revolution*, Marshall's *Life of Washington*, and books on the campaigns of Napoleon. "It is history," Lee believed, along with so many white Southerners living in what they considered a tragic era, "that teaches us to hope."[25]

A telling counterpoint to Grant's faith in the march of civilization and Lee's reveries of bygone glory can be found in the writings of Frances Ellen Watkins Harper. Renowned among reformers in the North as an antislavery activist, lecturer, and author, she embarked on a tour of the defeated South in 1867, to gauge the Southern temper and mark the freedpeople's hard-fought progress. In July of 1867, Harper wrote from South Carolina to a correspondent in Wilmington, Delaware; her letter was published in the *National Anti-Slavery Standard*. "The South is a sad place," she began. "It is so rife with mournful memories. . . . Here you listen to heart-saddening stories of grievous old wrongs, for the shadows of the past have not been fully lifted from the minds of the former victims of slavery." African Americans could neither escape from history nor escape into it. But Harper did not despair. "It is well for us to look hopefully to the future," she urged, "for the shadows bear the promise of a brighter coming day." Her tour, in which she addressed gatherings of former slaves, was proof that freedom of speech, which had been "an outlaw" in the South, was finally gaining ground. "The work goes bravely on." For those in the postwar world determined to seize the promise of freedom, this was the true meaning of Appomattox.[26]

ABBREVIATIONS

AAP   African American Perspectives: Pamphlets from the Daniel A.P. Murray Collection, Library of Congress, Washington, D.C. http://memory.loc.gov/ammem/app

APS   American Periodical Series http://www.proquest.com

CA   Chronicling America: Historic American Newspapers http://chroniclingamerica.loc.gov

CWLD   American Civil War: Letters and Diaries http://solomon.cwld.alexander-street.com

FWP   Born in Slavery: Slave Narratives from the Federal Writers' Project http://memory.loc.gov/ammem/snhtml

HSP   Historical Society of Pennsylvania, Philadelphia

LVA   Library of Virginia, Richmond

MOC   Eleanor S. Brockenbrough Archives, Museum of the Confederacy, Richmond, Virginia

MP   The Martyred President: Sermons Given on the Occasion of the Assassination of Abraham Lincoln http://beck.library.emory.edu/lincoln (sponsored by Emory University Libraries)

PAJ   Paul H. Bergeron, ed., *The Papers of Andrew Johnson: Volume 8, May–August 1865* (Knoxville: University of Tennessee Press, 1989).

PUSG   John Y. Simon et al., eds., *Papers of Ulysses S. Grant*, 30 vols. (Carbondale: Southern Illinois University Press, 1967–).

OR   *Official Records of the War of the Rebellion* Making of America Collection, http://ebooks.library.cornell.edu/m/moawar/waro.html

UVA   Small Special Collections, Alderman Library, University of Virginia, Charlottesville

VHS   Virginia Historical Society, Richmond

VSP   Valley of the Shadow Project http://valley.vcdh.virginia.edu

W&L   Special Collections and Archives, Washington and Lee University, Lexington, Virginia

NOTES

Chapter 1

1. Sheridan to Grant, April 5, 1865, *OR* 46 (3): 582; J. Warren Keifer, *A Forgotten Battle: Sailor's Creek, April 6, 1865* (Cincinnati: s.n., 1888?), p. 3; Philip H. Sheridan, *Personal Memoirs of P.H. Sheridan*, vol. 2 (New York: Charles L. Webster, 1888), pp. 175–80.
2. On Sheridan's standing at this juncture of the war, see Steven E. Nash, "'In the Right Place at the Right Time': Philip H. Sheridan," in *Grant's Lieutenants: From Chattanooga to Appomattox*, ed. Steven E. Woodworth (Lawrence: University Press of Kansas, 2008), pp. 155–71.
3. Philip H. Sheridan, *Personal Memoirs of P.H. Sheridan*, vol. 1 (New York: Charles L. Webster, 1888), pp. 461, 487–88; *Personal Memoirs*, vol. 2, pp. 51, 99.
4. Sheridan to Grant, April 5, 1865, *OR* 46 (3): 582; Henry Edwin Tremain, *Last Hours of Sheridan's Cavalry* (New York: Silver & Bowers, 1904), p. 141.
5. On the hard-war strategy, see Mark Grimsley, *The Hard Hand of War: Union Military Policy toward Southern Civilians, 1861–65* (New York: Cambridge University Press, 1997). Estimates of the number of troops with which Lee began the retreat range from 55,000 to 60,000. See Chris M. Calkins, *The Appomattox Campaign, March 29–April 9, 1865* (1997. Reprint, Lynchburg, Va.: Schroeder, 2011), p. 63; William Marvel, *A Place Called Appomattox* (Carbondale: Southern Illinois University Press, 2008), p. 201, and *Lee's Last Retreat: The Flight to Appomattox* (Chapel Hill: University of North Carolina Press, 2002), pp. 37, 202.
6. For reliable overviews of the Appomattox Campaign, see the National Park Service-sponsored publications: Noah Andre Trudeau, *The Campaign to Appomattox* (Ft. Washington, Pa.: Eastern National, 1995) and *Appomattox Court House* (Harpers Ferry, W.Va.: National Park Division of Publications, 2002).
7. On the condition of Lee's army in the spring of 1865, see Joseph T. Glatthaar, *General Lee's Army: From Victory to Collapse* (New York: Free Press, 2008). On the fate of the rations, see Calkins, *Appomattox Campaign*, p. 75.
8. Glatthaar, *General Lee's Army*, p. 461; Sheridan, *Personal Memoirs*, vol. 2, pp. 178–79; Sylvanus Cadwallader, *Three Years with Grant*, ed. Benjamin P. Thomas (1955. Reprint, Lincoln: University of Nebraska Press, 1996).

Notes to Pages 11–17

9. On the relationship of Grant, Meade, and Sheridan, see Ethan S. Rafuse, "'Wherever Lee Goes . . .': George G. Meade," in Woodworth, ed., *Grant's Lieutenants,* pp. 76–83 (quotation on p. 79).

10. Glatthaar, *General Lee's Army,* p. 461; Sheridan, *Personal Memoirs,* vol. 2, pp. 175–80; Ulysses S. Grant, *Personal Memoirs of U. S. Grant* (1885. Reprint, New York: Penguin Books, 1999), pp. 587–88.

11. For a detailed account of the battle, see Chris M. Calkins, *Thirty-Six Hours before Appomattox: The Battles of Sailor's Creek, High Bridge, Farmville and Cumberland Church* (Farmville, Va.: Farmville Herald, 2006), pp. 5–17, 29–32.

12. Report of Bvt. Maj. Gen. George A. Custer, April 15, 1865, *OR* 46 (1): 1129; Report of Maj. Gen. Philip H. Sheridan, May 16, 1865, *OR* 46 (1): 1107; Jeffrey D. Wert, *Custer: The Controversial Life of George Armstrong Custer* (New York: Simon & Schuster, 1996), pp. 73–105, 159 (quotation).

13. On Grant's reconfiguration of the senior command, see Jean Edward Smith, *Grant* (New York: Touchstone, 2001), p. 399. On Wright, see Benjamin Franklin Cooling, "Chasing 'Old Jube': David Hunter, Lewis Wallace, and Horatio Wright," in Woodworth, ed., *Grant's Lieutenants,* pp. 147–49, 153.

14. Calkins, *Thirty-Six Hours,* pp. 8–13; J. Warren Keifer, *Official Reports of J. Warren Keifer, Brevet Major General of Volunteers, USA* (Springfield: Daily Republic Steam Job Rooms, 1866), pp. 46–47 and *A Forgotten Battle,* pp. 5–7; Wright to Major-General Alexander S. Webb, April 6, 1865 *OR* (3): 604–5; Reports of Maj. Gen. Horatio G. Wright, April 29, 1865, *OR* 46 (1): 906–7. There is some controversy over which Union unit—the Fifth Wisconsin or Custer's cavalry division—captured General Ewell. See Donald C. Pfanz, *Richard S. Ewell: A Soldier's Life* (Chapel Hill: University of North Carolina Press, 1998), pp. 525–26.

15. Elisha Hunt Rhodes, *All for the Union: The Civil War Diary and Letters of Elisha Hunt Rhodes* (New York: Vintage, 1992), pp. 219–21.

16. On Humphreys, see Richard J. Sommers, "Andrew Atkinson Humphreys," in *Biographical Dictionary of the Union,* ed. John T. Hubbell and James W. Geary (Westport, Conn.: Greenwood Press, 1995), pp. 266–67, and Henry L. Abbot, *Memoir of Andrew Atkinson Humphreys* (Washington, D.C.: s.n., 1885). For Humphreys' movements, see his dispatches dated April 6, 1865 to Meade's chief of staff, Alexander S. Webb, *OR* 46 (3): 598–600; Reports of Maj. Gen. Andrew A. Humphreys, April 10 and 21, 1865, *OR* 46 (1): 673–82 and his memoir, *The Virginia Campaign of '64 and '65* (New York: Charles Scribner's Sons, 1885), pp. 373–81.

17. There are some discrepancies in scholarly accounts of the overall tally of prisoners and casualties; my statistics come from Christopher M. Calkins, "Sailor's Creek," in *The Civil War Battlefield Guide,* ed. Frances H. Kennedy, 2nd ed. (Boston: Houghton Mifflin, 1998), p. 427.

18. Calkins, *Thirty-Six Hours,* p. 2 and "Sailor's Creek," p. 427 (Lee quotation); Sheridan, *Personal Memoirs,* p. 180.

19. Royall W. Figg, *Where Only Men Dare to Go, Or the Story of a Boy Company, C.S.A.* (1885. Reprint, Baton Rouge: Louisiana State University Press, 2008), p. 217.

20. Sheridan to Grant, April 6, 1865, *OR* 46 (1): 610; Smith, *Grant,* p. 398; David W. Lowe, ed., *Meade's Army: The Private Notebooks of Lt. Col. Theodore Lyman* (Kent, Ohio: Kent State University Press, 2007), p. 364.

21. On Ord see William B. Feis, "Grant's Relief Man: Edward O. C. Ord," in Woodworth, ed., *Grant's Lieutenants,* pp. 173–94.

22. Calkins, *Thirty-Six Hours*, pp. 37–45, and *Appomattox Campaign*, p. 101; Wert, *Custer*, p. 29.
23. Humphreys, *Virginia Campaigns*, pp. 378, 386–87 and April 21, 1865, report, *OR* 46 (1): 683.
24. Chris M. Calkins, *The Battles of Appomattox Station and Appomattox Court House, April 8–9, 1865* (Lynchburg, Va.: H.E. Howard, 1987), pp. 3–4.
25. Report of Wright, April 29, 1865, *OR* 46 (1): 907–8; Grant, *Personal Memoirs*, p. 594; Sheridan, *Personal Memoirs*, vol. 2, 188–89.
26. Sheridan, *Personal Memoirs*, vol. 2, p. 189; Grant, *Personal Memoirs*, p. 594; Smith, *Grant*, pp. 398–99; James L. Morrison Jr., "John Gibbon," in *Biographical Dictionary of the Union*, p. 198 (first quotation); John Gibbon, *Personal Recollections of the Civil War* (New York: G.P. Putnam's Sons, 1928), pp. 306–7 (second quotation).
27. Gibbon, *Personal Recollections*, p. 307; Grant to Lee, April 7, 1865, *OR* 46 (3): 619.
28. Lieut. Col. C. A. Whittier to General N. A. Miles, April 7, 1865, *OR* 46 (3): 626–27.
29. Grant to Meade, April 7, 1865, *OR* 46 (3): 621; Richard J. Sommers, "Charles Griffin," in *Biographical Dictionary of the Union*, p. 215 (quotation); Grant, *Personal Memoirs*, pp. 594–95; Frank P. Cauble, *The Surrender Proceedings: April 9, 1865 Appomattox Court House* (Lynchburg, Va.: H.E. Howard, 1987), p. 2.
30. For use of the "effusion of blood" formula, see Jared Sparks, *The Writings of George Washington* (Boston: Little, Brown, 1855), p. 530; John S. C. Abbott, *The History of the Civil War in America* (New York: H. Bill, 1863–66), pp. 178, 382, 470, and Grant, *Personal Memoirs*, p. 306.
31. Joan Waugh, *U. S. Grant: American Hero, American Myth* (Chapel Hill: University of North Carolina Press, 2009), p. 94 (quotation).

Chapter 2

1. Lee to Grant, April 7, 1865, *OR* 46 (3): 619; Calkins, *Appomattox Campaign*, p. 135.
2. James Longstreet, *From Manassas to Appomattox* (1895. Reprint, New York: Da Capo Press, 1992), pp. 618–19; Charles Marshall, *Lee's Aide-de-Camp*, ed. Frederick Maurice (1927. Reprint, Lincoln: University of Nebraska Press, 2000), pp. 254–55; Lee to Grant, April 7, 1865, *OR* 46 (3): 619.
3. Glatthaar, *General Lee's Army*, pp. 337–38, 435; Jeffrey D. Wert, "Introduction" to Longstreet, *From Manassas to Appomattox* (1895. Reprint, New York: Da Capo Press, 1992), pp. xi–xii (quotation).
4. Edward Porter Alexander, *Fighting for the Confederacy: The Personal Recollections of General Edward Porter Alexander*, ed. Gary Gallagher (Chapel Hill: University of North Carolina Press, 1989), p. 527. On the Pendleton incident, see W. N. Pendleton, "Personal Recollections of General Lee," *Southern Magazine* 15 (1874), and Susan P. Lee, *Memoirs of William Nelson Pendleton* (Philadelphia: J.B. Lippincott, 1893), pp. 401–3; Longstreet, *From Manassas to Appomattox*, pp. 618–19; Marshall, *Lee's Aide-de-Camp*, pp. 254–55, and Armistead L. Long, *Memoirs of Robert E. Lee: His Military and Personal History* (New York: J.M. Stoddart, 1886), pp. 416–17. Pendleton claimed that Gordon and Longstreet were party to his initiative; Gordon and Longstreet later denied taking part in such a meeting. On this controversy, see Cauble, *Surrender Proceedings*, pp. 10–11.

5. Alexander, *Fighting for the Confederacy*, p. 527; Longstreet, *From Manassas to Appomattox*, pp. 618–19; Marshall, *Lee's Aide-de-Camp*, pp. 254–55; Long, *Memoirs of Robert E. Lee*, pp. 416–17; William C. Davis, ed., "On the Road to Appomattox," *Appomattox Commemorative Issue of Civil War Times* (Leesburg, Va.: Primedia History Group, 2005), p. 60 (Mahone quotation). The Davis article transcribes and contextualizes a detailed account of the Appomattox campaign by William Mahone; the account is a 73-page letter that Mahone wrote sometime between 1890 and 1894 on stationery of the Hotel Chamberlin in Washington, D.C., likely at the behest of Longstreet. The Mahone letter is also available through Auburn University's Special Collections Library at http://www.lib.auburn.edu/archive/find-aid/242.htm.

6. Longstreet, *From Manassas to Appomattox*, pp. 618–19; Long, *Memoirs of Robert E. Lee*, pp. 416–17. On the Fort Donelson surrender, see Waugh, *U. S. Grant*, p. 54.

7. On Lee's hope that Southern victories might effect a "political revolution" in the North, see Ethan S. Rafuse, *Robert E. Lee and the Fall of the Confederacy, 1863–1865* (Lanham, Md.: Rowman & Littlefield, 2008), pp. 20, 24, 41, 203, 206, and Gary Gallagher, "Introduction" to Marshall, *Lee's Aide-de-Camp*, p. xiv (Marshall quote).

8. Steven E. Woodworth, "The Last Function of Government: Confederate Collapse and Negotiated Peace," in *The Collapse of the Confederacy*, ed. Mark Grimsley and Brooks D. Simpson (Lincoln: University of Nebraska Press, 2001), pp. 13–39 (quotation on p. 14); William C. Davis: *An Honorable Defeat: The Last Days of the Confederate Government* (New York: Harcourt, 2001), pp. 28–30 (second quotation on p. 29).

9. Davis, *An Honorable Defeat*, pp. 5–8, 30; Woodworth, "The Last Function of Government," pp. 13–39; James M. McPherson, "No Peace without Victory, 1861–1865," *American Historical Review* 109 (February 2004): 12–14.

10. On this incident, see Feis, "Grant's Relief Man," pp. 191–93, and Longstreet, *From Manassas to Appomattox*, pp. 586–87 (Lee and Grant quotations), 647–48.

11. Davis, *An Honorable Defeat*, pp. 40–46.

12. Morris Schaff, *The Sunset of the Confederacy* (1912. Reprint, New York: Cooper Square Press, 2002), pp. 161–62.

13. Grant to Lee, April 8, 1865, *OR* 46 (3): 641.

14. Waugh, *U. S. Grant*, p. 65, and "'I Only Knew What Was In My Mind': Ulysses S. Grant and the Meaning of Appomattox," *Journal of the Civil War Era* 2 (September 2012), pp. 307–18.

15. Waugh, *U.S. Grant*, p. 65; Grant, *Personal Memoirs*, pp. 306–8.

16. Grant, *Personal Memoirs*, pp. 111–21; Brooks D. Simpson, *Let Us Have Peace: Ulysses S. Grant and the Politics of War & Reconstruction, 1861–1868* (Chapel Hill: University of North Carolina Press, 1991), pp. xvi–9.

17. Thomas J. Goss, *The War within the Union High Command: Politics and Generalship during the Civil War* (Lawrence: University Press of Kansas, 2003), pp. 170–73; Simpson, *Let Us Have Peace*, p. 25; John Y. Simon, "Grant, Lincoln, and Unconditional Surrender," in *Lincoln's Generals*, ed. Gabor S. Boritt (Lincoln: University of Nebraska Press, 1994), pp. 189 (quotation), 195–98; Waugh, *U. S. Grant*, pp. 72–73 and "I Only Knew What Was In My Mind," pp. 316–21.

18. McPherson, "No Peace without Victory, 1861–1865," 1–18.

19. Ibid., pp. 12–14.

20. Calkins, *Battles of Appomattox Station*, pp. 28–38; Report of Bvt. Major General Wesley Merritt, April 20, 1865, *OR* 46 (1): 1120–21.

21. Sheridan, *Personal Memoirs*, vol. 2, pp. 189–90; Report of Bvt. Major General Wesley Merritt, p. 1121.

22. Alexander, *Fighting for the Confederacy*, p. 528; Davis, ed., "On the Road to Appomattox," p. 63 (Mahone quotation).

23. Lee to Grant, April 8, 1865, *OR* 46 (3): 641.

24. William J. Cooper Jr., *Jefferson Davis, American* (New York: Vintage, 2000), pp. 564–65.

25. On antebellum Virginians' nostalgia for the past, see Susan Dunn, *Dominion of Memories: Jefferson, Madison, and the Decline of Virginia* (New York: Basic Books, 2007), pp. 5, 12, 14, 19, 44, 83–84, 126; for evidence of the centrality of "restoration" to Lee's thinking after the war, see Michael Fellman, *The Making of Robert E. Lee* (Baltimore: Johns Hopkins University Press, 2000), pp. 276–81, and Lee to E. M. Bruce, September 25, 1865, Robert E. Lee Letters (transcriptions), W&L. On Lee's secession crisis, see Varon, "'Save in Defense of My Native State': A New Look at Robert E. Lee's Decision to Join the Confederacy," in *Secession Winter: When the Union Fell Apart*, ed. Robert Cook (Baltimore: Johns Hopkins University Press, 2013), pp. 34–57.

26. Lee to Bruce, September 25, 1865, W&L. On Lee's apotheosis as the symbol of Confederate nationalism, see Gary W. Gallagher, *The Confederate War* (Cambridge: Harvard University Press, 1999), *Lee & His Army in Confederate History* (Chapel Hill: University of North Carolina Press, 2001), and Gallagher, ed., *Lee the Soldier* (Lincoln: University of Nebraska Press, 1996).

27. Davis, *Honorable Defeat*, pp. 108–9.

28. John Brown Gordon, *Reminiscences of the Civil War* (1903. Reprint, Baton Rouge: Louisiana State University Press, 1993), pp. 435–36; Fitzhugh Lee to Lee, April 22, 1865, Papers of Fitzhugh Lee, UVA. For the argument that there was some dissent at this final council of war, with Gordon and Fitz Lee questioning the viability of an attack, see Cauble, *Surrender Proceedings*, pp. 14–15; the evidence on behalf of such a case is weak.

29. Lowe, ed., *Meade's Army*, p. 367 (Lyman quote); Cadwallader, *Three Years with Grant*, pp. ix, 318–20 (Rawlins quotes); Grant, *Personal Memoirs*, pp. 597–98.

30. On Grant's rejection of restoration, see Simon, "Grant, Lincoln, and Unconditional Surrender," pp. 189–90.

31. Grant to Lee, April 9, 1865, *OR* 46 (3): 664.

32. Grant telegraph to Stanton, April 9, 1865, *PUSG* 14:371.

33. Calkins, *Battles of Appomattox Station*, pp. 19, 79; Noah Andre Trudeau, *Out of the Storm: The End of the Civil War, April–June 1865* (Baton Rouge: Louisiana State University Press, 1995), pp. 134–38.

34. Calkins, *Battles of Appomattox Station*, pp. 19, 79.

35. Report of Maj. Gen. Edward O. C. Ord, April 26, 1865, *OR* 46 (1): 1162; Report of Major-General Philip H. Sheridan, May 16, 1865, *OR* 46 (1): 1109; Report of Maj. Gen. John Gibbon, April 24, 1865, *OR* 1 (46): 1175.

36. Sheridan, *Personal Memoirs*, vol. 2, pp. 192–93; Calkins, *Battles of Appomattox Station*, pp. 105–15.

37. Gordon, *Reminiscences*, 438; Lee to Davis, April 12, 1865, *OR* 46 (1): 1266; Edward Porter Alexander, "Lee at Appomattox," *Century Magazine* (April 1902),

reprinted in *Battles and Leaders of the Civil War*, vol. 5, ed. Peter Cozzens (Urbana: University of Illinois Press, 2002), pp. 643–44. For a timetable of these movements, see Calkins, *Battles of Appomattox*, pp. 210–11, and Cauble, *Surrender Proceedings*, pp. 18–20. On Lee's assessment of the morning's developments, see Rafuse, *Robert E. Lee*, pp. 238–39.

38. Alexander, "Lee at Appomattox," pp. 643–44.

39. Ibid. Elucidating Lee's rejection of the guerrilla option, the military historian Robert R. Mackey has argued persuasively that "the Confederacy tried irregular warfare during the war, and in each attempt was thwarted by the Union army." Robert R. Mackey, *The Uncivil War: Irregular Warfare in the Upper South, 1861-1865* (Norman: University of Oklahoma Press, 2004), p. 197.

40. Longstreet, *From Manassas to Appomattox*, p. 624; Davis, ed., "On the Road to Appomattox," p. 65 (Mahone quotation).

41. Lee to Grant, April 9, 1865, *OR* 46 (3): 664.

42. Grant, *Personal Memoirs*, p. 598; Lee to Grant, April 9, 1865, *OR* 46 (3): 664 (letter requesting suspension of hostilities); Cauble, *Surrender Proceedings*, pp. 2–26.

43. Joshua Lawrence Chamberlain, *The Passing of the Armies: An Account of the Final Campaign of the Army of the Potomac, Based Upon Personal Reminiscences of the Fifth Army Corps* (1915. Reprint, Gettysburg, Pa: Stan Clark Military Books, 1994), pp. 240–41.

44. Roy P. Stonesifer, "George Armstrong Custer," in *Biographical Dictionary of the Union*, p. 123; Calkins, *Battles of Appomattox*, p. 134; Longstreet, *From Manassas to Appomattox*, pp. 626–27; Cauble, *Surrender Proceedings*, p. 31; Custer, as quoted in Wert, *Custer*, p. 133; Thomas W. Cutrer, ed., *Longstreet's Aide: The Civil War Letters of Major Thomas J. Goree* (Charlottesville: University Press of Virginia, 1995), pp. 166–67.

45. Sheridan, *Personal Memoirs*, pp. 196–98; Gordon, *Reminiscences*, pp. 440–42. There is some controversy over the exact nature of Custer's encounter with Longstreet; Cauble reviews the evidence and concludes that "Longstreet's exact language may be doubtful but it seems reasonable to believe that Custer did demand an unconditional surrender and that his demand met with a firm refusal from Longstreet." Cauble, *Surrender Proceedings*, pp. 35–37.

46. Gibbon, *Personal Recollections*, p. 318; Calkins, *Battles of Appomattox*, p. 136 (Ayres quotation).

47. Marshall, *Lee's Aide-de-Camp*, pp. 266–67; Longstreet, *From Manassas to Appomattox*, pp. 624–25; Davis, ed., "On the Road to Appomattox," p. 65.

Chapter 3

1. Lee to John Letcher, August 28, 1865; Lee to Matthew Fontaine Maury, September 8, 1865, Lee-Jackson Foundation Papers, W&L. On Lee's reverence for the Revolutionary generation, see Richard B. McCaslin, *Lee in the Shadow of Washington* (Baton Rouge: Louisiana State University Press, 2001), p. 209.

2. Grant, *Personal Memoirs*, pp. 615–17, 625, 640.

3. Ibid., p. 599.

4. Cadwallader, *Three Years with Grant*, p. 323 (Rawlins quotation); Grant to Lee, April 9, 1865, *OR* 46 (3): 665.

5. Orville E. Babcock, "Account of Lee's Surrender Attested by General Grant," Orville E. Babcock Papers, Newberry Library, Chicago; on Grant's staff, see Smith, *Grant*, pp. 301–2.

6. Babcock, "Account of Lee's Surrender."

7. Frederick Cushman Newhall, *With General Sheridan in Lee's Last Campaign* (Philadelphia: J.B. Lippincott, 1866), pp. 217–18. The same exchange is described in George A. Forsyth, *Thrilling Days in Army Life* (New York: Harper & Brothers, 1900), pp. 186–87.

8. Longstreet, *From Manassas to Appomattox*, pp. 627–28. On the laws of war and the difference, as the Civil War generation understood it, between "civilized wars" and civil wars, see John Fabian Witt, *Lincoln's Code: The Laws of War in American History* (New York: Free Press, 2010), especially pp. 267–74, and 286–87. Witt demonstrates that nearly 1,000 war crimes trials, prosecuted by the North as part of its strategy for breaking the Southern insurgency, took place during the war. The vast majority (85%) of those charged with violating the laws of war were noncombatants and guerrillas; their transgressions covered a "stunningly wide array of conduct," from the murder of Union sympathizers to assisting desertion to forging discharge papers to trading with the enemy. Confederate soldiers brought before military commissions were most commonly charged with spying, parole violations, oath breaking, and recruiting within Union lines.

9. On Marshall, see Gallagher, "Introduction," *Lee's Aide-de-Camp*, p. xiv. On Taylor, see Gary W. Gallagher, "Introduction," to Walter H. Taylor, *General Lee: His Campaigns in Virginia, 1861–1865* (1906. Reprint, Lincoln: University of Nebraska Press, 1994), pp. v–xv, and R. Lockwood Tower, ed., *Lee's Adjutant: The Wartime Letters of Colonel Walter Herron Taylor, 1862–1865* (Columbia: University of South Carolina Press, 1995), p. 23.

10. Trudeau, *Campaign to Appomattox*, p. 38 (first quotation); Fitzhugh Lee to Lee, "A Report of the Final Days," Papers of Fitzhugh Lee, UVA (second and third quotations).

11. Marshall, *Lee's Aide-De-Camp*, p. 268. On McLean, see Frank P. Cauble, *Biography of Wilmer McLean* (Lynchburg, Va.: H.E. Howard, 1987), p. 40.

12. Marshall, *Lee's Aide-De-Camp*, p. 269; Babcock, "Account of Lee's Surrender"; Grant interview with John Russell Young, *New York Herald*, July 24, 1878; Grant, *Personal Memoirs*, pp. 601–3; Sheridan, *Personal Memoirs*, vol. 2, pp. 201–2; "General Ely Samuel Parker," in *Generals in Bronze: Interviewing the Commanders of the Civil War*, ed. William B. Styple (Kearny, N.J.: Belle Grove, 2005), pp. 23–26 (Styple's book compiles interviews conducted after the war by New York sculptor and illustrator James E. Kelly). Only two men—Grant and Marshall—who were present for the duration of the surrender conference left detailed accounts of it; Lee never prepared his own account. Seven others, who were in the McLean parlor for some but not all of the meeting—Sheridan, Parker, Porter, Badeau, Sharpe, Morgan, and Cadwallader—also left detailed accounts. Others still, who were at the house, or in the vicinity, but not in the room (Forsyth, Gibbon, Chamberlain, Newhall, and Merritt) recorded their versions of the event. For a judicious resolution of some of the conflicting details in these accounts, see Cauble, *Surrender Proceedings*, pp. 45–61.

13. Marshall, *Lee's Aide-De-Camp*, p. 269; Babcock, "Account of Lee's Surrender"; Grant interview with John Russell Young, *New York Herald*, July 24, 1878 (Grant quotations); Grant, *Personal Memoirs*, pp. 601–3; Sheridan, *Personal Memoirs*, vol. 2, pp. 201–2; Cauble, *Surrender Proceedings*, pp. 48–49.

14. Frank R. Levstik, "Ely Samuel Parker," in *Biographical Dictionary of the Union*, pp. 392–93; Arthur C. Parker, *The Life of General Ely S. Parker* (1919. Reprint, Lynchburg, Va.: Schroeder, 2005).

15. Grant to Lee, April 9, 1865, *OR* 46 (3): 665; Grant, *Personal Memoirs*, pp. 603–4; Parker, *Life of General Ely S. Parker*, pp. 130–31.

16. Newhall, *With General Sheridan*, pp. 219–20; Horace Porter, *Campaigning with Grant*, pp. 472–76. There are some discrepancies in the first-hand accounts on the question of when Grant introduced his officers to Lee—namely whether he did so at the outset of the conference or during the copying of the terms. The evidence supports the conclusion that there were two rounds of introductions. There is also some confusion over who exactly was present in the room and for how long; Cauble offers a plausible, well-reasoned assessment. Cauble, *Surrender Proceedings*, pp. 55–56.

17. Grant, *Personal Memoirs*, pp. 604–5.

18. Lee to Grant, April 9, 1865, *OR* 46 (3): 666; Grant, *Personal Memoirs*, p. 605; Horace Porter, *Campaigning with Grant* (1907. Reprint, New York: Konecky and Konecky, 1992), pp. 476–77; Parker, *Life of General Ely S. Parker*, pp. 130–31; Styple, ed., "General Ely Samuel Parker," p. 25.

19. Newhall, *With General Sheridan*, pp. 219–20; Marshall, *Lee's Aide-de-Camp*, pp. 272–74; Sheridan, *Personal Memoirs*, vol. 2, p. 202; Grant, *Personal Memoirs*, p. 608.

20. Grant, *Personal Memoirs*, pp. 101, 601; Grant interview, *New York Herald*, July 24, 1878.

21. Grant, *Personal Memoirs*, pp. 33, 219, 317, 336, 610–13.

22. Ibid., pp. 114–19.

23. Grant to Andrew Johnson, March 30, 1866, *PUSG* 16:143; "Grant's Testimony before the House Committee on the Judiciary, July 18, 1867," in Edward McPherson, *The Political History of the United States of America during the Period of Reconstruction* (Washington, D.C.: Philp & Solomons, 1871), pp. 299–304.

24. McPherson, "Grant's Testimony," p. 305. Gary Gallagher, in explicating the meanings for nineteenth-century Americans of the Union, has noted that support for sectional reunion was premised, among most Northerners, on the idea that their victorious citizen-soldiers "held the moral high ground" over the defeated Confederates. Gary W. Gallagher, *The Union War* (Cambridge, Mass.: Harvard University Press, 2011), p. 153.

25. "At Appomattox: Incidents of Lee's Surrender" (interview with George H. Sharpe), *Philadelphia Weekly News*, June 30, 1877; "Michael R. Morgan Account," typescript supplied to author by Patrick Schroeder, Historian, Appomattox Court House National Park, June 2011 (original in Field Artillery Museum, Fort Sill, Okla.), pp. 27–30; Styple, ed., "General Ely Samuel Parker," p. 26; Adam Badeau, *Grant in Peace: From Appomattox to Mount McGregor* (Hartford, Conn.: S.S. Scranton, 1887), pp. 19–20.

26. Badeau to James H. Wilson, May 8, 1865, Adam Badeau Papers, Firestone Library, Princeton University, N.J. (Badeau quotations); Badeau, *Grant in Peace*, pp. 20–21; Parker, *Life of General Ely S. Parker*, pp. 132–37; "Michael R. Morgan Account," p. 30.

27. Babcock, "Account of Lee's Surrender"; Porter, *Campaigning with Grant*, pp. 475–86; "Michael R. Morgan Account," p. 27; Michael R. Morgan, "Feeding General Lee's

Army," *Southern Historical Society Papers* 21 (January–December 1893): 360–61; *Philadelphia Weekly News*, June 30, 1877; Adam Badeau, *Military History of Ulysses S. Grant*, vol. 3 (New York: D. Appleton, 1881), p. 606; Cadwallader, *Three Years with Grant*, p. 328.

28. Porter, *Campaigning with Grant*, pp. 481–82; Parker, *Life of General Ely S. Parker*, p. 133.

29. "Gen. George A. Forsyth on Lee's Surrender," in Styple, ed., *Generals in Bronze*, p. 5; Porter, *Campaigning with Grant*, p. 485; Wesley Merritt, "Note on the Surrender of Lee," *Century Illustrated* 6 (April 1902): 844.

30. Humphreys to Officers and Soldiers of the Second Army Corps, April 10, 1865, *OR* 46 (1): 687; Reports of Bvt. Maj. Gen. Charles Griffin, April 29, 1865, *OR* 46 (1): 842; Reports of Maj. Gen. Horatio G. Wright, April 22, 1865, *OR* 46 (1): 908; Report of Bvt. Maj. Gen. Wesley Merritt, *OR* 46 (1): 1121; Report of Brig. Gen. Thomas C. Devin, *OR* 46 (1): 1127; Custer to Soldiers of the Third Cavalry Division, April 9, 1865, *OR* 46 (1): 1133; Keifer, "Farewell Order," in *Official Reports of J. Warren Keifer*, p. 46.

31. Grant, General Orders No. 108, *PUSG* 15:120–21.

32. Marshall, *Lee's Aide-de-Camp*, pp. 269–74, and *Appomattox: An Address Delivered before the Society of the Army and Navy of the Confederate States* (Baltimore: Guggenheimer, Weil, 1894), pp. 7, 9–10, 20, and "Appomattox Courthouse," *Southern Historical Society Papers* 21 (January–December 1893): 353–60.

33. Marshall, *Lee's Aide-de-Camp*, pp. 269–74.

34. Longstreet, *From Manassas to Appomattox*, pp. 624 (exchange with Venable).

35. Ibid.; "Farewell Address," *OR* 46 (1): 1267.

36. William G. Nine and Ronald G. Wilson, *The Appomattox Paroles, April 9–15, 1865* (Lynchburg: H.E. Howard, 1989), p. 3. A copy of General Order No. 9 purporting to be Marshall's original—and containing a "lost paragraph," featuring a belligerent reference to the Yankees as the "hated foe," that Lee allegedly excised from the final version—sold at auction in 2005. Historians generally do not accept this document as original, although its existence has garnered some press attention. See *Washington Times*, April 2, 2004.

37. On the Southern critique of Northern capitalism, see Eugene Genovese and Elizabeth Fox-Genovese, *The Mind of the Master Class: History and Faith in the Southern Slaveholders' World View* (New York: Cambridge University Press, 2005); John M. McCardell, *The Idea of a Southern Nation: Southern Nationalists and Southern Nationalism, 1830–1860* (New York: W.W. Norton, 1979); Drew Faust, ed., *The Ideology of Slavery: Proslavery Thought in the Antebellum South, 1830–1860* (Baton Rouge: Louisiana State University Press, 1981). On the gendered dimensions of that critique, see Elizabeth R. Varon, *Disunion! The Coming of the American Civil War, 1789–1859* (Chapel Hill: University of North Carolina Press, 2008).

38. Lee to Davis, April 12, 1865, *OR* 46 (1): 1265–67; Civil War Pocket Diaries of Francis Conway Fitzhugh, April 9, 1865, UVA.

39. Venable, as quoted in Long, *Memoirs*, p. 421; Susan P. Lee, *Memoirs of William Nelson Pendleton*, p. 404; George G. Meade to Margaretta Meade, April 10, 1865, George G. Meade Collection, HSP.

40. Badeau to James H. Wilson, May 8, 1865, Badeau Papers, Princeton; Styple, ed., "General Ely Samuel Parker," pp. 26–27; Gary W. Gallagher, "From Petersburg to

Appomattox: An End and A New Beginning," in *Appomattox Court House*, p. 77; Gibbon, *Personal Recollections*, p. 327.

41. Nine and Wilson, *Appomattox Paroles*, pp. 4–8; Gibbon, *Personal Recollections*, pp. 328–37; John Gibbon to Mrs. Gibbon, April 11, 1865, John Gibbon Papers, HSP.

42. Nine and Wilson, *Appomattox Paroles*, pp. 6–16.

43. Alexander, *Fighting for the Confederacy*, pp. 538–40; Edward G. Longacre, *Fitz Lee: A Military Biography of General Fitzhugh Lee, C.S.A.* (Lincoln: University of Nebraska Press, 2005), pp. 188–89; Gibbon, *Personal Recollections*, pp. 339–40.

44. The Wise story is related in Gibbon, *Personal Recollections*, pp. 335–37; A. B. Lawrence, "Echoes from Appomattox," n.d., newspaper clipping in John Gibbon Papers, vol. 3, Newspaper Scrapbook, HSP.

45. Nine and Wilson, *Appomattox Paroles*, pp. 13–17; Glatthaar, *General Lee's Army*, p. 470; Long, *Memoirs*, p. 425 (quotation); Walter H. Taylor, *Four Years with General Lee* (New York: Appleton, 1878), p. 154.

46. Lee to Walter H. Taylor, July 31, 1865 and Lee to R. H. Anderson, July 31, 1865, in Lee Papers, W&L. Lee's own estimates of Confederate strength in the immediate aftermath of the surrender were shaped by Lt. Col. Briscoe G. Baldwin's April 14, 1865 report "on the Ordnance Department State of Affairs," in which Baldwin offered that on the morning of April 9, the Confederate infantry had 7,892 armed men. As the historian Chris M. Calkins explains, Baldwin's estimate is belied by the number of weapons stacked in the formal surrender ceremony (between 15,000 and 27,000), as well as by figures gleaned from the *Official Record*. On the Baldwin letter, see Calkins, *Appomattox Campaign*, pp. 196–97; for Calkins's detailed tabulation of the numbers of Union and Confederate soldiers in the Appomattox campaign, see his *The Final Bivouac: The Surrender Parade at Appomattox and the Disbanding of the Armies, April 10–May 20, 1865* (Lynchburg, Va.: H.E. Howard, 1988), pp. 204–16.

47. Thomas L. Rosser, *Riding with Rosser*, ed. S. Roger Keller (Shippensburg, Pa.: Burd Street Press, 1997), pp. 73–75; Thomas T. Munford, Special Orders No. 6, April 21, 1865, *OR* 46 (3): 1395.

48. William B. Feis, "Jefferson Davis and the 'Guerrilla Option': A Reexamination," in Grimsley and Simpson, eds., *Collapse of the Confederacy*, pp. 117–19.

49. W. W. Blackford, *War Years with Jeb Stuart* (New York: Charles Scribner's Sons, 1946), p. 293; Davis, ed., "On the Road to Appomattox," p. 66.

50. Lee to Davis, April 20, 1865, in *The Wartime Papers of Robert E. Lee*, ed., Clifford Dowdey (1961. Reprint, New York: Da Capo, 1987), pp. 938–39.

51. Glatthaar, *General Lee's Army*, p. 464; Calkins, *Final Bivouac*, p. 201. Patrick Schroeder, historian of the Appomattox Court House National Historical Park, estimates that Lee may have had as many as 33,000 troops at Appomattox, when you include the cavalry that escaped, captures during the battles at Appomattox Station and Appomattox Court House, soldiers in Walker's disbanded artillery, and all those who drifted off without paroles. Communication with the author, August 31, 2011. See also Calkins, *Appomattox Campaign*, p. 198.

52. Lee to Walter H. Taylor, July 31, 1865, and Lee to R. H. Anderson, July 31, 1865, in Lee Papers, W&L; Long, *Memoirs*, pp. 425–27; Gordon, *Personal Reminiscences*, pp. 443–45; Taylor, *Four Years with General Lee*, p. 191 (quotation).

53. Cauble, *Surrender Proceedings*, pp. 97–98.

54. Long, *Memoirs*, p. 425; Gordon, *Personal Reminiscences*, p. 444.

55. "Honor Answering Honor" (Brunswick, Maine: Bowdoin College, 1965): copy of Joshua L. Chamberlain letter to his sister Sarah, April 13, 1865, furnished to author by Patrick Schroeder, June 2011; Chamberlain, *Passing of the Armies*, pp. 258, 270–71.

Chapter 4

1. *Grant's Petersburg Progress*, April 5, 1865, UVA.
2. James C. Mohr, ed., *The Cormany Diaries: A Northern Family in the Civil War* (Pittsburgh: University of Pittsburgh Press, 1982), p. 533.
3. Ibid., pp. 538–40.
4. Farnham Lyon "A Letter from Appomattox," in *Twice Told Tales of Michigan and Her Soldiers in the Civil War*, ed. Minnie Dubbs Millbrook (Ann Arbor: Michigan Civil War Centennial Observance Commission, 1966), p. 73; David Lane, *A Soldier's Story: The Story of a Volunteer, 1862–1865* (privately published, 1905), pp. 258–61, CWLD.
5. Jacob J. Zorn, *A Sergeant's Story: Civil War Diary of Jacob J. Zorn*, ed. Barbara M. Croner (Apollo, Penn.: Closson Press, 1999), 165; Stephen Minot Weld to Hannah, April 24, 1865, in Stephen Minot Weld, *War Diary and Letters of Stephen Minot Weld, 1861–1865* (1912. Reprint, Boston: Massachusetts Historical Society, 1979), 396; George H. Allen, "Memoir of George Allen," in *Forty-six Months with the Fourth R.I. Volunteers in the War of 1861 to 1865* (J.A. & R.A. Reid Printers, 1887), p. 389, CWLD.
6. John Smith to "Dear Mother," April 11, 1865, John L. Smith Letters and Diaries: War Letters, 1862–1865, HSP; Henry Miner to Dear Mother and Father, April 13, 1865, Henry Miner Letters, LVA.
7. Charles Mattocks, *"Unspoiled Heart": The Journal of Charles Mattocks of the 17th Maine*, ed. Philip N. Racine (Knoxville: University of Tennessee Press, 1994), pp. 269–70; Henry Matrau, *Letters Home: Henry Matrau of the Iron Brigade*, ed. Marcia Reid-Green (Lincoln: University of Nebraska Press, 1991), pp. 59–60, 114.
8. Holman S. Melcher, *With a Flash of His Sword: The Writings of Major Holman S. Melcher, 20th Maine Infantry*, ed. William B. Styple (Kearny, N.J.: Belle Grove, 1904), p. 217; Gerald F. Linderman, *Embattled Courage: The Experience of Combat in the American Civil War* (New York: Free Press, 1987).
9. April 9 and 10, 1865, entries, William Hotchkiss Diaries, 1864–65, UVA; Henry Miner to "Dear Mother and Father," April 13, 1865, Henry Miner Letters, LVA; Melcher, *With a Flash of His Sword*, p. 217; A. O. Roe to the *New York Evangelist*, April 12, 1865, *New York Evangelist*, April 27, 1865, APS.
10. John H. Westervelt, *Diary of a Yankee Engineer: The Civil War Story of John H. Westervelt, Engineer, 1st New York Volunteer Engineer Corps*, ed. Anita Palladino (New York: Fordham University Press, 1997), p. 226; Linderman, *Embattled Courage*, p. 65.
11. John W. Haley, *The Rebel Yell & the Yankee Hurrah: The Civil War Journal of a Maine Volunteer*, ed. Ruth L. Silliker (Camden, Maine: Down East Books, 1985), pp. 206–10, 265.
12. On Republican ideology, see Eric Foner, *Free Soil, Free Labor, Free Men: The Ideology of the Republican Party before the Civil War* (New York: Oxford University Press, 1995). George C. Rable, *God's Almost Chosen Peoples: A Religious History of the*

American Civil War (Chapel Hill: University of North Carolina Press, 2010), pp. 52–56, 155, 353; Haley, *Rebel Yell*, p. 265.

13. John L. Smith to Dear Mother, April 15, 1865, Smith Letters, HSP.

14. Zorn, *A Sergeant's Story*, p. 165; Henry J. Millard to "Dear Sister Hattie," April 26, 1865, in *Yankee Correspondence: Civil War Letters between New England Soldiers and the Home Front*, ed. Nina Silber and Mary Beth Sievens (Charlottesville: University of Virginia Press, 1996), p. 53; John L. Smith to "Dear Mother" April 15, 1865, Smith Letters, HSP; Stanton P. Allen, *Down in Dixie* (Boston: D. Lothrop, 1893), pp. 461–63.

15. Alvin Voris, *A Citizen-Soldier's Civil War: The Letters of Brevet Major General Alvin C. Voris*, ed. Jerome Mushkat (DeKalb: Northern Illinois University Press, 2002), pp. 253, 255, 260, 263.

16. Hallock Armstrong to Mary Armstrong, April 10, 12, 15, 1865, in Mary A. Armstrong, *Letters from a Pennsylvania Chaplain at the Siege of Petersburg, 1865* (privately published, 1961), pp. 24–28, CWLD; *New York Evangelist*, April 27, 1865; Rhodes, *All for the Union*, p. 222.

17. Augustus J. Ricks, *Carrying the News of Lee's Surrender to the Army of the Ohio* (Cincinnati, OH: H.C. Sheridan & Co., 1887), pp. 9–10; Alexander G. Downing, *Downing's Civil War Diary*, ed. Lynthus B. Clark (Des Moines: Iowa State Department of History and Archives), p. 268, CWLD; Jeffrey L. Patrick and Robert J. Willey, *Fighting for Liberty and Right: The Civil War Diary of Bluffton Miller, First Sergeant, Company K, Seventy-Fifth Indiana Volunteer Infantry* (Knoxville: University of Tennessee Press, 2005), p. 332.

18. Millard, in Silber and Sievens, eds., *Yankee Correspondence*, p. 53; Rhodes, *All for the Union*, p. 222.

19. Cauble, *Biography of Wilmer McLean*, pp. 49–51 and *Surrender Proceedings*, pp. 112–15; Wert, *Custer*, p. 225; Armstrong, *Warrior in Two Camps*, p. 111; Porter, *Campaigning with Grant*, p. 487.

20. Cadwallader, *Three Years with Grant*, p. 330; Millbrook, ed., *Twice Told Tales*, pp. 74–75; Cauble, *Biography of Wilmer McLean*, p. 50; Alanson M. Randol, *Last Days of the Rebellion*, in *Civil War Unit Histories*, pt. 3, microfiche from U.S. Army Military Institute, Carlisle, Pa. (Bethesda, Md.: University Publications of America, 1992), pp. 11–12.

21. Cauble, *Surrender Proceedings*, pp. 114–15; Smith to "Dear Mother," April 11, 1865, Smith Letters, HSP; Calkins, *Final Bivouac*, pp. 182–83.

22. Zorn, *A Sergeant's Story*, p. 165; Calkins, *Final Bivouac*, pp. 182–83.

23. On Waud, see "A Civil War Sketch Artist," http://www.loc.gov/exhibits/treasures/trm041.html.

24. On Brady's visit to Richmond, see *Richmond Whig*, April 7, 22, and 25, 1865, and William A. Frassanito, *Grant and Lee: The Virginia Campaigns, 1864–1865* (Gettysburg, Pa.: Thomas, 1983), pp. 378–416. The author would like to thank Arden Alexander of the Prints and Photographs Division at the Library of Congress for helping track down information on the Ord negatives.

25. Webb Garrison, *Brady's Civil War* (London: Salamander Books, 2000), p. 206 (quotation).

26. *New York Times*, May 25, 1893.

27. Edward G. Longacre, *Army of Amateurs: General Benjamin F. Butler and the Army of the James, 1863–1865* (Mechanicsburg, Pa.: Stackpole Books, 1997), pp. 243–44; Calkins, *Battles of Appomattox Station*, pp. 88–93.

28. Calkins, *Battles of Appomattox Station*, pp. 88–93, 100–101; Joseph T. Wilson, *The Black Phalanx: African American Soldiers in the War of Independence, the War of 1812 & the Civil War* (1887. Reprint, New York: Da Capo, 1994), pp. 458–59; "Too Exuberant Joy," in *War Anecdotes and Incidents of Army Life*, ed. Albert Lawson (Cincinnati: E.H. Beasley, 1888), p. 142.

29. On Williams, see John Hope Franklin, *George Washington Williams* (Chicago: University of Chicago Press, 1985); on Yeocum, see *Christian Recorder*, August 25, 1887; on Whipper, see Eric Foner, *Freedom's Lawmakers* (Baton Rouge: Louisiana State University Press, 1996); on Simmons, see "Eulogy on William J. Simmons," in W. Bishop Johnson, *Sermons and Addresses* (Lynchburg: Virginia Seminary Steam Print, 1899), pp. 4–5, AAP, and Miriam DaCosta-Willis, ed., *The Memphis Diary of Ida B. Wells* (Boston: Beacon Press, 1995), pp. 121–27; on Costley, see Carl M. Adams, "The First Slave Freed by Abraham Lincoln: A Biographical Sketch of Nance Legins (Cox-Cromwell) Costley, circa 1813–1873," *For the People: A Newsletter of the Abraham Lincoln Association* 3 (Autumn 1999): 1–2.

30. Frank H. Taylor, *Philadelphia in the Civil War 1861–1865* (Published by the City: Philadelphia, 1913), p. 188; Report of Col. Samuel C. Armstrong, April 20, 1865, OR 46 (1): 1237. For background on the USCT, see, for example, Dudley Taylor Cornish, *The Sable Arm: Black Troops in the Union Army, 1861–1865* (Lawrence: University Press of Kansas, 1956); James M. McPherson, *The Negro's Civil War: How American Blacks Felt and Acted during the War for the Union* (New York: Pantheon, 1965); Joseph T. Glatthaar, *Forged in Battle: The Civil War Alliance of Black Soldiers and White Officers* (Baton Rouge: Louisiana State University Press, 2000); John David Smith, ed., *Black Soldiers in Blue: African American Troops in the Civil War Era* (Chapel Hill: University of North Carolina Press, 2002); J. Matthew Gallman, "In Your Hands That Musket Means Liberty: African American Soldiers and the Battle of Olustee," in *Northerners at War: Reflections on the Civil War Home Front* (Kent, Ohio: Kent State University Press, 2010), pp. 242–50.

31. John Cimprich, *Fort Pillow, a Civil War Massacre and Public Memory* (Baton Rouge: Louisiana State University Press, 2005), p. 62 (quotation); Gregory J.W. Urwin, *Black Flag over Dixie: Racial Atrocities and Reprisals in the Civil War* (Carbondale: Southern Illinois University Press, 2005).

32. White officers and chaplains of USCT regiments, too, appreciated the symbolism of the USCT role in Lee's defeat; for example, Thomas S. Johnson, chaplain of the 127th USCT, expressed satisfaction that his regiment had a "share in the glory" of defeating the "Generalissimo of the C.S.A." McCoslin and Johnson quoted in Noah Andre Trudeau, *Like Men of War* (New York: Little, Brown, 1998), p. 423; *Christian Recorder* (Philadelphia), July 29, 1865; R. J. M. Blackett, ed., *Thomas Morris Chester, Black Civil War Correspondent* (Baton Rouge: Louisiana State University Press, 1989), pp. 302, 313, 332.

33. Luman Tenney to his mother and sisters, April 8, 1866, in Frances Andrew Tenney, ed., *War Diary, 1861–1865* (Cleveland, Ohio: Evangelical, 1914), p. 195, CWLD; Stephen Tripp, "The Cavalry at Appomattox," *Maine Bugle* 5 (July 1898): 213–14; Mohr, ed., *Cormany Diaries*, p. 539; Report of Surg. Charles P. Heichhold, April 25, 1865, and Report of Col. William W. Woodward, April 27, 1865, OR 46 (1): 1231, 1243.

34. George W. Williams, *History of the Negro Race in America from 1619 to 1880* (New York: G.P. Putnam's Sons, 1883), pp. 341–44; Franklin, *George Washington Williams*, p. 4.

35. *Christian Recorder* (Philadelphia), April 29, 1865; Blackett, ed., *Thomas Morris Chester*, pp. 302, 313, 332; Wilson, *Black Phalanx*, pp. 378, 392, 406, 458.

36. George Washington Williams, *A History of the Negro Troops in the War of the Rebellion, 1861–1865* (New York: Harper & Brothers, 1888), p. 326; Leila Amos Pendleton, *A Narrative of the Negro* (Washington, D.C.: R.L. Pendleton, 1912), pp. 90, 157–67. On the literary tradition of blacks as the "redeemer race," see Mia Bay, *The White Image in the Black Mind: African-American Ideas about White People, 1830–1925* (New York: Oxford University Press, 2000).

37. Williams, *History of the Negro Troops*, pp. 289–93.

38. George Washington Williams, "Centennial: The American Negro from 1776–1876; Oration Delivered at Avondale, Ohio, 1876," Ohio Historical Society, http://dbs.ohiohistory.org/africanam/det.cfm?ID=803.

39. Varon, *Disunion!*, pp. 64, 78, 330–39.

40. William J. Simmons, *Men of Mark: Eminent, Progressive and Rising* (Cleveland, Ohio: Geo. M. Rewell, 1887), pp. 49–57; Johnson, *Sermons and Addresses*, p. 7.

41. The Woodlin letter is reproduced in Robert E. Bonner, *The Soldier's Pen: Firsthand Impressions of the Civil War* (New York: Hill and Wang, 2006), pp. 219–20.

42. Richard Barksdale Harwell, ed., *A Confederate Diary of the Retreat from Petersburg, April 3–20, 1865* (Atlanta: Emory University Library, 1953), pp. 11, 15, 17.

43. Papers of Henry Augustine Minor, UVA; "Memoir of Dr. [Hodijah Baylies] Mead," UVA, p. 102.

44. John Walters, *Norfolk Blues: The Civil War Diary of the Norfolk Light Artillery Blues*, ed. Kenneth Wiley (Shippensburg, Pa.: Burd Street Press, 1997), p. 223; Edward M. Boykin, *The Falling Flag: Evacuation of Richmond, Retreat and Surrender at Appomattox* (New York: E.J. Hale & Son, 1874), pp. 64–65; Diary of Lt. Robert Poole Myers, MOC; W. S. White, "Stray Leaves from a Soldier's Journal," *Southern Historical Society Papers* 12 (December 1883): 552; Randolph H. McKim, *A Soldier's Recollections: Leaves from the Diary of a Young Confederate* (New York: Longmans, Green, 1910), p. 268.

45. Henry A. Chambers, *Diary of Captain Henry A. Chambers*, ed. T. H. Pearce (Wendell, N.C.: Broadfoot's Bookmark, 1983), p. 262; W. R. Houghton and M. B. Houghton, *Two Boys in the Civil War and After* (Montgomery, Ala.: Paragon Press, 1912), 151; Edward A. Moore, *The Story of a Cannoneer under Stonewall Jackson* (New York: Neale, 1907), p. 302; Edward M. Boykin, *The Falling Flag* (New York: E.J. Hale & Son, 1874), pp. 64–65.

46. Jason Phillips, *Diehard Rebels: The Confederate Culture of Invincibility* (Athens: University of Georgia Press, 2007), pp. 8, 60–61, 144, 170 (Chambers quotation).

47. Herman H. Perry, "Appomattox Courthouse: Account of the Surrender of the Confederate States Army, April 9, 1865," *Southern Historical Society Papers* 20 (January–December 1892): 56; Herman Perry, Copy of General Order No. 9, MOC (the author is grateful to John Coski for providing her with a scan of this document); John E. Roller, "Incidents of the Retreat to Appomattox," n.d., Papers of John Edwin Roller, UVA, p. 12.

48. Roller, "Incidents," pp. 6, 9; George P. Clarke Diary, April 5, 7, 1865, LVA; Giles B. Cooke Diary, April 9, 1865, VHS.

49. George Shreve, "Narrative of the Stuart Horse Artillery, C.S.A.," George Shreve Papers, 1922, LVA, p. 48; Shreve obituary, *Santa Cruz Sentinel*, October 20, 1940, http://www.santacruzpl.org/history/articles/1143/; George Cary Eggleston, *A Rebel's Recollections* (1874. Reprint, Gretna, La.: Pelican, 2010), p. 244.

50. Eggleston, *A Rebel's Recollections*, pp. 222–23; John L. Smith to Mother, April 15, 1865, HSP. On Confederate administrative and logistical inefficiency, see for example, Paul Escott, *After Secession: Jefferson Davis and the Failure of Confederate Nationalism* (Baton Rouge: Louisiana State University Press, 1992); Glatthaar, *General Lee's Army*, p. 467; Andrew F. Smith, *Starving the South: How the North Won the Civil War* (New York: St. Martin's Press, 2011).

51. William Edward Wiatt, *Confederate Chaplain William Edward Wiatt: An Annotated Diary* (Lynchburg, Va.: H.E. Howard, 1994), p. 237; Walters, *Norfolk Blues*, pp. 224–25.

52. Frank Potts, *The Death of the Confederacy: The Last Week of the Army of Northern Virginia as Set Forth in a Letter of April, 1865* (Richmond: Privately Printed for Allen Potts, 1928), pp. 12–13.

53. Henry Robinson Berkeley Diary, June 24, 1865, VHS; J. C. Painter Pocket Diary, April 25, 1865, MOC.

54. Wiatt, *Confederate Chaplain*, p. 238; G. Ward Hubbs, ed., *Voices from Company D: Diaries by the Greensboro Guards, Fifth Alabama Infantry, Army of Northern Virginia* (Athens: University of Georgia Press, 2003), p. 371; Chambers, *Diary*, p. 262.

55. Rable, *God's Almost Chosen Peoples*, pp. 389–90; Figg, *Where Men Only Dare to Go*, p. 219.

56. Moore, *Story of a Cannoneer*, pp. 302–7.

57. Minor, "Dr H. A. Minor's Account of General Lee's Surrender," Papers of Henry Augustine Minor, UVA; Henry Kyd Douglas, *I Rode with Stonewall: The War Experiences of the Youngest Member of Jackson's Staff* (Chapel Hill: University of North Carolina Press, 1940), pp. 332–33.

58. Cooke Diary, April 13, 1865, VHS; John Bell Vincent Diary, April 11 and 12, 1865, VHS; Chambers, *Diary*, p. 264; "Memoirs of Confederate Surgeon [Hodijah Baylies] Meade," UVA (this is a second mss. collection by Meade, the same surgeon featured in the Mead [*sic*] collection cited in n. 43); Samuel Pickens, April 14, 1865, in Hubbs, ed., *Voices from Company D*, pp. 372–73.

59. Eggleston, *A Rebel's Recollections*, pp. 252–53; James C. Birdsong, "Reminiscences of Civil War Service," p. 6, LVA; Potts, *Death of the Confederacy*, p. 15.

60. Walters, *Norfolk Blues*, p. 225–26.

61. John M. Coski, "We Are All to Be Paroled," *Museum of the Confederacy*, Fall 2010, pp. 5–9; Gregory A. Coco, "A Priceless Legacy," *Civil War Times*, March–April 2006, pp. 38–45; Edgar Warfield, *Manassas to Appomattox: The Civil War Memoirs of Pvt. Edgar Warfield, 17th Virginia Infantry* (1936. Reprint, McLean, Va.: EPM Publications, 1996), p. 174; Abner Crump Hopkins Memoir, n.d, VHS.

Chapter 5

1. Grant to Stanton and Stanton to Grant, April 9, 1865, OR 46 (3): 663–64.

2. Michael Burlingame, *Abraham Lincoln: A Life*, vol. 2 (Baltimore: Johns Hopkins University Press, 2008), pp. 779–99.

3. Ibid., p. 800 (Stanton quote); *New York Tribune*, April 11, 1865; *Philadelphia Press*, April 11, 1865; Margaret Leech, *Reveille in Washington, 1860–1865* (1941. Reprint: New York: New York Review Books, 2011), pp. 460–73; Roy P. Basler, ed., *Collected Works of Abraham Lincoln*, vol. 8 (New Brunswick, N.J.: Rutgers University Press, 1953), pp. 393–95.

4. Basler, ed., *Collected Works of Abraham Lincoln*, vol. 8, pp. 393–95.

5. Lincoln, "Last Public Address," in Basler, ed., *Collected Works of Abraham Lincoln*, vol. 8, pp. 399–405.

6. Ibid.; Richard Carwardine, *Lincoln: A Life of Purpose and Power* (New York: Knopf, 2006), pp. 235–44 (quotation on 240).

7. Carwardine, *Lincoln*, p. 241. Lincoln also objected to Section 12 of the Wade-Davis bill, which declared slavery dead in the rebel states by Congressional fiat; he favored instead the passage of a constitutional amendment abolishing slavery, as the position more consistent with Republican Party principles. See James Oakes, *Freedom National: The Destruction of Slavery in the United States, 1861–1865* (New York: W.W. Norton, 2013), pp. 454–56.

8. Lincoln, "Last Public Address," in Basler, ed., *Collected Works of Abraham Lincoln*, pp. 399–405.

9. Ibid.

10. Garry Wills, *Lincoln at Gettysburg: The Words That Remade America* (New York: Simon and Schuster, 2006); Ronald C. White, *Lincoln's Greatest Speech: The Second Inaugural* (New York: Simon and Schuster, 2006).

11. On nineteenth-century understandings of progress, see Daniel Walker Howe, *What Hath God Wrought: The Transformation of America, 1815–1848* (New York: Oxford University Press, 2007), p. 3.

12. Andrew S. Coopersmith, *Fighting Words: An Illustrated History of Newspaper Accounts of the Civil War* (New York: New Press, 2004), pp. xiii–xxii; Jennifer L. Weber, *Copperheads: The Rise and Fall of Lincoln's Opponents in the North* (New York: Oxford University Press, 2006), pp. 163–64.

13. *New York Tribune*, April 10, 11, 12, 1865.

14. *New York Tribune*, April 10, 11, 13, 1865; Greeley, as quoted in Henry Luther Stoddard, *Horace Greeley: Printer, Editor, Crusader* (New York: G.P. Putnam's Sons, 1946), p. 231.

15. *National Anti-Slavery Standard* (New York), April 15, 1865.

16. *Christian Recorder* (Philadelphia), April 8, 1865; *Scientific American* (New York), April 15, 1865; *New York Times*, April 10, 1865; *New York Herald*, April 14, 1865; *Independent* (New York), April 13, 1865.

17. *Liberator* (Boston), April 14, 1865; *Christian Advocate and Journal* (New York), April 13, 1865; *Anglo-African* (New York), as quoted in Coopersmith, *Fighting Words*, p. 252.

18. Joshua McCarter Simpson, "Let the Banner Proudly Wave. Written After the Surrender of Lee," in *The Emancipation Car; Being an Original Composition of Anti-Slavery Ballads* (1874. Reprint: Miami, Fla.: Mnesmosyne, 1969), pp. 143–46.

19. William E. Gienapp, *Abraham Lincoln and Civil War America* (New York: Oxford University Press, 2002), pp. 169–70; *New York Times*, April 12, 14, 1865; *New York Tribune*, April 14, 1865. In the summer of 1864, when Lincoln's reelection prospects had seemed dim, Raymond had urged the president to make a peace offer to Davis of reunion without emancipation. Raymond expected that Davis would rebuff the overture and would thereby prove to Lincoln's Copperhead critics that a negotiated settlement was not possible. But it was Lincoln who rebuffed Raymond; there would be no exchange of emancipation for peace.

20. *New York Herald*, April 10, 11, 12, 13, 14, 1865.

21. Ibid; *Franklin Repository* (Penn.), April 19, 1865, VSP.

22. *Philadelphia Inquirer*, April 11, 1865; *Philadelphia Press*, April 11, 1865; *St. Louis Democrat*, April 12, 1865.

23. *Philadelphia Inquirer,* April 10, 1865; *Boston Daily Advertiser,* April 17, 1865; *New Haven Daily Palladium* (Conn.), April 10, 1865; *Sacramento Daily Union,* May 15, 16, 1865; *Philadelphia Press,* April 11, 1865.

24. *New York News,* as quoted in *Philadelphia Inquirer,* April 11, 1865; Coopersmith, *Fighting Words,* p. 254 (direct quotation and *New York World* quotation).

25. *Detroit Free Press,* April 11, 12, 13, 14, 1865; *Valley Spirit,* April 12, 1865, VSP; *Harrisburg Patriot & Union* (Penn.), quoted in Coopersmith, *Fighting Words,* p. 253; *New York Tribune,* April 14, 1865.

26. *New York Herald,* April 10, 11, 12, 13, 1865; *New York Times,* April 12, 13, 1865.

27. *Constitutional Union* (Washington, D.C.), April 11, 1865; *Brooklyn Daily Eagle,* April 10, 1865; *New York World,* quoted in Coopersmith, *Fighting Words,* p. 255.

28. *New York Tribune,* April 10, 1865; *New York Times,* April 11, 1865; Maria Lydia Daly, *Diary of a Union Lady, 1861–1865,* ed. Harold Earl Hammond (Lincoln: University of Nebraska Press, 2000), pp. 351–52; George Templeton Strong, *Diary of the Civil War, 1860–1865,* ed. Allan Nevins (New York: Macmillan, 1962), pp. 578–79.

29. Sophia Stockett Sellman to Henry, April 10, 1865, Sophia Stockett Sellman Letters, LVA; Caroline Cowles Richards Clarke, *Village Life in America 1852–1872, Including the Period of the American Civil War as Told in the Diary of a School-Girl* (New York: Henry Holt, 1913), pp. 177–79, CWLD; William Harry Miller, comp., *Postmarked Hudson: The Letters of Sarah A. [sic, E.] Andrews to Her Brother, James A. Andrews, 1864–1865* (Hudson, Wisc.: Star-Observer Printer, 1955), p. 76; *Hartford Daily Courant,* April 14, 1865.

30. Strong, *Diary of the Civil War,* pp. 578–79; Daly, *Diary of a Union Lady,* p. 352; Sidney George Fisher, *A Philadelphia Perspective: The Civil War Diary of Sidney George Fisher,* ed. Jonathan W. White (New York: Fordham University Press, 2007), pp. 250–51.

31. Caleb Gurney, *Portsmouth: Historic and Picturesque* (1902), p. 121; *Portsmouth Journal* (N.H.), April 15, 1865; Portsmouth, N.H. *Daily Morning Chronicle,* April 11, 13, 1865; J. Dennis Robinson, "The Newspaper Riot of 1865," http://www.seacoastnh.com/History/As-I-Please/The-Newspaper-Riot-of-1865/.

32. Nicole Etcheson, *A Generation at War: The Civil War Era in a Northern Community* (Lawrence: University Press of Kansas, 2011), p. 163; Karla Jean Husby and Eric J. Wittenberg, eds., *Under Custer's Command: The Civil War Journal of James Henry Avery* (Washington, D.C.: Potomac Books, 2002), pp. 141–42.

33. Strong, *Diary of George Templeton Strong,* pp. 580–81.

34. Jon Grinspan, "'Sorrowfully Amusing': The Popular Comedy of the Civil War," *Journal of the Civil War Era* 1 (September 2011): 313–14.

35. Petroleum V. Nasby [David Ross Locke], *Divers Views, Opinions, and Prophecies* (Cincinnati, Ohio: R.W. Carroll., 1867), pp. 300–303.

Chapter 6

1. William S. McFeely, *Grant: A Biography* (New York: W.W. Norton, 1980), p. 223; Burlingame, *Lincoln: A Life,* pp. 804–5; Gienapp, *Abraham Lincoln,* p. 201 (quotations); Allen C. Guelzo, *Abraham Lincoln: Redeemer President* (Grand Rapids, Mich.: Wm. B. Eerdmans Publishing, 1999), p. 433.

2. On the assassination as a turning point, see for example Thomas Reed Turner, *Beware the People Weeping: Public Opinion and the Assassination of Abraham*

Lincoln (Baton Rouge: Louisiana State University Press, 1982), which features a chapter entitled "Good Feeling Turns to Fury." See also John R. Neff, *Honoring the Civil War Dead: Commemoration and the Problem of Reconciliation* (Lawrence: University Press of Kansas, 2005), p. 91; Elizabeth D. Leonard, *Lincoln's Avengers: Justice, Revenge, and Reunion after the Civil War* (New York: W.W. Norton, 2004), p. xii; Harold Holzer, Craig L. Symonds, and Frank J. Williams, eds., *The Lincoln Assassination: Crime and Punishment, Myth and Memory* (New York: Oxford University Press, 2010), pp. 1–2. The scope and depth of modern scholarship on the assassination is evident in the recent compendium by Edward Steers Jr., *The Lincoln Assassination Encyclopedia* (New York: Harper Perennial, 2010).

3. Turner, *Beware the People Weeping*, p. 80; Leonard, *Lincoln's Avengers*, pp. 8–9; James De Normandie, *The Lord Reigneth: A Few Words on Sunday Morning, April 16, 1865, after the Assassination of Abraham Lincoln*, UVA.

4. Turner, *Beware the People Weeping*, p. 127; Leonard, *Lincoln's Avengers*, p. xii.

5. Michael W. Kauffman, *American Brutus: John Wilkes Booth and the Lincoln Conspiracies* (New York: Random House, 2004), pp. 209–11; Gienapp, *Abraham Lincoln*, pp. 199–200; Guelzo, *Abraham Lincoln*, pp. 427–28; Neely, *Last Best Hope*, pp. 190–91; Michael Burlingame, *Lincoln and the Civil War* (Carbondale: Southern Illinois University Press, 2011), p. 128.

6. Kauffman, *American Brutus*, p. 207; Burlingame, *Lincoln*, p. 815; *New York Herald*, April 16, 1865; Richard H. Steele, *Victory and Mourning: A Sermon Occasioned by the Death of Abraham Lincoln, Late President of the United States, Preached in the First Reformed Dutch Church, New Brunswick NJ, June 1st, 1865* (New Brunswick, N.J.: Terhune & Van Anglen's Press, 1865), p. 15, MP; Henry J. Raymond, *The Life and Public Services of Abraham Lincoln* (New York: Derby & Miller, 1865), p. 713; *In Memoriam. Abraham Lincoln Assassinated at Washington, April 14, 1865: Being a Brief Account of the Proceedings of Meetings, Action of Authorities and Societies, Speeches, Sermons, Addresses and Other Expressions of Public Feeling on Reception of the News* (Buffalo, N.Y.: Matthews & Warren, 1865), pp. 19, 27.

7. Coopersmith, *Fighting Words*, p. 275; Ann Hartwell Britton and Thomas J. Reed, eds., *To My Beloved Wife and Boy at Home: The Letters and Diaries of Orderly Sergeant John F. L. Hartwell* (Madison, N.J.: Fairleigh Dickinson University Press, 1997), pp. 350–51; Wilbur Fisk, *Anti-Rebel: The Civil War Letters of Wilbur Fisk* (Croton-on-Hudson, N.Y.: Emil Rosenblatt, 1983), p. 323; Jenkin Lloyd Jones, *An Artilleryman's Diary* (Wisconsin History Commission, 1914), p. 395, CWLD; Melcher, *With a Flash of His Sword*, p. 224; Ellis Spear, *Civil War Recollections of General Ellis Spear*, Abbot Spear et al., eds. (Orono, Maine: University of Maine Press, 1997), p. 185; Charles H. Lynch, *The Civil War Diary, 1862–1865, of Charles H. Lynch, 18th Con. Vols.* (Hartford, Conn.: Case Lockwood & Brainard, 1915), p. 149; Husby and Wittenberg., eds., *Under Custer's Command*, p. 143; Richard L. Kiper, *Dear Catherine, Dear Taylor: The Civil War Letters of a Union Soldier and His Wife* (Lawrence: University Press of Kansas, 2002), p. 385.

8. Mechler, *With a Flash of His Sword*, p. 224; Spear, *Civil War Recollections*, p. 185; Allen, *Down in Dixie*, pp. 471–72; Jacob Post, *Discourse on the Assassination of President Lincoln Preached in Camp by Rev. Jacob Post, Chaplain of the 184th Regiment N.Y.V. at Harrison's Landing, Virginia, April 23, 1865* (Oswego, N.Y.: S.H. Parker, 1865), pp. 1–9.

9. James Shaw, "Our Last Campaign and Subsequent Service in Texas," in *Personal Narratives of Events in the War of the Rebellion* (Providence: Rhode Island Soldiers & Sailors Historical Society, 1903), pp. 30–32. As an essay by Thomas P. Lowry notes, not all Union soldiers mourned Lincoln's death. There were in the ranks a small minority with Copperhead leanings who were never reconciled to Lincoln's way of war, even after Lee's surrender had seemingly vindicated it. Some of these Copperheads proved incapable of restraint. Thus the court-martial files of the War Department reveal that "nearly seventy *Union* soldiers and sailors were prosecuted for exclaiming, in some very heated language, that they were delighted to hear of the assassination." Elijah Chapman, a cook in the Tenth Veterans Reserve Corps, openly approved the assassination on the grounds that "Lincoln took off his hat to Negroes and ignored white men." The common penalty for such intemperate talk, Lowry explains, was a prison sentence. Thomas P. Lowry, "Not Everybody Mourned Lincoln's Death," in Holzer, Symonds, and Williams, eds., *Lincoln Assassination*, pp. 95–96, 111.

10. Edward Steers Jr., *Blood on the Moon: The Assassination of Abraham Lincoln* (Lexington: University Press of Kentucky, 2001), pp. 14, 293; Neff, *Honoring the Civil War Dead*, pp. 76–77; *Christian Recorder* (Philadelphia), April 29, 1865.

11. Steers, *Blood on the Moon*, p. 293; Whitman, "O Captain! My Captain!" in *Poems and Songs of the Civil War*, ed. Lois Hill (New York: Gramercy, 1990), p. 139; J. E. Rankin, *Moses and Joshua: A Discourse on the Death of Abraham Lincoln, Preached in the Winthrop Church, Charlestown, Wednesday Noon, April 19, 1865* (Boston: Dakin and Metcalf, 1865), pp. 7–8, MP.

12. Neff, *Honoring the Civil War Dead*, p. 94; Paul H. Bergeron, *Andrew Johnson's Civil War and Reconstruction* (Knoxville: University of Tennessee Press, 2011), p. 67.

13. Rankin, *Moses and Joshua*, p. 12; C. B. Crane, *Sermon on the Occasion of the Death of President Lincoln, Preached in the South Baptist Church, Hartford, Conn., Sunday April 16, 1865* (Hartford, Conn.: Case, Lockwood, 1865), pp. 27–28, MP; Frank L. Robbins, *A Discourse on the Death of Abraham Lincoln Delivered in the Greenhill Presbyterian Church on Sunday Evening, April 23, 1865* (Philadelphia: Henry B. Ashmead), p. 13, MP; Marvin R. Vincent, *Sermon on the Assassination of Abraham Lincoln Delivered in the First Presbyterian Church, Troy on Sunday Morning, April 23, 1865* (Troy, N.Y.: A.W. Scriber, 1865), pp. 37–39, MP.

14. Thomas Tousey, *Discourse on the Death of Abraham Lincoln Preached at the Presbyterian Church, Palmyra, N.Y., April 19th, 1865* (Rochester, N.Y.: C.D. Tracy, 1865), pp. 19–23, MP; Henry Fowler, *Character and Death of Abraham Lincoln. A Discourse Preached at Auburn, N.Y., April 23, 1865* (Auburn, N.Y.: Wm. J. Moses, 1865), pp. 15–16, MP.

15. Coopersmith, *Fighting Words*, pp. 275–76 (quotation); Samuel T. Spear, *The Punishment of Treason. A Discourse Preached April 23D, 1865 in the Southern Presbyterian Church of Brooklyn* (Brooklyn: Union Steam Presses, 1865), p. 20, MP; Gilbert Haven, *The Uniter and Liberator of America. A Memorial Discourse on the Character and Career of Abraham Lincoln: Delivered in the North Russell Street M.E. Church, Boston, Sunday, April 28, 1865* (Boston: James P. Magee, 1865), pp. 24–25, MP.

16. *Zion's Herald and Wesleyan Journal* (New York), April 19, 1865; *White Cloud Kansas Chief*, April 20, 1865, CA; Robert F. Engs and Corey M. Brooks, *Their Patriotic Duty: The Civil War Letters of the Evans Family of Brown County, Ohio* (New York: Fordham University Press, 2007), p. 342; Lydia Maria Child to Sarah Shaw [after

April 15, 1865] in *The Real War Will Never Get in the Books: Selections from Writers during the Civil War*, ed. Louis P. Masur (New York: Oxford University Press, 1993), p. 50.

17. Letter from Emma Yarnell, April 18, 1865, in *Life and Letters of Elizabeth L. Comstock* (Philadelphia: John C. Winston, 1895), p. 511, CWLD; *La Crosse Daily Democrat*, August 15, 1864, http://www.wisconsinhistory.org/teachers/lessons/civilwar/pomeroy/pdf/abraham_15.pdf; Ruth Ann Tucker, "M. M. 'Brick' Pomeroy: Forgotten Man of the Nineteenth Century," (Ph.D. diss., Northern Illinois University, 1979), pp. 106–8, http://murphylibrary.uwlax.edu/digital/lacrosse/BrickPomeroy/; *New York News*, as quoted in Coopersmith, *Fighting Words*, p. 274.

18. Turner, *Beware the People Weeping*, p. 50; Coopersmith, *Fighting Words*, p. 273; *Philadelphia Press*, April 17, 1865.

19. Emma Hardinge, *The Great Funeral Oration on Abraham Lincoln* (New York: American News Company, 1865), pp. 20–21, MP.

20. A. D. Mayo, *The Nation's Sacrifice. Abraham Lincoln. Two Discourses, Delivered on Sunday Morning, April 16, and Wednesday, April 19, 1865, in the Church of the Redeemer, Cincinnati, Ohio* (Cincinnati: Robert Clarke & Co., 1865), p. 28, MP; Herrick Johnson, *"God's Ways Unsearchable": A Discourse, on the Death of President Lincoln, Preached before the Third Presbyterian Congregation in Mozart Hall, Pittsburgh, Pa., Sunday April 23, 1865* (Pittsburgh: W.G. Johnson, 1865), p. 9, MP.

21. Phillips Brooks, *The Life and Death of Abraham Lincoln, A Sermon Preached at the Church of the Holy Trinity, Philadelphia, Sunday Morning, April 23, 1865* (Philadelphia: Henry B. Ashmead, 1865), pp. 7 11, 13, 17, 20, 24; J. G. Holland, *Eulogy on Abraham Lincoln, Late President of the United States, Pronounced at the City Hall, Springfield, Mass., April 19, 1865* (Springfield: L. J. Powers, 1865), pp. 12–17.

22. C. M. Butler, *Funeral Address on the Death of Abraham Lincoln, Delivered in the Church of the Covenant, April 19, 1865* (Philadelphia: Henry B. Ashmead, 1865), pp. 28–29; Richard Eddy, *The Martyr to Liberty. Three Sermons Preached in the First Universalist Church, Philadelphia. Sunday, April 16th, Wednesday April 19, and Thursday, June 1st* (Philadelphia: Horace W. Smith, 1865), pp. 23–24, MP.

23. Guelzo, *Abraham Lincoln*, p. 451; *Philadelphia Daily Evening Bulletin*, April 20, 1865.

24. Holland, *Eulogy on Abraham Lincoln*, pp. 12–17; Fowler, *Character and Death of Abraham Lincoln*, p. 15.

25. *National Anti-Slavery Standard* (New York), May 6, 1865.

26. *Connecticut Herald*, April 22, 1865; *National Anti-Slavery Standard* (New York), April 22, 1865; *Central Press* (Bellefonte, Penn.), April 28, 1865, http://digitalnewspapers.libraries.psu.edu.

27. *Christian Recorder* (Philadelphia), April 22, 29, 1865.

28. Bergeron, *Andrew Johnson's Civil War*, pp. 72–73; Bruce Levine, *The Fall of the House of Dixie: How the Civil War Remade the American South* (New York: Random House, 2013), pp. 283–87.

29. *Highland Weekly News* (Hillsborough, Highland County, Ohio), April 27, 1865, CA; *National Anti-Slavery Standard* (New York), April 29, 1865; U.S. Congress, *Report of the Joint Committee on the Conduct of the War, at the Second Session Thirty-Eight Congress* (Washington, D.C.: GPO), pp. 14–19; *Brooklyn Eagle*, April 29, 1865; *Franklin Repository* (Chambersburg, Penn.), May 10, 1865.

30. *Sacramento Daily Union*, May 15, 1865; *New York Times*, May 5, 1865.

31. Richard Nelson Current, "The Martyr and the Myth: The Lincoln Nobody Knows," in Holzer, Symonds, and Williams, eds., *Lincoln Assassination*, p. 234.

32. Gary Gallagher, *The Union War* (Cambridge, Mass.: Harvard University Press, 2012), pp. 12–23; *Independent Republican* (Montrose, Penn.), May 30, 1865.

33. Abial Edwards to Anna Conant, May 26, 1865, http://armyheritage.org/images/ stories/Education_Images/Edwards/Edwards_Letter_18650526_Army_ Grand_School.pdf and http://www.carlisle.army.mil/ahec/AHM/civilwarimagery/ edwards_Grand_Review.cfm.

34. Grant, *Personal Memoirs*, p. 615.

Chapter 7

1. Judith W. McGuire, *Diary of a Southern Refugee during the War* (1867. Reprint, New York: Arno Press, 1972), pp. 351–53.

2. Ibid., p. 353; Sallie Brock Putnam, *Richmond during the War: Four Years of Personal Observation* (1867. Reprint, Lincoln: University of Nebraska Press, 1996), p. 375.

3. http://www.encyclopediavirginia.org/Newspapers_in_Virginia_During_ the_Civil_War_Confederate; Judkin Browning, ed., *The Southern Mind under Union Rule: The Diary of James Rumley, Beaufort, North Carolina, 1862–1865* (Gainesville: University Press of Florida, 2009), p. 171; Coopersmith, *Fighting Words*, pp. 258–63, 310.

4. "Mary Custis Lee—'Our Poor Unhappy Country,'" in Katharine M. Jones, *Heroines of Dixie: Confederate Women Tell Their Story of the War* (New York: Bobbs-Merrill, 1955), pp. 403–4.

5. Elizabeth Preston Allan, *The Life and Letters of Margaret Junkin Preston* (Boston: Houghton, Mifflin, 1903), pp. 207–8, 214; Stacey Jean Klein, *Margaret Junkin Preston, Poet of the Confederacy: A Literary Life* (Columbia: University of South Carolina Press, 2007), pp. 60–62; Lois Hill, ed., *Poems and Songs of the Civil War* (New York: Gramercy Books), p. 127.

6. Emma Holmes, *The Diary of Miss Emma Holmes 1861–1866*, ed. John Marszalek (Baton Rouge: Louisiana State University Press, 1994), pp. 442–43.

7. *Anderson Intelligencer* (Anderson Court House, S.C.), April 27, 1865, CA. For articles estimating the Confederate army at 8,000 and Union army at 200,000, see for example *Southern Watchman* (Athens, Ga.), April 26, 1865; *Edgefield Advertiser* (Edgefield, S.C.), April 26, 1865, CA; *Columbia Phoenix* (S.C.), April 21, 1865, CA; Kate Cumming, *The Journal of Kate Cumming, A Confederate Nurse, 1862–1865*, ed. Richard Harwell (1866. Reprint, Savannah, Ga.: Beehive Press, 1975), p. 253; McGuire, *Diary of a Southern Refugee*, p. 353; Grace Brown Elmore, *Heritage of Woe: The Civil War Diary of Grace Brown Elmore, 1861–1868*, ed. Marli F. Wiener (Athens: University of Georgia Press, 1997), p. 115.

8. Diary of Mary Washington (Cabell) Early, April 7, 9, 1865, VHS; *Anderson Intelligencer*, April 27, 1865.

9. For uses of the phrase "overwhelming numbers" in the Southern press, see for example *Macon Telegraph* (Ga.), May 8, 1861; February 19, 21, 1862; *Weekly Raleigh Register* (N.C.), March 5, 1862; *Fayetteville Observer* (N.C.), April 10, 1862; December 29, 1864; January 23, 1865; *Charleston Courier*, April 22, 1862; *New Orleans Daily Picayune*, December 22, 1862; *Richmond Daily Dispatch*, May 20, 1864; *Daily South Carolinian* (Columbia), May 28, 29, 1864; Cornelia Phillips Spencer, *The Last Days of the War in North-Carolina* (New York: Watchman, 1866), pp. 235–36.

10. John B. Jones, *A Rebel War Clerk's Diary*, ed. Earl Schenck Miers (Baton Rouge: Louisiana State University Press, 1993), p. 535; Cornelia Peake McDonald, *A Woman's Civil War: A Diary, with Reminiscences of the War from March 1862*, ed. Minrose C. Gwin (Madison: University of Wisconsin Press, 1992), p. 232; John N. Fain, ed., *Sanctified Trial: The Diary of Eliza Rhea Anderson Fain, a Confederate Woman in East Tennessee* (Knoxville: University of Tennessee Press, 2004), pp. 322–23.

11. Emma LeConte, *When the World Ended: The Diary of Emma LeConte*, ed. Earl Schenck Miers (Lincoln: University of Nebraska Press, 1987), pp. 90–91; Sarah Morgan, *The Civil War Diary of a Southern Woman*, ed. Charles East (New York: Touchstone, 1992), p. 606; Diary of Mary Washington (Cabell) Early, April 11, 17, 1865, VHS.

12. Letter of Thomas S. Bocock, June 23, 1865, UVA; Elmore, *Heritage of Woe*, pp. 116–17; Elizabeth R. Baer, ed., *Shadows in My Heart: The Civil War Diary of Lucy Rebecca Buck of Virginia* (Athens: University of Georgia Press, 1997), p. 319.

13. *North Carolina Standard*, as quoted in Coopersmith, *Fighting Words*, p. 258; Steven E. Nash, "'The Other War Was but the Beginning': The Politics of Loyalty in Western North Carolina, 1865–1867," in *Reconstructing Appalachia: The Civil War's Aftermath*, ed. Andrew L. Slap (Lexington: University Press of Kentucky, 2010), pp. 107–9.

14. Coopersmith, *Fighting Words*, pp. 259 (first and second quotations), 260 (*Houston Tri-Weekly Telegraph* quotation).

15. *Augusta Constitutionalist*, as quoted in Coopersmith, *Fighting Words*, p. 259; *Edgefield Advertiser* (S.C.), April 26, 1865, CA.

16. John Levering, "Recollections of the Civil War, 1861–66" (bound volume), p. 483–84, UVA; *Brownlow's Knoxville Whig and Rebel Ventilator*, April 19, 1865, CA; Samuel M. Janney, *Memoirs of Samuel M. Janney, Late of Lincoln, Loudoun County, Va.* (Philadelphia: Friends' Book Association, 1881), pp. 233–34.

17. Aaron Sheehan-Dean, *Why Confederates Fought: Family & Nation in Civil War Virginia* (Chapel Hill: University of North Carolina Press, 2007), p. 181.

18. Judkin Browning, *Shifting Loyalties: The Union Occupation of Eastern North Carolina* (Chapel Hill: University of North Carolina Press, 2011), p. 56.

19. William W. Freehling, *The South vs. The South: How Anti-Confederate Southerners Shaped the Course of the Civil War* (New York: Oxford University Press, 2001); Thomas G. Dyer, *Secret Yankees: The Union Circle in Confederate Atlanta* (Baltimore: Johns Hopkins University Press, 1999); Elizabeth R. Varon, *Southern Lady, Yankee Spy: The True Story of Elizabeth Van Lew, A Union Agent in the Heart of the Confederacy* (New York: Oxford University Press, 1998), p. 199.

20. Varon, *Southern Lady, Yankee Spy*, p. 199; Robert Tracy McKenzie, *Lincolnites and Rebels: A Divided Town in the American Civil War* (New York: Oxford University Press, 2009), pp. 204–8, 227.

21. Varon, *Southern Lady, Yankee Spy*, pp. 194–95.

22. While many scholars note that Appomattox was a freedom day, none have offered a sustained account of its place in the process or memory of emancipation; recent studies of black freedom commemorations have mentioned Appomattox only in passing, if at all. On the surrender and emancipation, see for example Leon Litwack, *Been in the Storm So Long: The Aftermath of Slavery* (New York: Knopf, 1979), pp. 171–72; Melvin Patrick Ely, *Israel on the Appomattox: A Southern Experiment in Black Freedom from the 1790s through the Civil War* (New York: Knopf,

2004), pp. 416–17; Oakes, *Freedom National*, p. 482. On commemorations of emancipation, see Mitch Kachun, *Festivals of Freedom: Meaning and Memory in African American Emancipation Celebrations, 1808–1915* (Amherst: University of Massachusetts Press, 2003), p. 118; William Blair, *Cities of the Dead: Contesting the Memory of the Civil War in the South, 1865–1914* (Chapel Hill: University of North Carolina Press, 2004), pp. 137, 163; Kathleen Ann Clark, *Defining Moments: African American Commemorations and Political Culture in the South, 1863–1913* (Chapel Hill: University of North Carolina Press, 2005).

23. Peter Randolph, *From Slave Cabin to the Pulpit. The Autobiography of Rev. Peter Randolph: The Southern Question Illustrated and Sketches of Slave Life* (Boston: J. H. Earle, 1893), pp. 57–58; Booker T. Washington, *Up From Slavery* (1901. Reprint, New York: Penguin, 2000), p. 13.

24. Samuel Spottford Clement, *Memoirs of Samuel Spottford Clement Relating Interesting Experiences in Days of Slavery and Freedom*, ed. Sara Ovington (Steubenville, Ohio: Herald, 1809), pp. 9–10, at Documenting the American South, http://docsouth.unc.edu/neh/clement/clement.html; Michael Bedour Chesson and Leslie Jean Roberts, eds., *Exile in Richmond: The Confederate Journal of Henri Garidel* (Charlottesville: University Press of Virginia, 2001), pp. 375–76; Letitia Burwell, *A Girl's Life in Virginia before the War* (New York: Frederick A. Stokes, 1895), p. 184.

25. Mitchell, Texas Narratives, vol. 16, pt. 3, p. 112; Holmes, Alabama Narratives, vol. 1, p. 195; Harrison, Arkansas Narratives, vol. 2, pt. 3, pp. 185–86, FWP; Charles L. Perdue Jr., Thomas E. Barden, and Robert K. Phillips, *Weevils in the Wheat: Interviews with Virginia Ex-Slaves* (Charlottesville: University Press of Virginia, 1976), p. 39. For background on the WPA interview process, and on both the shortcomings and the richness of the interviews as a window into "black folk thought," see Bay, *The White Image in the Black Mind*, pp. 115–16.

26. Wesley John Gaines, *The Negro and the White Man* (Philadelphia: A.M.E., 1897), pp. 71–72.

27. Radford, Georgia Narratives, vol. 4, pt. 4, pp. 346–47; Johnson, South Carolina Narratives, vol. 14, pt. 3, p. 45, all in FWP.

28. Washington, Arkansas Narratives, vol. 2, pt. 7, p. 49; Harris, Virginia Narratives, vol. 17, p. 24; Jones, Georgia Narratives, vol. 4, pt. 4, p. 345; Dorum, Arkansas Narratives, vol. 2, pt. 2, p. 180, in FWP; *Pittsburgh Courier*, May 20, 1939.

29. Kachun, *Festivals of Freedom: Memory and Meaning in African American Emancipation Celebrations*, p. 118 (Mecklenburg quotation); see also W. Fitzhugh Brundage, *The Southern Past: A Clash of Race and Memory* (Cambridge, Mass.: Harvard University Press, 2005), p. 80. See also the *Baltimore Afro-American*, March 17, 1905.

30. Washington, Arkansas Narratives, vol. 2, pt. 7, pp. 55–56, FWP; Perdue, Barden, and Phillips, *Weevils in the Wheat*, pp. 29, 103.

31. *Brownlow's Knoxville Whig and Rebel Ventilator*, April 19, 1865, CA; Dyer, *Secret Yankees*, pp. 222–23.

32. LeConte, *When the World Ended*, pp. 90–91; Mary Chesnut, *Mary Chesnut's Civil War*, ed. C. Vann Woodward (New Haven, Conn.: Yale University Press, 1981), p. 791; Charlotte St. J. Ravenel, in *Two Diaries from Middle St. John's, Berkeley, South Carolina, February–May1865: Journals Kept by Miss Susan R. Jervey and Miss Charlottes St. J. Ravenel* (Pinopolis, S.C.: St. John's Hunting Club, 1921), pp. 44–46; "The Jones Family," in *Voices from the Reconstruction Years, 1865–1877,*

ed. Glenn M. Linden (Fort Worth, Tex.: Harcourt Brace, 1999), p. 7; Wise, *The End of an Era*, pp. 454–55.

33. McDonald, *A Woman's Civil War*, p. 235; Chesnut, *Mary Chesnut's Civil War*, p. 791; *Shreveport News* as quoted in *New Orleans Times*, May 7, 1865.

34. *Houston Tri-Weekly Telegraph*, and *North Carolina Standard*, as quoted in Cooper-smith, *Fighting Words*, pp. 278–80.

35. *Shreveport News* as quoted in *New Orleans Times*, May 7, 1865; Morgan, *The Civil War Diary of a Southern Woman*, pp. 606–7.

36. *Nashville Daily Union*, May 13, 1865.

37. Donald Robert Beagle and Brian Albin Giezma, *Poet of the Lost Cause: A Life of Father Ryan* (Knoxville: University of Tennessee Press, 2008), pp. 89–104; Abraham Joseph Ryan, "The Conquered Banner," in *Civil War Poetry: An Anthology*, ed. Paul Negri (Mineola, N.Y.: Dover, 1997), pp. 103–4.

38. David O'Connell, *Furl That Banner: The Life of Abram J. Ryan, Poet-Priest of the South* (Macon, Ga.: Mercer University Press, 2006), p. 62; Beagle and Giezma, *Poet of the Lost Cause*, pp. 110–11.

39. Beagle and Giemza, *Poet of the Lost Cause*, p. 106, 121; O'Connell, *Furl That Banner*, pp. 10, 82.

Chapter 8

1. Richard S. Ewell to Lee, April 17, 1865, Lee Headquarters Papers, VHS; Paul D. Casdorph, *Confederate General R. S. Ewell, Robert E. Lee's Hesitant Commander* (Lexington: University Press of Kentucky, 2004), pp. 325, 338–49.

2. Ewell to Lee, April 17, 1865, VHS.

3. For Lee as conciliator, see for example Freeman, *R. E. Lee*, vol. 4, p. 219; Gene Smith, *Lee and Grant* (New York: McGraw-Hill, 1984), p. 302; Manfred Weidhorn, *Robert E. Lee* (New York: Atheneum, 1988), p.128; McCaslin, *Lee in the Shadow of Washington*, pp. 192–94; Charles Bracelen Flood, *Lee: The Last Years* (New York: Houghton Mifflin, 1981), p. 51; Jay Winik, *April 1865: The Month That Saved America* (New York: Harper, 2001). For a trenchant critique of this tradition, see Alan T. Nolan, *Lee Considered: General Robert E. Lee and Civil War History* (Chapel Hill: University of North Carolina Press, 1991), pp. 135–52.

4. *Richmond Whig*, April 17, 1865.

5. *Richmond Whig*, April 21, 1865; *New York Times*, April 30, 1865; William A. Frassanito, *Grant and Lee: The Virginia Campaigns, 1864–1865* (Gettysburg, Penn.: Thomas, 1983), p. 418.

6. Frassanito, *Grant and Lee*, p. 416; Pryor, *Reading the Man*, p. 429; Bob Zeller, *The Blue and the Gray in Black and White: A History of Civil War Photography* (Westport, Conn.: Praeger, 2005), p. 167.

7. *Providence Journal* as quoted in *Bangor Daily Whig & Courier*, May 1, 1865.

8. *New York Herald*, April 29, 1865.

9. Ibid.; Varon, "'Save in Defense of My Native State.'"

10. *New York Herald*, April 29, 1865.

11. Ibid.; Nolan, *Lee Considered*, p. 29. For Lee's wartime laments on Confederate recruiting, see for example Dowdey, ed., *Wartime Papers of Robert E. Lee*, pp. 650–51, 654–55, 843–44, 847–50.

12. Flood, *Lee*, p. 51; Pryor, *Reading the Man*, p. 432.

13. *New York Herald*, April 29, 1865.

14. Ibid.
15. *New York Evening Post*, as quoted in the *Liberator* (Boston), May 5, 1865; *Harper's Weekly*, May 13, 1865; *Anglo-African* (New York), August 26, 1865.
16. *New York Evening Post*, as quoted in the *Liberator* (Boston), May 5, 1865; *New York Times*, as quoted in *Zion's Herald and Wesleyan Journal* (New York), May 17, 1865.
17. *Placerville News* as quoted in *Daily Miners' Register* (Central City, Colo.), May 21, 1865; *Cleveland Daily Herald*, May 30, 1865.
18. *New York Times*, June 4, 1865.
19. Bergeron, "Introduction," *PAJ*, 8:xxviii–xxix.
20. Paul H. Bergeron, *Andrew Johnson's Civil War and Reconstruction* (Knoxville: University of Tennessee Press, 2011), p. 75.
21. Bergeron, *Andrew Johnson's Civil War*, pp. 74–76; Brooks D. Simpson, Leroy P. Graf, and John Muldowny, eds., *Advice after Appomattox: Letters to Andrew Johnson, 1865–1866* (Knoxville: University of Tennessee Press, 1987), pp. 39–41.
22. Foner, *A Short History of Reconstruction*, pp. 94–95.
23. On Johnson's motivations, see for example Annette Gordon-Reed, *Andrew Johnson* (New York: Henry Holt, 2011), pp. 99–103; Hans L. Trefousse, *Andrew Johnson: A Biography* (New York: W.W. Norton, 1989), p. 228. For his comments to the delegation of Charlestonians, see Interview with South Carolina Delegation, June 24, 1865, *PAJ*, 8:280–85. On Johnson and the suffrage issue, see Bergeron, *Andrew Johnson's Civil War*, pp. 91–92.
24. John W. Gorham to AJ, June 3, 1865, *PAJ*, 8:173–74; Browning, ed., *The Southern Mind under Union Rule*, p. 178.
25. North Carolina Blacks to AJ, May 10, 1865; Delegation Representing the Black People of Kentucky to AJ, June 9, 1865; Committee of Richmond Blacks to AJ, June 10, 1865; South Carolina Black Citizens to AJ, June 29, 1865, all in *PAJ*, 8:57–58, 203–4, 211–13, 317–19.
26. Thaddeus Stevens to AJ, May 16, 1865; Joseph Noxon to AJ, May 27, 1865; John A. Dix to AJ, May 28, 1865; Truman Woodruff to AJ, June 20, 1865; Amasa Walker to AJ, July 18, 1865, all in *PAJ*, 8:80, 119, 125, 266, 433–34.
27. Pro Patria et Preside to AJ, May 14, 1865; A Southern Man to AJ, May 31, 1865, in *PAJ*, 8:69–70, 159–60.
28. Richard Lowe, *Republicans and Reconstruction in Virginia, 1856–1870* (Charlottesville: University Press of Virginia, 1991), pp. 31–35.
29. "Equal Suffrage. Address from the Colored Citizens of Norfolk, Va. to the People of the United States," *From Slavery to Freedom: The African-American Pamphlet Collection, 1822–1909*, AAP; William Still, *The Underground Rail Road* (Philadelphia: Porter & Coates, 1872), pp. 254–59; Wilson, *The Black Phalanx*.
30. Lowe, *Republicans and Reconstruction*, pp. 34–35.
31. Witt, *Lincoln's Code*, pp. 183–84, 267–68, 322–24 (quotation on 323); William Blair, *Why Didn't the North Hang Some Rebels? The Postwar Debate over Punishment for Treason* (Milwaukee: Marquette University Press), pp. 6–8, 16–31; *San Francisco Evening Bulletin*, June 5, 1865.
32. *Norfolk Post* (excerpt of and commentary on *Petersburg News*), June 22, 1865.
33. Lee to Grant, June 13, 1865, and Lee to AJ, June 13, 1865, Lee Papers (microfilm), VHS; Grant to Edwin M. Stanton, June 16, 1865, *PUSG*, 15:149–50.
34. McFeely, *Grant*, pp. 233–35; *New York Times*, June 7, 1865.
35. Grant to Edwin M. Stanton, June 16, 1865, *PUSG*, 15:149–50; Trudeau, *Robert E. Lee*, p. 202 (Johnson quote).

36. Flood, *Lee*, p. 63; Smith, *Grant*, p. 418; Trudeau, *Robert E. Lee*, p. 202; Pryor, *Reading the Man*, pp. 452–54; Lee to John Letcher, August 28, 1865; Lee to Matthew Fontaine Maury, September 8, 1865; Lee to E. M. Bruce, September 25, 1865, all in Lee and Lee-Jackson Papers, W&L.
37. Thomas, *Robert E. Lee*, pp. 380–81; Flood, *Lee*, pp. 200–201.
38. Fellman, *Making of Robert E. Lee*, p. 277; Dennett, *The South As It Is*, pp. 20–21; Lee to Washington College Board of Trustees, August 24, 1865, Lee Papers, W&L; *Lancaster Intelligencer* (Penn.), October 11, 1865; *Boston Daily Advertiser*, October 11, 1865.
39. Lee to P. G. T. Beauregard, October 3, 1865, Lee Papers, W&L; Thomas, *Robert E. Lee*, pp. 370–71.
40. Grant to Maj. Gen. Henry W. Halleck, May 6, 1865, *PUSG*, 15:11; Brooks D. Simpson, *Let Us Have Peace: Ulysses S. Grant and the Politics of War & Reconstruction, 1861–1868* (Chapel Hill: University of North Carolina Press, 1991), pp. 108–9; Thomas, *Robert E. Lee*, pp. 370–71. Among Grant's many concerns were conditions in Mexico: he feared that "harsh treatment of former Confederates might chase them into the arms of the French and Mexican monarchists who conducted war with the liberals under Benito Juarez." Blair, *Why Didn't the North Hang Some Rebels?*, pp. 12–13. While thousands of "last-ditch" Confederates did seek refuge in Mexico (and, to a lesser extent, in Cuba and Brazil), "Far fewer Confederates experimented with exile than threatened to do so," explains Bruce Levine. "And most of those who did go abroad eventually straggled back into the restored Union, where they joined the great mass of former slave owners determined to salvage something from the wreckage of the world they had known and that some had dreamed would last forever." Bruce Levine, *The Fall of the House of Dixie: The Civil War and the Social Revolution that Transformed the South* (New York: Random House, 2013), pp. 293–94.
41. *Army and Navy Journal* (New York), September 2, 1865 (Dana quotations); Witt, *Lincoln's Code*, pp. 322–24; Blair, *Why Didn't the North Hang Some Rebels?*, pp. 6–8, 16–31.
42. Blair, *Why Didn't the North Hang Some Rebels?*, pp. 19–21; *Constitutional Union* (Washington, D.C.), June 10, 1865.
43. Grant to Edwin M. Stanton, June 20, 1865, *PUSG*, 15:204.
44. Grant to Edwin M. Stanton, June 20, 1865, *PUSG*, 15:175.
45. Grant to S. Bishop and Co., June 22, 1865, *PUSG*, 15:539; McFeely, *Grant*, pp. 151, 251; Waugh, *U. S. Grant*, p. 120.

Chapter 9

1. Simpson, Graf, and Muldowny, eds., *Advice after Appomattox*, pp. 80–85.
2. "Voices of the Past: The Letters of Abial Edwards," at http://armyheritage.org/images/stories/Education_Images/Edwards/Edwards_Letter_18651022_Occupation_Force.pdf.
3. Smith, *Grant*, p. 421; McFeely, *Grant*, p. 241.
4. Brooks D. Simpson, "Grant's Tour of the South Revisited," *Journal of Southern History* 54 (August 1988): 425–48.
5. Simpson, Graf, and Muldowny, eds., *Advice after Appomattox*, pp. 212–15.
6. Foner, *Short History of Reconstruction*, pp. 104–9.
7. Simpson, *Let Us Have Peace*, pp. 116, 122–27.

8. "General Robert E. Lee," *The Old Guard* 4 (January 1866): 56–58; Lee to C. Chauncey Burr, January 5, 1866, Lee Papers (microfilm), VHS.

9. Ulysses S. Grant, *Report of Lieutenant General U.S. Grant, of the Armies of the United States, 1864–'65* (Washington, D.C.: Government Printing Office, 1865); *Charleston Daily News*, December 30, 1865, CA.

10. Eric Foner, *Forever Free: The Story of Emancipation & Reconstruction* (New York: Vintage, 2006), pp. 114–15. On the legal origins and implications of the Civil Rights act, see George Rutherglen, *Civil Rights in the Shadow of Slavery: The Constitution, Common Law, and the Civil Rights Act of 1866* (New York: Oxford University Press, 2013).

11. Simpson, *Let Us Have Peace*, p. 128.

12. *Appendix to the Cong. Globe*, 39th Cong., 1st sess., March 2, 1866, pp. 140–41 (Wilson speech).

13. *Cong. Globe*, 39th Cong., 1st sess., March 2, 1866, p. 1159 (Windom speech); March 8, 1866, pp. 1264–65 (Broomall speech).

14. Whitelaw Reid, *After the War: A Southern Tour. May 1, 1865, to May 1, 1866* (Cincinnati, Ohio: Moore, Wilstach & Baldwin, 1866), pp. 295–300.

15. Sidney Andrews, *The South since the War* (1866. Reprint, Baton Rouge: Louisiana State University Press, 2004), pp. 2, 29, 115.

16. John Richard Dennett, *The South As It Is, 1865–1866* (1866. Reprint, New York: Viking Press, 1965), pp. 3, 63, 87, 348, 358.

17. J. T. Trowbridge, *The South: A Tour of Its Battle-Fields and Ruined Cities* (Hartford, Conn.: L. Stebbins, 1866), pp. 235, 587–90.

18. *Christian Recorder* (Philadelphia), August 26, 1865, March 31, 1866.

19. *Cong. Globe*, 39th Cong., 1st sess., January 30, 1866, pp. 501–2 (Cowan); pp. 506–7 (Johnson); March 1, 1866, p. 1122 (Rogers).

20. *Valley Virginian* (Augusta Co.), February 21, 1866.

21. J. D. B. De Bow, "The Future of the United States," and W. W. Boyce, "President Johnson's Policy of Reconstruction," *De Bow's Review*, January 1866, pp. 4, 16–20.

22. De Bow, "Editorial Notes and Miscellanies," *De Bow's Review*, February 1866, p. 220; "General Grant's View of the Southern Situation," *De Bow's Review*, April 1866, pp. 439–40; De Bow, "Editorial Notes and Miscellanies," *De Bow's Review*, March 1866, p. 331.

23. John Hope Franklin, *Reconstruction after the Civil War* (Chicago: University of Chicago Press, 1961), p. 58.

24. Lee Testimony, U.S. Congress, *Report of the Joint Committee on Reconstruction, at the First Session, Thirty-Ninth Congress* (Washington, D.C.: GPO, 1866), pt. 2, 129–31.

25. Ibid., pp. 129–36.

26. Franklin, *Reconstruction*, pp. 58–59; U.S. Congress, *Report of the Joint Committee on Reconstruction*, pt. 2, pp. 51–59. White Southern Unionists who testified offered their own version of the golden moment lost argument, one that emphasized how Johnson's indiscriminate pardons had returned the "worst class of secessionists" to power. "There is as much disaffection and disloyalty as there was at any time during the war, and a hundredfold more than there was immediately after the evacuation [of Richmond] and the surrender of the army," Virginia Unionist John Minor Botts noted. Hans L. Trefousse, ed., *Background for Radical Reconstruction: Testimony Taken from the Hearings of the Joint Committee on Reconstruction, the Select Committee on the Memphis Riots and Massacres, and the Select Committee on the New Orleans Riots—1866 and 1867* (Boston: Little, Brown and Co., 1970), pp. 111–14.

27. For overviews of the debate over Lee's views on race, see Nolan, *Lee Considered*, esp. chs. 2 and 7, and Pryor, *Reading the Man*, chs. 16 and 25. For the story of Lee preventing a lynching, see Franklin L. Riley, ed., *General Robert E. Lee after Appomattox* (New York: Macmillan, 1922), pp. 129–30.

28. U.S. Congress, *Report of the Joint Committee on Reconstruction*, pp. xx–xxi. On paternalism, see Lacy Ford, *Deliver Us from Evil: The Slavery Question in the Old South* (New York: Oxford University Press, 2009).

29. *Chicago Tribune*, March 30, 1866; *National Anti-Slavery Standard* (New York), April 7, 1866.

30. *Lancaster Intelligencer* (Penn.), April 11, 1866.

31. Stanton Garner, *The Civil War World of Herman Melville* (Lawrence: University Press of Kansas, 1993), pp. 35, 360, 380–81; Masur, ed., *The Real War Will Never Get in the Books*, p. 209; Herman Melville, *Battle-pieces and Aspects of the War* (New York: Harper & Brothers, 1866), pp. 229–37.

32. Melville, *Battle-pieces*, pp. 229–37.

33. Ibid., pp. 229–37.

34. Garner, *Civil War World of Herman Melville*, pp. 430–41.

35. *Richmond Examiner*, March 21, 29, 30, 1866.

36. Ibid.

37. U. S. Grant, "Endorsement," February 17, 1866, *PUSG*, 16:70–73; Simpson, *Let Us Have Peace*, pp. 130–32.

38. Grant to AJ, March 14, 1866, *PUSG*, 16:114.

39. On the Pickett and Johnson cases, see Grant to Johnson, March 16 and 30, 1866, *PUSG*, 16:120–22, 143–44 and Grant's testimony before the House Judiciary Committee, July 18, 1867, *PUSG*, 17:220–21; Witt, *Lincoln's Code*, pp. 303, 322–23; Lesley J. Gordon, *General George E. Pickett in Life & Legend* (Chapel Hill: University of North Carolina Press, 1998), pp. 160–61.

40. Grant to Johnson, March 16 and 30, 1866, *PUSG*, 16:120–22, 143–44; Witt, *Lincoln's Code*, pp. 183–84, 267–68; 298; Brian D. McKnight, *Confederate Outlaw: Champ Ferguson and the Civil War in Appalachia* (Baton Rouge: Louisiana State University Press, 2011), pp. 163–78.

41. Stephen Fox, *Wolf of the Deep: Raphael Semmes and the Notorious Confederate Raider CSS Alabama* (New York: Alfred A. Knopf, 2007), pp. 242–45.

42. Raphael Semmes, *Memoirs of Service Afloat, During the War between the States* (Baltimore: Kelly, Piet & Co., 1868), pp. 823–29; *Army and Navy Journal*, February 17, 1866; Fox, *Wolf of the Deep*, pp. 246–50.

43. Foner, *Short History of Reconstruction*, p. 113; Simpson, *Let Us Have Peace*, p. 133; *Norfolk Post* as quoted in *National Anti-Slavery Standard* (New York), April 14, 1866; Dennett, *The South As It Is*, pp. 355–56. On April 3, 1866, the Supreme Court in *Ex Parte Milligan* ruled on the legality of Lincoln's wartime suspension of habeas corpus and declaration of martial law: the court found that military trials of civilians were unconstitutional where civil courts remained open. For the negative impact of this decision on Judge Advocate General Holt's efforts to bring Jefferson Davis to justice, see Elizabeth Leonard, *Lincoln's Forgotten Ally: Judge Advocate General Joseph Holt of Kentucky* (Chapel Hill: University of North Carolina Press, 2011), pp. 244, 268.

44. *Cong. Globe*, 39th Cong., 1st sess., April 4, 1866, pp. 1756–57; *Christian Recorder*, April 7, 1866; *Independent* (New York), April 5, 1866; "The Political Situation," *New Englander and Yale Review*, April 1866, pp. 359, APS.

45. *Independent* (New York), April 5, 1866; *National Anti-Slavery Standard* (New York), April 14, 1866. For the most detailed account of this incident in modern scholarship, see Pryor, *Reading the Man*, pp. 260–70.

46. *Independent* (New York), April 5, 1866; Pryor, *Reading the Man*, pp. 270–71.

47. George L. Prentiss, "The Political Situation," *American Presbyterian and Theological Review*, April 1866, pp. 298, APS.

48. *Zion's Herald and Wesleyan Journal* (New York), April 18, 1866; *National Anti-Slavery Standard* (New York), April 21, 1866; *Christian Recorder* (Philadelphia), April 21, 1866; *Cong. Globe*, 39th Cong., 1st sess., April 7, 1866, pp. 1837–39; Frederick Douglass, "Reconstruction," *Atlantic Monthly*, December 1866, pp. 761–65.

49. Pollard, *The Lost Cause*, pp. 746–52.

50. Ibid.

51. Terrell Armistead Crow and Mary Moulton Barden, eds., *Live Your Own Life: The Family Papers of Mary Bayard Clarke, 1854–1886* (Columbia: University of South Carolina Press, 2003), pp. 186–89, 196–97, 226–28.

52. Ibid.

53. Hannah Rosen, *Terror in the Heart of Freedom: Citizenship, Sexual Violence, and the Meaning of Race in the Postemancipation South* (Chapel Hill: University of North Carolina Press, 2009), pp. 61–69.

54. Ibid., pp. 81–82.

55. Grant to Stanton, July 7, 1866, *PUSG*, 16:233; Smith, *Grant*, p. 425.

56. *New York Times*, May 24, 1865; Simpson, *Let Us Have Peace*, pp. 137–38; transcript of Grant interview from the *Chicago Tribune*, September 14, 1866, *PUSG*, 16:256–59.

57. *New York Times*, May 24, 1865.

58. *New York Times*, May 24, 1865; Longstreet, *From Manassas to Appomattox*, pp. 636–37. Grant admired Joe Johnston's farewell address to his troops in North Carolina, in which Johnston had urged them to "discharge the obligations of good and peaceful citizens"; the "good tone and spirit" of Johnston's speech distinguished him from "others who did not appear so well." Grant Testimony, July 18, 1867, *PUSG*, 17:222.

59. On Mosby, see John S. Mosby, *Mosby's Memoirs* (1917. Reprint, New York: Barnes & Noble, 2006). On Mahone, see Jane Dailey, *Before Jim Crow: The Politics of Race in Postemancipation Virginia* (Chapel Hill: University of North Carolina Press, 2000), and Kevin M. Levin, "William Mahone, the Lost Cause, and Civil War History," *Virginia Magazine of History and Biography* 113 (2005): 379–412. On Longstreet, see William Garrett Piston, *Lee's Tarnished Lieutenant: James Longstreet and His Place in Southern History* (Athens: University of Georgia Press, 1990); Dowdey, *Lee*, p. 687.

60. For excerpts from and coverage of Wise's speech, see for example *Army and Navy Journal* (New York), May 19, 1866; *The (St. Albans) Vermont Transcript*, May 18, 1866; *Brownlow's Knoxville (Tn.) Whig*, June 6, 1866. In a letter to Lee, Wise explained that he would never request a presidential pardon because such a request was a tacit admission of guilt. "Lee responded perfunctorily," Wise's biographer Craig M. Simpson explains; "ever superior and devotedly self-sacrificial," Lee had requested a pardon "as an example for his men and the South." Craig M. Simpson, *A Good Southerner: The Life of Henry A. Wise of Virginia* (Chapel Hill: University of North Carolina Press), 1985, p. 291.

61. *Army and Navy Journal* (New York), May 19, 1866.
62. *New York Times*, May 24, 1865; Grant, *Personal Memoirs*, pp. 610–12.
63. *New York Times*, May 24, 1865; Foner, *Short History of Reconstruction*, p. 145.

Epilogue

1. Grant to Julia Grant, September 9, 1866, *PUSG*, 16:308; Bergeron, *Andrew Johnson's Civil War*, pp. 126–29.
2. *Valley Virginian* (Augusta Co.), February 27, 1867; *Cong. Globe*, 39th Cong., 2nd sess., February 15, 1867, p. 1365.
3. Grant Testimony, July 18, 1867, *PUSG*, 17: 210–233 (first and second quotations on 216 and 228); *Harper's Weekly*, December 14, 1867 (third quotation); *Gallipolis Journal* (Ohio), July 25, 1867, CA; David O. Stewart, *Impeached: The Trial of President Andrew Johnson and Fight for Lincoln's Legacy* (New York: Simon and Schuster, 2009), p. 93 (last quotation).
4. Waugh, *U. S. Grant*, p. 109; Thomas, *Robert E. Lee*, p. 391. For a text of the "White Sulphur Manifesto," see *Staunton Spectator* (Va.), September 8, 1868.
5. *Independent* (New York), April 13, 1865 (Greeley quote); *Detroit Free Press*, April 9, 1865; *London Times*, April 25, 1865.
6. *Round Table* (New York), April 7, 1866, APS.
7. Mark E. Neely Jr., Harold Holzer, and Gabor S. Boritt, *The Confederate Image: Prints of the Lost Cause* (Chapel Hill: University of North Carolina Press, 1987), pp. 68–75; *Edgefield Advertiser* (S.C.), January 10, 1866.
8. See Neely, Holzer, and Borritt, eds., *Confederate Image*, pp. 79–85.
9. Benjamin Perley Poore, *Perley's Reminiscences of Sixty Years in the National Metropolis* (Philadelphia: Hubbard, c. 1886), p. 238.
10. G. V. Clark, "Our Fallen Heroes," in James T. Haley, *Afro-American Encyclopedia; Or, the Thoughts, Doings, and Sayings of the Race* (Nashville, Tenn.: Haley & Florida, 1895), p. 378; David W. Blight, *Race and Reunion: The Civil War in American Memory* (Cambridge: Belknap Press of Harvard University Press, 2001), pp. 300, 324–25; T. Thomas Fortune, "It Is Time to Call a Halt," in *Lift Every Voice: African American Oratory, 1787–1900*, ed. Philip S. Foner and Robert J. Branham (Tuscaloosa: University of Alabama Press, 1998), pp. 713–28.
11. *Brooklyn Daily Eagle*, April 9, 1875; *Lancaster Intelligencer* (Penn.), January 29, 1868.
12. *Testimony Taken by the Joint Select Committee to Inquire into the Condition of Affairs in the Late Insurrectionary States: Georgia*, vol. 1 (Washington, D.C.: GPO, 1872), p. 316; *Cong. Record*, 43rd Cong., 2nd sess., January 6, 1875, pp. 269–71.
13. Elder, *Texas Narratives*, vol. 16, pt. 2, pp. 17–20, FWP.
14. Caroline E. Janney, "War over a Shrine of Peace: The Appomattox Peace Monument and the Retreat from Reconstruction," *Journal of Southern History* 77 (February 2011): 91–120.
15. Ibid.
16. *Christian Recorder* (Philadelphia), September 10, 1885; Leila Amos Pendleton, *A Narrative of the Negro* (Washington, D.C.: R.L. Pendleton, 1912), pp. 90, 157–67.
17. Frances Ellen Watkins Harper, *Iola Leroy, or Shadows Uplifted* (Boston: James H. Earle, 1892), p. 138; *Philadelphia Tribune*, April 18, 1914.
18. *Chicago Defender*, February 11, 1911, April 12, 1913, April 11, 1914. See also Paula J. Giddings, *Ida: A Sword Among Lions* (New York: Amistad, 2008), p. 636.

19. *Baltimore Afro-American*, July 12, 1902; *Pittsburgh Courier*, April 27, 1912. This somber interpretation is echoed in modern scholarship in the work of the historian David Blight, whose *Race and Reunion* charts how "Grant's lenient terms" had "transfigured" by the turn of the century into "a slow surrender of a different kind." In their determination to reconcile with white Southerners and restore "order" to the unstable South, Northern whites abandoned their commitment to black citizenship, capitulated to Jim Crow segregation, and embraced the gospel of white solidarity. This long retreat, which was well under way by the time Reconstruction formally ended in 1877, "drained the war of political meaning." Blight, *Race and Reunion*, pp. 214, 356. My emphasis, by contrast, is on the staying power of Appomattox as a symbol in the black freedom struggle and on the surrender's many political uses.

20. W. Fitzhugh Brundage, *The Southern Past: A Clash of Race and Memory* (Cambridge, Mass.: Harvard University Press, 2008), pp. 102–4; Mitch Kachun, *Festivals of Freedom: Memory and Meaning in African American Celebrations of Emancipation, 1808–1915* (Amherst: University of Massachusetts Press, 2003), pp. 257–58. The most important factor in the demise of black commemorations of Appomattox is generational change. The passing from the scene of ex-slaves and black veterans who had firsthand memories of April 9 surely contributed to the decline of the tradition, as did the fact that World War I and then World War II supplanted the Civil War as the test cases for how America would reward black patriotism. But it may also be that the fading of Appomattox can be understood as part of a broader reorientation of African American culture. The historians Fitz Brundage and Mitch Kachun, in studies of black festive culture, have suggested that celebrations of emancipation dwindled in the 1920s and 1930s, as a vanguard of activists and scholars representing the "New Negro" movement rejected both the "civilizationist" ideology and what they deemed the sentimental approach to commemorating African American history.

21. Philip Glass website, "Appomattox," http://www.philipglass.com/music/compositions/appomattox.php; Cy Musiker, "'Appomattox' Makes Its Debut," October 7, 2007, http://www.npr.org/templates/story/story.php?storyId=15011594; Winik, *April 1865*, p. 383.

22. Lee to John Letcher, August 28, 1865; Lee to Matthew Fontaine Maury, September 8, 1865; Lee to Lord Acton, December 15, 1866, Lee Papers, W&L.

23. Grant, *Personal Memoirs*, pp. 615–17, 625, 634–36, 640.

24. Ibid., pp. 116–17, 336.

25. Ibid., p. 634; Franklin L. Riley, "What General Lee Read after the War," in *General Robert E. Lee after Appomattox* (New York: Macmillan, 1922), pp. 157–81 (Lee quotations on 160 and 161).

26. Frances Ellen Watkins Harper, "Affairs in South Carolina," in *A Brighter Coming Day: A Frances Ellen Watkins Harper Reader*, ed. Frances Smith Foster (New York: Feminist Press, 1990), pp. 124–25.

INDEX

Note: Page numbers in *italics* indicate photographs and illustrations.

abolitionists
    antislavery press, 121, 123, 144, 189, 216, 232
    and the Civil Rights bill, 234
    and class divisions in the South, 168
    and criticisms of Lee, 232
    and cross-racial unity, 100
    De Bow's Review on, 219
    and Lee's background, 36
    and Lee's postwar interview, 187
    and Lee's restoration efforts, 190, 202
    and Lincoln's assassination, 145, 149
    and magnanimity policy, 206
    and news of Appomattox surrender, 115,
        120, 131, 133
    and Reconstruction plans, 120–25, 192, 199
    and vindication theme, 2, 121–24
    and Whittier, 213
    See also emancipation
Acton, John Dahlberg, 256
African American soldiers.
        See United States Colored Troops
African Methodist Episcopal (AME) Church,
    101, 123, 253
Afro-American (Baltimore), 254
Alabama, 228–29
Alexander, Edward Porter, 18, 24, 35, 42, 43, 72
Allen, George H., 82
Allen, Richard, 100
Allen, Stanton P., 87, 139
Amelia Court House, 9, 11–12
American Anti-Slavery Society, 123
amnesty
    Amnesty Proclamation, 51 (Lincoln), 192
        (Johnson)

debate on scope of, 129
and Johnston's surrender, 151–52
Lee's amnesty oath, 203
Lee's application for, 200
and Lee's postwar interview, 189
and Lee's surrender, 131
and Lincoln's assassination, 144–45
and pardon terms, 32–33
and peace negotiations, 27–28
and Reconstruction plans, 117–18, 191–93,
    197
and Southern reactions to Appomattox,
    72–73, 163
and surrender conference, 51, 62, 72
See also paroles
Anderson, Richard H., 12, 24
Andersonville Prison camp, 229–30
Andrews, Sidney, 215
Anglo-African (New York), 124, 190
Antietam, Battle of, 25
Antiwar Democrats. *See* Copperheads
apple tree myth, 247–50, *248*
Appomattox (2007), 255
"Appomattox" (Dinkins), 254–55
Appomattox Club, 254
Appomattox Court House, *83*
    and apple tree lore, 249–50
    and final battles of Civil War, 9, 18, 33–34,
        37, 40–41
    and myth of Appomattox, 247
    and surrender conference, 1, 46, 49–51, 53,
        55–56, 74
    and surrender negotiations, 44–45
    symbolic significance of, 84–85

Appomattox Station, 18, 21, 24, 33–34, 40,
    41–42, 270n51
April 1865: The Month that Saved America
    (Winik), 255
Arkansas, 166
armistice, 37
Armstrong, Hallock, 87–88
Army of Northern Virginia
    and Northern calls for amnesty, 129
    and Ewell, 183
    and final battles of Civil War, 8, 11, 14, 18,
        20, 35
    and "overwhelming numbers" theme,
        73–74, 77, 102–3
    USCT perceptions of, 97–98
    and soldiers' reactions to Lee's surrender,
        85, 101–12
    and Southern civilians' reactions to
        Appomattox, 162, 166
    and surrender conference, 1, 56, 59, 68–69,
        72, 76–77
    and surrender negotiations, 23, 29–31,
        35–36, 37, 44, 126
Army of Tennessee (Confederate), 65, 162
Army of the James, 9, 16–17, 20, 40–41, 93, 97
Army of the Potomac
    and criticisms of Grant, 238
    and final battles of Civil War, 7, 9, 11–12, 20,
        40
    and the Grand Review, 154–55, *155*
    and Reconstruction plans, 199
    and surrender conference, 77–78
Army of the Tennessee (Union), 17, 88
artifacts of surrender conference, 89–92, *91*,
    93
artillery units
    at Appomattox Station, 33, 270n51
    and "overwhelming numbers" theme, 66,
        161
    and parole at Appomattox, 111
    and Sailor's Creek, 13–14
    and surrender conference, 66
    and surrender negotiations, 42
    and surrender terms, 57, 58, 270n51
Atlanta, Georgia, 8, 168
Attucks, Crispus, 99
Augusta Constitutionalist, 166
Avery, James Henry, 132, 138
Ayres, Romeyn B., 46–47

Babcock, Orville E., 50–51, 53–55, 57, 64, 90
Badeau, Adam, 54, 57, 63
Banks, Nathaniel, 118

Barnard, John G., 57
Bartlett, Joseph J., 45
Battle-Pieces (Melville), 224
Bayne, Thomas, 197–98, 222
Beagle, Donald Robert, 178
Beauregard, P. G. T., 204, 215
Belgian Congo, 98
Belle Isle prison, 221
Bennett, Ellis, 173–74
Bennett, James, 125
Bergeron, Paul, 192
Berry, Fanny, 172
Big Sailor's Creek, 12. *See also* Sailor's Creek,
    battles of
Bingham, John A., 210
Birdsong, James, 111
black citizenship, 95, 119, 120–21, 123. *See also*
    black suffrage; Civil Rights bill
Black Codes, 193, 213
The Black Phalanx (Wilson), 98
black suffrage, 119, 150, 192–96, 210–11, 216,
    234, 256–57
Blackford, William, 75
Blaine, James G., 210
Blanton House, 23
Blight, David, 291n19
Blow, Henry, 220–21
Bocock, Thomas S., 164–65
Booth, John Wilkes, 135–36, *143*, 144, 150,
    154, *249*
Boritt, Gabor S., 247
Boston Daily Advertiser, 204, 215
Botts, John Minor, 287n26
Bowers, Theodore S., 54, 55, 58–59
Boyce, W. W., 219
Boykin, Edward M., 102
Brady, Mathew, 91–92, 184, *185*
Breckinridge, John C., 27, 28–29
Brooklyn Daily Eagle, 129, 250
Brooks, Phillips, 147
Broomall, John Martin, 214
Brown, John M., 197–98
Browning, Judkin, 168
Brownlow, William G., 166, 169, 174
Brundage, W. Fitzhugh, 291n20
Bryant, William Cullen, 190
Buchanan, James, 31
Buck, Lucy, 165
Buckner, Simon, 29, 153
Burlingame, Michael, 137
Burr, C. Chauncey, 211–12
Burwell, Letitia, 171
Butler, Benjamin, 17, 32, 93

Butler, Josiah, 147
Byrd, Susie, 173

Cadwallader, Sylvanus, 11, 38, 57, 64, 89, 125, 267n12
Caldwell, John, 251
Camp Nelson, 94
Camp William Penn, 94, 101
Campaigns of the Army of the Potomac (Swinton), 238
Campbell Court House, 24, 38
capitalism, 70
cavalry
    and final battles of Civil War, 7–9, 11–12, 14, 15, 17–19, 40
    and surrender conference, 65–66, 73, 270n51
ceasefires, 27, 44–46, 51, 53
Central Press (Bellefonte, Pa.), 150
Chamberlain, Joshua L., 45, 77–78
Chambers, Henry A., 102, 104, 109
Chambersburg, Pennsylvania, 229
Charleston Daily News, 212
Cheney, James, 137
Chesnut, Mary, 174, 175
Chester, Thomas Morris, 95–97, 98
Chicago Tribune, 215, 223, 238
Child, Lydia Maria, 145
Christian Advocate and Journal (New York), 124
Christian Recorder (Philadelphia), 95, 101, 123, 216–17, 231–32, 234
Cincinnati Gazette, 214
Civil Rights Act, 244
Civil Rights bill, 213–14, 216–17, 218, 231–35, 244
civil rights movement, 137
Clark, G. V., 249–50
Clarke, Caroline Cowles, 131
Clarke, George P., 106
Clarke, Mary Bayard, 235–36
Clarke, Sidney, 233–34
Clay, Henry, 31
clemency for defeated Confederates
    and African American soldiers, 99, 101
    and the Civil Rights bill, 217–18
    and Confederate soldiers' view of, 72–73, 110
    and Grant's rationale for, 30–32, 62, 205–6, 245
    and Johnston's surrender, 153
    and Lincoln's assassination, 143–50
    and Union soldiers' reactions to Lee's surrender, 86–87

    and Reconstruction plans, 121–22
    and Southern civilians' reactions to Appomattox, 164–65
    and Southern Unionist divisions on, 169
    and Whittier poem, 213
    See also paroles
Clement, Samuel Spottford, 170–71
Clifton House, 38
Clover Hill, 33, 72
commemorations of Appomattox, 173, 224, 252–53, 291n20
Commercial (Cincinnati), 224
Conant, Anna, 155–56
"Concord Hymn" (Emerson), 178
The Confederate Image (Neely, Holzer, and Boritt), 247–48
Confederate nationalism, resilience of, 167
Connecticut Herald, 150
"The Conquered Banner" (Ryan), 176–79, 179
Constitutional Union (Washington, D.C.), 129
Continental Congress, 204
Cook, Thomas M., 185–89, 189–90
Cooke, Giles B., 106, 110
Cooper Institute, 146
Coopersmith, Andrew S., 127, 165–66, 175
Copperheads
    and black suffrage, 217
    and the Civil Rights Bill, 231–32
    and "The Conquered Banner," 178–79
    criticisms of Johnson, 232
    and Custer, 45
    Grant's opinion of, 32, 39, 61–62, 242–43
    and Grant's tactics, 22
    and the Joint Committee on Reconstruction, 228
    and Lee's political calculations, 26–27, 36
    and Lincoln's assassination, 136–39, 143–46, 149–50, 279n9
    and Lincoln's reelection, 27
    and news of Appomattox surrender, 115, 120–21, 124–25, 127–29, 132–33
    and parole terms, 191
    and peace negotiations, 276n19
    reaction to war's end, 115, 126–27
    and Reconstruction plans, 120–22, 211
    resistance to Grant, 256–57
    resistance to Reconstruction, 236
    and restoration theme, 3
    and soldiers' reactions to Lee's surrender, 86
    and surrender terms, 205
    in Union Army, 279n9
Cormany, Samuel, 80–81, 97

Cornwallis, Charles, 21
Coski, John, 112
Costley, Nance, 94
Costley, William H., 94
Cowen, Edgar, 217–18
Crane, C. B., 142
Crawford, Lucy Redman, 173
CSS *Alabama*, 230
Cumberland Church, 18
Cumming, Kate, 162
Current, Richard Nelson, 153
Custer, George Armstrong, 12–13, 33–34, 45, 66, 132
Custer, Libby, 89
Custis, George Washington Parke, 232

Daly, Maria Lydia, 130–31
Dana, Charles A., 205
Danville, Virginia, 9, 24, 36, 75, 163
Danville Register, 163
Davis, Jefferson
   and apple tree lore, 248–49, *249*
   calls for retribution, 110, 188–89, 192
   and capture of Richmond, 8–9, 36, 106–7
   captured, 196
   and the Hampton Roads Peace Conference, 27, 28
   and Lincoln's assassination, 137, *143*, 144, 149
   mansion of, 91–92
   and news of Appomattox surrender, 122
   and press coverage of surrender, 128, 131
   and reactions to Lee's surrender, 80, 117
   and the *Richmond Examiner*, 227
Davis, Jefferson (*continued*)
   Southern devotion to, 215
   and surrender conference, 70–72, 75–77
   and surrender terms, 151, 153
Davis, William C., 27–28
Dawson, Sarah Fowler Morgan, 164
De Bow, J. D. B., 218–20
De Bow's Review, 218–19
De Normandie, James, 136–37
Delaware, 168
Democratic Party, 134, 179, 206, 231, 240. *See also* Copperheads; War Democrats
Dennett, John Richard, 215, 216, 231
Dent, Frederick T., 57
desertions, 11, 74–75, 106–7, 162, 167, 229
"Dixie," 116
Dorum, Fannie, 173
Doubleday, Ulysses, 93

Douglass, Frederick, 100, 110, 234, 254
Downing, Alexander G., 88
draft riots, 132

Early, Jubal, 7
Early, Mary Washington (Cabell), 162, 164
Eddy, Richard, 147–48
Eden, R. C., 80
Edgefield Advertiser (S.C), 162, 166, 247–48
Edwards, Abial Hall, 155, 208–9
"effusion of blood" phrasing, 20–23, 29, 76, 152
Eggleston, George Cary, 106, 111
Elder, Lucinda, 251–52
11th Iowa Infantry, 88
Elmore, Grace Brown, 162, 165
emancipation
   and calls for clemency, 122
   and Lee's postwar interview, 187
   and peace negotiations, 26–27
   and Reconstruction plans, 120–21
   and Southern restoration efforts, 208
   and spread of surrender news, 169–74
   and surrender negotiations, 30, 32
   and the Wade-Davis Bill, 118, 276n7
   See also abolitionists
Emancipation Proclamation, 30, 169, 170, 172
Emerson, Ralph Waldo, 178
English Civil War, 51, 246
Evangelist (New York), 144
Evans, Andrew, 145
Evans, Clement, 40
Evers, Medgar, 137
Ewell, Lizinka, 183
Ewell, Richard S., 9, 12–14, 21, 24, 183–84
Ex Parte Milligan, 288n43
exceptionalism, 246–47

Fain, Eliza Rhea Anderson, 164
Farewell Address (Lee)
   and battle over meaning of surrender, 68–70
   and "The Conquered Banner," 178
   and Lee's postwar interview, 189–90
   and "overwhelming numbers" theme, 79, 103
   and Reconstruction politics, 188
   and soldiers' reactions to Lee's surrender, 107–8, 109, 112
   and Southern civilians' reactions to Appomattox, 157, 163, 166
   and surrender conference, 74, 76–77
   text, *105*

Farmville, Virginia, 9, 11, 17–19, 49
Federal Writers' Project, 171–73
Feis, William B., 75
Ferguson, Champ, 229–30
Fessenden, William Pitt, 210
Fifth Corps (Army of the Potomac), 7, 21, 40, 77, 85
5th Michigan Cavalry Regiment, 132
54th Massachusetts Infantry, 145
Figg, Royall W., 109
"fire-eaters," 36
First Corps (Army of Northern Virginia), 12
Fisher, Sidney George, 131
Fisk, Wilbur, 138
Five Forks, Battle of, 7, 21
Foner, Eric, 194, 210, 213, 234
food shortages, 64, 67, 102, 104–6
Ford, Gerald, 203
Ford's Theater, 135, 156
Forsyth, George A., 65
Forsyth, J. W., 50–51
Fort Donelson, 25, 29
Fort Fisher, 8
Fort Wagner, 95
Forten, James, 100
Fortune, T. Thomas, 250
Foster, Joshua Lane, 132, 136
Foster, Robert S., 40, 93–94, 97
Fourteenth Amendment, 243
4th Rhode Island Volunteers, 82
Fowler, Henry, 144
Franklin, John Hope, 220, 221
Franklin Repository, 125
"free soil" principles, 87
Freedmen's Bureau, 209, 211–13, 220–22, 236
Freehling, William, 168
Freeman's Journal and Catholic Register (New York), 178
French Revolution, 246
From Slave Cabin to Pulpit (Randolph), 170

Gaines, Wesley John, 172
Gallagher, Gary W., 52, 71, 155, 268n24
Garidel, Henri, 171
Garner, Cornelius, 173–74
Garner, Stanton, 225, 227
Garrison, William Lloyd, 123
Gary, Martin, 46
General Orders No. 3, 213
General Orders No. 9, 69–70, 71, 75. *See also* Farewell Address
General Orders No. 108, 66

Gettysburg, Battle of, 11, 25, 45, 253
Gettysburg Address (Lincoln), 120
Gibbon, John, 19–21, 40–41, 46–47, 72–73, 93
Giezman, Bran Albin, 178
Glass, Philip, 255
Glatthaar, Joseph T., 76
Goodman, Andrew, 137
Gordon, John Brown, *251*
    on declining morale, 107
    farewell address, 70–71
    and final battles of Civil War, 12, 14–15, 17–18, 37–38, 40–41, 47
    and Grant's tour of the South, 209
    and Lee's inner circle, 24
    and myth of Appomattox, 250–52
    and stacking-of-arms ceremony, 110
    and surrender conference, 53, 70–72, 74, 77–78
    and surrender negotiations, 44–45
    and truces, 45, 46
Goree, Thomas J., 45
Gorham, John, 195
Goss, Thomas J., 32
gradual emancipation, 222
Grand Review, 154–55, *155*, 226
Grant, Ulysses S.
    and apple tree symbol, 250
    and black remembrance of Appomattox, 173
    elected president, 246
    and final battles of Civil War, 7–12, 13, 16–17, 18–22, 25–26, 33–35, 42
    and the Hampton Roads Peace Conference, 31
    and the Joint Committee on Reconstruction, 228
    key commanders of, 81
    and Lee's amnesty oath, 203–7
    and Lee's treason indictment, 200–202
    and Lincoln's assassination, 148, 150, 156
    memoirs, 59–61, 257
    political background of, 31–33
    and press coverage of surrender, 126
    reception after war, 200–201, *201*
    and Reconstruction plans, 209–10, 210–11, 245–46
    and reputation as merciless, 22, 109, 211
    strategic style, 2, 79–80, 82
    and surrender conference, 48–52, 54–59, 59–65, 65–68, 70–73, 76–78
    and surrender negotiations, 23–25, 28–31, 33–40, 42–47

Grant, Ulysses S. (*continued*)
  and surrender terms, 1–2, 56–59, 89,
    152–53, 205, 245, 291n19
  symbolic significance of, 256–57
  and vindication view of Lee's surrender,
    2–4
Grant's Petersburg Progress, 80
Greeley, Horace, 121–22, *122*, 123, 128–29,
    206, 246
Greensboro Guards, 109
Griffin, Charles, 21, 40–41, 45, 46, 72
Grimes, Bryan, 40
Grinspan, Jon, 133
Gurley, Phineas, Densmore, 148–49

habeas corpus, 51, 288n43
Haley, John W., 85–86
Halleck, Henry, 32, 205
Hampton Roads Peace Conference, 27
Hancock, Winfield Scott, 14
hard-war strategy
  and Butler, 110
  Copperhead press on, 127
  and emancipation, 32
  and final battles of Civil War, 16, 40
  and Grant's surrender terms, 125
  impact on Lee's army, 8
  and Lee's postwar interview, 188
  and the Lieber Code, 230
  and Southern reactions to Appomattox,
    103–4, 163
Harper, Frances Ellen Watkins, 234, 253–54,
    257–58
Harper's Weekly, 90–91, 153–54, *154*, 190
Harris, Della, 173
Harrisburg Patriot & Union, 127
Harrison, William, 171
Hartwell, F. L., 138
Haven, Gilbert, 144
Heichhold, C. P., 97
Henry, Patrick, 91
Heth, Henry, 46
High Bridge, 17–18, *19*
History of the Negro Race in America
    (Williams), 98
History of the Negro Troops in the War of the
    Rebellion (Williams), 99
Holden, William W., 165, 192, 209
Holland, Josiah, 147, 149
Holmes, Emma, 160
Holmes, Joseph, 171
Holt, Joseph, 137, 198
Holzer, Harold, 247

Hopkins, Abner Crump, 112
Houghton, W. R., 102
House Judiciary Committee, 245
Houston Tri-Weekly Telegraph, 165–66, 175
Howard, Jacob M., 245
Humphreys, Andrew A., 12, 14–15, 18, 21, 41, 43
hunger and malnutrition, 9, 102, 104–6
immigrants, 70
Independent (New York), 123, 232, 233
Ingalls, Rufus, 57
Iola Leroy (Harper), 253–54
"Iron Brigade," 83
Iroquois League of Five Nations, 55, 65

Jacksonian Democrats, 168
Janney, Caroline, 252
Janney, Samuel M., 167
"John Brown's Body," 88, 248
Johnson, Andrew, *193*
  and calls for amnesty, 151–52
  and class divisions in the South, 168
  and the Joint Committee on
    Reconstruction, 220–21, 224, 227–34
  and Lee's treason indictment, 199
  and Lincoln's assassination, 142–44, 148,
    150, 156, 175–76
  paroles and pardons, 183, 191, 287n26
  and Reconstruction plans, 180, 194–95,
    208–9, 213–14, 218–19
  and restoration theme, 3
  "Swing Round the Circle" tour, 243
Johnson, Bradley T., 229
Johnson, Bushrod, 24
Johnson, Herrick, 146–47
Johnson, James H., 172
Johnson, Reverdy, 217–18
Johnston, Joseph
  farewell address, 289n58
  and final battles of Civil War, 7, 9, 19, 74–75
  and the Joint Committee on
    Reconstruction, 230
  and the Republican Party, 239
  Southern devotion to, 215
  and surrender conference, 65, 74–75
  surrender of, 135, 151–53
  and surrender terms, 151–52, 176, 229–30
Joint Committee on Reconstruction, 210,
    220–36, 239
Jones, Caroline, 174
Jones, John B., 163
Jones, Will, 251
Juarez, Benito, 286n40
Julian, George, 210

Kachun, Mitch, 255, 291n20
Keifer, J. Warren, 13, 66
Kentucky, 168
King, Martin Luther, Jr., 137
Knoxville Whig and Rebel Ventilator, 166–67
Ku Klux Klan, 250

La Crosse Daily Democrat, 145
Lane, David, 81
Lawrence, A. B., 73
laws of war, 229–30
LeConte, Emma, 164, 174
Lee, Fitzhugh
  and final battles of Civil War, 17, 37–38, 40
  and General Lee's inner circle, 24
  and surrender conference, 52, 73–75
Lee, George Washington Custis, 15
Lee, Henry, III ("Light Horse Harry"), 257
Lee, Mary Custis, 159, 236
Lee, Robert E., 26, 185
  and apple tree lore, 249
  and black remembrance of Appomattox, 173
  ceremonial sword, 253
  Farewell Address, 68–70, 74–77, 79, 103, 105, 107–9, 112, 117, 157, 163, 166, 178, 188, 189–90
  and final battles of Civil War, 7–22, 35, 41–42, 47
  and the Hampton Roads Peace Conference, 28–29
  ideological entrenchment, 255–56
  influence of, 183–84
  and the Joint Committee on Reconstruction, 220–29, 232–34, 236
  and Lincoln's assassination, 143, 144, 149
  negotiations with Grant, 38–39
  Northern opinions of, 189–91
  and parole terms, 200–207, 289n60
  political philosophy, 37
  postwar press coverage of, 184–89
  and Reconstruction plans, 211–12
  and restoration theme, 3–4, 36–37, 202–3, 220–21, 256
  Southern reverence for, 215, 242
  strategic style, 2
  and surrender conference, 48–56, 58–59, 60, 60–65, 67–77, 78
  and surrender terms, 1, 4, 56–59, 239
  and treason indictment, 196–200
Lee, William Henry Fitzhugh ("Rooney"), 52
"Lee in the Capitol" (Melville), 225
Leopold II, King of Belgium, 98

"Let the Banner Proudly Wave. Written after the Surrender of Lee" (Simpson), 124
Letcher, John, 205
Levine, Bruce, 286n40
Libby prison, 91, 221
Liberator, 123
Lieber, Francis, 198
Lieber Code, 229–30
Lincoln, Abraham, 143
  assassination of, 135–38, 141, 142–45, 148–50, 156, 174–76, 191–92, 199, 279n9
  court cases argued by, 94
  and Grand Review, 226
  Grant's support for, 39
  and the Hampton Roads Peace Conference, 31
  and memorial observances, 254
  and news of Appomattox surrender, 115–17
  and Reconstruction plans, 117–20, 166
  reelection, 8, 27, 31, 33, 125
  and Second Inaugural, 148–49
  and surrender conference, 48, 61
  and surrender terms, 163
  and vindication theme, 2–3
Lincoln, Mary Todd, 135
Lincoln, Robert Todd, 57
Linderman, Gerald F., 85
Little Rock, Arkansas, 166
Little Round Top, 45
Little Sailor's Creek, 12–13. *See also* Sailor's Creek, battles of
Liuzzo, Viola, 137
Locke, David Ross, 133–34
Long, Armistead L., 24, 77
Longstreet, James, 241
  conversion to Republican Party, 239–40
  encounter with Custer, 45, 266n45
  and final battles of Civil War, 17–18, 37–38, 41–42
  and surrender conference, 45–46, 51–52, 53, 72, 266n45
  and surrender negotiations, 23–24, 28–29, 37–38
"The Lord Reigneth" (De Normandie), 136
The Lost Cause (Pollard), 234–35
Lost Cause ideology, 234, 247, 252–54
Louisiana, 117–19
L'Ouverture, Toussaint, 99
Lowe, Richard, 197
Lowry, Thomas P., 279n9
Lyman, Theodore, 38

lynchings, 252
Lyon, Farnham, 81, 89

Magnanimity. *See* clemency for defeated
    Confederates
Mahone, William
    account of Appomattox campaign, 264n5
    conversion to Republican Party, 239–40
    and final battles of Civil War, 17–18, 24–25,
        35
    and General Lee's inner circle, 24
    and surrender conference, 75
    and surrender negotiations, 42–43
Manassas Junction, 75
Marble, Manton, 127
Marshall, Charles
    and surrender conference, 51–54, 59–60,
        67–68, 70, 75, 77
    and surrender negotiations, 23, 43
Marshall, John, 52
martial law, 213, 245–46
Maryland, 168
Matrau, Henry C., 83
Mattocks, Charles, 82–83
Mayo, A. D., 146
McClellan, George, 224
McClure, Alexander, 125
McCreery, C. H., 80
McDonald, Cornelia Peake, 163–64, 175
McGuire, Judith W., 158, 159, 162
McKenzie, Robert Tracy, 169
McKim, Randolph H., 102
McLean, Wilmer, 75, 85, 90
McLean House, 54
    and accounts of Lee's surrender, 161
    and Brady photographs, 181
    and mementos of surrender conference,
        89–92
    and myth of Appomattox, 242
    and surrender conference, 52–54, 57,
        58–59, 65, 67, 73, 75
McMaster, James, 178
McPherson, James, 32
Meade, George G.
    and final battles of Civil War, 11–12, 14–15,
        18, 21
    headquarters with Grant, 38
    and surrender conference, 49, 51, 55, 71, 75
    and truces, 44
Meade, Hodijah Baylies, 102, 110
Meade, Margaretta, 71
Medals of Honor, 82–83
Melcher, Holman S., 84, 138–39

Melville, Herman, 224–27
mementos of surrender conference, 89–92, *91*,
    93
memorial services, 254
Memphis, Tennessee, 236–37
Men of Mark: Eminent, Progressive, and Rising
    (Simmons), 100–101
Merritt, Wesley, 33–35, 46, 66
Mexican War, 1, 31, 54, 68, 184
Mexico, 286n40
military commissions, 51
Millard, Henry J., 87, 88–89
Miller, Bluffton, 88
Miller Memorial Baptist Church
    (Philadelphia), 254
Milton, John, 159
Miner, Henry, 82
Minor, Henry Augustine, 102, 110
Missouri, 168
Mitchell, Charley, 171
mob violence, 146, 237
Moore, Edward A., 102, 109
Moore, Thomas W. C., 89
Morgan, Michael Ryan, 57, 59, 63–64
Morgan, Sarah, 176
Mosby, John Singleton, 8, 239–40
Munford, Thomas T., 52–53, 74–75
Museum of the Confederacy, 112
Myers, Robert Poole, 102
mythology of Appomattox, 1, 246–50

A Narrative of the Negro (Pendleton), 253
Nasby, Petroleum Vesuvius (pen name), 133–34
Nashville Daily Union, 176
Nast, Thomas, 153–54, *154*, 238
Nation, 215
National Anti-Slavery Standard, 123, 150, 152,
    223–24, 234, 258
National Park Service, 253
Neely, Mark E., 247
Neff, John C., 140
The Negro and the White Man (Gaines), 172
New Deal, 169–70
New Englander and Yale Review, 232
New Haven Palladium, 126
New Hope Church, 41
New Orleans, Louisiana, 117–18
New York Age, 250
New York Daily News, 127, 145
New York Evening Post, 190
New York Herald
    and Bennett, 125
    and criticisms of Lee, 191

on final battles of Civil War, 11
Lee's interviews in, 186, 239
and Lincoln's assassination, 138
on mementos of surrender conference, 89
on surrender conference, 57
on surrender negotiations, 38
New York Times
and criticisms of Lee, 190, 191
Grant interview, 238
and Lincoln's assassination, 138
on surrender terms, 124–25, 153
New York Tribune, 121–23, 125
New York World, 127, 130
Newhall, Frederick, 51, 57
Norfolk, Virginia, 197–98
Norfolk Light Artillery Blues, 102
Norfolk Post, 199, 231
Norris, Mary, 232
Norris, Wesley, 232–33
North Carolina, 192
North Carolina Standard, 165, 176
Northrop, Lucius B., 107
Norton, Daniel, 222

oaths of allegiance, 32, 117–18, 123, 190–92,
197, 203, 267n8
Old Guard, 211, 236
Olustee, Florida, 95
118th Pennsylvania Infantry, 82, 86
Open Letter to His Serene Majesty Leopold II
(Williams), 98
orchard peace conference myth, 246–47,
247
Ord, Edward O. C.
and artifacts of the peace conference, 89,
91–92, 93, 184
and final battles of Civil War, 16–17, 19–20,
21, 40–41
and the Hampton Roads Peace Conference,
28
and surrender conference, 46, 51, 52,
54–55, 57
Overland campaign, 21–22, 95, 163
"overwhelming numbers" theme
and African American soldiers, 97
and "The Conquered Banner,"
177–78
and the Copperhead press, 127
criticisms of, 82, 126, 150, 242
Ewell on, 183
and Lee's restoration efforts, 204
and myth of Appomattox, 242

and perceptions of surrender, 48, 68–71,
79–82, 102–3, 106, 108, 126, 160–63,
215–16
and surrender conference, 77–78

Paine, Lewis, 135–36
Painter, J. C., 108
"Palm Sunday" (Nast), *154*
Paradise Lost (Milton), 159
Pardons. *See* amnesty; clemency for defeated
Confederates
paroles
and debate on surrender terms, 183, 191,
200–207
and Johnston's surrender, 152
Lee's parole, 191
parole certificates, 72–74, *73*, 76, 111–12
terms of, 30, 32–33, 191
Parker, Ely S., 49, 54–59, *56*, 64–65, 71, 89
Parks, George, 232
paternalism, 222–23, 229, 242
Peace Democrats. *See* Copperheads
Peace Party, 165, 192
Pease, Charles E., 49
Peirce, Taylor, 138
Pemberton, John C., 30, 153
Pendleton, William N., 24–25, 71–72
Pendleton, Lelia Amos, 253
Perry, Herman H., 104
Petersburg, Virginia, 8, 80, 95, 101
Petersburg News, 199
Philadelphia Inquirer, 126
Philadelphia Press, 126
Phillips, Jason, 103–4
Phillips, Wendell, 149–50
Pickens, Samuel, 109, 110
Pickett, George E., 7, 24, 229–30
Pierpont, Francis H., 197, 199
piracy, 230
Pittsburgh Courier, 173, 254
Poe, Edgar Allan, 178
Pollard, Edward A., 227, 234–35
Pollard, H. Rives, 227–28
Pomeroy, Marcus "Brick," 145
Porter, David, 33
Porter, Horace, 54, 57, 64–65, 89, 92–93
Portsmouth, New Hampshire, 131–32
Portsmouth Journal, 132
Post, Jacob, 139
postwar politics, 2
Potts, Franklin, 108, 111
Prentiss, George L., 233
Preston, Margaret Junkin, 159–60

prisoners of war, 15, 30–31, 91, 183, 190–91, 221. *See also* paroles
Proclamation of Amnesty and Reconstruction (1863), 32–33, 117, 151
profiteering, 75
Providence Journal, 185
Pryor, Elizabeth Brown, 232–33
Putnam, Sallie Brock, 158, 159

Rable, George, 86, 109
Race and Reunion (Blight), 291n19
racial discrimination and conflict
    and Black Codes, 193–94
    cross-racial unity, 99–100
    and impact of surrender terms, 291n19
    and the Joint Committee on Reconstruction, 221, 222, 228–29, 232–33
    mob violence, 237, 251–52
    and Reconstruction process, 211, 212–13, 217–18, 236
    and Southern paternalism, 222–23, 229, 242
    and United States Colored Troops, 79, 95
Radford, Ruby Lorraine, 172
Radical Reconstruction, 243, 250, 252–53
Radical Republicans
    Copperhead press on, 127–28
    and Grant, 210–11
    and Lee's postwar interview, 189–90
    and magnanimity policy, 206
    and reactions to surrender, 110, 115, 118–19, 120, 123–24, 167, 128–29
    and Reconstruction plans, 192, 210, 213, 214
    resistance to Grant, 256–57
    and restoration efforts, 208–10
Randol, Alanson M., 89–90
Randolph, Peter, 170
Randolph House, 19
Rankin, J. E., 141–42
"The Raven" (Poe), 178
Ravenel, Charlotte S. J., 174
Rawlins, John A., 38, 49, 56, 57
Raymond, Henry J., 124–25, 129, *129*, 138, 276n19
readmission of Confederate states, 117–18, 192, 244. *See also* Reconstruction; Ten Percent Plan
Reconstruction
    and Arkansas, 166
    and impact of surrender terms, 291n19
    Lincoln's approach to, 117

and Lincoln's assassination, 137
and Louisiana, 117–19
and myths of Appomattox, 248
political struggles over, 191–97
and surrender terms, 179, 208–9
in Virginia, 197–200
Reconstruction Act, 244
Reeb, James, 137
Reid, Whitelaw, 214–15
relics of surrender conference, 89–92, *91, 93*
Republican Party
    and Civil Rights bill, 231
    and Grant's political career, 243
    and the Joint Committee on Reconstruction, 223–24
    and Lincoln's assassination, 142
    and moderate Republicans, 121, 124–26, 210–11, 214, 243
    and reactions to surrender, 3, 86, 115, 121, 128, 131, 132
    and Reconstruction plans, 197, 198, 243–44
    and slavery debates, 31–32
    and surrender terms, 209, 213–17
    See also Radical Republicans
Republican Union League, 133
restoration theme
    and the Joint Committee on Reconstruction, 220–21, 228, 231
    and Lee's postwar efforts, 3–4, 36–37, 202–3, 220–21, 256
    and Lee's postwar interview, 187
    and racial violence, 237
    and surrender conference, 48
    and surrender negotiations, 36
    and surrender terms, 3, 152
    and the "White Sulphur Manifesto," 246
retribution
    and Lee's treason indictment, 199
    and Lincoln's assassination, 136–37, 138, 142, 144, 145, 149–50, 174–75
    and reactions to Lee's surrender, 110
    Southern Unionist divisions on, 169
Rhodes, Elisha Hunt, 14, 88, 89
Richmond, Virginia, 7–9, 36, 101, 107, *159*, 168, 287n26
Richmond & Danville Railroad, 9
Richmond Examiner, 227–28
Richmond Howitzers, 102
Richmond Whig, 185
Richmond-Lynchburg Stage Road, 34
Ricks, Augustus, 88
River Queen meeting, 33, 115
Robbins, Frank L., 142

Roe, A. O., 85, 88
Rogers, Jackson, 217
Roller, John E., 104–5
Rosen, Hannah, 237
Rosser, Thomas L., 17, 74–75
Round Table (New York), 247
Rumley, James, 159, 195
Ryan, Abraham Joseph, 176–78

Sacramento Daily Union, 126
Sailor's Creek, battles of
    Confederate prisoners from, 106
    and Ewell's capture, 183
    and final battles of Civil War, 12–18, 24, 80
    and surrender conference, 76
    and surrender negotiations, 29
Salisbury, North Carolina, 229
San Francisco Bulletin, 199
Schroeder, Patrick, 270n51
Schurz, Carl, 208–9, 212
Schwerner, Micky, 137
secession, 31–32, 167–68, 186–87, 218–19, 221
Second Corps (Army of Northern Virginia), 77, 112, 183
Second Corps (Army of the Potomac), 12, 14–15, 17–18, 20
Second Inaugural Address (Lincoln), 120, 148–49
Sellman, Sophia Stockett, 130–31
Semmes, Raphael, 230
17th Maine, 82–83
7th Michigan Cavalry, 81
Seward, William, 135–36, 174, 203
Sharpe, George H., 57, 62–64, 72, 89
Shaw, James, 139–40
Shaw, Joseph, 146
Shaw, Robert Gould, 145
Shaw, Sarah, 145
Sheehan-Dean, Aaron, 167
Shenandoah campaign, 7–8
Sheridan, Philip H., *16*
    account of surrender conference, 267n12
    and final battles of Civil War, 7–9, 11–13, 15–21, 33–35, 40–41
    praised in press, 150
    and surrender conference, 50–51, 54–55, 57, 59, 77, 89
    and surrender negotiations, 44–46
    and truces, 46
Sherman, William T.
    and final battles of Civil War, 8
    and the Grand Review, 154–55, 226
    and Johnston's surrender, 151–52

and the Joint Committee on
    Reconstruction, 226
and reactions to Lee's surrender, 88
and Southern reactions to Appomattox, 162
Southern views of, 175–76
and surrender conference, 65
and surrender negotiations, 33
and surrender terms, 151
Shreve, George, 106
Shreveport News, 175–76
Sickles, Daniel E., 209
sieges, 8–9, 30, 50, 66, 95, 101
Simmons, William J., 94, 100–101
Simpson, Brooks, 211, 231
Simpson, Joshua McCarter, 124
Sixth Corps (Army of the Potomac), 12–14, 18, 66
slavery
    and the surrender as the dawn of freedom, 169–74, 253–54, 282n22
    and *De Bow's Review*, 218–19
    and final battles of Civil War, 8
    and Grant's political philosophy, 61
    and the Hampton Roads Peace Conference, 29
    and Lee's political philosophy, 37
    and Lee's postwar interview, 187
    slave codes, 193
    "slave power conspiracy," 86, 142, 147, 149
"Slavery is Dead (?)" (Nast), 238
Smith, Charles H., 40
Smith, Edmund Kirby, 153
Smith, Gerrit, 206
Smith, Jean Edward, 238
Smith, John L., 82, 86, 90, 107
South Side Railroad, 9, 17, 19, 24, 170
The South vs. the South (Freehling), 168
Southern Unionists, 3, 157, 167–69, 174, 207, 244, 256–57, 287n26
Spear, Ellis, 139
Spear, Samuel T., 144
Speed, James, 198, 202
Spencer, Cornelia Phillips, 163
St. John's Church, 91
St. Louis Democrat, 126
stacking-of-arms ceremony, 77, 86, 110, 111, 270n46
Stanton, Edwin M., 115, 137, 152, 198, 201–2, 206, 211
States and Union (Portsmouth, N.H.), 132
states' rights doctrine, 29, 32, 36–37, 194, 219, 235
Steele, Richard H., 138

Stephens, Alexander, 27, 210
Stevens, Thaddeus, 128, 192, 206, 210
Stone, Amherst, 174
Stoneman, George, 237
Strong, George Templeton, 130–31
Stuart, J. E. B., 7–8
Stuart Horse Artillery, 106
Sumner, Charles, 127–28, 192, 206, 210
supply lines, 8, 33, 34
"The Surrender at Appomattox" (Melville), 224–25
"Surrender Day" celebrations, 173
"Swing Round the Circle" tour, 243
Swinton, William, 238

taxes, 194
Taylor, Richard, 153, 239
Taylor, S. S., 172–73
Taylor, Walter H., 24, 52, 75, 77, 184
telegraph communications, 40, 59, 115, 130, 159
Ten Percent Plan, 117–19, 125, 128, 166–68
Tenney, Luman, 97
Third Corps (Army of Northern Virginia), 12
Third Methodist Episcopal Church (Philadelphia), 151
Thirteenth Amendment, 192
Thornton, William, 221–22
three-fifths compromise, 198
Tilton, Theodore, 123
Times (London), 247
Tousey, Thomas, 143–44
treason, 62, 150, 199–202, 221, 230
trench warfare, 9
Tripp, Stephen, 97
Trowbridge, J. T., 216
truces, 44–45, 52, 81
Trudeau, Noah Andre, 40
Trumbull, Lyman, 210, 212–13, 231
Turner, John W., 93–94, 146
Turner, Nat, 99
20th Maine Infantry, 138
Twenty-fifth Army Corps (Army of the James), 93
Twenty-fourth Army Corps (Army of the James), 20, 40, 73, 93

unconditional surrender, 25, 31, 42, 45
Underground Railroad, 101
Underwood, John C., 198–99, 202
United States Colored Troops (USCT)
    and apple tree lore, 249
    and Appomattox celebrations, 151
    banner of, 96
    and black suffrage, 217
    and Lincoln's assassination, 140
    and memory of Appomattox, 253
    and postwar occupation of South, 213, 237
    and prisoner exchange, 30
    and reactions to the surrender, 79, 95–101, 139–40, 157
    and role in the Appomattox campaign, 93–95
    and Reconstruction plans, 119, 198
universal suffrage, 216
Up From Slavery (Washington), 170
U.S. Congress
    and black suffrage, 198
    and the Civil Rights bill, 213–14, 216–17, 218, 231–35, 234–35, 244
    and Grant, 207
    and Johnson, 191–92, 194
    and Reconstruction plans, 117, 119–20, 196, 232
    and refusal to seat Southern representatives, 210–11
    and the Wade-Davis Bill, 118, 276n7
    See also Joint Committee on Reconstruction
U.S. Department of the Treasury, 115–16
U.S. Department of War, 130, 131
U.S. Senate, 250–51
U.S. Supreme Court, 288n43
US Army and Navy Journal, 230, 241–42

Valley of Virginia, 8
Valley Virginian, 218, 245
Van Lew, Elizabeth, 168–69
Vance, Zebulon, 165
Venable, Charles S., 24, 35, 47, 68, 77
Vicksburg, Battle of, 30, 33
Victorian culture, 84
"Victory and Mourning" (Steele), 138
vigilante violence, 222, 236. *See also* racial discrimination and conflict
Vincent, Marvin R., 142–43
vindication theme, 2–3, 48–49, 83–86, 61, 67, 95, 98–99, *154*
Virginia, politics in, 2, 36–37, 197–200, 220–23
"Virginia Capta" (Preston), 160
Voris, Alvin C., 87

Wade, Benjamin, 128, 210
Wade-Davis Bill, 118, 276n7

Walker, David, 100, 107
Walker, R. L., 33
Walters, John, 102, 107, 111
war crimes, 267n8
War Democrats, 115, 121, 142, 224
Warfield, Edgar, 112
Warren, Gouvernor K., 21
Washington, Booker T., 170, *170*
Washington, Eliza, 172–73
Washington, George, 21, 204, 207
Washington College, 203, 222, 225
Waud, Alfred, *60*, 90–91
Waugh, Joan, 30, 246
Weld, Stephen Minot, 81–82
Wells, Ida B., 94
West Virginia, 197
Westervelt, John H., 85
Whig Party, 31, 168
Whipper, William J., 94
Whipple, Rebekah M., 122
White, W. S., 102–3
"White Sulphur Manifesto," 246
white supremacy, 137, 193, 222. *See also* racial
    discrimination and conflict
Whitman, Walt, 140–41, 216
Whittier, Charles, 43
Whittier, John Greenleaf, 213

Wiatt, William Edward, 107, 108–9
Wilcox, Cadmus M., 46
Williams, George Washington, 94, 97–101
Williams, Seth, 23–24, 29–30, 57, 64
Wilson, Henry, 210, 213
Wilson, Joseph T., 98, 197–98
Windom, William, 214
Winik, Jay, 255
Wirz, Henry, 229–30
Wise, Henry A., 73, 240–41, 242, 289n60
Wise, John S., 86, 174–75
Witt, John Fabian, 205, 267n8
Wood, Benjamin, 127
Woodlin, William P., 101
Woodward, William W., 93
Woodworth, Steven E., 27
Works Progress Administration (WPA),
    171–73, 251
Wright, Horatio, 12, 14–15, 21, 41

"Yankee Doodle," 116
Yarnell, Emma, 145
Yeocum, William, 94
Yorktown, Battle or, 21

Zion's Herald, 144, 234
Zorn, Jacob J., 81, 87, 90